177
Summer
?
defining
Orthodox
American
Postmodern

245
Brace
on
method

Liberalism
?
Democracy
From
Europe
To
USA
?
ITS
Americanism
?
definition
of
Orthodox
Along
with the
rist of
The
APJA.

Liberalism and the Emergence of American Political Science

Liberalism and the Emergence of American Political Science

A Transatlantic Tale

ROBERT ADCOCK

OXFORD
UNIVERSITY PRESS

Oxford University Press is a department of the University of
Oxford. It furthers the University's objective of excellence in research,
scholarship, and education by publishing worldwide.

Oxford   New York
Auckland   Cape Town   Dar es Salaam   Hong Kong   Karachi
Kuala Lumpur   Madrid   Melbourne   Mexico City   Nairobi
New Delhi   Shanghai   Taipei   Toronto

With offices in
Argentina   Austria   Brazil   Chile   Czech Republic   France   Greece
Guatemala   Hungary   Italy   Japan   Poland   Portugal   Singapore
South Korea   Switzerland   Thailand   Turkey   Ukraine   Vietnam

Oxford is a registered trademark of Oxford University Press
in the UK and certain other countries.

Published in the United States of America by
Oxford University Press
198 Madison Avenue, New York, NY 10016

Library of Congress Cataloging-in-Publication Data
Adcock, Robert.
Liberalism and the emergence of American political science: a transatlantic tale / Robert Adcock.
pages cm
Summary: "This book situates the origins of American political science in relation to the transatlantic
history of liberalism. In a corrective to earlier accounts, it argues that, as political science took shape in
the nineteenth century American academy, it did more than express a pre-existing American liberalism,
rather adapting multiple contemporary European liberal arguments to speak to particular challenges
of mass democratic politics and large-scale industry as they developed in America."— Provided by
publisher.
ISBN 978-0-19-933362-2 (hardback)
1. Liberalism—United States—History—19th century.   2. Political science—United States—
History—19th century.   3. Political culture—United States—History—19th century.   I. Title.
JC574.2.U6A42 2014
320.510973'09034—dc23
2013034095

9 8 7 6 5 4 3 2 1
Printed in the United States of America
on acid-free paper

For Alison

CONTENTS

ACKNOWLEDGMENTS

This book is the culmination of almost a decade and a half of intellectual exploration and writing in the history of political science. As I look back, three critical junctures in the path that led here call for special acknowledgment. First, I would like to thank John Gunnell and James Farr, whose scholarship first inspired me as a graduate student to take up the history of political science as a research specialty. Second, I thank Mark Bevir, whose incisive observation that the dissertation I had started on the history of comparison in political science was, in its own way, also a history of liberalism has shaped this book even more than it did that dissertation. Third, I thank Mark Vail for encouraging me, as I pondered my way from dissertation to a first book, to give more attention to political economy so as to better elucidate political science's relation to varieties of liberalism.

There are many others—and more I fear than I will remember here—to thank. My attentiveness to comparison is one of many debts to David Collier, while Shannon Stimson modeled for me just how much political theorists might learn from J. S. Mill's *Principles of Political Economy*. Also from my time at UC Berkeley, I thank Daniel Geary and Andrew Jewett, who as fellow graduate students in a different department first encouraged me to think that a political scientist might write about his field's past in a way historians could appreciate. More generally I thank the multiple additional historians—including Martin Jay, Dorothy Ross, James Kloppenberg, Angus Burgin, Trygve Throntveit, and Mark Solovey— whose discussions with me have repeatedly reaffirmed my interdisciplinary aspirations.

I am grateful to multiple audiences and individuals for feedback on ideas and iterations of parts of this book as it made its way from proposal to manuscript. I thank my colleagues in junior faculty workshops in George Washington University's political science department, my political theory colleagues in the department and beyond, the faculty and students who made giving a Dunbar lecture in Tulane's University political science department such a pleasure, the Research in American and Comparative Politics Workshop at Boston University, and the History, Institutions and Politics Workshop at Harvard University. For one-on-one feedback, I am grateful to Elizabeth Saunders, Steven Kelts, Ingrid Creppell, Martyn Thompson, Emily Hauptmann, Patrick Thaddeus Jackson, Jennifer Burns, and Prithvi Datta.

I thank GWU's Columbian College for a Facilitating Fund Award early in this project, and Tristan Volpe and Dina Bishara for their excellent research assistance. My thanks to Harvard University Archives for the aid of the staff in my work with the papers of A. Lawrence Lowell, and for permission to quote from Lowell's letters. I am, moreover, much indebted to Harvard's Department of Government for providing me with office and library resources as the bulk of this book's final manuscript was completed during 2011–2012. I thank my editor David McBride for his expeditious shepherding of the manuscript through the review process at Oxford University Press, and the anonymous reviewers whose comments did so much to help me better articulate my approach and argument.

Finally, I thank both sides of my transatlantic family. My British parents, in moving their family to America a quarter-century ago, laid the first foundation for the transatlantic perspective of this book, and made it possible for me to attend university in a country where a chemistry major can, for better or worse, become a political scientist. My American parents-in-law, in spanning the globe with their travels and interests, fascinate and inspire, and it is a pleasure to write these lines in their home-away-from-home and my office-away-from-my-office in Columbia Plaza. Every day my beautiful daughter Lydia teaches me about the love of books and people. I dedicate this book to my wife Alison, whose aid to it exceeds acknowledgment.

Liberalism and the Emergence of American Political Science

Introduction

AMERICAN POLITICAL SCIENCE AND LIBERALISM IN
TRANSATLANTIC PERSPECTIVE

When the founders of America's republic debated the US Constitution they invoked a "science of politics" that drew largely from Scottish Enlightenment intellectuals and the Frenchman Montesquieu. By the mid-twentieth century, by contrast, the British scholar Bernard Crick could declare that "the idea of a science of politics has become in our age *distinctively American*...the study of politics in the United States today is something in size, content and method unique in Western intellectual history."[1] The Americanization of political science built on generations of intellectual and institutional development. After gaining a foothold in America's academy in the antebellum period, political science expanded and evolved concurrent with the dramatic growth of university ideals and institutions in the post–Civil War decades, and then became the object of its own professional association at the dawn of the twentieth century. This development has, for almost a century now, drawn the attention of political scientists revisiting their history with diverse aims.[2]

---

[1] Bernard Crick, *The American Science of Politics: Its Origins and Conditions* (Berkeley: University of California Press, 1959), v, xi; italics added.

[2] I date this mode of reflection from Charles Merriam's *American Political Ideas, 1865–1917,* which first pulled out from American thought more broadly a distinctively academic current of "greatly increased attention to the scientific study of politics." The individuals to whom Merriam gave the most attention when attributing origins, and sketching the growth, of "Systematic Studies of Politics"—Francis Lieber, Theodore Woolsey, John W. Burgess, Woodrow Wilson, W. W. Willoughby, and Frank Goodnow—remain to this day the pre-1920s figures most widely addressed in accounts of the development of American political science. Charles Edward Merriam, *American Political Ideas, 1865–1917: Studies in the Development of American Political Thought* (New York: Macmillan, 1920), chap. 13. For overviews of the extensive work in this area, from Merriam's day to the present, see John G. Gunnell's appendix "Telling the Story of Political Science" in *Imagining the American Polity: Political Science and the Discourse of Democracy* (University Park: Pennsylvania State University Press, 2004) and Robert Adcock, "A Disciplinary History of Disciplinary Histories," paper presented at the annual meeting of the Midwest Political Science Association, Chicago, April 11, 2013.

In offering a new study of the early-nineteenth- to early-twentieth-century emergence of American political science, I present the field's academic pioneers as active participants in the transatlantic transformation of the liberal tradition that took place during this period in response to changing political and economic realities. Two trends are central for my argument: first, the spread of democratic belief in popular sovereignty and the political capacity of the common man; second, the growth of large-scale industry, which altered the structure and power of social classes while confronting governments with novel policy demands. As these trends unfolded and interacted in countries on both sides of the Atlantic, they repeatedly challenged received liberal beliefs about the characteristics of modern society, the political institutions and economic policies best suited to it, and the contemporary threats to such institutions and policies.

There are distinctive rewards to charting changes in liberalism spurred by these trends as manifested in the emerging domain of American political science. Political science's pioneers in the American academy directly engaged European liberal arguments about ongoing political and economic changes. But they did so with attention to the particular character and challenges of democratic politics and large-scale industry as these developed in America. American political science hence took shape as a science that did more than just embody and express liberal beliefs. It also adapted liberal arguments to address American challenges and audiences. The pioneers of our field were, I argue, agents of the *Americanization of liberalism*.

Transatlantic Perspective and Varieties of Liberalism

The history in this book is framed by two principal interpretive decisions. First, I adopt a transatlantic perspective.[3] Pioneers of political science in the American academy drew widely from across British, French, and German intellectual currents. In doing so, they most frequently found exemplars in specifically liberal writers in those countries. But they then adapted these liberal transatlantic influences to address particularities of nineteenth-century American politics and economics. At the heart of this transatlantic conversation lay transatlantic comparisons. When liberals in Europe discussed mass suffrage, they usually argued with one eye looking across the Atlantic. Some saw in America a harbinger of a democratic future that Europeans would, sooner or later, have to address in their

---

[3] In adopting this orientation, I apply to the history of political science a perspective that has transformed the writing of American intellectual and cultural history during recent decades. For preeminent examples, see James T. Kloppenberg, *Uncertain Victory: Social Democracy and Progressivism in European and American Thought, 1870–1920* (Oxford: Oxford University Press, 1986), and Daniel T. Rodgers, *Atlantic Crossings: Social Politics in a Progressive Age* (Cambridge: Harvard University Press, 1998).

own politics. Others saw an exceptional nation, relevant to Europe principally as a contrast. In engaging with European liberalism, pioneers of political science in America's academy thus became involved in discussions that turned, in no small part, on claims about their own nation's political institutions, history, and economy. They encountered multiple liberal interpretations of how America led, lagged, or was traveling a path different from political and economic developments in Britain, France, or Germany.

Political science as it took shape in America focused upon using, debating, and remaking these liberal transatlantic comparisons. Some pioneers of the field believed that their nation was ahead of Europe, with lessons to teach about constitutional design, federalism, or mass suffrage. Others saw America as behind, with lessons to learn from Britain, France, or Germany about civil service or municipal reform, responsible political parties, or policy responses to the needs of industrial society. Leader and laggard interpretations could each be challenged by, or combined with, beliefs about American exceptionalism. In American political science, alternative lessons for America came to be advanced less by philosophical argument than by divergent comparisons between America's political and economic trajectory and those of major European nations.

By stressing comparisons I seek a fresh angle on the theme of American exceptionalism pursued in Dorothy Ross's *The Origins of American Social Science*.[4] All claims about American exceptionalism, whether in primary sources themselves or historical studies of past scholarship, presume a comparative frame. When we make that framing explicit, it is evident that Europe offered the pivotal comparisons for Americans in the nineteenth century—as it still does, to a large extent, even today. In recounting the emergence of political science in the American academy I explore a series of figures who forcefully articulated and drew practical lessons from transatlantic comparisons between America and major European countries. Their works offer a venue in which we can follow concrete claims being made about the ways in which America was (or was not, or would not remain) exceptional, relative to which European countries, and with what political and policy implications.

My second interpretive decision is to showcase the emergence of political science specifically as it helps elucidate varieties of liberalism. I am interested in alternative liberal political visions, how these differ, and how they change over time in response to challenges to the beliefs, hopes, and fears that inform them. I hence offer a history structured in terms of, and in order to illuminate, multiple *liberalisms*. The way that I analytically differentiate between liberalisms is consciously designed to highlight changes among American political scientists in

---

[4] Dorothy Ross, *The Origins of American Social Science* (Cambridge: Cambridge University Press, 1991).

their views of the promise or perils of democracy and industry, and their accompanying uses of transatlantic comparisons.

I structure the narrative of my book around three subtypes of liberalism. First I recount the political vision that I call *democratized classical liberalism*, which crystallized in the 1830s among advocates of the possibility of a specifically liberal democracy, and reached a zenith after the American Civil War freed modern democracy from slavery's illiberal stain. By interpreting movement toward widespread suffrage as the grand political trajectory of the epoch, this midcentury vision located America at the forefront of modern history and made its politics pivotal for liberal reflection on what to hope, fear, and strive for in the present and future. By the 1880s, however, events and policy trends on both sides of the Atlantic increasingly jarred against the classical laissez-faire orientation in political economy of democratized classical liberalism.

Against this backdrop, I then recount how two divergent adaptations of midcentury liberalism shaped the late-century political visions I call *progressive liberalism* and *disenchanted classical liberalism*. Both of these visions viewed expansion in the social and economic roles of government, with Europe setting the pace, as the primary political trend of their day. Progressive liberals, on one hand, saw in such expansion the potential for a healthy ameliorative response to demands arising from industrialization, and they refashioned the concept of liberal democracy bequeathed by democratized classical liberalism to better fit this aspiration.[5] By contrast, those I label disenchanted classical liberals saw in the same expansion a revival of illiberal paternalism. They offered critical analyses of late-century political and policy trends that eschewed the midcentury hope of democratized classical liberalism that a more democratic politics could advance rather than imperil classical liberal economic policies.

Among these three liberalisms, progressive liberalism has been the most studied. Its sympathizers and critics alike, even as they disagree sharply in evaluative tone, agree on the integral relationship of this political vision to intellectual innovations in America's late-century academy.[6] However, neither the democratized

---

[5] In employing the phrase "progressive liberalism" I follow Dorothy Ross as well as Raymond Seidelman and Edward Harpham (who use it as a synonym for "liberal progressivism"). See Dorothy Ross, "Socialism and American Liberalism: Academic Social Thought in the 1880s," *Perspectives in American History* 11 (1977–78), 7 n 1; Raymond Seidelman and Edward J. Harpham, *Disenchanted Realists: Political Science and the American Crisis, 1884–1984* (Albany: State University of New York Press, 1985), 239. The British counterpart to progressive liberalism is often labeled simply "new liberalism." Its parallels and interactions with American progressive liberalism have been explored, with special attention to the generation that follows those examined in this book, by Marc Stears, *Progressives, Pluralists, and the Problems of the State: Ideologies of Reform in the United States and Britain, 1909–1926* (Oxford: Oxford University Press, 2002).

[6] For sympathetic treatments of progressive liberalism, see Kloppenberg, *Uncertain Victory*, and Rodgers, *Atlantic Crossings*. For critical treatments from different perspectives, see Seidelman and

classical liberalism that had preceded progressive liberalism, nor the disenchanted classical liberalism that competed with it, has received as much attention.[7] Yet all three of these liberal political visions found, as I spotlight in the chapters that follow, forceful articulation among pioneers of American political science. If we are to interpret the political science that emerged in America's academy between the early nineteenth and early twentieth centuries as an identifiably liberal science, we should also, I propose, attend to the fact that the emerging science was far from monolithic in the substantive details of its liberalisms.

Connecting American Political Science to the "Liberal Tradition"

In connecting the emergence of American political science to liberalism, I take up a relation most influentially treated in Bernard Crick's *The American Science of Politics*.[8] Yet, whereas Crick approached this topic under the influence of Louis Hartz's then-recent *The Liberal Tradition in America*,[9] I revisit it against the backdrop of the often sharp criticisms of Hartz that are commonplace in more contemporary scholarship on American liberalism.[10] My interpretive choices about "the liberal tradition," and how to connect American political science to it, hence make my history more a corrective to than an extension of Crick's classic book.

The revisionary aspect of this history is most immediately evident in my differentiation of multiple liberalisms. Crick drew from Hartz a conception of "the American liberal tradition" as an enduring monolith. He emphasized the "unity"

Harpham, *Disenchanted Realists*, and Dennis J. Mahoney, *Politics and Progress: The Emergence of American Political Science* (Lanham, MD: Lexington Books, 2004).

[7] I build here on the recent lead of Leslie Butler, who has extended the transatlantic agenda among historians from the progressive liberal focus of the earlier works of Kloppenberg and Rodgers to midcentury classical liberals and their disenchantment in late century. Leslie Butler, *Critical Americans: Victorian Intellectuals and Transatlantic Liberal Reform* (Chapel Hill: University of North Carolina Press, 2007).

[8] Crick, *American Science of Politics*. On Crick's book and its reception, see Michael Kenny, "History and Dissent: Bernard Crick's *The American Science of Politics*," *American Political Science Review* 100, no. 4 (2006), 547–53.

[9] Louis Hartz, *The Liberal Tradition in America: An Interpretation of American Political Thought since the Revolution* (New York: Harcourt, Brace and World, 1955).

[10] For recent examples of the extensive scholarly commentary Hartz's classic has generated, see Mark Hulliung, ed., *The American Liberal Tradition Reconsidered: The Contested Legacy of Louis Hartz* (Lawrence: University Press of Kansas, 2010). For a careful attempt to disentangle Hartz's "actual purpose, intention, and argument" from the ways in which his work has come to be received and debated over decades of commentary, see John G. Gunnell, "Louis Hartz and the Liberal Metaphor: A Half-Century Later," *Studies in American Political Development* 19 (Fall 2005), 196–205.

and "unanimity of American liberalism," and its "continuity" over time. From this perspective Crick could sweepingly declare that even "the Progressive Era gave rise to no new political thought."[11] By contrast, I emphasize variety and change. As a result, for example, when I reach the Progressive Era, I elucidate how alternative intellectual departures from midcentury democratized classical liberalism gave shape to two late-century liberal political visions with divergent conceptions of democracy and the role of the state in an industrial society. In differentiating my own stress on variety and change from Crick's stress on unity and continuity, I do not intend to deny the existence of commonalities across American political scientists whom I locate under my different subtypes of liberalism. I am, after all, still treating them together as fellow participants in the liberal tradition.

While my stress on variety and change is, by itself, insufficient to entail a thoroughgoing disagreement with Crick, where disagreement does arise is in my treatment of political scientists as *agents* of variety and change. Crick introduced "the American liberal tradition" into his study as a sweeping societal "context" external to the development of political science in the American academy. He then treated the "massive agreement about the nature and aims of American life" of this "pre-existent American liberalism" as constraining and directing the content and character of political science as it emerged in the academy.[12] By contrast, I conceive "the liberal tradition" as just one evolving current within American political thought, and I characterize political scientists as active agents in its production, reproduction, and remaking over time.[13] Moreover, I present pioneering political scientists as helping to import "the liberal tradition" into American thought and Americanize it, whereas for Crick "the liberal tradition" was a "pre-existent" consensus that already dominated American political thought before academic political science took root.

Despite these differences, historians of American political science might observe that my approach retains a basic similarity to Crick's. We both use the concept of liberalism in analyzing nineteenth-century Americans who themselves neither self-identified as "liberals" nor construed American politics or thought in terms of "liberalism." Talk of liberalism only became prominent among America's

---

[11] Crick, *American Science of Politics*, vi, 13, 234, 240, 80–83. Though Crick's use of Hartz is well in line with the dominant image of *The Liberal Tradition in America*, there are alternative uses of Hartz's book that find resources within it to analyze change and contestation within American thought. For example, see Philip Abbott, "Still Louis Hartz after All These Years: A Defense of the Liberal Society Thesis," *Perspectives on Politics* 3, no. 1 (2005), 93–109; and Catherine A. Holland, "Hartz and Minds: *The Liberal Tradition* after the Cold War," *Studies in American Political Development* 19 (Fall 2005), 227–33. Given the range of uses to which Hartz's multifaceted book may be put, I situate my own study as a corrective explicitly of Crick's *use* of Hartz more than of Hartz himself.

[12] Crick, *American Science*, vi, 8.

[13] For a philosophical account and defense of "tradition" as I conceive it, see Mark Bevir, *The Logic of the History of Ideas* (Cambridge: Cambridge University Press, 1999).

political scientists beginning during the 1930s, on the heels of its entry into the discourse of American politics between the 1910s and 1930s.[14] Any account of earlier American political scientists in terms of "liberalism" thus unavoidably involves conceptual projection. In so doing, I aim to make explicit the grounds upon which this projection rests.

My projection of "liberalism" onto nineteenth-century American political scientists has three historical anchors. First, in chapter 1, I introduce liberalism with reference to what the words "liberalism" and "liberal" meant as they first entered into political use in early- to mid-nineteenth-century Europe, and with specific attention to the range of views of American democracy found among these liberals. When I then move across the Atlantic to begin tracing the emergence of American political science, I carry the language of "liberalism" with me. I support doing so by showing that political science during its initial steps in America's academy articulated a political vision—the vision I call democratized classical liberalism—that was introduced in chapter 1 as a position also developing at the same time within European liberal debates about democracy.

My second historical anchor is the identification of transatlantic ties that directly connect American political scientists to Europeans who were liberals in the politics of their own countries. (Several of these Europeans, indeed, served at one time or another in government or elected assemblies as members of Liberal parties.) Taken together, these ties establish that American political science took shape in the context of transatlantic networks of intellectual and political elites connecting the pioneers of the science to the vicissitudes of liberalism in nineteenth-century Europe.[15] Even as "liberal" and "liberalism" lacked resonance in nineteenth-century American politics, the political visions of American political scientists were, I argue, informed by their ties to European liberalism.

The third anchor for my projection of "liberalism" comes in the conclusion of my study, when I step back from my history of political scientists to show how this history illuminates the way the words "liberal" and "liberalism" were used as they finally did enter American political discourse between the 1910s and 1930s. The contours of their earliest American uses differed notably from their earliest

---

[14] The course of this conceptual change in political science is summed up as follows by John Gunnell: "Liberalism was appropriated by political scientists from the language of politics, often by those who favored the politics of the Roosevelt administration. It was then abstracted and equated generically with democracy, and reified and applied retrospectively to functionally or categorically similar ideas and modes of action before being further concretized as a description of American politics and ideas." Gunnell, *Imagining the American Polity*, 195. See also John G. Gunnell, "The Archaeology of American Liberalism," *Journal of Political Ideologies* 6, no. 2 (2001), 125–45.

[15] My study takes the form of a historical narrative, but its content parallels sociological insights about mechanisms structuring the transnational flow of people and ideas as explicated in Johan Heilbron, Nicolas Guilhot, and Laurent Jeanpierre, "Toward a Transnational History of the Social Sciences," *Journal of the History of the Behavioral Sciences* 44, no. 2 (2008), 146–60.

European uses as discussed in chapter 1. This contrast provides linguistic start and end points to the process I have called the *Americanization of liberalism*. The contrast is bridged temporally and intellectually by my account of American political scientists. My most general goal in projecting "liberalism" onto emerging American political science is to show that following changes in the beliefs of pioneering political scientists about democracy and industry leads us step by step from debates among liberals in early- to mid-nineteenth-century Europe to the contests over the meaning of "liberalism" as this word first acquired political resonance in America a full century later.

The History of Political Science: Situating My Approach

Political scientists have long written about the past of their field. But only within the last generation has this activity become, as John Gunnell put it, "a distinct research specialty."[16] The onset of this specialization in the late 1980s to early 1990s involved two developments. First, a series of methodological discussions charged earlier studies of the past of political science with being insufficiently historical.[17] Second, the substantive studies of Gunnell and James Farr inaugurated a new approach to the history of political science centering on conceptual change.[18] One of the best ways to identify my own approach is to spell out how it is indebted to, and departs from, these developments in the recent history of histories of political science.

---

[16] John G. Gunnell, "The Historiography of Political Science," in *The Development of Political Science: A Comparative Survey*, ed. David Easton, John G. Gunnell, and Luigi Graziano (London: Routledge, 1991), 16.

[17] In addition to Gunnell's "Historiography of Political Science," see James Farr, "The History of Political Science," *American Journal of Political Science* 32, no. 4 (1988), 1175–95; John S. Dryzek and Stephen T. Leonard, "History and Discipline in Political Science," *American Political Science Review* 82, no. 4 (1988), 1245–60; James Farr, John G. Gunnell, Raymond Seidelman, John S. Dryzek, and Stephen T. Leonard, "Can Political Science History Be Neutral?" *American Political Science Review* 84, no. 2 (1990), 587–607.

[18] James Farr, "Political Science and the Enlightenment of Enthusiasm," *American Political Science Review* 82, no. 1 (1988), 51–69; James Farr, "The Estate of Political Knowledge: Political Science and the State," in *The Estate of Social Knowledge*, ed. JoAnne Brown and David K. van Keuren (Baltimore: Johns Hopkins University Press, 1991), 1–21; John G. Gunnell, "American Political Science, Liberalism, and the Invention of Political Theory," *American Political Science Review* 82, no. 1 (1988), 71–87; John G. Gunnell, *The Descent of Political Theory: The Genealogy of an American Vocation* (Chicago: University of Chicago Press, 1993). As examples of continuing development of this approach, see Brian C. Schmidt, *The Political Discourse of Anarchy: A Disciplinary History of International Relations* (Albany: State University of New York Press, 1998) and Gunnell, *Imagining the American Polity*.

One prominent theme in the methodological discussion of the late 1980s and early 1990s was a concern that studies of the past of political science had been divided and distorted by their involvement with grand battles over the discipline's overall direction. John Dryzek and Stephen Leonard complained that many histories had been written in "Whig" or "skeptic" mode. Writing from a "teleological" standpoint, "Whigs" had portrayed changes in political science "in terms of triumph over the limited perspectives of past practitioners." The "obverse" stance of "skeptics" had led, by contrast, to histories of political science written "in terms of unremitting error."[19] Gunnell subsequently concluded his 1991 survey "The Historiography of American Political Science" by advocating for efforts "to distinguish between a historical and instrumental approach to the past," and to put aside "rhetorical history," as remedies to rehabilitate "the history of political science which has for too long been overwhelmed by the plots of progress and decline."[20]

In light of such criticisms, I am wary of imposing a narrative arc of triumph or error, progress or decline, on my own history. Since I structure this history around three subtypes of liberalism and change between them, such an arc would be implied if I singled out one subtype as superior. My aim is thus, not simply to give substantial space to all three of the liberalisms I distinguish, but to present each of their political visions with equal charity. I seek to convey the plausibility internal to each vision given the concerns and commitments of its holders. By doing so, I stress that there were multiple reasonable ways that liberalism could be, and was, articulated and adapted by political scientists in nineteenth-century America.

Further features of my approach stand out in relation to the conceptual approach to the history of political science inaugurated by Farr and Gunnell. They prioritized historical recovery of the concepts that past political scientists themselves used. This involved, as Gunnell put it, "approaching the history of political science as a discursive practice" with the aim of charting "its internal conceptual development," and thus, as Farr put it, studying "the development of political science" with "an ear to its practitioners' own language."[21] I am directly indebted to the injunction to heed the language of the past in the way I treat "political science" and decide which Americans to consider as political scientists for the sake of this study. Giving this injunction an institutional twist, I take as my guide the actual use of "political science" in the naming, first of academic chairs, then of schools

[19] Dryzek and Leonard, "History and Discipline in Political Science," 1253–54.

[20] Gunnell, "Historiography of Political Science," 29.

[21] Gunnell, "Historiography of Political Science," 29; James Farr, "From Modern Republic to Administrative State: American Political Science in the Nineteenth Century," in *Regime and Discipline: Democracy and the Development of Political Science*, ed. David Easton, John G. Gunnell, and Michael B. Stein (Ann Arbor: University of Michigan Press, 1995), 131.

and departments, and finally the American Political Science Association (APSA). The Americans I examine in this book all held such a chair, taught in such a school or department, or became a president of the APSA.

Relying on past institutional language to guide my treatment of political science has two principal payoffs. First, it enables me to chart a major conceptual change. The earliest uses of "political science" in America's academy inherited from European precursors a wide remit that encompassed political economy (the forerunner of the later economics discipline), with history another core area, or a close ally. As Collini, Winch, and Burrow stressed in introducing *That Noble Science of Politics*, their study in nineteenth-century British intellectual history, political science in this older sense is a "subject which no longer appears on modern maps of knowledge, at least not as the extensive though vaguely delimited empire it once was."[22] Following the inheritance of the older wider sense of political science from Europe into America's nineteenth-century academy makes it possible, in turn, to grasp the institutional innovation involved in the 1903 founding of the APSA to represent the "special interests" of "Political Science, as distinguished from History and Economics."[23]

The second payoff of following the institutionalized use of "political science" is that the phrase's initially wider sense brings within the remit of my study individuals who, if approached via the lens of later disciplinary divisions, might be left aside as "historians" or "economists." In recent scholarship the extent to which intertwining with history informed political science during its emergence in the American academy has been amply treated.[24] But in also including within my study figures and themes of what was then called "political economy," I make a more novel, and moreover pivotal, move. This enables me to offer a narrative that supplements more studied issues of political science's relation to democracy with attention to industrialization and its tense interplay with democracy. In sum,

[22] Stefan Collini, Donald Winch, and John Burrow, *That Noble Science of Politics: A Study in Nineteenth-Century Intellectual History* (Cambridge: Cambridge University Press, 1983), 3. On the German instantiation of political science in this older, wide, and practical sense, see David F. Lindenfeld, *The Practical Imagination: The German Sciences of the State in the Nineteenth Century* (Chicago: University of Chicago Press, 1997).

[23] I quote here from the circular letter sent to several hundred individuals in October 1903 inviting them to attend the meeting that formally founded the American Political Science Association that December. "The Organization of the American Political Science Association," *Proceedings of the American Political Science Association* 1 (1904), 9.

[24] Ross, *Origins of American Social Science*; Robert Adcock, "The Emergence of Political Science as a Discipline: History and the Study of Politics in America, 1875–1910," *History of Political Thought* 24, no. 3 (2003), 459–86; James Farr, "The Historical Sciences of Politics," in *Modern Political Science: Anglo-American Exchanges since 1870*, ed. Robert Adcock, Mark Bevir, and Shannon Stimson (Princeton, NJ: Princeton University Press, 2007), 66–96.

attending to the past usage of "political science" opens up the central substantive opportunity I take advantage of in this book.

Indebted as I am to the conceptual change approach, the manner in which I proceed from the opportunity of attending to political economy to the crafting of my own synthetic narrative ultimately steps away from the language of the past. As already discussed, in characterizing the responses of American political scientists to democracy and industry as episodes in the liberal tradition, I apply a label of "liberal" they did not apply to themselves. Since I rely in doing so on historical anchors in the uses of "liberalism" in nineteenth-century Europe and twentieth-century America, this first step in framing my narrative takes only a limited step beyond the language of the past. Where I unapologetically apply analytical categories of my own construction is with my subtypes of liberalism. I apply these subtypes to structure a synthetic narrative that deliberately spotlights changes in views of democracy and industry, and in uses of transatlantic comparisons, and does so in a manner intended to speak to how political scientists discuss liberalism today.

Taken as a whole my approach in this book thus proceeds at three different levels. In my talk of "political science" I attend closely to the language of the past. In my talk of "liberal" and "liberalism" I project, but do so with identified anchors in the language of the past. Finally, when applying my three subtypes of liberalism, I retrospectively impose my own analytical typology. The heightened methodological self-consciousness accompanying specialization in the history of political science demands clarity about the existence of each of these methodologically distinct levels in my study. A single historical study, especially a book-length one, may interweave such levels so long as it does so self-consciously and carefully.

A Transatlantic Tale in Three Parts

This book has three parts. Part I establishes the transatlantic departure point for my treatment of the emergence of American political science. Its first chapter introduces the liberal tradition at the time when "liberalism" first entered European political usage, and singles out democratized classical liberalism as a distinctive political vision crystallizing in the context of the tradition's debates about democracy. Chapter 2 introduces the intellectual tradition of historicism and its methodological updating and debates as the research university took shape in early nineteenth-century Germany. Chapter 3 brings my study across the Atlantic and into the American academy through an extended examination of the Prussian émigré Francis Lieber, the first occupant of a chair of "Political Science" in America. Lieber's scholarship combined the political vision of democratized classical liberalism with historicist science. Taken together the three chapters of Part I hence serve to specify the content of the *political* and the *science* in political science as it first secured a foothold in America's antebellum academy.

Part II examines the expansion of American political science between the late 1860s and mid-1880s that accompanied the dramatic growth of university ideals and institutions during the post–Civil War decades. During this period "political science" carried a wide sense inherited from Europe and extending Lieber's encompassing conception of his field. In chapters 4 and 5, as I follow the institutional diffusion of wide political science, I concentrate my substantive attention on political economy as the particular area in which divides and ultimately divergence within the liberalism of political scientists came to the fore. I end Part II by interpreting the controversy-charged middle to late 1880s early years of the American Economics Association as the proverbial canary in the gold mine of wide political science. It publicized the divergence of progressive liberalism and disenchanted classical liberalism as alternative successors to the midcentury democratized classical liberalism to which America's initially wide political science had initially been wedded.

Part III elucidates the content of the *political* and the *science* in political science as the nineteenth century drew to a close. First I examine the two liberal political visions developed as the divergence that had first came to the fore in political economy was fleshed out in alternative conceptions of democracy and the emerging administrative state. Chapter 6 uses the figures of William Graham Sumner and A. Lawrence Lowell to examine disenchanted classical liberalism in this regard, and chapter 7 then uses Woodrow Wilson to examine progressive liberalism. Finally, chapter 8 shows how both of these currents of liberal political thought came during the 1890s to be combined with a new approach to political science that pursued a posthistorical analysis of "modern political systems." When the APSA was founded in 1903 it would provide a national-level professional home for practitioners of a liberal science that, in the substance of its *liberalism* and its *science*, had been transformed from the liberal science of Francis Lieber.

FROM EUROPE TO AMERICA

CHAPTER 1

The "Political" in Political Science

THE LIBERAL DEBATE ABOUT DEMOCRACY

I locate the substance of the "political" in nineteenth-century political science in the liberal tradition—specifically, in debates within this tradition regarding the promise or perils of democracy and its relation to industry. Analyzing these debates in terms of an evolving array of liberal political visions presumes an answer to the question of what makes these all liberal. This chapter thus begins by making explicit the general baseline conception of liberal political thought that my historical narrative presumes, and by identifying the two major axes of contention in the liberal tradition that will be examined through this narrative. My second section then discusses the leading role that beliefs about transformative social change played in fleshing out the substantive content of liberal political thought during the nineteenth century.

The rest of the chapter begins the book's historical narrative by introducing the political vision of *democratized classical liberalism*, the first of the three liberal visions central to my transatlantic tale of political science. Democratized classical liberalism crystallized in Europe during the 1830s in the context of a lively and long-running liberal debate about suffrage. In following this debate from early to mid century, I examine the argument in favor of property limits on suffrage made by prominent early-century liberals, and the subsequent response of democratized classical liberals—in particular, Alexis de Tocqueville and John Stuart Mill—who proposed that liberal commitments could be sustainably combined with a wider suffrage given certain social conditions. In facilitating liberal accommodation with a core democratic practice, democratized classical liberals thus stressed both the possibility and the prerequisites of a liberal democracy.

In surveying the early- to mid-nineteenth-century liberal debate about democracy, I attend especially to the role that the democratization of American politics played in the development of liberal thought. The expansion of universal white male suffrage to become a nationwide norm in 1820s America was a pivotal reference point for the democratized classical liberal political vision when it crystallized in the 1830s. By relating liberal beliefs about democracy to changing experiences with democracy on both sides of the Atlantic, spotlighting incipient anxiety about how industrial development would interact with democratization, and noting parallels between European liberal arguments and those that Americans made about their own politics, I establish a departure point for carrying the political side of my narrative across the Atlantic to America in later chapters.

Liberal Political Thought as a Historical Tradition

I approach liberalism historically as a broad tradition of political thought, evolving over time as its participants have addressed practical questions. Substantively this approach is akin to that of Andreas Kalyvas and Ira Katznelson in their *Liberal Beginnings*. They treat liberalism as having developed at "critical junctures" when it addressed "pressing political and institutional matters," and they thereby advance an account of "liberalism that is more historical, more unpredictable, more heterogeneous and relational, and more oriented to practical affairs."[1] Kalyvas and Katznelson's study runs from 1750 to the 1820s, traveling from the Scottish Enlightenment to the American founding, and then back across the Atlantic to the francophone liberals Germaine de Staël and Benjamin Constant. The chapters of my study run from 1810 to the early twentieth century, offering a practically oriented transatlantic account, which starts here from the same pair of francophone liberals with whom Kalyvas and Katznelson end, and which by the close of Part III has advanced to address five of the earliest presidents of the American Political Science Association, founded in 1903.[2]

Any narrative of liberalism as an evolving tradition will be decisively shaped by where it enters the flowing historical stream of liberal thought. My book begins in Europe in the era of Napoleon's defeat and the return of the Bourbon dynasty to the French throne. The regime of the Bourbon Restoration was based upon the Charter of 1814, granted by Louis XVIII following his return to France.[3] Modeled on Britain's constitution, the Charter created a Chamber of Deputies, and it was in relation to this elected assembly that the word *libéralisme* first

---

[1] Andreas Kalyvas and Ira Katznelson, *Liberal Beginnings: Making a Republic for the Moderns* (Cambridge: Cambridge University Press, 2008), 14.

[2] I self-consciously use the word "pair" in referring to de Staël and Constant to allude to their extended and close personal interaction. To situate the political thought of these liberals beside their complex personal relations, from their first meeting in 1794 to de Staël's death in 1817, see Renee Winegarten, *Germaine de Staël & Benjamin Constant: A Dual Biography* (New Haven, CT: Yale University Press, 2008).

[3] On the Charter and the relation of French liberals to it, see Aurelian Craiutu, *Liberalism under Siege: The Political Thought of the French Doctrinaires* (Lanham, MD: Lexington Books, 2003), 70–75.

acquired a common political use in French. During the Bourbon Restoration the word came to label supporters of the authority of the elected Chamber. Some of them held ministerial and other government positions in the 1810s. But after the government turned reactionary in 1820 following the assassination of the king's nephew, all liberals were aligned in opposition.[4] It was also during 1815–1830 that the word "liberalism" first acquired a clear political usage in Britain, where it came to label the more radical wing of the parliamentary opponents of the then-governing Conservative Party.[5] By the late 1830s, its use was broadening. Thus, John Stuart Mill in 1839 argued that all proreform currents within British politics—from Whig supporters of moderate reform through "the Ultra-Radicals and the Working Classes"—should cooperate so that the Conservatives would have to compete against "the whole Liberal party, not some mere section of it."[6]

Political events of the early 1830s carried liberals in both France and Britain into power. The 1830 July Revolution in France ended the reign of the restored Bourbons and led to the new constitutional monarchy of Louis Philippe in which liberals were the dominant political force. In Britain, general elections in 1830 and 1831 ended decades of Conservative dominance and paved the way for passage of the 1832 Reform Act, which extended suffrage into the liberal-supporting middle classes. The 1830s and 1840s were hence a period of liberal political ascendancy in both France and Britain. But, at midcentury, the fate of liberalism in the nations diverged. In France, liberals lost power after Louis Napoleon's coup against parliamentary institutions and founding of the Second Empire in 1851–1852.[7] In Britain, by contrast, the power of liberalism continued. The Whig Party formally became the Liberal Party in the 1850s, while continuing its dominance of British politics, winning most elections, and hence forming most governments.

---

[4] This context played a major role in perhaps the first characterization of "liberal" in political terms for an American audience. In 1831 the *Encyclopedia Americana*, edited by the Prussian political émigré Francis Lieber (who would, as we will see in chapter 3, later become America's first professor of political science), explained: "In modern times, the word *liberal* has received a peculiar political meaning. The two great parties throughout the European continent are composed of those who adhere to the ancient *regime*, and object to the principle of equal rights, and of those who, adhering to the latter, are thence called *liberals*.... The word *liberal* received the most distinct signification, in a political point of view, in France, during the years preceding the revolution of 1830. It then meant the party opposed to the ultras and the hierarchists." "Liberal," in *Encyclopedia Americana*, vol. 7, ed. Francis Lieber (Philadelphia: Carey and Lea, 1831).

[5] G. de Bertier de Sauvigny, "Liberalism, Nationalism and Socialism: The Birth of Three Words," *Review of Politics* 32, no. 2 (1970), 150–55.

[6] John Stuart Mill, "Reorganization of the Reform Party," in *Essays on England, Ireland, and the Empire*, ed. John. M Robson, *Collected Works of John Stuart Mill*, vol. 6 (Toronto: University of Toronto Press, 1982), 467.

[7] The baseline commitments I identify below as bounding my use of "liberalism" entail that the Cobden trade treaty and other economic moves of the later Second Empire did not make that Empire "liberal" since it remained illiberal in its political institutions.

As "liberal" and "liberalism" came to label political movements, the words also came to label the individuals who gave these movements intellectual articulation, and the views that they espoused. These intellectuals were directly engaged with contemporary politics. Many were, at some point, members of Parliament, and several became party leaders and statesmen. The most read today are Alexis de Tocqueville and John Stuart Mill. But there were multiple other figures in the lively intellectual life of early- to mid-nineteenth-century European liberalism. In France, between de Staël and Constant's generation and that of Tocqueville, there stands the towering figure of François Guizot: one of the most politically power-ful of French liberals in the period of liberalism's greatest power in France, and also hugely intellectually influential in his time as a historian of modern Europe. In Britain, J. S. Mill's mature political vision took shape against the backdrop of the criticism leveled against his father James Mill's radical politics by the younger Mill's generational contemporary, T. B. Macaulay, who went on to become a prom-inent liberal statesman-historian akin in key ways to Guizot. It is with reference to this broader liberal milieu that the political vision articulated by Tocqueville and J. S. Mill from the 1830s on stands out as distinctive. They were far from radi-cal democrats, but I label the political vision they expounded *democratized* classi-cal liberalism in order to spotlight their openness to democracy *relative* to many other prominent liberals in Europe at the time, such as Guizot or Macaulay.

Any conception of liberal political thought capable of encompassing the breadth of the liberal tradition should have space within it for these and other diverse figures of the decades in which "liberalism" first acquired political resonance.[8] I conceive of liberal political thought as a broad tradition marked by contained contention. The common ground of de Staël and Constant, Guizot and Tocqueville, the Mills and Macaulay, does not lie at the level of philosophical foundations, for among them we find arguments appealing, alternatively, to inalienable rights, to divine providence, and to utility. But whichever of these foundations they appealed to, the *practical* political conclusions of their arguments converged upon two base-line commitments regarding institutions of domestic governance: constitutional government and representative institutions.[9] It is these two commitments that

[8] Approaching seventeenth- or eighteenth-century political thinkers in terms of "liberalism" entails retrospectively projecting a label that first acquired political resonance in the context of the nineteenth century movements I have pinpointed. This is no reason to rule out such projections. But they should proceed on the basis of a clear conception of what it is to be "liberal" that can encompass the actual political meaning this term later acquired. For example, the conception I make explicit here could encompass Locke, Montesquieu, Smith, Madison, among others who are often discussed as liberal. It would not, however, encompass Rousseau or Hobbes since neither meets the requirement of commit-ment to representative institutions that I state below.

[9] I include the word "domestic" since liberals did not necessarily support constitutional represen-tative government in *all* societies. During the last decade and a half, scholarship on liberal views of empire has brought much attention to the fact that liberal commitments to constitutional representa-tive government did not automatically extend beyond Western nations. When considering Europe's

delimit the boundaries within which a thinker must fall to be considered a liberal for the purposes of my study.

First, liberals are committed to *constitutional* government. They believe that the government should exercise its powers through the institutions, and within the confines, of a recognized constitution (codified or not), and that the government has an attendant duty to provide an equitable rule of law and to respect civil liberties. Second, liberals are committed to *representative* government. They believe an elected assembly, whose debates and decisions are public, should play a lead role in legislation and should critically scrutinize government policy and actions. That assembly cannot be a mere talking shop that the government may heed, ignore, or manipulate as it wishes. This second commitment is especially crucial for bounding liberalism. Because constitutionalism is a commitment shared throughout much Western political thought, it is the commitment to representative government that more often does the heavy lifting in distinguishing specifically *liberal* thought.

These baseline commitments leave open ample space for disagreements among liberals, and they debated one another along multiple axes of contention during the nineteenth century. It has long been standard to retrospectively parse the liberalisms of this century around a division over the extent of government's social and economic roles. On one side of this familiar divide is "classical liberal" advocacy of laissez-faire (which, we will see in later chapters, was interpreted alternately in moderate or more uncompromising ways). On the other side are liberals labeled as "progressive" (or "modern liberals," "social liberals," etc.),[10] who call for government to take on expanded responsibilities, especially in responding to social problems believed to accompany an industrial economy. This standard divide is prominent in my own study, especially in its later chapters as the historical narrative advances into the 1880s and beyond.

The drama of liberal debate over the extent of government's responsibilities should not, however, obscure other areas of debate in nineteenth-century

non-Western colonies, some major liberals advocated despotic forms of government that they rejected at home. For major examples of this now expansive literature, see Uday Singh Mehta, *Liberalism and Empire: A Study in Nineteenth-Century British Liberal Thought* (Chicago: University of Chicago Press, 1999); Jennifer Pitts, *A Turn to Empire: The Rise of Imperial Liberalism in Britain and France* (Princeton, NJ: Princeton University Press, 2005); Karuna Mantena, *Alibis of Empire: Henry Maine and the Ends of Liberal Imperialism* (Princeton, NJ: Princeton University Press 2010); Yvonne Chiu and Robert Taylor, "The Self-Extinguishing Despot: Millian Democratization," *Journal of Politics* 73, no. 4 (2011), 1239–50.

[10] There is little consensus about what to call the nonclassical liberal side of the divide established by the category of "classical liberal." Most recently the divide has been reframed as one between "classical" and "high liberalism." See John Tomasi, *Free Market Fairness* (Princeton, NJ: Princeton University Press, 2012), chaps. 1 and 2.

liberalism. In connecting the liberal tradition to the "political" in political science, my book stresses a less studied axis of contention: disagreement over the particular political institutions and ideals that are possible and preferable in modern nations. Liberals all advocated constitutional and representative government, but they were not wedded to any single institutional model. Some were republicans, but others favored constitutional monarchies, as in Britain, that combined a monarch of limited powers with a powerful representative assembly. Liberals also diverged over crucial details of the representative assemblies that they all advocated. There was, for instance, no one liberal view of the proper relationship between elected representatives and those who elect them. And most importantly, liberals disagreed on the desired extent of the suffrage. These practical institutional questions were informed, moreover, by a theoretical disagreement about whether elected representative assemblies were, or should aim to be, compatible with the democratic principle of popular sovereignty.

These questions about institutions and ideals, which I treat together as the "liberal debate about democracy," constituted a—arguably *the*—principal axis of contention and differentiation in the liberal tradition during the decades in which my study begins. To concretely illustrate this point, I will sketch briefly some selected examples of arguments advanced by leading early- to mid-nineteenth-century liberals.

First, let us turn to *Considerations on the Principal Events of the French Revolution*, the seminal liberal treatment of the French Revolution that Germaine de Staël was completing when she died in 1817. This work interwove a history of events with liberal political reflections upon those events. De Staël distinguished a set of common liberal positions—which she preferred to rest upon an "invariable principle" of "imprescriptible rights"—from the practical choices about the "form of government" then much debated among liberals.

> In the code of liberty we have the means of distinguishing that which is founded on invariable principle from that which belongs to particular circumstances. Imprescriptible rights consist in—equality under the law, individual liberty, the liberty of the press, freedom of religion, the right of admission to public employments, and the grant of taxes by the representatives of the people. But the form of government, whether aristocratic or democratic, monarchical or republican, is but an organization of powers; and powers themselves nothing but the guarantees of liberty.[11]

---

[11] Germaine de Staël, *Considerations on the Principal Events of the French Revolution*, ed. Aurelian Craiutu (Indianapolis, IN: Liberty Fund, 2008), 211. De Staël's *Considerations* was first published in English translation in 1818. In labeling the work as a seminal one I have in mind the many parallels noted by its editor Aurelian Craiutu to the now more famous liberal interpretation of the French Revolution advanced in the 1850s in Alexis de Tocqueville, *The Old Regime and the French Revolution*, trans. Stuart Gilbert (New York: Anchor Books, 1983).

While advocating "representative government" as the "point toward which the human mind" was directing itself in her day, de Staël believed that political institutions should vary in their details to suit particular national circumstances. Hence, even as she celebrated "the independence of the United States" as having been "desired by all liberal minds," she also argued that the Constituent Assembly of the first years of the French Revolution went astray in drafting a constitution after it was "seized with a philosophical enthusiasm, proceeding in part, from the example of America." In de Staël's view this enthusiasm led the Constituent Assembly to decisions that were unsuited to France's circumstances at the 1789–1791 outset of the Revolution. More akin to England than America, France's situation at the time had, she held, favored an English-model combination of an elected representative assembly, an upper house of the hereditary nobility, and a constitutional monarch with a formally absolute veto over legislation.[12]

To interpret de Staël's liberal commitment to representative government as if it entailed, or should have entailed, unwavering commitment to a single constitutional form would obscure the practical dimension of her political thought. Her concern with practical judgment about what is possible and preferable in particular circumstances led her to advocate differing constitutional models for France as its situation changed. During the middle to late 1790s, for example, de Staël had contended that "in the present circumstances, republican government alone can give France peace and freedom."[13] By acknowledging the significance of clauses such as "the present circumstances," our view of de Staël's liberalism, and the liberal tradition more generally, can and should include prescriptions both for constitutional monarchy or for a republic.[14]

Early nineteenth-century liberal political thought also pursued theoretical reflection into the relationship between the democratic ideal of popular sovereignty and elected representative assemblies. Commitment to such assemblies was, for most liberals, informed by a belief and hope that these assemblies could embody, and thus politically empower, deliberative *reason*. But this belief and hope stood in a recognized tension with responsiveness to the popular *will*, which, they noted, might be far from exemplifying deliberative reasoning. For example,

[12] De Staël, *Considerations*, 24–25, 72–73, 180–81, 211–15. For an overview of the debate between the American and English model that de Staël passed judgment on, see Joyce Appleby, "America as a Model for the Radical French Reformers of 1789," *William and Mary Quarterly*, 3rd series, 28, no. 2 (1971), 267–86.

[13] Winegarten, *De Staël & Constant*, 72–73.

[14] I diverge on this point from Kalyvas and Katznelson's treatment of de Staël in *Liberal Beginnings*, which tends to see her as more fully liberal in the middle to late 1790s when she advocated republican institutions for France. In doing so they unpack the liberal commitment to representative government into a particular commitment to a republic, and indeed even a specifically democratic republic. Such a conception of liberalism would exclude many of the political actors and intellectuals labeled "liberal" as the term acquired common political usage in the nineteenth century.

when de Staël reflected upon what had led France's Constituent Assembly astray, she not only pointed to its "enthusiasm" about America, but also the Assembly's responsiveness to the popular mood. After bewailing "the disastrous effect of popular clamor on the decisions of enlightened men," she in turn declared: "It is scarcely possible for a reflecting mind to exercise sufficient deliberation to understand all the questions relative to political institutions; what then, can be more fatal than to submit such questions to the arguments, and, above all, the sarcasms of the multitude?"[15]

The anxiety that informed de Staël's view that the "class which is called to govern by virtue of its knowledge and education" must deliberate at some remove from the popular will provided a basis for the more elaborate political theory of representative government expounded by the younger French liberal Guizot in the 1820s. Following the lead of other liberals, Guizot conceived of representative government as the telos of modern political history, declaring that

> ever since the birth of modern societies their condition has been such, that in their institution, in their aspirations, and in the course of their history, the representative form of government, while hardly realized as such by the mind, has constantly loomed more or less distinctly in the distance, as the port at which they must at length arrive, in spite of the storms which scatter them, and the obstacles which confront and oppose their entrance.[16]

Contending, however, that during "the endeavour after it [representative government], men have often ignored its principles and mistaken its nature," Guizot intertwined political philosophy with political history to advance a theory of representative government as a progressively developing pursuit of the sovereignty of reason. Emphasizing the difference between reason and will, Guizot conceived the sovereignty of reason as competing with, and preferable to, any will-based concept of sovereignty. From this standpoint the *democratic* ideal of popular sovereignty appeared as the successor to the early-modern absolutist ideal of monarchical sovereignty. The abstract notion of the popular will had simply taken the position previously given to the king's will. Both concepts of sovereignty were will-based and, as such, all too capable of being used to justify despotism. Just as

---

[15] De Staël, *Considerations*, 214. The next sentence quotes p. 231.

[16] François Guizot, *The History of the Origins of Representative Government in Europe*, trans. Andrew R. Scoble (Indianapolis, IN: Liberty Fund, 2002), 12. This work is based on lectures Guizot gave in Paris in 1820–1822, after he had left public life due to the reactionary turn of the Bourbon government, and later revised for their publication in 1851, after the 1848 revolution had ended the political career he had restarted with great success following the 1830 revolution.

liberals supported representative assemblies against monarchical sovereignty, so they should also, Guizot taught, distinguish and defend the authority and deliberative activity of representative assemblies from appeals to the new democratic form of will-based sovereignty.[17]

These brief snapshots of arguments from francophone liberals should suffice to suggest that liberalism in the early nineteenth century was far from equating representative government with democracy. A tendency toward this equation certainly would develop in the liberal tradition over the course of the century. But to historically chart when and how the liberal commitment to representative government came to be *democratized*, we have to avoid the premature reading of democratic content into liberal political thought.[18] Only then can we grasp the content and import of changes in the liberal tradition between the works of de Staël and Guizot, and a later work like J. S. Mill's *Considerations on Representative Government*.

Mill's 1861 *Considerations* exemplifies the midcentury flourishing of the democratized classical liberal political vision. While Mill's work reiterated the standard liberal commitment to representative government, in doing so he restated the content of that commitment by presenting representative *democracy* as its ideal form.[19] Mill shifted between "representative government," "popular government," "representative democracy," and "democracy," in a manner that blurred older conceptual distinctions and paved the way toward these phrases coming to be used by later liberals (including American political scientists) as largely synonymous. This conceptual elision was not a marker of sloppiness. Rather, it was symptomatic of the more particular liberal vision and project that Mill advanced. Whereas Guizot pitted the sovereignty of reason *against* popular sovereignty, Mill favored institutions, practices, and principles that sought an accommodation between deliberative reasoning and popular will (or, as political scientists today might say, he advocated "deliberative democracy"). If some of Mill's moves *liberalized* democracy, others *democratized* liberalism, and both kinds of moves together advanced the political vision that I label democratized classical liberalism, and that I outline in greater detail later in this chapter.

[17] Craiutu, *Liberalism under Siege*, chap. 5.

[18] In emphasizing the evolving relationship between liberalism and democracy I am indebted to Guido de Ruggiero, *The History of European Liberalism*, trans. R. G. Collingwood (Oxford: Oxford University Press, 1927).

[19] John Stuart Mill, *Considerations on Representative Government*, in *Essays on Politics and Society*, ed. John. M. Robson, *Collected Works of John Stuart Mill*, vol. 19 (Toronto: University of Toronto Press, 1977). See esp. chaps. 2, 3, 7.

Nineteenth-Century Liberalism: Social Transformations as a Basis for Political Thought

Liberal political thought in the nineteenth century offered more than a series of shifting visions of representative government. These visions were embedded in theories of history that situated, explained, and extolled representative government in light of grand processes of social change that were believed to make a liberal political order both viable and desirable. Nineteenth-century liberals talked comfortably and commonly of social transformations—"enlightenment," "civilization," "progress," or later in the century, "evolution"—that they understood as having developed over centuries, and as leading to the present cultural, economic, and political situation of their own nations. Liberal thinkers positioned themselves as the interpreters—at their most ambitious even the vanguard—of social change. They believed that this standpoint sharpened their ability to grasp what was possible and preferable in their own day and thereby to inform practical judgments on contemporary political choices.

The implications of this standpoint for liberal political thought were well understood by J. S. Mill. Crediting "the influences of European, that is to say, Continental, thought" on his mature political views of the 1830s onward, Mill declared in his *Autobiography*:

> I derived, among other ideas... these in particular: That the human mind has a certain order of possible progress, in which some things must precede others, an order which governments and public instructors can modify to some, but not to an unlimited extent: That all questions of political institutions are relative, not absolute, and that different stages of human progress not only *will* have, but *ought* to have, different institutions: That government is always either in the hands, or passing into the hands, of whatever is the strongest power in society, and that what this power is, does not depend on institutions, but institutions on it: That any general theory or philosophy of politics supposes a previous theory of human progress, and that this is the same thing with a philosophy of history.[20]

Applying this standpoint in *Considerations on Representative Government*, where he presented his own political theory in its fullest form, Mill avowed that "the main point of superiority in the political theories of the present" arose from their recognition of the "truth" that "institutions need to be radically different, according to the stage of advancement reached." It was on this basis that Mill judged his

[20] John Stuart Mill, *Autobiography* (New York: Liberal Arts Press, 1957), 104–5 (italics in original).

own treatment of democracy to be an advance over the earlier view of radicals, such as his father, who claimed "representative democracy for England or France by arguments which would equally have proved it the only fit form of government for Bedouins or Malays."[21]

While J. S. Mill is especially explicit about relating political questions to grand processes of social change, the proclivity of nineteenth-century liberals to elaborate the substance of their political thought in this way had found perhaps its now most read exemplification in Constant's 1819 lecture "The Liberty of the Ancients Compared with That of the Moderns."[22] Constant here characterized the political institutions and ideals of ancient republics as suited to a social order of small slaveholding city-states recurrently at war, and set that social order in polar contrast to a modern Europe of large states engaged in extensive commerce. He used this contrast to suggest that France had gone astray during the Republican period of its Revolution under leaders who were overly wedded to ancient republican models. Ignoring the distinctive character of modern societies, French republican leaders had pursued projects doomed to fail. Moving from criticism to advocacy, Constant suggested that these anachronistic yearnings had obscured the kind of liberty—a liberty of individual freedoms secured by representative government—which was best suited to modern societies, and which had already been realized in Britain and the United States.[23]

Constant's lecture exemplified a basic framework of ideas about social change pervasive in nineteenth-century liberal political thought. These were as follows: First, a distinctive modern social order has come (or is coming) into being. Second, this social transformation alters what is politically possible. Third, more specifically, it makes representative government not simply possible but preferable. Fourth, it rules out older political institutions and ideals as anachronisms unsuitable for modern societies. This framework of ideas sustained a mode of argument that liberals deployed against a diverse array of alternative political ideals and institutions: not just ancient republics, but also medieval feudal aristocracy and early-modern absolute monarchy.[24]

---

[21] Mill, *Considerations on Representative Government*, 393–94.

[22] Benjamin Constant, "The Liberty of the Ancients Compared with That of the Moderns," in *Political Writings*, ed. Biancamaria Fontana (Cambridge: Cambridge University Press, 1988).

[23] Starting with the example of Constant's lecture, Karuna Mantena suggests that the charge that radical republicans of the French Revolution pursued anachronistic agendas "initiated a fundamental reevaluation of ancient society" that gave distinctive shape, through the ancient versus modern contrast, to "nineteenth-century social theory's account of modernity." Mantena, *Alibis of Empire*, 58–67.

[24] In stressing how beliefs about social change limit the space of possibility within liberal political thought I extend an insight of Wolin's discussion of "Liberalism and the Decline of Political Philosophy." Sheldon S. Wolin, *Politics and Vision: Continuity and Innovation in Western Political Thought* (Boston: Little, Brown, 1960), chap. 9.

Nineteenth-century liberals did not originate this emphasis on social trans-formation. They inherited it from the eighteenth-century thinkers, especially of the Scottish Enlightenment, who had analyzed the "modern" in terms of the cre-ation of a "commercial society," and expounded liberal institutions and ideals as the political order best suited to such a society. The inheritance was direct in the case of Constant, who had studied at the University of Edinburgh as a teenager in the mid-1780s. He had put what he learned there to practical effect in the middle to late 1790s when he brought anachronism-charging arguments to bear within French political debates about the best constitution for what was then the French Republic.[25]

To get a sense for how liberal conceptions of the modern differed and changed over time, we can turn from Constant to Guizot, twenty years younger, and not yet born when Constant was a student in Edinburgh. The most celebrated and influential of Guizot's works was his *History of Civilization in Europe*. First pre-sented as an acclaimed series of lectures at the Sorbonne in 1828—with a young and receptive Tocqueville in the audience—the lectures became, when pub-lished, a highly popular book that was translated into multiple languages and made its way across the Atlantic to be assigned in multiple American colleges. If Constant's 1819 lecture testified to the legacies of Enlightenment thought in nineteenth-century liberalism, a decade later Guizot's classic articulated a new direction for liberal conceptions of the modern.

Whereas Constant's theory of history deployed an ideal-typical contrast between modern and ancient societies, Guizot directed the bulk of his histori-cal attention to the centuries that fell chronologically between Constant's two poles. Indeed, the "modern" for Guizot did not refer just to the present or very recent past, but to a continuous process of development, unfolding from the fall of Rome on, which had to be considered as a whole to appreciate the distinctive character of modern European civilization. Guizot echoed Constant in assert-ing that the ancient Greeks and Romans had conceived liberty only as "politi-cal liberty" and not as "personal liberty." However, returning to a view favored earlier by Montesquieu, he located "the love of individual liberty" as having been brought into European civilization by the Germanic barbarians who conquered the western half of the Roman Empire, rather than as part of the more recent rise of commerce.[26]

---

[25] On Constant's use of argument from anachronism during the Thermidorian Republic of the middle to late 1790s, and the use of the specific ancient/modern liberty version of this argument by de Staël toward the end of this period, see François Furet, *The French Revolution, 1770–1814* (Oxford: Blackwell, 1996), 169–71, 203–6.

[26] François Guizot, *History of Civilization in Europe*, ed. George Wells Knight (New York: D. Appleton, 1896), 57–58.

In displacing commerce from the center of a liberal theory of history, Guizot did not just replace it with the Germanic invasions or any other single factor. Instead, he made variety itself his chief theme. The barbarian conquerors had interacted with, without eliminating, the peoples, institutions, and ideals already existing in Europe as legacies from the ancient world and the rise of Christianity. It was the resulting plurality that, Guizot argued, gave the civilization of modern Europe "its immense superiority." Looking at other civilizations in history, "whether in Asia or elsewhere, including even those of Greece and Rome, it is impossible not to be struck with the unity of character which reigns among them." Drawing out his comparison, Guizot proclaimed:

> How different from all this is the case as respects the civilization of modern Europe! Take ever so rapid a glance at this, and it strikes you at once as diversified, confused, and stormy. All the principles of social organization are found existing together within it; powers temporal, powers spiritual, the theocratic, monarchic, aristocratic, and democratic elements, all classes of society, all the social situations, are jumbled together, and visible within it; as well as infinite gradations of liberty, of wealth, and of influence.

This social plurality generated liberal political consequences through the contentions it sustained. The "various powers" had been "in a state of continual struggle among themselves, without any one having sufficient force to master the others, and take sole possession of society." Whereas in all other civilizations "the predominance of one principle" eventually culminated in tyranny, "the variety of elements of European civilization, and the constant warfare in which they have been engaged, have given birth in Europe to that liberty, which we prize so dearly."[27]

The argument from social plurality and conflict to liberty did dual service for Guizot. In addition to using it to differentiate modern European civilization from other civilizations, he also used it to illuminate cross-national political differences within Europe. Taking up the continental Europe versus England comparison freighted with import in liberal political thought, Guizot held that "different social elements" had tended to develop "more successively" on the continent, with each having an era in which it came more to the fore. English history, by contrast, had involved "a simultaneous development of the different forces, and a sort of negotiation and compromise between their pretensions and interests." Guizot proposed that this "greatly contributed to make England arrive more quickly than any of the continental states, at the end and aim of all society, that is to say, the establishment of a government at once regular and free."[28] The political lesson of

[27] Guizot, *Civilization in Europe*, 26–33.
[28] Guizot, *Civilization in Europe*, 369–72.

Guizot's grand survey of modern European history was, therefore, to offer a fresh foundation for the veneration of England's post-1688 institutions commonly found among French liberals, from Montesquieu, through de Staël and Constant, to Guizot himself.

Guizot's sweeping historical treatment of the distinctiveness and value of modern society was one of the continental European works with the greatest and most permanent impact (second only to Tocqueville's *Democracy in America*) on J. S. Mill's mature political thought as it took shape from the 1830s onward. In his *Considerations on Representative Government*, where Mill extolled "the function of Antagonism" as served by variety in the membership of a representative assembly, he underscored the significance of this function by declaring, in Guizot-like terms, that

> No community has ever long continued progressive, but while a conflict was going on between the strongest power in the community and some rival power; between the spiritual and temporal authorities; the military or territorial and the industrious classes; the king and the people; the orthodox, and religious reformers. When the victory on either side was so complete as to put an end to strife, and no other conflict took its place, first stagnation followed, and then decay.[29]

What Mill stated here in 1861 as a given fact, he had formulated some two decades earlier, in his 1840 review of Tocqueville's *Democracy in America*, as a "principle of improvement" that had been "profoundly remarked by M. Guizot."[30]

One of the most interesting features of Mill's 1840 reception of Guizot's plurality theory was his concern to relate it to the earlier liberal theory of progress, still employed by Constant in 1819, that wedded progress to the rise of commerce. Speaking at one point like an Enlightenment thinker, Mill credited to the "spirit of commerce and industry...nearly all that advantageously distinguishes the present period from the middle ages." But he then nuanced this older belief by proposing that "the benefits" commerce and industry "conferred on humanity were unqualified" for as long, but only for as long, "as other coordinate elements of improvement existed beside it, doing what it left undone, and keeping its exclusive tendencies in equipoise." When applying this blend of older and newer liberal

---

[29] Mill, *Considerations on Representative Government*, 458–59.

[30] John Stuart Mill, "De Tocqueville on Democracy in America [II]," in *Essays on Politics and Society*, ed. John M. Robson, *Collected Works of John Stuart Mill*, vol. 18 (Toronto: University of Toronto Press, 1977), 197. A fuller exploration of Mill's debts to Guizot would supplement this 1840 engagement with the more extended comments of Mill's 1845 "Guizot's Essays and Lectures on History," in *Essays on French History and Historians*, ed. John M. Robson, *Collected Works of John Stuart Mill*, vol. 20 (Toronto: University of Toronto, 1985), 257–94.

theories of history to interpret the practical demands of his own time, Mill worried that the power of commerce and industry was reaching a point where it could itself threaten progress, and warned that "with its complete preponderance would commence an era either of stationariness or of decline."[31]

Putting Liberal Political Thought in Motion: Dilemmas of Democracy and Industry

These examples make clear that the "modern" was far from a stable reference point for early- to mid-century liberalism. The older Scottish Enlightenment conception of modern society as commercial society was increasingly unable to give practical purchase on contemporary issues. Political and economic transformations had begun that would, through the decades ahead, repeatedly challenge received liberal beliefs, posing dilemmas that spurred new reflection, debate, and positions in the liberal tradition.[32] Two processes of change are especially significant for my narrative: first, the spread of democratic belief in popular sovereignty and the political capacity of the common man, with associated shifts in political practices; and second, the growth of large-scale industry, which altered the structure and power of social classes while confronting governments with new policy demands from this evolving cast of societal actors.

These transformative processes, usually characterized in retrospect as "democratization" and "industrialization," developed over the course of the nineteenth century in often surprising ways, across multiple countries on both sides of the Atlantic, over many decades. Attentiveness to the historical twists and turns of each process, and interplay between them, helps us to see that the array of changes we group together as the rise of mass democracy and mass industry posed a succession of specific dilemmas for liberals in different countries at different times.[33] By structuring my narrative in terms of a *series* of dilemmas, rather than any

[31] Mill, "Tocqueville on Democracy in America," 197.

[32] In looking to "dilemmas" to recount and explain changes in a "tradition" I draw methodologically on the approach to the history of ideas articulated by Mark Bevir in *The Logic of the History of Ideas* (Cambridge: Cambridge University Press, 1999). Substantively, in following how the liberal tradition responded to ongoing social change, and situating the development of social science in relation to this dynamic, I follow the lead of Richard Bellamy. But where Bellamy studies European thought in the period 1870–1930, my study begins with earlier Europeans, and my American focus when dealing with post-1870 thought leads my exploration of these shared themes to overlap his only with regard to the figure of John Stuart Mill. Richard Bellamy, *Liberalism and Modern Society: A Historical Argument* (University Park: Pennsylvania State University Press, 1992).

[33] The complex evolving character of nineteenth-century democratization, and its interaction with industrialization, is succinctly and compellingly stressed in Daniel Ziblatt's synthetic review of recent scholarship. Daniel Ziblatt, "How Did Europe Democratize?" *World Politics* 58, no. 2 (2006), 311–38.

overarching dilemma, this book will show how liberal responses to democracy and industry created, not a single new liberalism, but several alternative liberalisms over the course of the nineteenth century. The first of these—democratized classical liberalism—responded to suffrage expansions in America that made once commonplace liberal arguments regarding property qualifications appear outmoded and in need of replacement, or at least refinement, to address America's experience with democracy.

THE LIBERAL ARGUMENT FOR PROPERTY
QUALIFICATIONS: DEMOCRATIZATION AS A DILEMMA

Just as Constant's lecture of 1819 illustrates how liberals used beliefs about social change to flesh out their political thought, so his position on suffrage illustrates how liberal arguments, once formulated, were vulnerable to being undermined by subsequent events. During his lecture Constant rhapsodized about "the exercise of political liberty" in recent French elections in terms that readers today might assume imply wide democratic participation.[34] But elections in Bourbon Restoration France—in which Constant repeatedly competed as a candidate, first being elected to the Chamber of Deputies about six weeks after this lecture— involved an electorate of fewer than 100,000 in a nation of some 30 million.[35] They were hence far from democratic.

While Constant favored a broader electorate, he was no advocate of universal suffrage. In his 1815 *Principles of Politics Applicable to All Representative Governments* he argued that the franchise should reach "the least prosperous part of the property holders" but not go any further. Constant's belief that "[p]roperty alone makes men capable of exercising political rights" rested on a claim that only property holders combine "interests" favorable to "the love of order, justice and conservation" with "the leisure indispensable for the acquisition of understanding." Constant differentiated, moreover, between types of property to single out "landed property," in contrast to "industrial property," as the type of property that best promotes a "spirit" and "character" proper to political activity, and therefore the best basis of the franchise.[36]

---

[34] Constant, "Liberty of the Ancients," 327. In interpreting the passage we may note that, when giving this lecture on February 13, 1819, Constant was himself standing for election. This illuminates his use of Lafayette's earlier election to the Chamber of Deputies as an example since Constant was standing in the department that had elected Lafayette. He had, moreover, been solicited to stand by the same lawyer-newspaperman who had promoted Lafayette. Dennis Wood, *Constant: A Biography* (London: Routledge, 1993), 226–30. If Constant was praising those who on March 25 would elect him to the Chamber, we may interpret this rhapsodic passage in the manner of campaign rhetoric.

[35] Frederick B. Artz, "The Electoral System in France during the Bourbon Restoration, 1815–30," *Journal of Modern History* 1, no. 2 (1929), 205–18; Craiutu, *Liberalism under Siege*, 231–35.

[36] Benjamin Constant, *Principles of Politics Applicable to All Representative Governments*, in *Political Writings*, 207, 214–21. The stance on suffrage taken in the published version of Constant's *Principles*

Constant's position on the suffrage may appear archaic in light of impending political and economic transformations. But support for property qualifications was standard among French liberals during the early nineteenth century. Their thought on the topic was informed less by an unmoored fear of the people than by recent French political history. Universal suffrage had been introduced during the French Revolution for the 1792 election of the National Convention.[37] It was the Convention that made France a Republic, convicted Louis XVI of treason and sent him to the guillotine, replaced the new Constitution of 1791 with another new constitution in 1793 only to postpone actually implementing that constitution, and most notoriously created the Committee of Public Safety, during whose Reign of Terror in 1793–1794 tens of thousands were executed.

Although the Convention only existed for three years, it had a long afterlife as an anxiety-inducing example of the fact that a powerful representative assembly might act in ways inimical to constitutionalism. As advocates of elected representative assemblies who were also committed to constitutional government, liberals had to address the revealed potential for tension between these commitments. When French liberals like Constant promoted property qualifications using the argument that these limits on suffrage favor the election of assemblies likely to be a bulwark of, rather than a threat to, the rule of law and security of property, they argued in the lingering shadow of the democratically elected National Convention of 1792–1795.

The French experiment with universal suffrage provided a charged example, not only in France, but also in America's young republic. During the middle to late 1790s, competing views of recent events in France played a notable role in America's first party system. The Federalists emerged as anxious critics of France's republic, drawing from it warnings about the perils of democracy that they believed applied also in America. While politically surpassed by Jefferson's Democratic Republicans from 1800 on, the Federalist viewpoint did not disappear overnight. For example, John Adams—whose presidency had been scarred by tension over French events—still invoked the specter of revolutionary France at the 1820–1821 Massachusetts State Constitutional Convention. Adams held that the French Revolution had "furnished an experiment [of universal suffrage], perfect and complete in all its stages and branches," which taught that Massachusetts had been wise to include property qualifications in its 1780 constitution (which

---

was also advanced in the longer unpublished 1810 version. See Benjamin Constant, *Principles of Politics Applicable to All Governments*, ed. Etienne Hofmann, trans. Dennis O'Keefe (Indianapolis, IN: Liberty Fund, 2003), 166, 175.

[37] On the details of the suffrage and other features of elections in France during the first decade of the revolution, see Malcolm Crook, *Elections in the French Revolution: An Apprenticeship in Democracy, 1789–1799* (Cambridge: Cambridge University Press, 1996).

he had largely written), and when revising that constitution should persist in rejecting universal suffrage.[38]

The voice of John Adams might be dismissed as a relic of a past era, except for the fact that, in supporting property qualifications, he had multiple younger counterparts. Later in 1821, at New York's Constitutional Convention, James Kent—then chancellor (head of the judiciary) of the state, and almost three decades younger than Adams—argued in terms paralleling Adams. Refusing "to bow before the idol of universal suffrage," Kent characterized such a suffrage as an "extreme democratic principle... regarded with terror, by the wise men of every age, because in every European republic, ancient and modern, in which it has been tried, it has terminated disastrously, and been productive of corruption, injustice, violence, and tyranny." Rejecting the exceptionalist belief that Americans were "a peculiar people... exempted from the passions which have disturbed and corrupted the rest of mankind," Kent saw no escape for America from the "tendency of universal suffrage... to jeopardize the rights of property, and the principles of liberty." In arguing specifically for retaining a landed property qualification for the electorate of New York's state senate, Kent echoed Constant as he avowed that "freeholders of moderate possessions" were inspired "with a correct spirit of freedom and justice" that made them "the safest guardians of property and the laws."[39]

Recognizing these American parallels to Constant's argument for property qualifications serves two purposes. First, it reminds us that a forthright rejection of democracy in the name of "property and the laws" could resonate in the early nineteenth century, not only among European liberals comfortable with constitutional monarchy, but also among Americans who took pride in the absence of monarchy and hereditary aristocracy in their young republic. As Russell Hanson stressed in his study of changing views of democracy in America, "democracy did not assume a place of preeminence among American political ideals until well into the nineteenth century."[40] When the 1820s began, there remained Americans who were concerned to draw a line between republicanism and democracy. One speaker at Massachusetts' Constitutional Convention made this point so strongly as to denounce universal suffrage as "anti-republican" on the grounds that it would admit voters "of a character most liable to be improperly influenced or corrupted" and thereby pave a path toward "despotism."[41]

[38] Merrill D. Peterson, ed., *Democracy, Liberty, and Property: The State Constitutional Conventions of the 1820s* (Indianapolis, IN: Liberty Fund, 2010), 68–70.

[39] Peterson, *Democracy, Liberty, and Property,* 172–77.

[40] Russell L. Hanson, *The Democratic Imagination in America: Conversations with Our Past* (Princeton, NJ: Princeton University Press, 1985), 58.

[41] Peterson, *Democracy, Liberty, and Property,* 57.

The second purpose served by recognizing the transatlantic reach of the liberal argument for property qualifications is to focus attention on when, where, and how this argument became problematic. It was undermined in America during the 1820s, as movement away from property qualifications came to be interpreted as an unstoppable nationwide trend. That trend had begun earlier, in the constitutions of some of the newer states admitted to the Union, and against this backdrop calls for reform had grown in older states like Massachusetts and New York, leading to the constitutional conventions of the 1820s. At their conventions in 1820–1821 Massachusetts and New York both expanded the vote by replacing freehold property limits with taxpaying qualifications, and in the years ahead they would fall fully in line with the movement toward "universal suffrage" (which at this time meant universal white male suffrage).[42] It is especially telling that, even as he was defending property limits in 1821 at New York's Convention, Kent characterized this democratic movement as a nationwide trend sweeping away all before it. He thus observed:

> It is not to be disguised that our governments are becoming downright democracies, with all their good, and all their evil. The principle of universal suffrage, which is now running a triumphant career from Maine to Louisiana, is an awful power, which, like gunpowder, or the steam engine, or the press itself, may be rendered mighty in mischief as well as in blessings.[43]

Acknowledging the trend away from property qualifications created a dilemma for those who believed such qualifications had secured property and the rule of law. If taken seriously, the trend entailed that this belief could, from now on, only inform a lament, but no viable agenda for political action or actors. Much rethinking was needed to craft a successor political vision, which rather than rejecting democracy wholesale, would instead reframe political thought and action in terms of good versus bad variants of democracy. This framework would direct attention toward identifying and promoting those institutions, or social conditions, which can buttress the security of property and rule of law within a political system where democratic suffrage is a given.[44] This rethinking, which gained

---

[42] Talk of "universal suffrage" and "democracy" at this time did not, as we do today, look upon racial and gender exclusions from political rights as inimical to these concepts. Exclusionary assumptions regarding what was *not* at stake when American politics was characterized in terms of a rising tide of "universal suffrage" and "democracy" would, in turn, be extended by American political science as it developed in subsequent decades. In later chapters, when I treat political scientists engaging "democracy," racial and gender exclusion will be a constant background fact. At no point was such exclusion recognized by the political scientists that I study as a challenge to their view of post-1820s America as a "democracy."

[43] Peterson, *Democracy, Liberty, and Property*, 165.

[44] If we date "democratization," not from the first use of a democratic suffrage in France in the 1790s, but from the point and place in time in which such suffrage came to be taken for granted even by those

momentum in America during the 1820s, would feed into the political theory and agenda of the new American Whig Party of the 1830s.

On the other side of the Atlantic, America's political democratization spurred a broader range of responses. One response, as we will see in the next section, was to interpret America as characterized by exceptional conditions that made its democratization irrelevant or even entirely misleading as a source of examples for European liberals. An alternative response, however, was to interpret democratization as a transatlantic rather than a solely American trend, and therefore as a process that European nations would also, sooner or later, undergo. This interpretation implied that the dilemma facing Americans who had favored property qualifications was also a concern for European liberals. Their challenge was to reconcile inherited liberal commitments with a future political democratization by identifying reforms that could help liberal institutions and ideals to survive such a transformation, or perhaps even to thrive under democratic political conditions. This was the challenge Tocqueville's *Democracy in America* so influentially took up.

The novelty of Tocqueville's democratized classical liberal vision stands out against the backdrop of the views advanced by de Staël, Constant, and Guizot during the decades prior to the 1835 first volume of Tocqueville's classic.[45] Whereas these earlier figures had all favored property qualifications of one type or another, Tocqueville encouraged French liberals to accept universal suffrage as a long-term outcome, and to direct their practical energies toward reforms that would make France better able to become politically democratic without sacrificing liberal institutions and ideals. Well aware that just such a sacrifice had occurred in France in the 1790s, Tocqueville used the more recent example of America's political democratization to show that liberalism and democracy were not inevitably incompatible. As he explained in a letter to a friend soon after his first volume appeared: "To those for whom the word democracy is synonymous with destruction, anarchy, spoliation, and murder, I have tried to show that under a democratic government the fortunes and the rights of society may be respected, liberty preserved, and religion honored."[46]

---

who initially opposed it, and political arguments updated accordingly, then democratization as I treat it here maps onto Huntington's classic conception of the "first wave of democratization" beginning in the United States during the 1820s. Samuel Huntington, *The Third Wave: Democratization in the Late Twentieth Century* (Norman: University of Oklahoma Press, 1991), 16–17. For more recent scholarship on the first wave of democratization, see Ziblatt, "How Did Europe Democratize?"

[45] The two parts of Tocqueville's book published in 1835 were originally each designated as a volume. I, however, follow the norm in today's editions of treating the parts of the work published in 1835 as together making up one single volume, and four further parts published in 1840 as together making up volume 2 of Tocqueville's classic.

[46] Tocqueville to Eugène Stoffels, February 21, 1835, in *Memoir, Letters, and Remains of Alexis de Tocqueville*, 2 vols. (London: Macmillan, 1861), 1: 397.

Tocqueville sought further to persuade liberals that representative government based on a property-limited suffrage could not be sustained over the longer term. To make this argument, he started from recent American experience, but pushed beyond it to project the trend of American political change into a grander generalization:

> When a people begins to touch the electoral qualification, one can fore-see that it will sooner or later make it disappear completely. That is one of the most invariable rules that govern societies. As one moves the limit of electoral rights back, one feels the need to move it back more; for after each new concession the forces of democracy increase and its demands grow with its new power. The ambition of those who are left below the property qualification becomes irritated in proportion to the great number of those who are found above. The exception finally becomes the rule; concessions succeed each other relentlessly and there is no stop-ping until they have arrived at universal suffrage.[47]

In pronouncing this rule "invariable," Tocqueville moved to transform liberal beliefs about what was politically possible. As he, on the one hand, expanded the range of the possible by rejecting the early-century fear that democratic suffrage was incompatible with liberalism, he also, on the other hand, narrowed the range of possible futures to exclude nondemocratic liberal political systems. He pushed liberals to believe that the elections essential to representative government must, in time, be put on a democratic basis.

The distinctive character of Tocqueville's liberalism is further brought out if we situate it, not only relative to his unapologetically elitist predecessors within French liberalism, but also against the radical democratic current within British liberalism in the years preceding the 1832 reform of Britain's Parliament. Many who supported the 1832 Reform Act were—as J. S. Mill noted when later encour-aging the act's diverse supporters to work together as a broad "Liberal party"—"terrified at Universal Suffrage."[48] But others were advocates of universal suffrage who supported the act as a first step toward that end. These radicals offer another telling contrast to Tocqueville. They had looked to America to support the pos-sibility of a liberal democracy before he did, but had embedded that possibility in a liberal political vision that diverged significantly from his.

The expansion of suffrage in America had been eagerly watched and invoked by radical supporters of a large-scale suffrage extension in Britain. They made much of the fact that no collapse in the rule of law or security of property had followed

---

[47] Alexis de Tocqueville, *Democracy in America*, trans. Harvey C. Mansfield and Delba Winthrop (Chicago: University of Chicago Press, 2000), 55.
[48] Mill, "Reorganization of the Reform Party," 467, 479.

the arrival of universal suffrage in an ever-increasing number of American states. This liberal interpretation of America's advancing democratization was, by 1820, already used in Jeremy Bentham's *Radicalism Not Dangerous*, and in the years running up to the 1832 reform it became a common mantra among supporters of wide suffrage.[49] These radicals differed on a crucial point from the democratized classical liberal political vision Tocqueville and J. S. Mill would later advance in the 1830s. The radicals viewed America's recent political experiences as supporting their belief that an extensive suffrage could and should be *immediately* introduced in European nations. By contrast, Tocqueville would view recent American political events as the culminating step in a much more extended process. When drawing practical lessons from that process for contemporary France, he pushed French liberals to accept universal suffrage as a future outcome, and start reforms now to prepare for it, but did not consider it time yet to follow America in extending universal suffrage. Stressing this contrast when interpreting *Democracy in America* for British readers in 1840, J. S. Mill would declare of Tocqueville: "No one is more opposed than he is to that species of democratic radicalism, which would admit at once to the highest of political franchises, untaught masses."[50]

LIBERALISM, DEMOCRACY, AND AMERICAN EXCEPTIONALISM: ECONOMIC DEVELOPMENT AS A DILEMMA

Thus, the democratized classical liberal political vision that crystallized in the 1830s diverged, on one side, from more elitist early-century liberals in believing liberal democracy to be *possible*. On the other side, it diverged from more radical early-century liberals in holding that liberal democracy was possible only under specific *conditions*, which then held in America, but not Europe. In a third divergence, it broke with a major current of British Whig thought over the issue of whether these American-style conditions might become more or less widespread in the future, and whether their spread could be promoted. Both sides of this latter divide agreed—as J. S. Mill put it when summarizing Tocqueville's views in 1840—that democracy is "desirable only under certain conditions." But only democratized classical liberals believed that, as Mill went on to declare, these "conditions [were] capable, by human care and foresight, of being realized."[51]

This final divergence substantively hinged on arguments about American exceptionalism. As we saw with de Staël, the belief that America might be a poor political model for European nations had long had supporters within European

[49] David Paul Crook, *American Democracy in English Politics, 1815–1850* (Oxford: Clarendon Press, 1965), chap. 2.

[50] Mill, "Tocqueville on Democracy in America," 159.

[51] Mill, "Tocqueville on Democracy in America," 158.

liberalism. This belief gained newer content and import after universal suffrage became increasingly standard in America. Exceptionalism offered a mode of argument that could credit recent American political change with showing liberal democracy to be possible, but contain its practical implications by contending that this outcome required conditions so distinctive that they could never be realized in Europe.

During the debates over parliamentary reform in Britain, Whig reformers, who favored a small suffrage expansion limited to bringing the rising middle classes into political life, turned to political economy to flesh out this exceptionalist argument. In 1829 the young T. B. Macaulay—who would be elected to Parliament as a Whig the following year—famously employed what he called "the noble Science of Politics" in cutting criticism of James Mill's political theory. While making much of issues of method, the political take-home of the criticism was to challenge the support that James Mill, along with Jeremy Bentham and others in the circle of "philosophical radicals," gave to the call for broad suffrage in Britain. For Macaulay, a cardinal sin of James Mill's "*a priori* method" was to ask the question of what is desirable in political institutions in abstraction from the specific conditions of a given nation.[52] Attending to such conditions would, however, undermine the radicals' inference from the nonthreatening results of universal suffrage in America to confidence about introducing a broad suffrage in Britain.[53] Stressing that economic conditions in America were exceptional, Macaulay contended:

> The case of the United States is not in point. In a country where the necessaries of life are cheap and the wages of labour high, where a man who has no capital but his legs and arms may expect to become rich by industry and frugality, it is not very decidedly even for the immediate advantage of the poor to plunder the rich; and the punishment of doing so would very speedily follow the offence. But in countries in which the great majority live from hand to mouth, and in which vast masses of wealth have been accumulated by a comparatively small number, the case is widely different. The immediate want is, at particular seasons, craving imperious, irresistible. In our own time it has steeled men to the fear of the gallows, and urged them on the point of the bayonet. And, if

---

[52] Thomas Babington Macaulay, "Mill on Government," in *Macaulay: Prose and Poetry*, ed. G. M. Young (Cambridge, MA: Harvard University Press, 1952), 608, 581.

[53] While I illustrate this argument using Macaulay's celebrated criticism of James Mill, the form and substance of the argument did not originate with Macaulay. It was being used as early as 1818 by Sir James Mackintosh (a lifelong friend of Constant from their time as students together in Edinburgh in the 1780s) to criticize Bentham's call for broad suffrage. On Mackintosh's argument, and more broadly, British Whig views of America's democracy, see Crook, *American Democracy*, 22–24 and chap. 3.

these men had at their command that gallows and those bayonets which now scarcely restrain them, what is to be expected?[54]

Macaulay artfully defended his exceptionalist argument by appealing to common ground in classical liberal political economy that he shared with Bentham and James Mill. He contended that doctrines they endorsed in their political economy—specifically, Malthus's theory of population—supported his fear about suffrage. America's economic conditions were a product of its exceptionally low ratio of population to land. By contrast, the far higher level of inequality in Britain, which Macaulay saw making a broad suffrage threatening there, was the normal "state of things," and "[i]f there be the least truth in the doctrines of the school to which Mr. Mill belongs, the increase of population will necessarily produce it everywhere." Macaulay expected that, as America's population grew in the future, so would inequality. The conditions that made broad suffrage nonthreatening in America at present were hence exceptional, not only in transatlantic, but also in temporal terms.

Macaulay's argument shared with the later democratized classical liberal political vision an attention to the prerequisites of liberal democracy. Like J. S. Mill particularly, Macaulay gave special attention to economic conditions.[55] Mill, however, offered a distinctively democratized classical liberal vision that looked optimistically to economic policy change (e.g., repealing the Corn Laws to start free trade in grain and lower the cost of food for workers), self-restraint by the working classes (having fewer children, and saving more), and the diffusion among workers of familiarity with classical liberal political economy, to make a future of universal suffrage less threatening in Britain. Already in his 1840 review of Tocqueville Mill held that some of Britain's working class were "becoming, in point of condition and habit, what the American working people are,"[56] and he expressed optimism that liberal economic and education reforms would hasten this shift. In contrast, Macaulay pessimistically projected transatlantic convergence in the opposite direction. He expected that, as America's economy grew and industry developed there, inequality would grow, and its politics would change to illustrate the conflict between democracy and classical liberal views of property that he saw as normal. Macaulay hence archly and darkly announced in 1829: "As for America, we appeal to the twentieth century."[57]

[54] Macaulay, "Mill on Government," 602.

[55] Tocqueville, by contrast, argued that "mores" were more important than "material well-being" in explaining the maintenance of a liberal democracy in America. Tocqueville, *Democracy in America*, 264–302. The common feature of Tocqueville and Mill as democratized classical liberals was not substantive agreement on all details of what the conditions of a liberal democracy are, but agreement that with the right reforms these conditions could in time be developed in Europe as well as in America, and universal suffrage then extended without threatening the liberal rule of law and security of property.

[56] Mill, "Tocqueville on Democracy in America," 166.

[57] Macaulay, "Mill on Government," 602. Almost three decades later Macaulay would restate and extend his views on how economic development would interact with America's democratized politics

In predicting that the United States would undergo economic changes that would interact with democratic politics in such a way as to challenge liberalism, Macaulay expressed an anxiety already stated in America itself. When Massachusetts' Constitutional Convention met in 1820–1821 the state was just beginning to industrialize. Francis C. Lowell, a scion of Boston's elite, had returned from visiting Britain in the early 1810s planning to start textile manufacturing on a larger scale than ever before in America by using water-powered machine looms. In 1813 he and partners from his elite circles pooled their capital in the Boston Manufacturing Company (BMC), one of America's first joint-stock companies. In 1814 Lowell completed his efforts to develop a working loom and demonstrated it to his fellow BMC proprietor, Nathan Appleton, who would later recall "the state of admiration and satisfaction with which we sat by the hour, watching the beautiful movement of this new and wonderful machine, destined as it evidently was, to change the character of all textile industry."[58] Lowell also helped secure the profitability of the BMC's mill in Waltham, Massachusetts, via successful lobbying in Washington, DC, regarding the rate on textile imports in the Tariff of 1816. In sum, as the 1810s came toward a close, the future of capital-intensive larger-scale industry looked particularly promising. During the 1820s, corporate offspring of the BMC would develop the Massachusetts town of Lowell—named for the BMC's then-deceased founder—into a showcase of mass industry based on water-powered machinery.

At the Massachusetts Convention of 1820–1821, the contemporary context of incipient industrialization was brought directly into the debate about suffrage by Josiah Quincy, a former Federalist Party congressman, and future mayor of Boston as well as Harvard president. Quincy announced that "[e]verything indicates that the destinies of the country will eventuate in the establishment of a great manufacturing interest in the Commonwealth." Rather than turn, as John Adams did, to the past example of revolutionary France to question the desirability of universal suffrage, Quincy framed the issue "prospectively" in light of

in a letter exchange with the American H. S. Randall. For these letters see George Otto Trevelyan, *The Life and Letters of Lord Macaulay*, 2 vols. (New York: Harper, 1875), 2: Appendix, Lord Macaulay on American Institutions. Macaulay declared to Randall, for example: "Your fate I believe to be certain, though it is deferred by a physical cause. As long as you have a boundless extent of fertile and unoccupied land, your laboring population will be far more at ease than the laboring population of the Old World, and, while that is the case, the Jefferson politics may continue to exist without causing any fatal calamity. But the time will come when New England will be as thickly peopled as Old England. Wages will be low, and will fluctuate as much with you as with us. You will have your Manchesters and Birminghams, and in those Manchesters and Birminghams hundreds of thousands of artisans will assuredly be out of work. Then your institutions will be fairly brought to the test" (408).

[58] Nathan Appleton, *The Introduction of the Power Loom and the Origin of Lowell* (Lowell, MA: Penhallow, 1858), 9. In this paragraph I draw on Appleton's pamphlet, while taking additional information from Frances W. Gregory, *Nathan Appleton: Merchant and Entrepreneur, 1779–1861* (Charlottesville: University Press of Virginia, 1975), chaps. 10 and 11.

how such suffrage might operate in an industrial future. Predicting that factory workers would be "absolutely dependent upon their employers," he projected a future in which there would be "one, two, or three manufacturing establishments [in every county of the Commonwealth], each sending as the case may be, from one hundred to eight hundred votes to the poll depending on the will of one great employer, one great capitalist." This would, Quincy warned, endanger the "rights, liberties and properties" of "the yeomanry of the country." But this future threat could be forestalled so long as property qualifications were retained, since those poor enough to potentially become dependent upon manufacturing employment would thereby be kept out of the state's electorate.[59]

The way in which Quincy appealed to incipient industrialization to justify opposition to universal suffrage might seem archaic today. But it had broader resonance at the time, as is seen in the fact that James Kent deployed the same argument as part of his multifaceted defense of freehold qualifications for New York's senate at that state's 1821 convention. Kent argued:

> We are destined to become a great manufacturing as well as commercial state. We have already numerous and prosperous factories of one kind of another, and one master capitalist with his one hundred apprentices, and journeymen, and agents, and dependents, will bear down at the polls, an equal number of farmers of small estates in his vicinity.... Large manufacturing and mechanical establishments, can act in an instant with the unity and efficiency of disciplined troops. It is against such combinations, among others, that I think we ought to give to the freeholders, or those who have interest in land, one branch of the legislature for their asylum and their comfort.[60]

The way in which Quincy and Kent projected politics going awry in America if industry developed against a backdrop of universal suffrage was rather different in its details from that of Macaulay. Quincy and Kent pointed toward a threatening concentration of political power in the hands of "capitalists" rather than property-less workers. Taken together, however, the anxieties articulated on both sides of the Atlantic in the 1820s about the future interaction of democracy and industry in America shared a broader framework of beliefs. First, the figures making these arguments all saw America's economic future, as Kent put it, as a move away from "plain and simple republics of farmers" to "a great nation, with great commerce, manufactures, population, wealth, luxuries, and with the vices and

---

[59] Peterson, *Democracy, Liberty, Property,* 60.
[60] Peterson, *Democracy, Liberty, Property,* 177.

miseries that they engender."[61] Second, none of them proposed measures to try to stop or slow this course of economic change. They framed it as an inexorable process, just as Tocqueville would suggest with regard to democratization. Third, they expected economic development to generate novel forms of inequality that would alter the dynamics and outcomes of democratic politics in ways inimical to classical liberalism.

In reacting to this prospect by rejecting democracy, these figures spoke in an idiom more suggestive of liberalism's past than its future. But in highlighting political economy they pointed to dilemmas that, from the moment of its birth, the democratized classical liberal political vision would have to address to sustain its hopes for a liberal democracy. The liberal proclivity to think in terms of grand processes of historical change was generating not one, but two new narratives in the early to mid nineteenth century: one of inexorable democratization that would, over time, demand more extensions of political equality; the other of inexorable economic change creating new social inequalities. Taken together, these narratives set up guiding themes and dilemmas of "the political" in political science when it began to develop in the nineteenth-century American academy.

---

[61] Peterson, Democracy, Liberty, Property, 175.

CHAPTER 2

The "Science" in Political Science

THE HISTORICIST DEBATE ABOUT METHOD

Whereas chapter 1 introduced liberalism as a tradition of political thought within which I will situate pioneers of political science in the American academy, this chapter introduces the "science" in political science: the *methodological* tradition within which I will also locate these figures. A methodological tradition centers upon beliefs—sometimes explicitly articulated and debated, at other times implicitly taken for granted—about the premises and practices proper to, or incompatible with, a scientific treatment of political phenomena. We have already seen such beliefs put to work in Macaulay's 1829 criticism of James Mill for using an "*a priori* method" whose abstraction from particular national conditions was, Macaulay charged, inimical to "the noble Science of Politics." Macaulay's criticism here exemplified a methodological tradition—the *historicist* tradition—that would be the main locus of appeals to, and arguments over, method in political science as it took shape in America's nineteenth-century academy.

The first part of this chapter introduces historicism as a transnational tradition originating in the eighteenth century, and the once widespread species of it that I label *developmental historicism*. I then examine the early- to mid-nineteenth-century rise of self-consciously scientific attention to method among German historicists, above all at the University of Berlin, which was founded in 1810 and became the archetype for the modern university. Methodological attention was soon followed by argument, in a famous debate at the university that formulated a contrast between "historical method" and "philosophical method" in the developmental historicist study of laws and institutions. We will later see this contrast carried across the Atlantic and handed down through generations, to continue to resonate among American political scientists as late as the 1890s.

In the final part of this chapter, I start to weave together the "science" and the "political" sides of my story as I examine selected midcentury combinations of developmental historicism and liberalism. In chapters 3 through 5, we will see that this combination was a common trait of political science as it took root in America's academy from the 1830s into the 1880s. My goal here is to set up a transatlantic backdrop for later chapters by introducing three midcentury Europeans—Johann Bluntschli, Henry Maine, and Edward Freeman—who, as we will see, had a notable impact on political science in America. Together these three Europeans exemplified both *political* variety within liberalism and *methodological* variety within developmental historicism, relative to which I will subsequently analyze American figures.

The Historicist Tradition: Embedded Exceptionalisms and Developmental Historicism

Historicism is often principally associated with Germany. That association is largely correct with regard to the most sophisticated nineteenth-century developments and debates about how to be scientific in method. But the prior emergence and crystallization of historicism during the eighteenth century had been a transnational intellectual phenomenon. Students of it diverge in how and where they draw a line between precursors and full-fledged historicists, but they give one or the other role to the Italian Giambattista Vico, the French Baron de Montesquieu, and the British Edmund Burke, in addition to the German Johann Gottfried Herder.[1]

Historicism was interwoven with the interest in qualitative social transformation whose importance for liberalism we have already stressed. The growth of this interest in the eighteenth century engaged and encouraged comparative and historical studies that highlighted temporal, cross-cultural, and cross-national social variety. Attention to such variety strained the capacities of natural law theory, which had long provided a principal methodological framework for political scholarship. Historicist moves are, for example, most evident in Montesquieu's mid-eighteenth-century classic *Spirit of the Laws* at moments when his interests carry him beyond the natural law and regime typology ordering schemes introduced early in that work.

The most extended such moment comes in the final part of *Spirit of the Laws.* In books 28, 30, and 31, Montesquieu pursued a historical study of laws and

---

[1] The classic study is Meinecke's *Die Entstehung des Historismus.* Friedrich Meinecke, *Historism: The Rise of a New Historical Outlook*, trans. J. E. Anderson (London: Routledge and Kegan Paul, 1972). I diverge from Meinecke's treatment of the move from precursors to full-fledged historicism as a distinctively German move (and the stress on the irrational and power politics this brings to the fore of his conception of "historicism"). But Meinecke's treatment of eighteenth-century Italian, French, and British thinkers is magisterial, and the major influence on my sketch here.

institutions of the Germanic tribes that had conquered the Western Roman Empire.[2] He explored how the evolution of these laws and institutions over multiple centuries gave shape to the feudal system, the monarchy, and the nobility of France. Montesquieu's study here exhibited two principal features of historicism. First, he singled out this evolution as exceptional. It was a historical process "which happened once in the world and which will perhaps never happen again."[3] Second, he engaged this process sympathetically. This made his approach very different from that of other Enlightenment figures, such as Voltaire, who looked back on the Middle Ages to condemn them as a time of barbarism and religious superstition with few, if any, redeeming features or legacies.

In sympathetically recounting in exceptionalist terms a lineage of institutional evolution that extended over centuries, the chapters closing the *Spirit of the Laws* exemplified an emergent historicism. But this was just one moment in a labyrinthine book that at other moments employed the framework of early-modern natural law theory. Such a blend was characteristic of eighteenth-century proto-historicist works, seen also, for example, in Vico. This blend also found political expression during the American Revolution, as natural rights arguments rooted in the natural law tradition were intermingled with arguments that justified the Revolution as defending institutions and rights that were the exceptional historical inheritance of the colonists as free Englishmen.

The disappearance of this once-common blend at the end of the eighteenth century marks the transition from emergent to full-fledged historicism. This break developed in the context of the French Revolution, which combined the appeal to natural rights of the 1789 Declaration of the Rights of Man and of the Citizen with a proud rupture from France's past. During the 1790s, as the Revolution was radicalized and war began between revolutionary France and other great powers, natural law was increasingly called into question as a framework for political thought, and historicism was elevated into a freestanding methodological tradition that started to supplant, rather than supplement, natural law. Historicism answered the challenge of making sense of the contrast between America's Revolution—which could be interpreted as legitimate and successful in creating a stable regime because it built upon historically established institutions and rights—and France's Revolution, which was seen as doomed by its bold rejection of the French past. Formulated by Edmund Burke in the early 1790s, this seminal historicist comparison soon spread more widely. For example, in 1800 it was elaborated in a German historical journal by Friedrich Gentz

---

[2] This study, in effect, builds at length upon Montesquieu's famous reference to the Germanic tribes in his admiring account of the English constitution in book 11: "the English have taken their idea of political government from the Germans. This fine system was found in the forests." Montesquieu, *The Spirit of the Laws*, trans. Anne M. Cohler, Basia C. Miller, and Harold Stone (Cambridge: Cambridge University Press, 1989), 166.

[3] Montesquieu, *Spirit of the Laws*, 619.

in a long essay that John Quincy Adams (then US minister to Prussia) translated and had published in America as *The Origins and Principles of the American Revolution Compared with the Origins and Principles of the French Revolution*.[4]

The revolutionary period was, therefore, a watershed in the history of historicism. By the time the revolutionary and Napoleonic wars finally ended in 1815, the articulation of historicism as a fully fledged scientific research program, consciously attentive to method, was under way at the University of Berlin. But before considering German academics, I return to the French liberal historian-politician Guizot to pursue two goals: First, to further explicate features of historicism, and second, by using another French figure in doing so, to counter tendencies to see Germany as *the* sole birthplace of historicism.

In chapter 1 I sketched the liberal content of Guizot's plurality argument in his classic *History of Civilization in Europe*. This work also warrants attention for its approach. In stressing the distinctiveness of European civilization as it had developed since the fall of Rome, Guizot exemplified the historicist concern with the exceptional. If historicists are concerned with the historical individuality of their chosen objects of study, this does not require that they deny the existence of any general phenomena. Indeed, such phenomena serve well as a backdrop against which to stress individuality. Before asking what made modern European civilization distinctive, Guizot first addressed what "civilization in general" consists in: by his account, "the progress of society" and "the progress of individuals." These reflections served, in the context of Guizot's work as a whole, to focus his argument about European exceptionalism. Thus, after his opening lecture "Civilization in General," Guizot then devoted his pivotal second lecture, entitled "European Civilization in Particular: Its Distinguishing Characteristics—Its Superiority—Its Elements," to introducing his liberal plurality argument.[5]

In elaborating the distinctiveness of modern European civilization, Guizot approached that civilization as a concrete historical whole with a discernible unity. It had, as such, its own general characteristics rooted in shared inheritances and experiences, and ongoing interactions and influences across its parts. But its unity was a complex one that did not entail uniformity in its parts. Guizot

---

[4] Friedrich von Gentz, *The Origin and Principles of the American Revolution, Compared with the Origins and Principles of the French Revolution*, trans. John Quincy Adams (Indianapolis, IN: Liberty Fund, 2009). This work was first published in 1800. John Quincy Adams's concern to immediately translate Gentz's work for publication in America might be related to the fraught 1800 presidential election, which pitted his Francophobic father and sitting president, John Adams, against the Francophilic Thomas Jefferson. In his preface to the translation, John Quincy Adams praised Gentz's work for saving America's "revolution from the disgraceful imputation of having proceeded from the same principles as that of France" and proving that the difference "between the America and French Revolutions" was, quite simply, "The difference between *right* and *wrong*" (3–4).

[5] François Guizot, *History of Civilization in Europe*, ed. George Wells Knight (New York: D. Appleton, 1896), Lectures I and II.

emphasized with veneration the emergence between the thirteenth and sixteenth centuries of a sense of distinct "nationality": in various regions of Europe, diverse social classes who had long lived alongside each one another came to see themselves as constituting together a "moral unity," a "nation" with a common interest and character that transcended and integrated them. The parallel emergence of nationality in different locations within Europe was a general movement in the historical development of European civilization considered as a whole.[6] But the nations that emerged were themselves, in turn, concrete historical wholes, each of which could itself be the object of historicist inquiry.

There was, as such, historical variety to be explored within the broader historical unity of European civilization, and Guizot in the 1820s also wrote national-level histories of England and France. More generally, historicists examined exceptionalism across highly varied levels: local, national, racial, and civilizational. Rather than consistently favor any of these levels, historicism promoted what might be called *embedded exceptionalisms*. Embedding the exceptional at one level within the exceptional at another level allowed the historicist tradition to reach from detailed studies of local history to universal histories that situated the history of Europe itself as a submovement—albeit the most important one— within the overall march of human history.

If embedded exceptionalism allowed historicists to work at different levels, the notion of development provided connections through time. A developmental orientation directed historicists to study past events in terms of how they drew on, extended, and reshaped longer-run processes that gave history structure and direction. These might reach across decades, centuries, millennia, or even all human history. The search for developmental predecessors, legacies, and revivals tying present to past, and the past to the ever further past, prevailed in the historicist tradition for much of the nineteenth century. I highlight this once widespread concern, and distinguish it from later forms of historicism more oriented to historical ruptures than continuities, by naming it *developmental historicism*.

One of the more illuminating questions we might ask of developmental historicists is this: the development of what? In Guizot, for instance, institutions had a principal role. What he offered was, first and foremost, a general *institutional* history of Europe, and one especially concerned with political and religious institutions.[7] In focusing on institutions Guizot again introduces to us a commonplace

---

[6] Guizot, *Civilization in Europe*, Lecture VIII.

[7] For a rounded picture of Guizot's work as an institutional historian, it is useful to read, beside his famous general history, the study of representative government he prepared as lectures in 1820–1822. The general history surveys a wide range of European institutions while stepping back from variety found within any one kind of institution. In contrast, Guizot's earlier lectures, by focusing on a single kind of political institution as it developed (or decayed) in France, Spain, and England, brought just such variety to the fore. See François Guizot, *The History of the Origins of Representative Government in Europe*, trans. Andrew R. Scoble (Indianapolis, IN: Liberty Fund, 2002).

feature of developmental historicism. Some of the most pervasive interests of developmental historicists lay in institutional frameworks of governance, as seen in studies in the history of political and church institutions, and in legal and constitutional history. If Guizot's scholarship stood apart from that of German contemporaries this was not because it was less historicist, but because it was less marked by the explicit emphasis on method brewing among academics in Berlin. Guizot thus offers a point of contrast against which to explore just what this new self-consciously scientific emphasis involved.

The University of Berlin, Scientific Advance, and the Historicist Debate over Method

The University of Berlin was founded in 1810 as part of a wave of reforms that strove to revitalize Prussia following the shock of its defeat and occupation by Napoleon. Specifically, the new university was to train civil servants and turn Prussia's capital city into a preeminent center for cutting-edge scholarship. The resources and relative academic freedom of the new university created an environment in which faculty brought scholarship across multiple fields to new levels of self-conscious sophistication. This research-promoting setting, and the knowledge production it supported, was accompanied by confidence among the faculty that they were making major, even revolutionary, scientific advances. As the faculty's scholarship was received elsewhere in the European academy, their sense of leading intellectual advance would be accepted and become a cornerstone of widely diffused academic narratives. In the human sciences more particularly, narratives of an early- to mid-nineteenth-century dawn of a new scientific era came to prevail in fields from law, history, and philology, to theology and philosophy. In all fields this new era was largely credited to scholars who were, had been, or had become, University of Berlin faculty.

In recalling this belief in a new scientific era in such fields as history and law, it is useful to first clarify a translation issue. Why translate the German *Wissenschaft* specifically in terms of "science" (and hence "scientific") rather than as "scholarship" (and "scholarly")? What matters here is that American figures we will meet in later chapters, the pioneers of political science in America's nineteenth-century academy, employed this translation. Moreover, in doing so, they advanced a view of their own efforts as scientific that they inherited as one trait of the broader methodological legacy of the University of Berlin's "Historical School." That school included multiple scholars in history and law, but most prominently for my purposes, Barthold Niebuhr in the earliest years of the university, and later Leopold von Ranke.

The Historical School's distinctive legacy can be illuminated by a contrast between it and Guizot. The French scholar and his German counterparts were all developmental historicists. But they diverged in their understanding of how their historical work stood in relation to that of prior generations. The Historical School saw itself as making a qualitative change, which its members interpreted as an advance toward a more accurate view of the past made possible by specialized research techniques. Guizot also saw a qualitative change, but interpreted it as largely due to the external impact of the upheaval of the revolutionary and Napoleonic decades. When introducing his lectures on the history of representative government, which he gave in 1820–1822, Guizot noted that dramatic changes, such as those of the preceding decades,

> take possession of all that exists in society, transform it, and place everything in an entirely new position; so that if, after such a shock, man looks back upon the history of the past, he can scarcely recognize it. That which he sees, he had never seen before; what he saw once, no longer exists as he saw it; facts rise up before him with unknown faces, and speak to him in a strange language. He sets himself to the examination of them under the guidance of other principles of observation and appreciation. Whether he considers their causes, their nature, or their consequences, unknown prospects open before him on all sides. The actual spectacle remains the same; but it is viewed by another spectator occupying a different place—to his eyes all is changed.[8]

The self-understanding of scholars acquires a different tenor depending on how they situate their work relative to their predecessors. In treating approaches pursued by Berlin faculty as examples of historicist *science*, I have in mind their self-understanding as agents of an ongoing intellectual advance facilitated by specialized methods. The same self-understanding would accompany the belief of pioneering American political scientists that they were extending lines of research that had become properly scientific in the hands of methodologically attentive German academics.

The growth of attention to method was soon accompanied by lively contention regarding the question of what specific methods were essential for scientific advance. Debate on this issue had already become pointed at the University of Berlin by the 1820s. Among faculty there who helped raise the methodological self-consciousness of historicism, minor issues paled before the heated dispute between the Historical School and the philosophical school of Hegel.[9]

---

[8] Guizot, *Origins of Representative Government*, 4.

[9] For a more detailed discussion of this dispute, see Georg G. Iggers, *The German Conception of History: The National Tradition of Historical Thought from Herder to the Present* (Middletown, CT: Wesleyan University Press, 1968), chap. 4. The way the dispute can play into retrospective accounts of "historicism" is evident in the contrast between Meinecke and Croce. Meinecke narrates

The Historical School embraced the critical treatment of source materials as a foundation for historicist science. What made scientific advance possible was not just the discovery and use of new source materials (though the school excelled at this), but the critical analysis of sources to assess in what respects, and to what extent, they could be relied on. Scientific scholars had to carefully and remorselessly interrogate the veracity of sources that they used. This attitude was exemplified in the way Niebuhr treated Roman history when he lectured at the new University of Berlin. Published first in 1811–1812, and again in a revised edition in 1827–1832 (when he was at the University of Bonn), Niebuhr's *History of Rome* sought via "searching criticism" of its sources "to lay open the groundworks of the ancient Roman people and state, which have been built over and masked, and about which the old writers preserved to us are often utterly mistaken."[10] This book was canonized in the self-narrative of the Historical School and its offspring as the founding work of scientific history. Niebuhr drew guidance and inspiration for his critical method from philology (the study of languages and texts). The method was later elaborated and applied to early-modern materials by Ranke. He, in turn, taught it to two generations of future scholars in the research seminar that he offered at the University of Berlin for many decades after his mid-1820s appointment there.[11]

The critical source method, foundational as it was for the Historical School's belief that it was at the forefront of scientific progress, struck the philosopher Hegel as profoundly limited. In his 1818 inaugural address as Professor of Philosophy at the University of Berlin, Hegel sharply pointed to scholars who studied history "in a *critical* and *learned* matter" but believed that "its content *cannot be taken seriously*." He aggressively held that philosophy, if properly construed and pursued, constituted "the *centre* of all spiritual life and of all science and truth." Philosophy,

---

historicism from a standpoint that judges it to have reached its climax in Ranke's works (whose legacy he saw himself continuing). Croce, by contrast, assaults Ranke from a stance that owes more to Hegel's side in this controversy. Meinecke, *Historism*. Cf. Bendetto Croce, *History as the Story of Liberty*, trans. Sylvia Sprigge (New York: Meridian Books, 1955), Part II. My own stance is to treat neither side as having a better claim than the other to embody a "truer" or "fuller" historicism.

[10] G. B. Niebuhr, *The History of Rome*, vol. 1, trans. Julius Charles Hare and Connop Thirlwall (Philadelphia: Thomas Wardle, 1835), xvi.

[11] For brief overviews of, and selections from, Niebuhr and Ranke, see Fritz Stern, ed., *The Varieties of History: From Voltaire to the Present* (New York: Meridian Books, 1956), 46–62. Since I am principally interested in how the Historical School played into the self-understanding of later American scholars, I skip much nuance here. Thus, for example, the school's emphasis on sources and their criticism had predecessors (and contemporaries). To narrate the school as if the critical method was born there, and only there, is a simplification. We also might note that the critical method was, for the school, necessary but not sufficient for historical scholarship. By rejecting false or dubious sources, it opened the way to constructing more accurate histories. When reflecting on the constructive moment in its work, the school stressed sympathetic identification and piercing beyond the surface of events to capture the dynamic movements of an underlying reality.

as Hegel understood it, grew out of "the *freedom of disinterested scientific activity*" and stood in contrast to "*purely critical drudgery with no content.*"[12]

Hegel's contrast was clarified in the introduction to his 1821 *Philosophy of Right*. Here he distinguished between "historical" and "philosophical" approaches to laws and institutions. A historical approach to the development of laws and institutions aimed to identify "circumstances, eventualities, needs, and incidents which led to their introduction." But such an approach could not, by itself, evaluate whether the "determinations of right" produced by those laws and institutions were actually "rightful and reasonable." The "truly essential issue" was this evaluative one, and it could not be pursued if scholarship on laws and institutions did not employ rational concepts, such as Hegel's own philosophy strove to articulate. Hegel agreed that law and institutions should be studied in a developmental historicist manner, but argued that these studies would be "more profound" if they drew on "philosophical insights."[13] Only if historicist studies were informed by philosophy—which for Hegel, as we saw in his inaugural, was the very center of "all science and truth"—would they gain the "content" whose lack Hegel had lamented in his inaugural. In sum, he saw concepts rationally clarified and systematized by philosophy as a necessary foundation of genuine progress in historicist science.[14]

The response of the Historical School to Hegel's argument received its most developed articulation from Ranke during the 1830s. Ranke identified history and philosophy as the "only two ways of acquiring knowledge about human affairs," each associated with its own "method." But, against Hegel, he defended the autonomy and sufficiency of the historical method. Ranke's defense ran along two tracks. First, he attacked the "immature philosophy" of the "philosophy of history" as accepting "*a priori* ideas"—for example, that "the human

[12] G. W. F. Hegel, *Political Writings*, ed. Laurence Dickey and H. B. Nisbet, trans. H. B. Nisbet (Cambridge: Cambridge University Press, 1999), 181–85 (italics in original). Hegel's dismissive attitude toward Niebuhr's much celebrated work would be made explicit later in his philosophy of history lectures, during which he pronounced: "Niebuhr's History can only be regarded as a *criticism* of Roman History, for it consists of a series of treatises which by no means possess the unity of history." G. W. F. Hegel, *The Philosophy of History*, trans. J. Sibree (New York: Dover, 1956), 281.

[13] G. W. F. Hegel, *Elements of the Philosophy of Right*, trans. H. B. Nisbet (Cambridge: Cambridge University Press, 1991), 29–32 (italics in original). Hegel's arguments may have been motivated in part by political opposition to the conservative views regarding legal reforms especially associated with Savigny, the leading Historical School figure in the study of law. But Hegel carried out his critique largely via the medium of methodological dispute.

[14] Reaffirming this position later in his philosophy of history lectures, Hegel would declare: "[I]n all that pretends to the name of science, it is indispensable that Reason should not sleep," where "Reason" meant, he went on to explain, "Thought conditioning itself in perfect freedom." Hegel, *Philosophy of History*, 11–13.

race moves along a course of uninterrupted progress, in a steady development towards perfection"—and simply seeking "to find them reflected in the history of the world."[15]

Ranke's second line of defense held that the synthetic aims of developmental historicism could be pursued independently of philosophy. The "highest" goal of the study of history was "to lift itself in its own fashion from the investigation and observation of particulars to a universal view of events." To do this "in its own fashion" historical scholarship would approach "the development of the world in general" by starting from reflection "on the particular" rather than the "preconceived ideas" of philosophers. Scholars should advance toward a general history, not by relating particulars through "universal concepts," but by relating them through their historical interactions. The main interactions to focus on, for Ranke, were between peoples as collectively embodied in states. Whereas in Hegel's view of world history certain states were prominent to the extent that he saw them as instantiating stages in the development of the Idea of Freedom, in Ranke's approach the prominence of states depended on the extent to which they shaped world history through their power and influence over other states.

The sharpness of the debate between the Historical School and Hegel should not lead us, however, to overlook their commonalities. They extolled different methods, but both in service of a developmental historicism with a confidently scientific aspiration. Parallels on a substantive level are also clear, especially when we consider Hegel and Ranke together in contrast to Guizot. Whereas Guizot's developmental historicism found its focal points in the development of "nation" and "civilization," for Hegel and Ranke the most important focal point was the development of the "state." These common traits would occupy a central place in the political science of Johann Bluntschli, who studied at Berlin the 1820s, and saw his midcentury scholarship as integrating the historical and philosophical methods. Through his works and his training of Americans who studied with him, Bluntschli would, in turn, significantly influence political science in America's academy.

---

[15] The quotes in this and the next paragraph are from Stern, *Varieties of History*, 58–60. A basic methodological issue at stake here concerned the relationship between historical synthesis and evaluative judgment. For Hegel, the two were interwoven with philosophically articulated rational concepts a common prerequisite to carrying through either. But for Ranke a distinction could and should be made. His famous line about writing a history that "wants only to show what actually happened (*wie es eigentlich gewesen*)" incorporated an aspiration to synthesis, but disavowed "the office of judging the past, of instructing the present for the benefit of future ages." *Varieties of History*, 57.

Bluntschli, Maine, and Freeman: Liberal Historicist Science and the Aryan Synthesis

Bluntschli stands out as a key connecting figure through whom the methodological self-consciousness and self-confidence that developmental historicism acquired at the University of Berlin came to influence pioneering political scientists in America. He also stands out, moreover, for combining this methodological orientation with liberalism. In both regards Bluntschli can be compared to two British scholars of law and institutions—Henry Maine and Edward Freeman—who also had a notable influence on American political science. Each of these figures located his scholarship at the methodological cutting edge of a self-consciously scientific developmental historicism, and each employed his *science* in work that was liberal in its *political* concerns and commitments. Considered together, these three Europeans exemplify the range of political and methodological variety within the combination of liberalism and developmental historicism that proved central to political science as it developed in America's nineteenth-century academy.

The works of Bluntschli, Maine, and Freeman in the 1850s–1870s also testify, finally, to the prominence that racial and cultural[16] groupings informed by studies of language families came to have in developmental historicism by midcentury. In the 1820s Ranke and Hegel had already distinguished Romance (or Latin) peoples (e.g., the French, Spanish, and Italians) and Germanic (or Teutonic) peoples (e.g., the Germans, English, and Scandinavians). But grouping along racial and cultural lines moved to a new level as the locating of the Germanic languages, classical Greek, and Latin together within the Indo-European linguistic family promoted a dramatic new manner of interpreting European history. The history of ancient Greece and Rome, and of Europe since the Germanic conquest of the Western Empire, came to be interpreted as submovements in the overall developmental history of racially kindred peoples who increasingly came to be identified as "Aryan."[17] What we may call "the Aryan synthesis" advanced together with a self-consciously scientific developmental historicism, and hence we find

---

[16] The German word *Volk*, and the distinctions German scholars drew using it, were often translated into English in the nineteenth century as "race," which was, at the time, conceptually linked not only to physical traits but also to language and cultural traits more broadly. After this introductory paragraph I follow the language of the day in discussing these groupings as racial.

[17] On the impact of the Aryan model on classics scholarship, see Martin Bernal's argument that this model supplanted an earlier synthesis stressing inheritances linking ancient Greece to non-Aryan societies of North Africa and the Mideast. Martin Bernal, *Black Athena: The Afroasiatic Roots of Classical Civilization*, vol. 1, *The Fabrication of Ancient Greece, 1785–1985* (New Brunswick, NJ: Rutgers University Press, 1987). On the rise of racial thinking more broadly through the first half of the nineteenth century and its ramifications in American politics, see Reginald Horsman, *Race and Manifest Destiny: The Origins of American Racial Anglo-Saxonism* (Cambridge, MA: Harvard University Press, 1981).

the liberal political visions of Bluntschli, Maine, and Freeman to be, at the same time, racialized visions.

BLUNTSCHLI: THE THEORY OF THE STATE
AND GERMAN LIBERALISM

From the late 1840s through the 1870s, the Swiss-German Bluntschli was one of the main scholars involved in the research and teaching of the sciences of the state (*Staatswissenschaften*) in German universities, working first at Munich and then at Heidelberg.[18] His scholarly interests encompassed institutional history, constitutional and international law, public administration, and idealist philosophy as applied to political phenomena. Bluntschli saw the earlier conflict between the Historical School and Hegel as having, from the 1840s onward, given way to an aspiration to reconcile them.[19] What this could entail is on display in Bluntschli's *Theory of the Modern State*, published in the mid-1870s toward the end of his career, but the culmination of over two decades of expansion and revision of a work first published in 1852.[20]

Bluntschli's *Theory of the Modern State* ambitiously pursued a "general" science of the state based on "universal history." Universal history did not, from his developmental historicist viewpoint, encompass all of the human past, but rather parts of the past held to have contributed to the march of history. What mattered specifically for his *Theory* were historical developments that contributed to the "progress of political civilization." These were, Bluntschli held, concentrated in the history of the branches of the Aryan peoples that had made their way to Europe. The historical basis of his work was, therefore, how the Aryan "manly genius for politics" had "unfolded and matured" in the course of European history. The primary agents of "a high and conscious political development" included the Greeks and Romans in antiquity, and the invading Teutonic tribes who gave shape to the Middle Ages; "modern political civilization" in turn developed from this "mixture of Greco-Roman and Teutonic elements." In the recent past and present,

[18] For an overall characterization of the *Staatswissenschaften*, and their changing shape in the nineteenth century, see the scrupulously researched work of David F. Lindenfeld, *The Practical Imagination: The German Sciences of the State in the Nineteenth Century* (Chicago: University of Chicago Press, 1997).

[19] Johann Caspar Bluntschli, *The Theory of the State* (Kitchener, ON: Batoche Books, 2000), 15–18, 70.

[20] Johann Caspar Bluntschli, *Lehre vom Modernen Stat*, 3 vols. (Stuttgart: J. G. Cotta, 1875–76). In using the unusual spelling *Stat* I cite directly from the title page of Bluntschli's book. The first volume of this work was translated in the 1880s under the title *The Theory of the State* by a team of faculty who taught modern history at Oxford. In my text I quote from a recent republication of that translation. For the initial work the *Lehre* developed from, see Johann Caspar Bluntschli, *Allgemeines Statsrecht Geschichtlich Begründet* (Munich: J. G. Cotta, 1852).

Bluntschli assigned major roles in "modern political development" to England and its American offspring, and to France and Prussia.[21]

Bluntschli's *Theory of the State* also drew directly on idealist philosophy. To avoid being "oppressed by the weight of the material, overwhelmed by the mass of historical experience, and above all, attracted and enchained by the past," Bluntschli drew especially on Hegel's concepts and distinctions to frame and interpret historical developments. He contended, at the same time, that bringing philosophy to engage with "the rich content of actual existence" would check its tendencies toward "barren formulae, empty husks" and "the delusions of ideology." His project was to integrate the "two sound methods of scientific enquiry"—the "historical method" and "philosophical method"—so they would keep each other from the "one-sided perversions" of "*mere empiricism*," on the one hand, and "*Abstract Ideology*" on the other.[22] The product was a current of developmental historicism, which I call the theory of the state, that drew on institutional history and idealist philosophy to produce something that was itself, neither one nor the other.

Bluntschli's *Theory of the Modern State* was integrative not only in its methodological character, but also in its political substance. It exemplifies a distinctive liberal vision most fully articulated during the mid-nineteenth century in Germany. This German liberalism shared in the commitments to representative and constitutional government, and the use of grand conceptions of social change, identified with the liberal tradition in chapter 1. But it combined these with an ethical conception of the state widespread in German political thought. This set German liberalism apart from classical liberalism, and looks ahead to traits of the progressive liberalism crafted in the 1880s by American academics who rejected classical liberalism.

Bluntschli's participation in the broader liberal tradition is highlighted in the way he, as had Constant and Guizot, emphasized qualitative differences between institutions and ideals of classical antiquity and those of modern states. The core distinctive trait of the modern state was, for Bluntschli, recognition of a right to individual freedom of all its inhabitants. This recognition was incompatible with slavery or serfdom. It entailed, moreover, a sphere of private life in which individuals were free to believe and act independent of state infringement. A modern state was "essentially a legal and political community." It left behind all claims to "dominate religion and worship" and supported "freedom of scientific enquiry and of expression of opinion." The state had to be limited if it was to be modern, and these limits were best embodied in a constitution.[23]

---

[21] Bluntschli, *Theory of the State*, 19–20, 54–55, 76–77.

[22] Bluntschli, *Theory of the State*, 18, 15 (italics in original).

[23] Bluntschli offers a summary of what he takes to be the distinctive features of the modern state in book 1, chap. 6, and I take my quotes here from that overview. The limits recognized by a modern state

Bluntschli's liberal commitments were further evident when he considered in more detail the political institutions of a modern state. Such a state had to have a representative government. Bluntschli saw a variety of specific institutional arrangements, falling under two basic "forms of the State," as meeting this criterion. First, there was constitutional monarchy. While this form of state had first fully developed in England, its roots and applications were far broader. Bluntschli glowingly characterized it as "the end of a history of more than a thousand years, the completion of the Romano-Germanic political life, the true political civilization of Europe." A second form of the modern state had also originated from "the political genius of the Anglo-Saxon race." Just as England pioneered constitutional monarchy, so "representative democracy, or the modern form of Republic, as the Americans prefer to call it, was developed in North America." The merit of this modern form of democracy over its classical predecessors arose from replacing mass citizen assemblies with elected assemblies. It was an advance over direct democracy to the extent to which it met "the great difficulty" of crafting electoral institutions "so as to secure that the best men both in intellect and character shall be chosen."[24] For Bluntschli, the modern state thus did not rule out—indeed it required—roles for a monarch or an elite of "the best men." In rejecting democracy unleavened by elite elements, Bluntschli advanced a teaching about the *forms* of the state that, as we saw in chapter 1, was common among European liberals more generally.

When we turn to Bluntschli's account of the *end* of the state, however, it becomes clear that we are dealing with a German liberalism notably different from the classical liberalism more common elsewhere in Europe, especially in Britain. Bluntschli here again stressed the ancient versus modern distinction. But rather than draw a contrast exalting the modern, he now identified the ancient and modern with opposing one-sided views to be transcended by integrating elements of both. He rejected the "ancient" view in which the "welfare of private men" was "unhesitatingly sacrificed to that of the State." But he equally rejected the "modern" view, "often maintained by English and American writers," which regarded the state

> simply as an institution or machine which gives to individuals security for their life, their property, and their personal freedom, or at most as an artificial creation designed to raise and promote the welfare and happiness of all individuals, or at any rate of the greater number.

were, for Bluntschli, external as well as internal; a modern state was willing to be limited in its actions by international law. Bluntschli was a pioneer in the study (and a strong proponent) of international law.

[24] Bluntschli, *Theory of the State*, 319, 370, 378–79.

Against the ancient view Bluntschli favored, as we have seen, a sphere of liberal private freedom supported by constitutional limits on government. Against the modern view, he argued that any satisfactory political theory had to recognize that "every now and then, the State is compelled, either for its own preservation, or in the interest of future generations, to make heavy demands from its present members." To take such situations seriously demanded a theory in which "the State is something better and higher than a mutual assurance society."[25]

A view of the state as "something better and higher" brings us to the ethical conception of the state prominent in nineteenth-century German thought more broadly, in German liberalism specifically, and in Bluntschli as an exemplar of this liberalism. Bluntschli's account of "the true end of the State" ascribed to it a high ethical purpose. It was to promote the development of the capacities and life of its people. The state was to pursue this end, not only by providing military security against external threats, and a legal system securing persons, private liberties, and property, but also by playing positive roles in the economic sphere and in the educational and cultural sphere. Giving similar weight to all four tasks, Bluntschli argued against overstressing any one of them at the expense of the others.[26]

Bluntschli combined these views with a significant rethinking of the division of powers that proposed multiple changes to Montesquieu's classic trifold division of legislative, judicial, and executive powers. For example, Bluntschli argued that the label "executive power" obscured the range and significance of independent decision-making by holders of this power. Instead he favored the label "governmental power." Most notably, Bluntschli added two "groups of organs and functions" to the three stated by Montesquieu. These reflected his German liberal stress on the state's positive roles. He summed up these additional powers as (1) "superintendence and care of the intellectual elements of civilization," and (2) "administration and care of material interests."[27] In adding these two powers, Bluntschli argued that they should be exercised in a manner different from the more familiar three powers. Whereas those powers involved "functions of the State" pursued in a "commanding" mode, state activity in relation to education, culture, and the economy should be pursued instead in an alternative "fostering" mode. It should avoid "employment of force," and rely "not so much on the authority of the State, as on technical knowledge and experience." What was key here

---

[25] Bluntschli, *Theory of the State*, 250–53. Regarding limits on the state, see also 265–66.

[26] Bluntschli, *Theory of the State*, 257–65.

[27] Bluntschli, *Theory of the State*, 409–12. The latter power of "Public Economy" includes "administration of the income and expenditure of the State," "maintenance of the economic welfare of the citizens," "support of commerce," "management of public works," and "control of local government."

was "a spirit of scientific and technical care" directed to serving "the interests at once of the welfare and the freedom of the community."[28]

The confidence with which German liberals like Bluntschli gave wide responsibilities to the state should be seen in connection with the "capable and trustworthy class of officials" they expected to exercise most state functions. Training such officials was a major task of university courses in the *Staatswissenschaften*, and Bluntschli's liberalism hence had a direct tie with his teaching duties. A large swath of the activities he attributed to the state were, Bluntschli argued, best handled by professionalized officials selected by exams or other meritocratic criteria without reference to social class. He called for such officials to handle, in addition to the educational and economic functions of the state, the judicial power and part of the "governmental power." In regard to the latter, he advocated distinguishing "political government (*politische Regierung*) in the general conduct of the State" from "administration (*Verwaltung*) in reference to details."[29] He sought here to distinguish between the legislature and leading figures within the government, who his liberalism dictated should be directly or indirectly electorally responsible, and holders of long-term state offices that should be professionalized. Looking across the Atlantic with evident distaste, Bluntschli singled out the spoils system of democratic America as the polar opposite of the "modern" approach to administration pioneered in Germany.[30]

Professionalized public offices were, for Bluntschli and German liberals in general, a key element of a modern political order. If the state was to promote the ethical end they assigned, it needed a professional administrative apparatus. This feature of German liberalism explains why, for Bluntschli, the "modern epoch" dated from 1740. That was the start of the reign of Frederick the Great, under whom Prussia's administrative apparatus was reformed along lines admired by German liberals. For this, among other reasons—including a policy of religious toleration, and a view of himself as "first servant of the State"—Frederick was declared by Bluntschli to be "the most significant representative of the modern State and the modern view of life." If Bluntschli's *Theory of the Modern State* gave major roles in modern political development to the English and Americans, it saved a lead role for Frederick, in whom "the liberal philosophy of the eighteenth century... ascended the throne of a rising State."[31]

[28] Bluntschli, *Theory of the State*, 411–12.

[29] Bluntschli, *Theory of the State*, 410.

[30] Bluntschli, *Theory of the State*, 418–20. For Bluntschli's views regarding a broader array of issues associated with professionalized public administration, see 413–30.

[31] Bluntschli, *Theory of the State*, 53, 318.

MAINE AND FREEMAN: LIBERAL PROGRESS, INSTITUTIONAL HISTORY, AND THE "COMPARATIVE METHOD"

Two other European developmental historicists who would exercise notable influence on political science in America's post–Civil War academy were the English liberal historians of law and institutions Henry Maine and Edward Freeman.[32] Like Bluntschli, they saw themselves as in the vanguard of scientific advance and employed the Aryan synthesis. But there were differences between them and Bluntschli evident in their manner of formulating a synthetic interpretation of European history. Whereas continental liberals made much use of distinctions between ancient and modern Europe, Maine and Freeman noted more legacies and parallels.[33] They crafted histories in which changes in laws and institutions *during* the multiple centuries of Greek and Roman history supplemented, without supplanting, the ancient versus modern contrast. In the hands of Maine and Freeman the laws and institutions of Aryan peoples, from the farthest reaches of the past to recent centuries, were studied with a British Whig concern for continuity as leavened, and indeed facilitated, by steady and tempered progressive changes.[34]

[32] Many more substantive facets of Maine's thought than I touch on here are examined in Karuna Mantena's excellent recent book. Karuna Mantena, *Alibis of Empire: Henry Maine and the Ends of Liberal Imperialism* (Princeton, NJ: Princeton University Press, 2010). On Maine's method see also Kenneth Bock, "Comparison of Histories: The Contribution of the Henry Maine," *Comparative Studies in Society and History* 16, no. 2 (1974), 232–62; John Burrow, *Evolution and Society: A Study in Victorian Social Theory* (Cambridge: Cambridge University Press, 1966), chap. 5.

[33] This contrast might be related to the different political situation facing liberals in Britain versus on the continent. Continental liberals had to contend both against the ways the republics of earlier Rome and Greece were invoked by radical republicans and the ways in which the later Roman Empire was invoked in the First and Second Napoleonic Empires. Since these illiberal uses of the ancients were far less important within British politics, liberals there could arguably explore continuities and parallels with the classical world with greater ease.

[34] The Britain versus continental European contrast I suggest in this paragraph is exemplified by setting Maine's 1861 *Ancient Law*, discussed in my main text in the next few pages, beside the French scholar Fustel de Coulanges's 1864 *The Ancient City*. In introducing his study of ancient Greek and Roman institutions, Coulanges noted his concern "to set in a clear light the radical and essential differences which at all times distinguished these ancient peoples from modern societies." He also made clear the practical ramifications of this concern as he declared that "liberty among the moderns" had been "put in peril" and "the march of modern society" impeded in the "last eighty years" by the tendency of looking to ancient examples when pursuing practical action in modern societies. Coulanges argued in his book that ancient institutions and liberty were interwoven with social beliefs and practices rooted in a religion radically different from the Christianity of modern societies. Fustel de Coulanges, *The Ancient City: A Study of the Religion, Laws, and Institutions of Greece and Rome*, trans. Willard Small (Garden City, NY: Doubleday, 1956), 11–13.

Change during the course of ancient history provided the substance of Maine's influential claim about progress in his 1861 *Ancient Law*. In the middle of that book, he famously proposed "movement *from Status to Contract*" as a "formula" summing up the process of social change he saw himself charting in ancient Rome. This process moved "from a condition of society in which all the relations of Persons are summed up in the relations of Family...towards a phase of social order in which all these relations arise from the free agreement of individuals." Maine followed this process, as refracted in changes in Roman law, through a millennium of Roman history. But he did so with more in mind than Rome. Maine believed he had identified the "one respect" in which the development of "the progressive societies has been uniform." Movement from status toward contract was not only a process that occurred in ancient Rome; it was ongoing in contemporary Europe. A society based on "the free agreement of individuals" was the end that progress moved toward in the past and the present.[35] In conceptualizing this end Maine articulated mid-Victorian classical liberalism in its heyday. His use of "Contract" identified as the measure of progress the ability of individuals to arrange the terms of their relations with one another by private contracts, which they were free to make and enter into based on their own judgment of their interests.

Maine's argument about progress was framed by an established contrast between "progressive" and "stationary" societies or civilizations (both Guizot and Hegel had also used it). He updated this contrast in light of a focus on legal change over centuries, which had become a major research agenda in the hands of Historical School scholars. Maine argued that there were mechanisms by which law in progressive societies kept up with the changing "social necessities" and "opinion" of an advancing society. In stationary societies, by contrast, law resisted change and thus stifled advance. Maine tied the two sides of this contrast together as divergent branches in a sweeping historical synthesis: early social development proceeded to the point at which legal codes were drafted, with societies thereafter dividing into two types. On one side were stationary societies, whose later history encompassed only limited further development. On the other side were the progressive societies marked by extensive continuing development. Here advances in "material civilization" remade the law rather than being inhibited by it.[36]

---

[35] Henry Sumner Maine, *Ancient Law: Its Connection with the Early History of Society, and Its Relation to Modern Ideas* (New York: Scribner, 1864), 163–65 (italics in original).

[36] Maine, *Ancient Law*, 20–24. There is ambiguity in *Ancient Law* about what Maine was claiming with regard to the early social development he portrayed as running up to the branching point when codes are written. At points he implied that this was common to all mankind. At other times he suggested that he was portraying early social developments common to "all branches of the Indo-European family of nations," but that he did not have the evidence to assess whether his claims applied beyond that family (11, 117).

Maine's "from Status to Contract" formula summarized the *direction* of development in progressive societies, and his branching framing situated those societies in a sweeping historical synthesis. But neither of these aspects of his thought constituted an account of the *dynamic* that drove progress. Maine's treatment of law reflected a classical liberal concern with conditions that can hinder a progressive dynamic thought to be based in society. Laws could stifle this dynamic, but they did not create it. To the extent Maine considered the springs of progress, he found its prime agent in intellectual change. In stating this view in his later work *Popular Government*, he declared that the "only intelligible meaning" of progress was "the continued production of new ideas," and identified "scientific invention and scientific discovery" as "the great and perennial source of these ideas."[37] In Maine's liberal vision of progress, new ideas fed new technologies and outlooks on life, and these, in turn, propelled the changes toward a social and legal order prioritizing free agreement of individuals.

For Maine, the progressive character of European civilization made European societies "a rare exception in the history of the world." To look further afield to the "totality of human life" showed that most human beings in world history lived in stationary societies where the primary temperament was conservative hostility to change. It was, Maine thus argued, "indisputable that much the greatest part of mankind has never shown a particle of desire that its civil institutions should be improved since the moment when external completeness was first given to them by their embodiment in some permanent record."[38]

While Maine thus shared Guizot's stress on European exceptionalism, he gave it distinct content. Whereas Guizot saw the barbarian invasions of the fifth century as starting Europe on its unique historical path, Maine looked further back to embrace ancient Europe as also sharing in—and indeed a primary source of—the exceptionality of modern Europe. What set European societies, ancient and modern, on their progressive path was, Maine judged, "one of the great secrets which inquiry has yet to penetrate." A partial explanation should, he thought, draw on his identification of the drafting of law codes as a developmental critical juncture. A fuller explanation would also include a role for the impact that Greek philosophy, and specifically "the theory of Natural Law," had exerted on Rome. It was only after this "stimulus was applied" that the "progress of the Romans in legal improvement" became "astonishingly rapid."[39] Maine would further extend this claim in his 1874 Rede Lecture at Cambridge University. Here he enthroned ancient Greece as the great spark of intellectual progress whose legacy had diffused to shape not only Roman law, but also the

---

[37] Henry Sumner Maine, *Popular Government* (Indianapolis, IN: Liberty Fund, 1976), 154.

[38] Maine, *Ancient Law*, 21–22.

[39] Maine, *Ancient Law*, 22–23, 13–19, 54–55.

intellectual achievements of modern Europe. It is worth quoting him at length on this point:

> Whatever be the nature and value of that bundle of influences which we call Progress, nothing can be more certain than that, when a society is once touched by it, it spreads like a contagion. Yet, so far as our knowledge extends, there was only one society in which it was endemic; and putting that aside, no race or nationality, left entirely to itself, appears to have developed any very great intellectual result, except perhaps Poetry. Not one of those intellectual excellencies which we regard as characteristic of the great progressive races of the world—not the law of the Romans, not the philosophy and sagacity of the Germans, not the luminous order of the French, not the political aptitude of the English, not that insight into physical nature to which all races have contributed— would apparently have come into existence if those races had been left to themselves. To one small people, covering in its original seat no more than a handsbreadth of territory, it was given to create the principle of Progress, of movement onwards and not backwards or downwards, of destruction tending to construction. That people was the Greek. Except the blind forces of Nature, nothing moves in this world which is not Greek in its origin. A ferment spreading from that source has vitalised all the great progressive races of mankind, penetrating from one to another, and producing results accordant with its hidden and latent genius, and results of course often far greater than any exhibited in Greece itself.[40]

As the close of this quote suggests, Greek thought was, for Maine, the starting spark, but not the culmination of intellectual advance. To stay true to the "ferment" born in Greece was to strive "onwards and not backwards," and to recognize when "destruction" was necessary for new advance. This attitude had informed the intellectual agenda of *Ancient Law*. While he praised the role natural law theory had played *in* the past, Maine sought in that book to consign it *to* the past. Natural law theory had done yeoman work serving progress in the ancient world, and in shaping modern international law. But, by the mid-eighteenth century, it had gone awry. The "remedial" function it played at its best had given way to a

---

[40] I quote from the lecture's republication as part of the appendix of addresses included in Henry Sumner Maine, *Village-Communities in the East and West*, 3rd ed. (New York: Holt, 1876), 237–39. The belief in Greece's critical import for progress was not Maine's alone. For example, we find John Stuart Mill declaring that the events of classical Greece "decided for an indefinite period the question, whether the human race was to be stationary or progressive." John Stuart Mill, "Grote's History of Greece [2]," in *Essays on Philosophy and the Classics*, ed. John M. Robson, *Collected Works of John Stuart Mill*, vol. 11 (Toronto: University of Toronto Press, 1978), 313.

"revolutionary or anarchical" role. From Maine's viewpoint, the tragedy of eighteenth-century intellectual life was that natural law thinking in this role surged
into the popular imagination at just the time when natural law theory and its associated ideas should, on intellectual grounds, have been dying out. Montesquieu had
already pioneered a new, more advanced, approach to law and institutions. But his
"Historical Method" paled in influence beside the works of Rousseau. More recently,
the intellectual star of the Law of Nature and its offspring the State of Nature had
begun to fade. The battle to advance beyond them was, however, still not complete.[41]

Ancient Law was a new contribution to the long-standing historicist effort to
supersede natural law theory and its associated ideas. Maine's attack was threefold.
First, he took on the theory frontally by applying historical method to the Law of
Nature itself, and to the issue of the origins of society so central to the State of Nature.
Second, he sought to exemplify how historical method could positively remake the
study of Roman law (an academic study that had, through recent centuries, helped to
revitalize, and then sustained, natural law theory). Third, he argued that in making
these substantive moves he was advancing a properly scientific approach to law and
institutions. This third strand of Maine's attack brings us back to the methodological
issues highlighted earlier in debates at the University of Berlin.

Maine drew significantly on the Historical School, and methodological parallels between them are therefore unsurprising. We find in Maine again the belief
that correct method is crucial to scientific inquiry; the view that this method
involves careful attention to getting the historical facts right; and the criticism of
opponents for allowing a priori theories to drive their findings. As the last point
suggests, Maine did not partake of the rapprochement involved in Bluntschli's
view of "historical method" and "philosophical method" as equally scientific
methods that work best if integrated. Maine was wedded to pursuing developmental historicist synthesis, but like the Historical School was confident that this
did not require turning to philosophy for articulated abstract concepts. At the
same time that Bluntschli was pursuing a theory of the state that strove to combine institutional history with Hegelian philosophy, Maine showed that a freestanding institutional history wary of philosophy retained its resonance.

In advocating historical method Maine employed, however, empiricist notions
foreign to both sides in the prior German debate. The stress on linguistically
informed textual criticism in the Historical School's position was replaced by a
generic praise of "sober research" that enabled Maine to analogize his approach
to practices in the natural sciences. During the opening pages of Ancient Law,
Maine compared his approach to that of a geologist and charged the study of law

---

[41] This paragraph summarizes Maine's arguments in his chapter "The Modern History of the Law
of Nature." See Maine, Ancient Law, chap. 4. For Maine's specific use of terms and phrases I quote, see
pp. 74, 83, 87.

with being methodologically laggard.[42] The study of law was, Maine bemoaned, still "prosecuted much as inquiry in physics and physiology was prosecuted before observation took the place of assumption." In this image of advance from "assumption" to "observation," Maine used an empiricist trope about natural science methods to claim the mantle of scientific advance for his attack on "[t]heories, plausible and comprehensive, but absolutely unverified such as the Law of Nature or the Social Compact."[43]

Maine's 1861 claim that his method paralleled the natural sciences places him in well-established company among British historicists. When Macaulay in 1829 had criticized James Mill, he had credited "inductive method" for the "rapid progress of the experimental sciences," tied *a priori* method" to "the verbal sophistry that flourished during the dark ages," and then gone on to caustically charge:

> Mr. Mill ... is an Aristotelian of the fifteenth century, born out of due season. We have here an elaborate treatise on Government, from which, but for two or three passing allusions, it would not appear that the author was aware that any governments actually existed among men. Certain propensities of Human Nature are assumed; and from these premises the whole science of Politics is synthetically deduced! We can scarcely persuade ourselves that we are not reading a book written before the time of Bacon and Galileo.[44]

Macaulay was, in turn, elaborating a theme Edmund Burke had deployed in his classic work of British historicism, his 1790 *Reflections on the Revolution in France*, where he stressed: "The science of constructing a commonwealth, or renovating it, or reforming it, is, like every other experimental science, not to be taught *a priori*."[45] What Maine offered in the methodological rhetoric and practice of *Ancient Law* was a blending of an established empiricist trope of British historicism with the more recent, and differently founded, scientific authority of the German Historical School.

Ancient Law captures, however, only one of two methodologically noteworthy moments within Maine's scholarship. After making his reputation with his first book, Maine spent most of the 1860s in India serving as a law member of the

---

[42] In Britain, the Benthamite John Austin's philosophical jurisprudence had, most recently, been in the ascendant.

[43] Maine, *Ancient Law*, 3. See also 115. Maine's continuing use of this methodological framing is evident in an address he gave at the University of Calcutta in 1865. There he portrayed recent intellectual changes in the study of language and history as resulting from applying "scientific modes of inquiry" pioneered in the physical sciences. Maine, *Village-Communities*, 264–69.

[44] Thomas Babington Macaulay, "Mill on Government," in *Macaulay: Prose and Poetry*, ed. G. M. Young (Cambridge, MA: Harvard University Press, 1952), 579–81.

[45] Edmund Burke, *The Portable Edmund Burke*, ed. Isaac Kramnick (New York: Penguin, 1999), 442.

Governor General's council. On returning to England in 1869 he was appointed to a Chair in Comparative Jurisprudence at Oxford. In works developed from his academic lectures, Maine promoted "the Comparative Method" as an exciting new approach offering opportunities to extend "the Historical Method" as extolled in *Ancient Law*.[46] Maine's friend Edward Freeman also began to promote the comparative method, and together they sparked a surge of excitement that would, as we will see, spread to the other side of the Atlantic. Wide use of the phrase "comparative method" among scholars of law and institutions in Britain and America begins with Maine and Freeman in the early 1870s. Perhaps most interestingly for political scientists today, Freeman, when titling lectures he gave in 1873, coined "Comparative Politics" to label studies that applied this method to political institutions.[47]

For Maine and Freeman the original and paradigmatic use of the comparative method had been by German scholars who revolutionized philology. It was by closely comparing languages that philologists had grouped diverse languages in a single Aryan language family.[48] It was, moreover, through comparisons that philologists sought to extend the genealogical reach of their work and reconstruct stages in the development of this language family for which direct evidence was fragmentary or nonexistent. These endeavors had fleshed out the Aryan synthesis, which postulated a mother tongue that, over millennia of branching and sub-branching, gave rise to the many historical and contemporary languages in the family. First pioneered in the study of language, the Aryan synthesis and the comparative method that created it had later been extended into studies of mythology and culture. Maine and Freeman sought, in turn, to extend this method another step by bringing it into their institutional studies. Freeman grandly expressed the sense of new possibilities associated with these developments:

> On us a new light has come. I do not for a moment hesitate to say that the discovery of the Comparative method in philology, in mythology—let

---

[46] Maine first waved the banner of "the Comparative Method" in the early pages of the 1871 first edition of *Village-Communities East and West*, which grew out of his initial set of lectures after his appointment at Oxford. On both Maine and Freeman on this method, see Stefan Collini, Donald Winch, and John Burrow, *That Noble Science of Politics: A Study in Nineteenth-Century Intellectual History* (Cambridge: Cambridge University Press, 1983), chap. 7.

[47] Edward Freeman, *Comparative Politics* (London: Macmillan, 1873).

[48] The terminology used to talk about this common descent—whether used to label languages, peoples, practices, or societies—was a matter of debate. Maine used the now prevalent term Indo-European in *Ancient Law*. By the 1870s he had adopted the term Aryan, which Freeman also favored. Both seem to have followed the lead of the Oxford faculty member, Max Müller. This German scholar of Sanskrit and comparative philology advocated Aryan as an alternative to Indo-European, which he found problematic because it might suggest that all languages and peoples in India and Europe shared a common ancestry. See Max Müller, "Aryan, as a Technical Term," in *Selected Essays on Language, Mythology, and Religion* (London: Longmans, Green, 1881), 1: 204–15.

me add in politics and history and the whole range of human thought—
marks a stage in the progress of the human mind at least as great and
memorable as the revival of Greek and Latin learning. The great contribution of the nineteenth century to the advance of human knowledge
may boldly take its stand alongside of the great contribution of the fif-
teenth. Like the revival of learning, it has opened to its votaries a new
world, and that not an isolated world, a world shut up within itself, but
a world in which times and tongues and nations which before seemed
parted poles asunder, now find each one its own place, its own relation to
every other, as members of one common primæval brotherhood.[49]

Maine and Freeman thus envisioned a comparative institutional history that
followed the methodological lead of comparative philology. The premise of their
aspiration was that not only languages, but also some institutions, had common
Aryan precursors that existed before recorded history. They strove to reconstruct
ancient Aryan institutions and chart later developments, down through branching and sub-branching lines of historical descent, to institutions found within the
historically documented past and the present societies of Aryan language speakers. In doing so, they employed two research practices.

The first practice, stressed particularly by Maine, sought out traces of older
institutions surviving in the present day. Maine built here on the combination
of his earlier work and his own experience. When analyzing early legal codes in
Ancient Law he had briefly compared ancient Indian laws to Rome's early code to
parse the exceptionalism of progressive societies by asking what made Roman law
different from that of "stationary" India. In doing so, Maine had already noted that
the Romans and Indians "sprang from the same original stock," and that there was
"a striking resemblance between what appears to have been their original customs."[50] He hence was ready to approach India during his time there as a reservoir
of survivals of the common Aryan past preserved by the stationary character of
its society. He returned from India convinced that, as he proclaimed in his 1874
Rede Lecture, it contained "a whole world of Aryan institutions, Aryan customs,
Aryan laws, Aryan ideas, Aryan beliefs, in a far earlier stage of growth and development than any which survive beyond its borders."[51] Pairing observation of such
survivals with historical knowledge about the past of Aryan societies in Europe
allowed for comparisons in which "observation comes to the aid of historical
enquiry, and historical enquiry to the aid of direct observation."[52] The research
practice that Maine promoted with regard to India could also be applied to some

[49] Freeman, *Comparative Politics*, 301–2.
[50] Maine, *Ancient Law*, 18.
[51] Maine, *Village-Communities*, 211.
[52] Maine, *Village-Communities*, 7.

tent with phenomena observed in Europe. Freeman, for example, believed that in the self-governing villages and cantons of Switzerland, he observed institutions once found throughout the Teutonic sub-branch of the Aryan peoples.[53]

The second practice associated with the comparative method of Maine and Freeman also assumed branching lines of development running forward from a shared historical origin. But it compared institutions across past societies, rather than comparing institutions from the past of one society with institutions observed in another society today. Freeman's *Comparative Politics* centered on this practice. It compared political institutions of ancient Greece, ancient Rome, and the Teutonic peoples who invaded the Roman Empire. His study built on the premise that Greek, Roman, and Teutonic societies descended from a common predecessor, and that a developmental interpretation of their political institutions was the key to a general synthetic view of the political history of western Europe.

While Maine and Freeman differed in details of their methods and their liberalism from Bluntschli, all three exemplify the methodological self-confidence of developmental historicism in its intellectual heyday. That confidence would prove attractive to American scholars eager to increase the international scientific credentials of their academy as it began to develop modern universities during the post–Civil War decades. Developmental historicism was, moreover, not only scientifically confident, but also familiar. It had already been pursued, and interwoven with liberal political substance, in the antebellum American college by the United States' first professor of political science, the Prussian émigré Francis Lieber. It is to Lieber that we now turn.

[53] Freeman, *Comparative Politics*, 238–40.

CHAPTER 3

Democratized Classical Liberalism in the Antebellum American College

THE ÉMIGRÉ POLITICAL SCIENCE OF FRANCIS LIEBER

The transatlantic origins of political science in America are concisely reflected in the fact that Francis Lieber—the first American academic to have "political science" in his title—was a Prussian political émigré. A liberal nationalist, born in 1800, who overstated his age in order to fight for Prussia in 1815 and almost died from the wounds he received at the battle of Waterloo, Lieber later became bitterly disappointed as Prussia's king failed to promulgate the constitution and representative government he had promised in rousing the people to fight Napoleon.[1] Under suspicion for his political views, Lieber was imprisoned for four months in 1819. Following his release, despite not being convicted of anything, he was kept under surveillance and restricted in his educational and employment options. The restrictions led him to take his PhD in 1820 at the University of Jena (in Saxe-Weimar, not Prussia) in the safely nonpolitical field of mathematics. After he was jailed, again without conviction, for eight months by Prussia's authorities in 1824–1825, Lieber decided to emigrate in 1826, going first to Britain, and then to America in 1827.[2]

---

[1] The limited powers of the estates-based provincial assemblies established by the Prussian king in 1823 led Lieber to judge them "in reality, nugatory." Far from "a fulfillment of his promise made in 1815 to give a constitution to his people," the king's creation of the assemblies was "an evasion and a mockery." "Constitution," in *Encyclopedia Americana*, vol. 3, ed. Francis Lieber (Philadelphia: Carey and Lea, 1830), 475; "Prussia," in *Encyclopedia Americana*, vol. 10, ed. Francis Lieber (Philadelphia: Carey and Lea, 1832), 388. On Lieber's volunteering and experience as a Prussian soldier, see Letters VI and VII of Francis Lieber, *Letters to a Gentleman in Germany, written after a Trip from Philadelphia to Niagara* (Philadelphia: Carey, Lea & Blanchard, 1834).

[2] For biographical details on Lieber see M. Russell Thayer, "The Life, Character, and Writings of Francis Lieber," in *Miscellaneous Writings of Francis Lieber*, 2 vols., ed. Daniel C. Gilman (Philadelphia: Lippincott, 1881), 1: 14–44; Thomas Sergeant Perry, ed. *The Life and Letters of Francis Lieber* (Boston: Osgood, 1882); Frank Freidel, *Francis Lieber: Nineteenth-Century Liberal* (Baton Rouge: Louisiana State University Press, 1947).

Embracing his new homeland, Lieber became an American citizen in 1832, obtained his first academic position as Professor of History and Political Economy at South Carolina College in 1835, and taught there for two decades before he was hired by Columbia College in New York in 1857. There he took up a new chair of history and political science, for which he personally requested that "political science" be used in its title. In Lieber's scholarship we find the political vision of democratized classical liberalism, as introduced in chapter 1, being combined with premises and practices of developmental historicist science, as introduced in chapter 2. This distinctive specification of the *political* and the *science* in political science thus formed the point of departure in the emergence of a self-conscious "political science" in America's academy.

My presentation of Lieber proceeds in four roughly chronological steps. First, I examine his popularly oriented writings in the years between his arrival in America and his appointment as a professor in 1835. By comparing them with the first volume of his friend Tocqueville's *Democracy in America*, published in 1835, I establish that Lieber entered America's academy with a democratized classical liberal political vision. Second, I turn to the treatise, *Manual of Political Ethics*, that Lieber wrote during his first years at South Carolina College. Here Lieber employed a blend of philosophical and historical methods evocative of the cutting edge of developmental historicism, and put this blend to work politically in extolling an Anglo-American exceptionalism centered on constitutionalism and judicial independence. Third, I examine Lieber's writings in political economy to flesh out my identification of his liberal vision as a *classical* liberalism. And more specifically, by comparing Lieber's arguments on trade unions and free trade to positions in J. S. Mill's *Principles of Political Economy*, I explicate a divide—at once both methodological and political—between uncompromising and moderate subspecies of classical liberalism. Finally, to conclude, I use Lieber's 1857 request to have "political science" in his Columbia title as a spur to elucidate the meaning this phrase had for Lieber. I argue that Lieber's "political science" bridged alternative usages associated, respectively, with the German *Staatswissenschaften* and the French *sciences politiques*. We find in Lieber more than a passive reception of European models. Lieber crafted a hybrid that creatively drew from distinct currents of European scholarship as he adapted transatlantic intellectual exchanges to his American setting to inaugurate an American political science not entirely mapping the earlier political science of any single European country.

Democratized Classical Liberalism as a Point of Departure: Lieber and Tocqueville

In chapter 1 I used a series of contrasts to distinguish the democratized classical liberalism that crystallized in the 1830s from other early- to

mid-nineteenth-century liberal political visions. I differentiate
from elitist early-century French liberals who supported prop⌐
suffrage in the belief that democracies are illiberal; and on the op⌐
of the spectrum, from early-century British radicals who, in promoti⌐
democracy with universally stated arguments, avoided issues about its c⌐
tions of possibility. Finally, I noted the more nuanced contrast between demo⌐
ratized classical liberalism and the views of the British Whig T. B. Macaulay,
who granted that a liberal democracy was possible under certain conditions, but
saw these conditions as exceptional to America and expected them to disappear
even there in the future. My first goal in discussing Francis Lieber is to show
that the political vision displayed in the popularly oriented works that he wrote
during his years in America prior to his 1835 academic appointment exemplifies
democratized classical liberalism.

Lieber's political vision may be introduced by way of a comparison with the
much better-known views of his contemporary and friend Tocqueville.[3] Born in
1800 and 1805, respectively, their friendship began when Tocqueville, and his
travel companion Gustave de Beaumont, met Lieber in Boston in September 1831
while touring America. The formal reason for the tour was to study America's
prisons, and after completing their report *On the Penitentiary System in the United
States*, the two Frenchmen turned to Lieber to translate it for publication in
America in 1833.[4] Thereafter, Lieber and Tocqueville maintained an extended
correspondence,[5] in which, among other things, they discussed their major works
as these appeared from the 1830s to the mid-1850s. After Tocqueville's *Ancien
Régime* was published, Lieber proudly reported to his friend that one American
reviewer had "grouped Montesquieu, de Tocqueville, and Lieber as forming a distinct class of modern political philosophers and distinguished by their rising from
the broad ground of history and human reality to the highest speculations, by
their true wisdom and by real statesmanship, the only modern publicists resem-
bling Aristotle."[6] I concentrate here on the early 1830s, when the democratized
classical liberalism of both Tocqueville and Lieber was taking form, as seen in

[3] In pairing Lieber and Tocqueville I follow David Clinton, who studies them alongside the British Bagehot. David Clinton, *Tocqueville, Lieber, and Bagehot: Liberalism Confronts the World* (New York: Palgrave Macmillan, 2003).

[4] Gustave de Beaumont and Alexis de Tocqueville, *On the Penitentiary System in the United States, and Its Application in France*, trans. Francis Lieber (Philadelphia: Carey, Lea & Blanchard, 1833).

[5] For Tocqueville's and Lieber's letters during the 1840s and 1850s see Aurelian Craiutu and Jeremy Jennings, eds., *Tocqueville on America after 1840: Letters and Other Writings* (New York: Cambridge University Press, 2009).

[6] Letter from Lieber to Tocqueville, May 30, 1857. *Tocqueville after 1840*, 232. Lieber politely refrained from telling Tocqueville that the reviewer, Samuel Tyler, also declared: "There is not a politi-cal idea, much less a principle of political science propounded by De Tocqueville which Lieber had not before announced in his 'Civil Liberty.'" Review as quoted in Freidel, *Francis Lieber*, 276.

Tocqueville's 1835 first volume of *Democracy in America*, Lieber's 1834 *Letters to a Gentleman in Germany*,[7] and selected Lieber contributions to the *Encyclopedia Americana*,[8] which appeared under his editorship in multiple volumes between 1829 and 1833.

In introducing democratized classical liberalism in chapter 1, I contrasted Constant's defense of property limits on suffrage to Tocqueville's belief that the suffrage in representative governments must, sooner or later, be put upon a democratic basis. Lieber shared Tocqueville's view that property limits were at odds with the tide of history. In his *Letters to a Gentleman*, he rejected "writers who wish to see the right of representation attached to landed property only" for supporting "a system, which, at one time, when the great mass of intelligence found a pretty fair standard in landed property, was sound, but which the noble struggle fought by the cities of the middle ages for all mankind, ought to be considered as having dismantled for ever."[9]

Arguments for basing a political system on property appeared anachronistic to Lieber and Tocqueville because they both approached this political issue in light of a shared conception of a grand social transformation from aristocracy (which they equated with feudalism) to democracy. In the "Constitution" entry in the 1830 third volume of the *Encyclopedia Americana*, Lieber divided "representative constitutions" between (1) an older type "founded on the union of feudal estates," and (2) a newer type establishing "the right of a general representation." He judged constitutions that were still "founded on the idea of estates" to be "inconsistent with the spirit of the age." Proceeding in turn to explicate this "spirit of the age" in broader social terms, he proclaimed:

> The democratic tendency of time must be acknowledged by every calm
> and unprejudiced observer, whether he thinks the effect good or bad,

---

[7] This work is not made up of actual letters, but of a wide-ranging series of essays, titled as a numbered set of letters, of which Lieber presented himself as the editor, though he had in fact written all the content. It was published under a different title in England as *The Stranger in America, Comprising Sketches of the Manners, Society, and National Peculiarities of the United States, in a Series of Letter to a Friend in Europe* (London: Bentley, 1835). In reviewing the book in 1836, alongside other works on America, John Stuart Mill would comment, rather sharply, that Lieber's "book contains something about America, with which he is in the highest good humour, and something about every other subject whatsoever, especially about the author himself." "State of Society in America," in *Essays on Politics and Society*, ed. John M. Robson, *Collected Works of John Stuart Mill*, vol. 18 (Toronto: University of Toronto Press, 1977), 97.

[8] Entries in the *Encyclopedia Americana* do not list their authors. In addition to the "Politics" entry, which has been attributed to Lieber by multiple historians of political science, I also tentatively attribute the entries "Constitution," "Estates," "France, History of," "History," "Liberal," "Prussia," and "Representative Government." I rely here on a combination of evidence from close parallels to Lieber's other writings in this period, parallels between these pieces, and comments in biographies of Lieber on subjects that he wrote about for the *Encyclopedia*.

[9] Lieber, *Letters to a Gentleman*, 269.

whether he belongs to the class which deems all virtue and nobleness of character concentrated in the middle ages, to those who believe in the final perfection of mankind, or to those who have no standard for measuring the state of a nation but statistical tables. Every thing, from the fashion of the dress to the cultivation of the intellect tends to a democratic equality.[10]

The belief that political judgments should take as given a sweeping social transformation toward democracy would be more famously and fully elaborated five years later by Tocqueville in the introduction of *Democracy in America.* Here Tocqueville elegantly sketched the previous seven hundred years of European history in terms of a "gradual and progressive development of equality." Adding a divine dimension missing from Lieber's formulation, Tocqueville declared that this "irresistible revolution" had "the sacred character of the sovereign master's will," and held that European nations had to "accommodate themselves to the social state that Providence imposes on them." Tocqueville then singled out America as the "one country in the world where the great social revolution I am speaking of seems nearly to have attained its natural limits," and hence, a country offering "lessons...from which we [the French] could profit," since "sooner or later we shall arrive, like the Americans, at an almost complete equality of conditions."[11]

The notion that America offered a key to unlock the character and challenges of the age was one that Lieber had brought to America with him. Writing to his family in June 1827 during his voyage to America, he had said:

In a few words I will try and explain to you my expectations in regard to America. I know that it will not be a paradise. I believe that the customs and influences of the Middle Ages were required for the development of the race then, but now new and greater ideas are dawning which Europe is too petrified and ossified to accept or adopt.... These new ideas will find their soil in America, and many have already taken root.[12]

---

[10] Lieber, "Constitution," 467. Lieber's particular appeal to a "democratic tendency of time" to reject estates-based representation was probably informed by recent moves in Prussia to revive representative government on a medieval estates basis. Arguing that "the institution of estates has become unsuited to the wants of the age: they have had their time, and have become obsolete," Lieber contended that "[t]hey serve at present only to frustrate the most just and reasonable demand of society—individual liberty, protected by equal laws, and an equal representation." Francis Lieber, "Estates," in *Encyclopedia Americana*, vol. 4, ed. Francis Lieber (Philadelphia: Carey and Lea, 1830), 587.

[11] Alexis de Tocqueville, *Democracy in America*, trans. Harvey C. Mansfield and Delba Winthrop (Chicago: University of Chicago Press, 2000), 55.

[12] Letter of June 10, 1827. Quoted from Perry, *Life and Letters*, 70.

Within a few years of arriving in America, Lieber was connecting these "new ideas" specifically with democracy. His experiences in an America in which Jacksonian democracy was swept into national power by the election of 1828, and his pleased surprise at the 1830 July Revolution that overthrew the restored Bourbons in France, appear to have solidified his incipient conception of an irresistible trans-atlantic march toward democracy. In January 1831, Lieber noted in his diary:

> What a change! In looking back on the year 1830 it seems of far greater importance than many preceding years... when the friends of liberty thought that the fulfillment of their dearest hopes must be long deferred, a revolution broke out as momentous as it was sudden.... Feudalism has had its days, and in the great course of events it has had to succumb to democratic principles. The struggle for deliverance may be prolonged, but cannot be eventually prevented.[13]

That same month Lieber summed up his perspective in a letter to the German historian Ranke. He explained that "for the present time, of which the key is the democratic principle,—I mean this only in opposition to the feudal principle and not with regard to form,—the United States and France seem to me to be the high-schools for history."[14]

It was with this conception of history thus fresh in his mind that Lieber met Tocqueville in Boston later in 1831. Questions of influence—between the two men, and shared influences on both—lie largely beyond this study.[15] For my purpose what matters is that the Prussian political émigré, who would later become America's first professor of political science, shared with his French friend the bold conception of a sweeping democratizing trajectory, in light of which they both interpreted the political present of the 1830s. Both men took as an irresistible backdrop of their age "the ascendancy which the popular principle has been continuously gaining over the aristocratic throughout the whole European race," as Lieber put it in 1834.[16]

Situating Lieber alongside Tocqueville illuminates common nuances in their approach to democracy. Both treated democracy in social as well as political

[13] Perry, *Life and Letters*, 89. The language and conception of a world-historical movement away from "feudalism" to an age of "democratic principles" found in Lieber's diary is directly employed in the *Encyclopedia Americana's* entries "France, History of" and "History" that I attribute to Lieber. Francis Lieber, "France, History of," in *Encyclopedia Americana*, vol. 5, ed. Francis Lieber (Philadelphia: Carey and Lea, 1830), 211; Francis Lieber, "History," in *Encyclopedia Americana*, vol. 6, ed. Francis Lieber (Philadelphia: Carey and Lea, 1831), 346.

[14] Perry, *Life and Letters*, 90.

[15] On such issues for Tocqueville in particular, see James T. Schleifer, *The Making of Tocqueville's Democracy in America*, 2nd ed. (Indianapolis, IN: Liberty Fund, 2000).

[16] Lieber, *Letters to a Gentleman*, 247.

terms, and in doing so, located democratic society as one side of a contrast pair whose opposite was aristocratic feudal society. Both saw transformation toward a democratic *society* as irresistible, but approached the *political* implications of this broad transformation as multifaceted, and able to be influenced by informed practical judgments and action. On the one hand, some political practices— such as estates-based representation or property qualifications for voting—were unsuited to a democratic society, and hence not practically sustainable. Never found, or rapidly disappearing, in democratic America, such practices would and should, Lieber and Tocqueville agreed, sooner or later disappear also in Europe. On the other hand, democratic politics could take varying governmental forms, some better and some worse from the standpoint of liberal political commitments. Democracy was potentially, but not necessarily, compatible with constitutional and representative government.

Both Lieber and Tocqueville focused their political hopes and advice on a reconciliation of liberal commitments with democracy, and both in the 1830s singled out America as relatively successful in combining them. When analyzing this success both allowed that America benefited from exceptional conditions. Tocqueville saw in "the particular and accidental situation in which Providence has placed the Americans... a thousand circumstances independent of men's will that facilitate the democratic republic in America."[17] In a similar fashion, Lieber observed that "a thousand favorable circumstances concur in America, to make it possible that a far greater amount of liberty can be introduced into all the concerns of her political society."[18] Specifically, both stressed the benefits deriving from America's geographical position, as Lieber described it, "at a great distance from Europe and all her intricate questions and diplomatic influences," which meant that America had, Tocqueville asserted, "no neighbors and consequently no great wars." Both also emphasized America's material condition of enjoying what Tocqueville characterized as "a boundless continent"—and Lieber "a boundless country"—in which a low population-to-land ratio favored widespread prosperity and relative equality, with attendant political benefits.[19]

Whereas Macaulay, a few years before, had appealed to this material condition to contend that America's liberal democracy presupposed conditions alien to populous Europe, Tocqueville and Lieber tempered the role of American exceptionalism in their arguments by also highlighting America's inheritance of ideas and institutions from Britain. In doing so both advanced a line of argument probably picked up via their warm interactions with Boston's elites, who were prone to find in the historical origins of New England the root of what they thought best about

---

[17] Tocqueville, *Democracy in America*, 265.
[18] Lieber, *Letters to a Gentleman*, 32.
[19] Lieber, *Letters to a Gentleman*, 31–33; Tocqueville, *Democracy in America*, 265–74.

America.[20] In his chapter "On the Point of Departure," Tocqueville went so far as to contend: "When, after having attentively studied the history of America, one carefully examines its political and social state, one feels profoundly convinced of this truth: there is not one opinion, one habit, one law, I could say one event, that the point of departure does not explain without difficulty."[21] Lieber was similarly assertive as he used the inheritance argument to specifically venerate America's liberal legacies from Britain—a nation with "civil liberty in its bones and marrow." In explaining why Americans were "eminently qualified for a government of law," he emphasized their descent

> from that noble nation to which mankind owes nearly all those great ideas, the realization of which forms the aim of all the political struggles on the European continent, and which the historian will single out as the leading and characteristic political features of the present age—namely, elective representation, two houses, an independent judiciary, liberty of the press, responsibility of ministers, a law standing above the highest ruler even if a monarch, and a proper independence of the minor communities in the state—that great nation which alone sends along with its colonies a germ of independent life and principle of self-action, (rendering the gradual unfolding of their own, peculiar law, possible,) and above all, that nation which first of all elevated itself it to the great idea of a lawful opposition.[22]

As Lieber's parenthetical attention here to "their own, peculiar law" suggests, neither he nor Tocqueville wanted the inheritance argument to obscure the differences between Britain and America. They used it to help explain common liberal institutions and ideas, but situated these as only one dimension of an American political system that was far more democratic than Britain's. Though both saw America's exceptional conditions promoting this difference, they also nuanced the inheritance argument to note that America's settlers did not descend from all of Britain, but from a subset of British society inclined toward democracy. Tocqueville saw America, especially New England, as largely settled by people from the middle classes. This destined the Americans to develop "not

---

[20] James T. Schleifer's close study of the development of Tocqueville's views establishes that he arrived in America principally stressing material conditions, but was persuaded by elite Americans he met in Boston about the import of historical origins. Schleifer, *Making of Democracy in America*, chaps. 3 and 4. Schleifer's analysis of the Bostonian influence on Tocqueville's arguments may justify, in turn, a hypothesis that Lieber (who lived in Boston for his first years in America and interacted frequently with elite figures there) was similarly influenced, and thus the parallels I note here between Lieber and Tocqueville may, in large part, reflect common Bostonian influences on them both.

[21] Tocqueville, *Democracy in America*, 29.

[22] Lieber, *Letters to a Gentleman*, 30–31.

the aristocratic freedom of their mother country, but the bourgeois and democratic freedom of which the history of the world had still not offered a complete model."[23] In Lieber's *Encylopedia Americana* entry "Representative Government," he likewise held that, while "the representative principle expanded in England more quickly than in the rest of Europe," it was the "democratic part" of that principle that had been "transported to another hemisphere," where it "branched forth with a new vigor, and produced a degree of liberty never known before."[24]

But Lieber and Tocqueville approached liberalism and democracy as only *potentially* compatible. A darker side of their liberal vision hence also considered the illiberal tendencies that could flourish in a democracy. Tocqueville famously examined the "tyranny of the majority" in the first volume of *Democracy in America*,[25] and Lieber likewise worried in his *Letters to a Gentleman* about "the monstrous idea"

> that liberty exists only where the majority can do what they please— while, on the contrary, the degree of existing liberty can justly be measured only by the degree of undoubted protection which the minority enjoys, and the degree to which the sovereign, be he one or many, or represented by the majority, is restricted, by fundamental laws, from acting on sudden impulses and impassioned caprices, to which a body of men is as subject as a single man.[26]

Lieber wedded this classic fear to the concept of "absolutism" by defining absolutism as existing wherever "the representative of sovereignty can act capriciously and uncontrolled."[27] It was only a small step from here to the phrase "democratic absolutism," which would feature prominently in the academic works Lieber began to author after obtaining his first faculty position in 1835.

It is fitting to end our discussion of the first volume of *Democracy in America*, published in 1835, with Tocqueville's view of what tempered tyranny of the

---

[23] Tocqueville, *Democracy in America*, 30, see also 35, 46.

[24] Francis Lieber, "Representative Government," in *Encyclopedia Americana*, 10: 561. This entry calls for a "history of representative governments" that would follow the "various manifestations of the representative principle" through history to its culmination in America's democratic variant of the principle. In the early 1830s Lieber planned to write such a history and sought, without success, federal funding to do so. On this never realized plan, see Friedel, *Francis Lieber*, 88–92.

[25] Tocqueville, *Democracy in America*, 235–49.

[26] Lieber, *Letters to a Gentleman*, 194–95. There are moments in Lieber's *Encyclopedia Americana* entries that hint at an equation of the "liberal" and "democratic." Francis Lieber, "Liberal," in *Encyclopedia Americana*, vol. 7, ed. Francis Lieber (Philadelphia: Carey and Lea, 1831), 533. But, by Lieber's 1834 *Letters to a Gentleman*, we already find clearly stated the fear of illiberal democracy that was to be a major theme in his subsequent scholarly treatises.

[27] Lieber, *Letters to a Gentleman*, 195.

majority in America, since a parallel view would appear as a key teaching of Lieber's 1838–1839 *Manual of Political Ethics*, to which we will turn next. A centerpiece of Tocqueville's view was a reverential account of the role of lawyers in America: "When one visits the Americans and when one studies their laws, one sees that the authority they have given to lawyers and the influence that they have allowed them to have in government form the most powerful barrier today against the lapses of democracy."[28] This grand pronouncement rested, in part, on his earlier, more specific, contention that "the power granted to American courts to pronounce on the unconstitutionality of laws" was "one of the most powerful barriers that has ever been raised against the tyranny of political assemblies."[29] It also rested on an argument that juries, by familiarizing ordinary Americans with legal principles and processes, helped "the spirit of the lawyer penetrate down to the lowest ranks of society." This "spirit" was "appropriate for neutralizing the vices inherent in popular government" because, in contrast to democratic "love of novelty," "enthusiasm," and "scorn for rules," lawyers (especially lawyers in the Anglo-American precedent-based legal system) had a "superstitious respect for what is old," a "taste for forms," and "habit of proceeding slowly." It was such counterbalancing that helped make America's democracy one that liberals could accept or even embrace. But it required that judges, the guardians and governors of the legal process, be able to resist democratic pressures. Tocqueville therefore fearfully predicted that "dire results" would follow from provisions in some state constitutions that made judges popularly elected.[30]

In expressing his fears about elected judges, Tocqueville took sides in a major political debate of the early Republic. Americans had long disagreed about whether the institutions and ideal of judicial independence that they had inherited from Britain remained appropriate in post-Revolution republican conditions. Among Jeffersonian advocates of a specifically *democratic* republic, the belief was widespread that bringing state-level institutions into line with popular sovereignty required selection, removal, tenure, or pay rules that would make local judges more popularly accountable than federal judges, who were controversially given great independence by the federal Constitution.[31] Contestation over this topic continued into the state constitutional conventions of the 1820s, where the agenda of issues under debate included judicial organization alongside suffrage qualifications.[32] The nationwide convergence toward universal (white

---

[28] Tocqueville, *Democracy in America*, 251.

[29] Tocqueville, *Democracy in America*, 98.

[30] Tocqueville, *Democracy in America*, 251–64.

[31] Richard E. Ellis, *The Jeffersonian Crisis: Courts and Politics in the Young Republic* (New York: Oxford University Press, 1971)

[32] Merrill D. Peterson, *Democracy, Liberty, and Property: The State Constitutional Conventions of the 1820s* (Indianapolis, IN: Liberty Fund, 2010), 12–13, 126–29.

male) suffrage highlighted in chapter 1 was not accompanied by convergei the ways that states organized their judiciaries. A decoupling of these two i was reflected in, and advanced by, arguments that accepted popular sovereignty, but held that judicial independence was compatible with such sovereignty, and indeed, promoted this independence as a critical institution helping to set good apart from bad variants of democracy.

One of the most influential proponents of this position was longtime (1811–1845) federal Supreme Court justice Joseph Story. Via his decisions on the Court, his teaching at Harvard's Law School from 1829 onwards, his celebrated *Commentaries on the Constitution of the United States* of 1833, and many public lectures and personal ties, Story spread his judge-empowering view of American constitutionalism far and wide. Tocqueville followed Story when discussing constitutional matters—indeed, so much so that Story sharply observed in 1840: "The work of De Tocqueville has had great reputation abroad, partly founded on their [Europeans'] ignorance that he has borrowed the greater part of his reflections from American works, and little from his own observations. The main body of his materials will be found in the Federalist, and in Story's Commentaries on the Constitution." This remark was made in a letter to none other than Lieber. Story had done much to help the émigré make his way in America, from contributing law articles to the *Encyclopedia Americana* to advocating Lieber for the South Carolina College position he obtained in 1835. Lieber dedicated his 1838–1839 *Manual of Political Ethics* to his benefactor, and Story offered his sharp remark about Tocqueville to set up a comparison in praise of Lieber and the text: "You know ten times as much as he does of the actual workings of our system and of its true theory."[33]

Lieber's *Manual of Political Ethics*: A Philosophic-Historic Vindication of American Constitutionalism

A Story-style interpretation of American constitutionalism is a common thread running through the three major treatises Lieber wrote while at South Carolina College—in addition to his *Manual of Political Ethics*, his 1837–1839 *Legal and Political Hermeneutics*,[34] and 1853 *On Civil Liberty and Self-Government*. The works accepted the principle of popular sovereignty, while unpacking it in ways

---

[33] Letter from Story to Lieber, May 9, 1840, quoted from William W. Story, ed., *Life and Letters of Joseph Story*, 2 vols. (Boston: Little and Brown, 1851), 2: 329–30. On Story, Lieber, and their relations, see the introduction to the recent collection of Story's contributions to the *Encyclopedia*. Joseph Story, *Joseph Story and the Encyclopedia Americana* (Clark, NJ: Lawbook Exchange, 2006).

[34] On this work, see James Farr, "Francis Lieber and the Interpretation of American Political Science," *Journal of Politics* 52, no. 4 (1990), 1027–49.

that, in practice, empowered judges. But there is more to each work, and most especially so with regard to method. Born and raised in Berlin, Lieber had seen the university there flourish in the 1810s, and later was aided and befriended by the celebrated historian Niebuhr.[35] Lieber was thus well positioned to explicate and extol the constitutionalism of his adopted land in a manner informed by what was, at the time, the leading edge of self-consciously scientific historicist scholarship.

In chapter 2, I introduced the controversy within historicist science between historical and philosophical methods, and Bluntschli's blending of them in his theory of the state. Lieber conceived his *Manual of Political Ethics* on similar methodological lines, explaining in a letter that the work "endeavored to reconcile the historic development of the State with its philosophic ground."[36] However, Lieber and Bluntschli diverged substantively in their preferred current of German political philosophy. Whereas Bluntschli, as we saw earlier, advanced a Hegelian ethical conception of the state, Lieber thought Hegel had "done infinite harm to the cause of science."[37] He instead built upon the earlier, more classical liberal, moment in German political philosophy exemplified by Kant.[38] This element of Lieber's philosophic-historic synthesis warrants our close attention for two reasons. First, the content and centrality given to the concept of the state in Lieber's *Manual of Political Ethics* was, relative to American academic discourse, arguably the single most innovative aspect of Lieber's large corpus of writings.[39] Second, Lieber's

[35] In 1821 Lieber had left Prussia with falsified exit documents to make his way to Greece intending to join the fight for Greek independence from the Ottoman Empire. Unable to find any forces to fight with, or to support himself, he left Greece disillusioned and penniless and made his way to Italy in 1822. The historian Niebuhr was then serving in Rome as Prussian ambassador, and when Lieber went to him for help, he generously aided the young man and brought him into his family as a tutor. See Francis Lieber, *Reminiscences of an Intercourse with Mr. Niebuhr the Historian, During a Residence with him in Rome, in the Years 1822 and 1823* (Philadelphia: Carey, Lea & Blanchard, 1835).

[36] Letter from Lieber to Hillard, December 3, 1838, quoted from Perry, *Life and Letters*, 132.

[37] Lieber then went on: "Instead of earnest, thoughtful investigation, and a discreet acknowledgement of previous experience, he [Hegel] is full of arrogance and presumption." Letter from Lieber to Mittermaier, September 13, 1834, quoted from Freidel, *Francis Lieber*, 112. Lieber's hostility to Hegel may have had a personal dimension due to his own friendship with, and admiration of, the historian Niebuhr against whom Hegel had aimed multiple barbs.

[38] I use Kant's well-known texts to illuminate this point, but in doing so I do not intend to judge whether Lieber was directly influenced by Kant or indirectly influenced via the assimilation of Kantian concepts and arguments among early-nineteenth-century scholars of the *Staatswissenchaften*. On the extent of this assimilation, and the assimilation of Adam Smith that frequently accompanied it, see David F. Lindenfeld, *The Practical Imagination: The German Sciences of the State in the Nineteenth Century* (Chicago: University of Chicago Press, 1997), 55–67.

[39] On Lieber in this regard, see James Farr, "From Moral Philosophy to Political Science: Lieber and the Innovations of Antebellum Political Thought," in Charles R. Mack and Henry H. Lesesne eds., *Francis Lieber and the Culture of the Mind* (Columbia, SC: University of South Carolina Press, 2005), 113–26.

innovation provided a philosophical grounding for Story's side in the debate about the judiciary's position in America's democracy.

Kant's political philosophy distinguished the *sovereign* from its agent and representative, the *government*. He contended, in addition, that the sovereign, "if considered in the light of laws of freedom, can be none other than the united people itself." In light of this stance, Kant moved, through the conceptual tie between sovereignty and the state, toward mapping the *state* onto the people as organized by a "civil constitution," understood to be "an act of general will whereby the mass becomes a people." Thus, Kant held: "A state is a union of an aggregate of men under rightful laws." For this pioneer of the German idea of the *Rechtsstaat*: "*Right* is the restriction of each individual's freedom so that it harmonises with the freedom of everyone else."[40] Lieber's *Manual of Political Ethics* reads like a parsing of Kant when it declares,

> Man… is a moral individual, yet bound to live in society. He is a being with free agency—freedom of action, but as all his fellowmen with whom he lives in contact, are equally beings with free agency, each making the same claim of freedom of action, there results from it the necessity, founded in reason, i.e. the law, that the use of freedom by one rational being must not contradict or counteract the use of liberty by another rational being. The relation which thus exists between these rational beings, this demand of what is just made by each upon each, is the relation of *right*, and the society founded upon this basis, which exists because right (*jus*) in its primordial sense exists and ought to exist between men, which has to uphold and insist upon it, which had to enforce it, since every man has a right to be a man, that is, a free-acting or rational being, because he is a man—this society is the state.[41]

Lieber conceived "the relation of *right*" as the foundation of society, but not the entirety of social relations. He understood society more broadly as made up of "men closely united by a variety of important relations and strongly affecting each other's welfare."[42] In differentiating among these varied relations, he favored the term "jural" to pick out the specific kind of relation constitutive of the state, and thereby identified the state with "*jural* society." Jural relations were the relations of right between free individuals that could and should be embodied in enforceable

---

[40] Kant, *Political Writings*, 2nd ed. Hans Reiss (Cambridge: Cambridge University Press, 1991), 138–43, 99–102, 73–74. On the Kantian character of Lieber's concept of the state, see also Bernard Edward Brown, *American Conservatives: The Political Thought of Francis Lieber and John W. Burgess* (New York: Columbia University Press, 1951), 26–34.

[41] Francis Lieber, *Manual of Political Ethics, Designed Chiefly for the Use of Colleges and Students at Law*, 2 vols. (Boston: Little and Brown, 1838–39), 1: 167. Italics in original.

[42] Ibid., 1: 139.

general laws. These relations were prior to such laws as the philosophical standard of justice that the laws should aim to realize. "The idea of the just, and the action founded upon this idea, called *justice*" was, Lieber hence held, "the broad foundation and great object of the state."[43]

Having characterized the state in these terms, Lieber next addressed the accompanying concept of sovereignty. The "train of the argument" led from one to other as follows:

> Society cannot exist without jural relations between its members, because no member ought to give up, or can give up his individuality. Society, considered as to its jural relations, or jural society, is the state. The necessary existence of the state, and that right and power which necessarily or naturally flow from it, is sovereignty. Sovereignty derives its power from no previous or superior one, but is the source of all vested power.[44]

Lieber's identification of the state with jural society underwrote two main features of his account of sovereignty. First, since sovereignty was the "vital principle of the state," defining the state as a society made it "contradictory in itself" to believe "that society, or the people" could "divest themselves of sovereignty and delegate it to someone else." The "sovereignty of society" was, Lieber taught, "natural, inherent, unavoidable, and imprescriptible, not made, granted, declared, or arrogated."[45] Second, placing the qualifier jural before society put limits on sovereign power. Sovereignty meant "something entirely different from absolute power, unbounded power."[46] If power was used to infringe, rather than sustain, jural relations—as, for example, in censorship, which infringed one of twelve "primordial rights" of free individuals that Lieber enumerated[47] —this use of power could not, by definition, be a proper act of sovereignty.

While the concept of the jural limited, in philosophical terms, what society could do with the sovereignty that Lieber's definition of the state put in its hands, to forestall democratic absolutism in practice was a matter of the institutional organization of power. Absolutism existed "wherever all power that can be obtained is undivided, unmodified, and *un-mediatised*, somewhere, whether apparently in an individual, or a body of men, or the whole people, which means in this case of course, the majority."[48] The antidote to absolutism was the division

---

[43] Ibid., 1: 171–76. Italics in original.
[44] Ibid..,1: 248.
[45] Ibid, 1: 250–51, 270.
[46] Ibid., 1: 196.
[47] For Lieber's enumeration of these "primordial rights," see Ibid., 1: 203–25.
[48] Ibid, 1: 385. Italics in original.

of power. Society could and should directly exercise *some* of its sovereign power, for example, via public opinion.[49] But other powers were to be exercised by a representative government on the behalf of society. The "great principle of representative government" was far more than an expedient due to the people being too numerous to assemble in modern society. It was good in itself for the people to "act through agents," since "[h]e who has power, absolute and direct, abuses it."[50]

As he favored dividing power between the state (jural society) and its agent, government, so Lieber favored, in turn, the division of power *within* government. He endorsed the legislative/executive/judicial division enshrined in American constitutionalism. And, more distinctively, he argued that in this regard "[n]othing" was "of so vital importance, of so momentous influence, as the independence of the judiciary." Elevating his tone to that of a paean, he declared: "The more deeply and earnestly we study history, the more sacred will appear this wonderful institution of an independent judiciary." Independence for Lieber meant, specifically, "a judiciary that in the administration of justice cannot be overawed by any one, or anything,... but which is strictly dependent upon the law and the spirit which made it."[51]

In sum, after presenting his largely Kantian philosophical foundation, which was highly innovative in the American intellectual context of his day, Lieber rested upon that foundation a far more familiar judge-empowering interpretation of American constitutionalism. His practical teaching in this regard paralleled closely that of Story in an 1834 speech arguing for the "science of government" to be taught "as a branch of popular education." Story characterized this science as involving "consideration of the true ends of government, and the means, by which those ends can be best achieved or promoted." In regard to ends, he identified "the great objects of all free governments" to be "the protection and preservation of the personal rights, the private property, and the public liberties of the whole people." He then contended that these ends were best served

> by constitutions of government, wisely framed and vigilantly enforced; by laws and institutions, deliberately examined and steadily administered; by tribunals of justice above fear, and beyond reproach, whose duty it shall be to protect the weak against the strong, to guard the unwary against the cunning, and to punish the insolence of office, and the spirit of encroachment and wanton injury.[52]

[49] Ibid, 1: 255–62.
[50] Ibid.,1: 383.
[51] Ibid., 1: 397–406.
[52] Joseph Story, "The Science of Government," in *The Miscellaneous Writings of Joseph Story*, ed. William W. Story (Boston: Little and Brown, 1852), 615, 619–21.

Veneration of such means led Lieber in his *Manual of Political Ethics* to single out America and Britain for special praise and integrate them in a shared exceptionalist narrative. Playing first on the patriotism of his American audience, Lieber declared, "I do not think that there is anything to which an American can point with greater pride than the decisions of his courts by which even legislative enactments have been declared unconstitutional." While such decisions were a highlight of American constitutionalism, they assumed the ideal and institution of an independent judiciary, and this was a transatlantic inheritance. Following back the line of this inheritance, Lieber next proclaimed, "England owes her greatness, in a high degree, to her independent judiciary, the independence of the law."[53] One of multiple themes sounded in his *Manual of Political Ethics*, an Anglo-American exceptionalism highlighting constitutionalism, common law, and judicial independence would subsequently become the centerpiece of Lieber's influential 1853 text *Civil Liberty and Self-Government*, which reverently expounded "Anglican Liberty" at length.[54] This was the most prominent exceptionalism within Lieber's developmental historicist political science. But, in line with chapter 2's account of embedded exceptionalism as a strategy of developmental historicism, Lieber also found exceptionalism at more particular and more general levels, as we will see in turning from his liberal constitutionalism to his liberal political economy.

Lieber's Political Economy: Industrialization and the 1840s Divide in Classical Liberalism

Prior to his 1835 appointment at South Carolina College, Lieber paid relatively little attention to political economy. His inaugural address there gave over twenty pages to elaborating his approach to history, but only three pages to political economy.[55] While in South Carolina, however, he came to develop and publicly promote strident stances on major issues in political economy. These aligned largely with the text that he used in teaching: the French classical liberal political economist J. B. Say's *Treatise of Political Economy*.[56] The stances Lieber advanced

---

[53] Lieber, *Political Ethics* 1: 383–84.

[54] Francis Lieber, *On Civil Liberty and Self-Government* (Philadelphia: Lippincott, 1953), chap. V-XX.

[55] Francis Lieber, "On History and Political Economy, as Necessary Branches of Superior Education in Free States," in Gilman, *Miscellaneous Writings of Lieber*, 1: 179–203. The subsequent growth of Lieber's engagement in this area was registered in his devoting as many pages to political economy as to history in his 1858 inaugural address at Columbia. See Francis Lieber, "History and Political Science Necessary Studies in Free Countries," in *Miscellaneous Writings of Francis Lieber*, 1: 329–68.

[56] Lieber taught using the 1834 American edition of Say's text. Jean-Baptiste Say, *A Treatise on Political Economy; or the Production, Distribution, and Consumption of Wealth*, 6th ed., trans. C. R. Prinsep and Clement C. Biddle (Philadelphia: Grigg, Elliot, 1834). On Say's significance in the field

in political economy are less innovative in the American academic context than other aspects of his scholarship, but they deserve our attention for multiple reasons. First, they give further content to my identification of Lieber's liberalism as a *classical* liberalism by linking it to *classical* political economy. Second, in both their timing and details, Lieber's views were tied to, and can thereby serve to introduce, debates about capital, labor, and tariffs spurred by industrial development in antebellum America. Finally, by comparing Lieber's arguments on trade unions and free trade to positions taken in J. S. Mill's 1849 *Principles of Political Economy*, I explicate a divide *within* classical liberalism between uncompromising and moderate interpretations of general principles espoused by classical political economy.[57]

PRIVATE PROPERTY, INDUSTRIALIZATION, AND THE DYNAMIC OF CAPITAL AND LABOR

A developmental conception of "civilization" provided a starting point for Lieber's views in political economy. While he was especially interested to chart civilization in terms of changes in political institutions and principles, he also saw a material side to this grand process. His 1834 *Letters to a Gentleman* already heralded "the inextinguishable desire of property" as an "original principle...planted deep in our breast to make it a foundation of all civilization." The book also saluted technology, specifically how steamboats and railroads were transforming transportation in America. Pairing these recent innovations with media technologies often celebrated for aiding the growth of public opinion, Lieber argued that "the history of civilization runs parallel with the history of communication, both physical and intellectual, as roads, canals, steamboats, printing-presses, newspapers."[58] As his teaching at South Carolina College immersed Lieber in political economy, he began to elaborate his valorization of property and technology. He first articulated an account of property and its significance for civilization, and then

---

of political economy, see Keith Tribe, "Continental Political Economy from the Physiocrats to the Marginal Revolution," in Theodore M. Porter and Dorothy Ross, eds., *The Cambridge History of Science*, vol. 7, *The Modern Social Sciences* (Cambridge: Cambridge University Press, 2003), 154–70.

[57] Lieber's teaching and writings on political economy have received relatively little attention from recent scholars of his thought. Indeed, none of the fifteen papers in a recent edited volume focused on his political economy. See Charles R. Mack and Henry H. Lesesne eds., *Francis Lieber and the Culture of the Mind* (Columbia, SC: University of South Carolina Press, 2005). The fullest treatment to date remains, I believe, that in Joseph Dorfman's classic *The Economic Mind in American Civilization, 1606–1865*, 2 vols. (New York: Viking, 1946), 2: 865–879.

[58] Lieber, *Letters to a Gentleman*, 60, 44. See also 198–200, where Lieber presents the transportation revolution as aligning prices and wages across different parts of the country, with this growth of a national-level economy, in turn, contributing "not a little to the stability of our political existence."

interwove that account with classical political economy to offer a classical liberal interpretation of the dynamic of labor and capital in the young, technology-based, industrial sector of America's economy.

Lieber's account of property, formulated in 1837, was initially presented in his *Political Ethics*, applied in his 1840 *Letter on International Copyright*, and finally and most importantly for my purposes, further elaborated and applied to industrial production in his 1841 *Essays on Property and Labour*.[59] The distinctive feature of Lieber's account lay in its integrating the view of property as a natural right commonplace in American political discourse with a developmental account of civilization and related historicist interest in the exceptionalism of the West. Thus we find, in the *Manual of Political Ethics*, a claim that private property is innate to humans:

> Property is nothing else than the application of man's individuality to external things, or the realization and manifestation of man's individuality in the material world. Man cannot be, never was, without property, without *mine* and *thine*. If he could he would not be man. In all stages of civilisation, at all ages of his life, we find him anxious to individualize things, to rescue them as it were from undefined generality—to appropriate.

Lieber quickly stressed, however, that his argument that "the idea of property is natural to man" did not entail that this idea "represents itself at once perfect to his mind in all its bearing." What "is truly natural to man" is not fully articulated in "man's savage or rude state"; to the contrary, it "unfolds itself more perspicuously with the progress of civilisation." Lieber illustrated his central developmental notion using "the right of property." Although "acknowledged at an early period" in "some limited form," during the course of civilization this right "became more clearly defined, more distinctly recognized in the various spheres of human activity and enterprise."[60]

After introducing this account in his *Manual of Political Ethics*, Lieber employed it in his *Essays on Property and Labour* to elucidate an exceptionalist comparison between "Asiatic and European civilization," seen as the "two great divisions" in

---

[59] See letter from Francis Lieber to Charles Sumner, August 27, 1837, in Perry, *Life and Letters*, 120–22; Lieber, *Political Ethics*, Bk 2, ch 2; Francis Lieber, *On International Copyright, in a Letter to the Hon. William C. Preston, Senator of the United States* (New York: Wiley and Putnam, 1840); Francis Lieber, *Essays on Property and Labour, as Connected with Natural Law and the Constitution of Society* (New York: Harper & Brothers, 1841). Attentive readers may note switching back and forth between "labour" and "labor." In referencing Lieber's work I reproduce the usage in his published texts, which shifts back and forth between these English and American-English spellings.

[60] Lieber, *Political Ethics*, Bk 2, ch 2, italics in original.

the "history of civilization." Lieber held that "the striking difference between man as he appears in Asia, and the Western man" lay in Western man's "consciousness of holding property as an inherent natural right, and not simply at the mercy of the ruler." This belief accompanied and supported greater security of individual property in the West. "Private property, and the unshackled right of acquiring it" there showed itself to be both "the basis of social advancement" and "the promoter of manly consciousness and individual independence." It was, furthermore, "a firm foundation-stone of the fabric of national liberty," and in all these respects, underlay "fundamental differences of European and Asiatic history."[61]

Lieber's belief in a mutually reinforcing progressive dynamic between private property, individual independence, social advancement, and national liberty faced a potential challenge from contemporary economic change in the very nations he celebrated as leaders of civilization. Early industrialization was, as we saw in chapter 1, accompanied by fears of a growing class of laborers permanently dependent on capitalists, with negative outcomes likely to follow if these workers had the right to vote. If Lieber's *Essays on Property and Labor* is free of such anxieties, this in good measure reflects its participation in the distinctively *American* Whig narrative of industrialization that had been transforming the political culture of Boston's elite in the very years, 1827–1833, during which Lieber made the city his first home in America.[62]

Having earlier turned to a future president of Harvard, Josiah Quincy, to illustrate elite fears of 1820, we can turn to Quincy's eventual successor in that role, Edward Everett, to sample the optimism about American industrialization that largely supplanted those fears a decade later. Everett was one of multiple prominent figures holding these views who assisted Lieber after his arrival in Boston.[63]

---

[61] Lieber, *Essays on Property*, 21–22, 192–93.

[62] On the transformation of attitudes toward industrialization among Boston's elites—in which "skeptics…raising questions about its moral and social consequences" gave way to widespread embrace of "the new economic order" by the early 1830s—see "From Federalism to Whiggery" in William F. Hartford, *Money, Morals, and Politics: Massachusetts in the Age of the Boston Associates* (Boston: Northeastern University Press, 2001), chap. 2.

[63] These elite Bostonians became Whigs as that party took shape in the early 1830s in support of Henry Clay and his pro-manufacturing "American System." My interest in the academy leads me to select Everett as the figure I use in the main text to illustrate American Whig optimism about industrialization. In Daniel Walker Howe's classic study of American Whig thought, Everett is quoted on this issue as a supplement to a central focus on textile entrepreneur Nathan Appleton, who we met briefly in Chapter 1. See Daniel Walker Howe, *The Political Culture of the American Whigs* (Chicago: University of Chicago Press, 1979), 97–108. Like Everett, Appleton was also a Bostonian friend of Lieber, and also contributed to the *Encyclopedia Americana*, notably writing the entries on Cotton Manufacture and the textile-manufacturing town, Lowell, which Appleton helped create. Lieber thought highly enough of Appleton's views to envision in a letter the benefits if Appleton, his fellow textile industry leader Abbott Lawrence, and others would "club together to issue a series of 'tracts for the people'" on such "important subjects, as on Government, Obedience to the Laws, Property, Labor, Social (Political) Economy,

As the first American to hold a PhD (earned at the University of Göttingen in 1817 in classics), Everett was well disposed to welcome the Prussian émigré, preceded as he was by a personal testimonial from Niebuhr, the historian of ancient Rome.[64] Everett effusively endorsed Lieber's *Encyclopedia Americana* in its 1828 published prospectus, and as the project became a reality, he wrote entries in classics. He was, moreover, one of the multiple Bostonians with whom Lieber would correspond for decades after the now naturalized American had left Boston.[65]

Everett's optimism about industrialization is vividly displayed in a Fourth of July address he gave in 1830 in Lowell, Massachusetts. Less than a decade old, this rapidly expanding center of water-powered, machine-based textile manufacturing was the concrete example facilitating change in attitudes about industrialization in Massachusetts. The entrepreneurs who created it sought to allay fears about the character of an industrial workforce by founding churches (with attendance a condition of employment), supervised dormitories for workers, and banks for workers' savings. Most of their largely female workers were young single women drawn from farming communities to work in manufacturing for only a limited number of years.[66] Everett's address celebrated Lowell as the prime example of America's "well-conducted manufacturing establishments," which were "demonstrating to the world" that "physical comfort, moral conduct, general intelligence, and all the qualities of social character which make up an enlightened New England community" were indeed "consistent with the profitable pursuit of manufacturing industry." For Everett, the young mill town testified to the promise of "a mutually beneficial connection between those who have nothing but their muscular power and those who are able to bring to the partnership the masses of property requisite to carry on an extensive concern." It showed that "labor and capital" could establish an "alliance" in industrial production without challenging the principle of private property—"that great principle by which a man calls what he has *his own*, whether it is little or much, (the corner stone of civilized life)."[67]

In taking private property to be "the corner stone of civilized life," Everett sounded a note akin to Lieber's paean to property in his *Manual of Political*

Trades Unions, & c.,—each tract to be sold very low, and at least five hundred thousand copies distributed." See letter from Lieber to Charles Sumner, January 1842, quoted from Perry, *Life and Letters*, 167.

[64] On the aid Niebuhr's testimonial gave to Lieber's reception among Boston's elite, see Perry, *Life and Letters*, 73.

[65] On Lieber's longstanding correspondence with those he had met in Boston during his first years in America, see Charles B. Robson, "Papers of Francis Lieber," *Huntington Library Bulletin* 3 (Feb., 1933), 137–38.

[66] Frances W. Gregory, *Nathan Appleton: Merchant and Entrepreneur, 1779–1861* (Charlottesville: University Press of Virginia, 1975), 187–91. See also Howe, *Political Culture*, 102–104.

[67] Edward Everett, "Fourth of July at Lowell," *Orations and Speeches on Various Occasions*, vol. 2 (Boston: Little and Brown, 1850), 47–68.

Ethics and *Essays on Property and Labor.* In the later work, when Lieber offered an account of the dynamic of capital and labor and applied it to issues of industrialization, he propounded a message of mutual benefit, and his most recurring example was textile manufacturing. After declaring in general terms that, since "there is nothing on earth which can pay for labour except capital," therefore all those "who have not yet acquired lasting property, are deeply interested in the increase and further accumulation" of capital, Lieber then illustrated his point using textile mills. "[T]he immense advantages obtained by machinery for the poorer classes" were, he held, exemplified by the consequences of the mills replacing handlooms. By reducing "the price of calico so much that millions can use it and decently dress themselves who before were doomed to go in rags," machinery benefited the poor as consumers. They were also benefited as sellers of labor since the "vastly increased demand" resulting from cheaper calico made "the employment of hundreds of thousands possible in weaving it by machinery." These benefits flowed from applying technology to production, but the cost of machinery could only be borne by "accumulative property," and capital did not "accumulate without security" of private property. Hence, property holders and laborers shared overlapping interests.[68]

Lieber did not, however, find this argument alone sufficient to defend private property in an industrial age. Recognizing that calls for "community of property" had "of late been renewed in some countries with redoubled activity," he proceeded to address this challenge from "modern socialists" in France and Britain. Tracing their growing appeal to discomfort with inequality, he granted that seeing "wealth accumulated in the hands of some individuals, while many others are known to live in penury or actual wretchedness from want... seems at first really to be a crying injustice."[69] Again turning to textile mills to make a general issue concrete, Lieber observed:

> One of the chief evils complained of in regard to the inequality of property... is, I believe, the unduly small share which the workman has in the ultimate profits derived from the product. While the owner of the factory makes thousands a year, the actual weaver, or person who attends the spinning machines, receives so small a share that, in some countries, he can barely exist upon it.[70]

In giving voice to this complaint, Lieber was not endorsing it, but identifying a standpoint he strove to undermine with multiple arguments. One, echoing the

---

[68] Lieber, *Essays on Property*, 94–104.
[69] Ibid., 164–65.
[70] Ibid., 179–80.

views of Everett and other American Whig friends of Lieber, contrasted America
to Europe. Everett's 1830 address had set Lowell off against the lurid backdrop of
the "old world," whose "manufacturing cities" presented "a state of things revolt-
ing to humanity... an amount of suffering, depravity, and brutalism, which formed
one of the great scandals of the age."[71] Lieber similarly allowed that "[n]o one can
deny that there are countries in which whole and numerous classes are depressed
into wretchedness, and even into barbarity," only to then ask, by contrast, "where
are these classes of depressed labouring men to be found in the United States"? He
held that, in his adopted land, the "complaint that the workman receives always
the smallest share of the profits" was "unfounded." "Never before" had "a country
existed in which industry, honesty, and frugality were so sure of success in acquiring a fair livelihood and an honourable standing in the community." The harsher
conditions of labor in Europe made it "no wonder" that complaints about labor's
lot arose there, but to take up "agitation or presumptuous theory started in foreign
parts" and import it across the Atlantic was "a mere handle for mischief."[72]

While Lieber thus made a charged appeal to American exceptionalism, he
also argued in general terms that classical political economy demonstrated that
inequality, while it might seem unjust, redounded to the ultimate benefit of labor.
High profits served the longer-term interests of the laboring classes by making
possible accumulation that could fund greater production in the future, and
thereby more demand, and a better lot, for laborers. Therefore,

> accumulated capitals are not spoliations of others, and, if honestly
> acquired, however great, imply no injustice whatever; but, on the con-
> trary, that, as Adam Smith expresses it, every saving and accumulating
> man is like the founder of an almshouse for all future generations. He is
> indeed more; for he lays the foundation for the support of labour for all
> generations to come, indeed forever, unless the beneficial effect of accu-
> mulation is arrested by a wasteful process, that is, by some unproductive
> consumption.[73]

Underlying this argument was the general principle of classical political economy
(usually called the wage-fund doctrine) that revenue was split between return to
capital and wages for laborers in proportion to the ratio of capital to the number of

---

[71] Everett, "Fourth of July," 63. For another example, nearer the time of Lieber's book, from another
Bostonian who had contributed to Lieber's *Encyclopedia Americana*, see Nathan Appleton, "Labor, its
Relations, in Europe and the United States, Compared," *Merchants' Magazine* 11, no. 3 (1844), 217–23.

[72] Lieber, *Essays on Property*, 202–203, 209–10.

[73] Ibid., 176. Lieber declared in an accompanying footnote: "Every sound work on Political
Economy shows this fact conclusively," and indeed, "perhaps none... more plainly and cogently than"
his own favored text in teaching the field, "Mr. Say's Political Economy."

laborers seeking employment. Therefore, as Lieber put it, "if there be much capital and little labour in the market, capital will receive a small share in the profits of the product, and vice versa."[74] This doctrine had decidedly classical liberal policy implications. It supported the view, forcefully stated by Lieber, that

> [t]here is no such thing as forcing wages up by legislation.... Legislation may remove impediments created by previous legislation, by which labour was prevented from obtaining the equivalent to which, in the natural and unimpeded course, it was entitled; but no legislation can possibly raise them by maximum or minimum prices. It has been tried full often enough, and has always ended in increasing misery.[75]

When responding to the inequality between returns to capital and labor in industrial-scale production, which he saw as a key source of the growing appeal of modern socialists, Lieber thus used two styles of argument to persuade his fellow Americans to reject such appeals. He assured them in a tone of exceptionalist promise that, unlike Europeans, they lived in a nation with wages high enough to ensure that "industry, honesty, and frugality give a support and independence." But he also, in a sterner style, appealed to classical political economy to dissuade them from attempting to improve wages by legislation. He warned that, since "capital must ever seek its best employment, which is there where profit and security are combined, every forced action makes it flow out of the country, and therefore withdraws so much from the fund which must sustain labour, and thus increases the evil."[76]

LIEBER VERSUS MILL ON UNIONS AND FREE TRADE: UNCOMPROMISING VERSUS MODERATE CLASSICAL LIBERALISM

In addition to rejecting legislative efforts to raise wages, Lieber also rejected any effort of workers to raise wages through collective action in trade unions. His position on this issue stands in notable contrast to the more moderate position advanced by J. S. Mill in his 1848 *Principles of Political Economy*.[77] By comparing

---

[74] Ibid., 187. Revisiting this argument about "the fund which must sustain labor" in his conclusion, Lieber held "no truth is more firmly established than that the equivalent given for labour or wages depends, in the natural course of things, upon demand and supply, upon capital productively employed by that labour." Ibid., 210.

[75] Ibid., 210–11.

[76] Ibid., 210–11.

[77] John Stuart Mill, *The Principles of Political Economy with Some of Their Applications to Social Philosophy*, ed. John M. Robson, *Collected Works of John Stuart Mill*, vols. 2–3 (Toronto: University of Toronto Press, 1965). This edition presents all textual variations of the many editions of Mill's

Lieber and Mill here, first on unions and then on free trade, I introduce a contrast between *uncompromising* and *moderate* modes of argument from the general principles of classical political economy to practical judgments. This contrast is, at once, a matter of methodological nuance within classical political economy, and a point of substantive political differentiation between subspecies of classical liberalism. Located at the very intersection of the *science* and the *political* in political science, it will play a recurring role in the chapters to come.

In treating trade unions, Mill and Lieber both offered arguments from political economy only after first engaging the then-fraught question of the legality of collective action by laborers. Mill could dispose of the legal question swiftly since he rejected "laws against combinations of workmen to raise wages" as a "governmental interference, in which the end and the means are alike odious."[78] Lieber, by contrast, when addressing unions as "[a] species of association, which has lately acquired great importance" in his *Manual of Political Ethics*, dwelt on the law at more length. While accepting "unions among the working classes for charitable purposes, and mutual support in distress" to be "lawful and highly laudable," he argued that, if laborers acted together to try to influence employment conditions, they engaged in a "conspiracy" illegal under common law. He appealed to multiple legal cases, including the recent 1835 *People v. Fisher* decision of New York's Supreme Court, which had ruled a union for this purpose illegal.[79] Lieber was thus shocked when, a few years after his *Manual of Political Ethics* had appeared, the Massachusetts Supreme Court in 1842 broke from precedent to rule in *Commonwealth v. Hunt* that a union of shoemakers trying to improve wages was legal under common law.[80] Writing to a Boston friend after the ruling, Lieber declared it "startling and unsound," and went on to complain:

> If men not only club together, but make a permanent society, not to sell certain articles under a certain price, and should, in addition, enact not to have intercourse with those who would do so, it would be an unlawful combination, because tyrannical to society. Is that of the shoemakers, who fix a certain price for their merchandise—i.e. labor—different?... In the case of trades-unions... the subject becomes peculiarly serious,

Principles, from 1848 to 1871. In quoting Mill as a comparison to Lieber, I present Mill's views as stated in his 1848 first edition, since that is the edition nearest in time to Lieber's arguments, and my general goal here is to introduce a divide within classical liberalism at it existed in the 1840s.

[78] Mill, *Principles*, 3: 929.

[79] Lieber, *Political Ethics*, book 4, chap. 3.

[80] On the shift in legal rulings about labor unions and conspiracy between the 1835 People v. Fisher case and 1842 Commonwealth v. Hunt case, see John W. Johnson, *Historic US Court Cases: An Encyclopedia*, 2nd ed. (New York: Routledge, 2001), 409–11.

because we know to what insufferable social tyranny, to what evil habits and fearful crimes they lead.[81]

The Massachusetts court decision that made Lieber's legal argument almost immediately outdated can serve to focus our attention toward other aspects of his stance on unions. His claims about unions in *Manual of Political Ethics* drew partly on political economy, and his position in this regard was more fully stated in *Essays on Property and Labor*. Lieber held that no "real and lasting good" could be produced "by associations whose object is to enforce, by combinations, wages higher than the natural price of labour." Relying on studies of the costs borne by striking workers who "stopped working, and were obliged to consume what they had saved" in Glasgow in 1838 and Paris in 1840, Lieber treated these costs as "useless consumption." More generally, he argued that, if a union did win a raise in wages, the unintended but inevitable longer-term consequences, by one mechanism or another, would be harmful for labor itself as well as society.

> If the members of a Trades' Union succeed in raising wages, the employer either continues to manufacture or not. If not, of course the means of support of labour are destroyed; if he does, without sufficient remuneration for his capital, he will soon remove it, and employ it in some other way. In this case the workmen of course lose their support, and society at large loses, because a loss is necessarily incurred at each violent change of investment or of productive channel. Should the employer raise the price of the product according to the rise of wages, others will undersell him, if not in his own country, certainly in foreign parts.[82]

In running through this chain of universally stated assertions, Lieber pursued a standard practice of classical political economy. But whereas Lieber treated such assertions as if they were given truths applying to any and all cases, Mill understood general claims in political economy to be abstract statements of general tendencies to which exceptions were empirically possible under particular conditions. For example, when explicating Ricardo's theory of rent in his *Principles*, Mill paused to stress the methodological point he considered fundamental to political economy:

> It is not pretended that the facts of any concrete case conform with absolute precision to this or any other scientific principle. We must never forget that the truths of political economy are truths only in the rough. . . it is impossible in political economy to obtain general theorems embracing

---

[81] Francis Lieber to G. S. Hillard, August 24, 1842. Quoted from Perry, *Life and Letters*, 171–72.
[82] Lieber, *Essays on Property*, 187–90.

the complications of circumstances which may affect the result in an individual case.[83]

Although this may, at first glance, appear an arcane point, taking it seriously supported Mill in a mode of argument from general principles to practical judgments that differed not only in form, but often also in its substantive policy implications, from that of Lieber. This divide—at once a methodological nuance and politically substantive—is well exemplified in the contrast between Lieber's use of political economy in discussing unions and Mill's.

Mill in his *Principles* accepted, and indeed gave one of the most famous presentations of, the wages-fund doctrine of classical political economy.[84] That doctrine underpinned Lieber's contention that a union wage gain would have long-term negative consequences. It also underlay Mill's general contention that efforts of "the working classes, by combining among themselves, to raise or keep up the general rate of wages" had to fail. Unlike Lieber, however, once Mill stated his general point, he identified exceptional conditions ("in trades where the workpeople are few in number, and collected in a small number of local centres") under which efforts to improve wages were "sometimes successful." After granting this as empirically possible, Mill evaluated its desirability. He argued that such a "partial rise of wages... ought to be regarded as a benefit" if (1) it was "not gained at the expense of the remainder of the working class," (2) the union that produced it was "voluntary" and not promoted "by threats or violence," and (3) the union did not aim, above and beyond improving wages or lowering hours, to such further goals as ending "task work" and "difference of pay" based on skill, which Mill judged to be "pernicious" goals since they would "place the energetic and the idle, the skilful and the incompetent, on a level."[85]

Given these demanding conditions, the contrast between Lieber and Mill on unions is not between an uncompromising critic and an uncompromising advocate. It is, instead, between an uncompromising critic and a moderate, whose moderation relies on relating general principles of political economy to practical judgments in a way sensitive to particular conditions. This contrast between uncompromising and moderate modes of argument from principles of classical

---

[83] Mill, *Principles*, 2: 422. Similarly, when taking up competition in his *Principles*, Mill had stressed that assuming "rents, profits, wages, prices" to be entirely "determined by competition" made it possible to formulate "principles of broad generality and scientific precision" about them, but warned that "in applying the conclusions of political economy to the actual affairs of life" it was essential to consider the extent to which competition was operative in the particular case under consideration and qualify conclusions accordingly. Ibid, 2: 239, 244.

[84] Very late in his life, toward the end of the 1860s, Mill would famously come to reject the doctrine. As mentioned in a previous footnote, I am presenting his views as of the 1848 first edition of his *Principles*.

[85] Ibid., 3: 929–34.

political economy, and the resulting divide between two subspecies of classical liberalism, can be further elucidated by comparing Mill and Lieber on another charged issue: free trade versus protection.

When Mill treats international trade in general terms during his *Principles*, he sings its praises, as we would expect of a classical liberal. He locates the principal economic "benefit of international exchange... in a more efficient employment of the productive forces of the world," and argues that, since international commerce is largely "a mode of cheapening production," the consumer is usually "the person ultimately benefited." The "economic advantages of commerce" were accompanied, for Mill, by even more laudatory noneconomic effects. International trade was "rendering war obsolete, by strengthening and multiplying the personal interests which are in natural opposition to it." Finally, "the great and rapid increase of international trade, in being the principal guarantee of the peace of the world," provided "the great permanent security for the uninterrupted progress of the ideas, the institutions, and the character of the human race."[86]

When Mill considers restrictions on a trade as a government policy, his stance is broadly critical. Yet his methodological openness to qualifying conditions led him to weigh carefully, rather than dismiss, alternative views. In doing so, he admitted two concessions. First, certain restrictions might be justified in terms of national defense. Mill suggested that the Navigation Laws, which had forced English commerce onto English-owned ships, had historically increased the numbers of ships and sailors England could muster, and thereby helped its "maritime power" surpass its one-time rival, the Dutch. But once superiority had been achieved, the laws were no longer necessary, and hence Mill's 1848 *Principles* advocated repeal of the Navigation Laws, as would happen in 1849. Second, there was one situation "in which, on mere principles of political economy, protecting duties can be defensible": for infant industries. This exception allowed for duties "imposed temporarily (especially in a young and rising nation) in hopes of naturalizing a foreign industry... suitable to the circumstances of the country." Again, the justification itself entailed limits on its extent: (1) "protection should be confined to cases in which there is good ground of assurance that the industry which it fosters will after a time be able to dispense with it," and (2) "nor should the domestic producers ever be allowed to expect that it will be continued to them beyond the time strictly necessary for a fair trial of what they are capable of accomplishing."[87]

Although Lieber and Mill shared a general preference for free trade, Lieber's uncompromising mode of economic policy argument was again evident in his hostility to any exceptions. He praised the repeal of the Navigation Laws in a

[86] Ibid., 3: 587–94.
[87] Ibid., 3: 913–22.

decidedly strident fashion. To his long-time correspondent, Carl Mittermaier, a professor at Heidelberg, he proclaimed: "these are grand successful, and true victories of peace and liberty! God bless all sincere free-traders!" To a friend in Boston, Lieber hailed the victory of "good sense and plain truth" over the view, he heard as "a schoolboy," that the Navigation Laws were "the foundation of Britain's greatness." Unlike Mill, Lieber's view of the repeal of these laws was not moderated by any notion that they had once been justified. He approached them as if they had always been wrong, but now at last the "plain truth" had won.[88]

By the late 1840s, Lieber was a public participant in an international movement of free trade advocacy. Galvanized by Richard Cobden's famous Anti–Corn Law League, which had built up mass public opposition to protection in England in the first half of the 1840s, the French classical liberal Frédéric Bastiat had begun a similar campaign in France in 1846, the year the Corn Laws were repealed in Britain. When Bastiat's popularizing assault on arguments against free trade was translated for American audiences as *Sophisms of the Protective Policy* in 1848, Lieber wrote an introductory letter published with the text. It heralded Bastiat's work as serving to "contribute to the spread of what we sincerely and firmly believe to be the cause of truth, of civilization, and of good will among men." Wedding the free trade cause to his own long-standing valorization of technology, Lieber added, more specifically:

> [W]hat else is Free Trade, but another name for road, canal, machinery, natural agent, railway, mail, wagon, plough, or whatever other abridgement of toil, removal of impediment, victory over elements, and increase of enjoyment and civilization can be named? All have but this one end, to get as much for as little labor as possible, so that the labor thus saved may be applied for the attainment of other objects, and that capital not be wilfully wasted.[89]

Lieber espoused free trade as forcefully in his classroom as he did in his introduction to the translation of Bastiat and his private letters. The South Carolina College class of 1849 printed Lieber's concluding political economy lecture to them as the pamphlet "Some Truths Worth Remembering." Here Lieber denounced protective tariffs as "veiled communism," while holding up free trade as the true "protection of every man's own," and at the same time, "the principle of the gospel of peace and good will, carried out in the world of exchange."[90] Lieber

---

[88] Lieber to Mittermaier, June 4, 1849; to Hillard, June 24, 1849. Quoted from Perry, *Life and Letters*, 218–19.

[89] Francis Lieber, "Introductory Letter," in Frédéric Bastiat, *Sophisms of the Protective Policy*, trans. D. J. McCord (New York: Putnam, 1848), 5, 10–11.

[90] Francis Lieber, "Some Truths Worth Remembering, Given, as a Recapitulation, in a Farewell Lecture to the Class of Political Economy of 1849" (Published by the class, 1849), 2–3, 5.

had begun the lecture, moreover, by stating a methodological viewpoint direc at odds with that we identified in Mill. Echoing a claim about the relationship theory to practice made in Bastiat's *Sophisms*, Lieber argued that "[i]n politicai economy, as in all other practical branches, there is nothing that can be true in theory, but false in practice."[91] This was no one-off lecture flourish. Almost twenty years later, when sharp rises in America's tariffs in the 1860s roused Lieber, late in life, to write his own Bastiat-style tract, *Notes on Fallacies Peculiar to American Protectionists*, he would declare again: "In political economy we know nothing in the abstract. That which is not true in practice is not true at all. Let us hear no more about being true in theory but not in practice."[92]

Lieber's "Political Science" in Transatlantic Perspective

As we have seen, political economy made up a notable strand of Lieber's teaching and writing, from the late 1830s through his *Notes on Fallacies Peculiar to American Protectionists* of 1869. Given this continuity it may, at first glance, seem odd that Lieber requested the removal of political economy from his academic title during his 1857 appointment to Columbia College. When Columbia's board elected Lieber to a newly created chair, it was as Professor of History and Political Economy. But as soon as his appointment was secure, Lieber asked that the chair be titled "History and Political Science."[93] The granting of his request led to the earliest use of "political science" in an American academic title. But this substitution of terms did not indicate any move between fields. Political economy was, for Lieber, a branch of political science, and as such, his request was for a more general title that encompassed political economy but also much else. When political science first found a formal place within America's academy, it thus carried a distinctively wide meaning.

Lieber's conception of political science built upon a venerable tradition. From Aristotle's treatment of economics within his *Politics*,[94] to Mill's locating of political economy as a "limited department" of the "general science of politics" in his *Principles*,[95] the notion of an overarching science of governance of which political economy was one part was a recurring trope of Western thought. From the late eighteenth century onward, elaborations of this encompassing science had

[91] Ibid., 1. For Bastiat on theory and practice, see *Sophisms of the Protective Policy*, 119–27.

[92] Francis Lieber, *Notes on Fallacies Peculiar to American Protectionists, or Chiefly Resorted to in America* (New York: American Free Trade League, 1869), 12.

[93] Lieber to Hamilton Fish, May 20, 1857. Quoted from Perry, *Life and Letters*, 295.

[94] Aristotle, *The Politics and The Constitution of Athens*, ed. Stephen Everson (Cambridge: Cambridge University Press, 1996), book 1.

[95] Mill, *Principles*, 889.

increasingly bifurcated into two intellectual currents: one turned to "society" as a central concept (in doing so, creating such phrases as "social science," and later "sociology"), whereas the other gave this role to the "state." The latter was dominant in Germany, the former in France. Seen in transatlantic perspective, the most unique trait of Lieber's political science was not its breadth, which was commonplace at the time, but its bridging of this bifurcation. Located in neither Germany nor France while engaged with intellectual currents in both—and the advocate of a theory of the state that, as we have seen, conceived the state as a society—Lieber crafted a wide political science that was, at one and the same time, the science/s of the state *and* equivalent to what we today usually call social science.

The wide sense of the range of his teaching and writing that informed Lieber's request to have "political science" in his Columbia title was one he had long held. In the dedicatory letter "To My Former Pupils" that prefaced his 1853 *Civil Liberty and Self-Government*, Lieber had identified himself as "Professor of History and of Political Philosophy and Economy."[96] When making his chair title request, Lieber explained similarly that he wanted it made explicit that his remit covered "*Government*, Political Philosophy, or, as our great master called it, Politics."[97] It was, moreover, in the 1832 *Encyclopedia Americana* entry for the Aristotelian term "Politics" that Lieber had first himself outlined a wide science of multiple branches. There he announced:

> POLITICS, in its widest extent, is both the science and the art of government, or the science whose subject is the regulation of man, in all his relations as the member of a state, and the application of this science. In other words, it is the theory and the practice of obtaining the ends of civil society as perfectly as possible.... Politics, therefore, extends to every thing which is the subject of positive laws; for it is by means of these that the purposes of a state or civil union are effected.... As the idea of *politics* depends upon that of *state*, a definition of the latter will easily mark out the whole province of the political sciences. By *state* we understand a society formed by men, with the view of better obtaining the ends of life by a union of powers and mutual assistance. This idea of state is the basis of a class of sciences.[98]

Lieber proceeded to explain that these "political sciences" were "divisible into the *abstract*, or purely philosophical, and the *historical* and *practical*." But the "order for studying them" best "adapted to the wants of the scientific student" would

---

[96] Lieber, *Civil Liberty*, viii.

[97] Lieber to Hamilton Fish, May 20, 1857. Quoted from Perry, *Life and Letters*, 295. Italics in original.

[98] Francis Lieber, "Politics," in *Encyclopedia Americana*, 10: 225. Caps and italics in original.

distinguish areas of study at a more fine-grained level. Over the next several pages, he successively identified twelve such areas:

1. Natural law
2. Abstract or theoretical politics
3. Political economy
4. Science of police[99]
5. Practical politics—"the art of administering the government of states"
6. History of politics
7. History of the European and American systems of states
8. Statistics—"knowledge of the actual conditions, resources, &c. of states"
9. Positive, public, and constitutional law
10. Practical law of nations
11. Diplomacy
12. Political practice—"whatever is necessary for the conduct of public affairs"[100]

Lieber's entry extended German academic models. His use of the Aristotelian "Politics" to name an encompassing science followed an old use, prominent earlier in German universities as the Latin *Politica*, and still found in the late eighteenth century in the use at the University of Göttingen of the German *Politik*.[101] *Politica* and *Politik* covered a wide domain including, as did Lieber's "Politics" entry, theoretical and practical areas, and external relations of states as well as domestic governance. More recently, growing German intellectual attention to the concept of the state had made *Staatswissenchaften* the rising new term for this encompassing domain in its most contemporary formulations. Lieber paralleled this trend in his plural use of "political sciences," and appeal to the concept of the state to demarcate the "province" of these sciences. His ordered listing of specific areas of specialized study appears, indeed, to be largely a direct translation of the ordering of areas covered in a popular 1820s

[99] This translates the German *polizeiwissenschaft*. For Lieber on this science, see "Police," *Encyclopedia Americana*, 10: 215. For a recent overview of the evolution of this science, from its sub-differentiation within the broader domain of the Aristotelian "Politics" during the seventeenth century, to its subsuming into the rising field of administration during the mid-to-late nineteenth century, see Lindenfeld, *Practical Imagination*, 16–20, 38–40, 81–84, 125–30, 199–201.

[100] Lieber, "Politics," 225–27.

[101] Lindenfeld, *Practical Imagination*, 16–20, 41–44; Michael Philipp, "The '*Politica*' of 17th Century Germany, as Reflected in the 'dissertationes politicae': Some Aspects of the Older Tradition in Academic Political Science." Paper presented at the "Sciences of Politics" International Conference, Tulane University, New Orleans, January 9, 2004. I thank Martyn Thompson of Tulane for sharing Philipp's fascinating paper with me.

work he cited, *The Sciences of the State in the Light of Our Time*, by German academic Karl Heinrich Ludwig Pölitz.[102]

A quarter-century after his "Politics" entry, when requesting the use of "political science" in his Columbia title, Lieber was keenly attentive to how this phrase would resonate in Europe. He noted in his request that he had not yet written about his new chair to European friends, and that "it would gratify me to tell them that I have been made professor of the greatest branches in the greatest city of the greatest Union—that of History and Political Science."[103] It is especially notable here that Lieber expected "political science" to resonate with both Tocqueville in France and his friend Mittermaier at Heidelberg University. Although Lieber's sketch of a wide science of politics in 1832 was derivative of German academic models, his friendship with Tocqueville had, since that time, also brought the French *sciences politiques* prominently to his attention.

This French phrase had come into use during the latter half of the eighteenth century as part of the formulation *sciences morales et politiques*, which was, in turn, institutionalized by the 1795 founding of the Académie des sciences morales et politiques. One of the younger of the limited (by election only) membership academies that together constituted the prestigious Institut de France, the Académie des sciences morales et politiques at first existed for less than a decade before Napoleon suppressed it. But it had been reestablished in 1832 due to the efforts of Guizot when he was France's minister of education. In 1838 Tocqueville won election to the academy after the success of the first volume of *Democracy in America*, and the next year he proposed to Lieber that the American might be elected a foreign member.[104] The possibility of membership for Lieber in the Académie (and thereby the prestigious Institut) thereafter peppered the Lieber-Tocqueville correspondence, and when Lieber visited Tocqueville in Paris in 1844, they together visited with the Académie's permanent secretary, the liberal historian François Mignet.[105] In the 1850s, Lieber would identify himself on the title page of *Civil*

---

[102] Karl Heinrich Ludwig Pölitz, *Die staatswissenschaften im lichte unsrer zeit*, 5 vols. (Leipzig: J. C. Hinrichs, 1827–28). The contents of the five volumes are (1) Natur- und völkerrecht; staats- und staatenrecht, und staatskunst; (2) Volkswirthschaftslehre; staatswirthschaftslehre und finanzwissenschaft, und polizeiwissenschaft; (3) Die geschichte des europäischen und amerikanischen staatensystems aus dem standpuncte der politik; (4) Staatenkunde und positives staatsrecht (verfassungsrecht); (5) Practisches (europäisches) völkerrecht; diplomatie; und staatspraxis. An entry on Pölitz, which describes him as a "professor of politics," comes after the "Politics" entry in the *Encyclopedia Americana*. Francis Lieber, "Pölitz," *Encyclopedia Americana*, 10: 227. For a recent sketch of Pölitz and his text *Die staatswissenschaften*, see Lindenfeld, *Practical Imagination*, 100.

[103] Lieber to Hamilton Fish, May 20, 1857. Quoted from Perry, *Life and Letters*, 295.

[104] Lieber to Tocqueville, September 20, 1839. Quoted from Perry, *Life and Letters*, 140.

[105] See letters in Crauitu and Jennings, *Tocqueville after 1840*, 62, 67, 75–76, 84, 146, 155. On the visit with Mignet, see Lieber's June 11, 1844, letter to his wife, in Perry, *Life and Letters*, 183. Lieber tells his wife: "We talked of the representative system and I was at home there."

Liberty and Self-Government as a corresponding member of the Institute of France, and in 1857, when he wrote Tocqueville about his Columbia chair, he asked his friend to see that "in the publications of the Institute I am called *Professeur de l'Historie et des Sciences Politiques au Columbia College, à New York.*"[106]

To get a sense for the content that was evoked by Lieber's equating his political science with the French phrase, we can look to Tocqueville's own use of it. Most famously employed in his claim that "[a] new political science is needed for a world altogether new" in the introduction of *Democracy in America,*[107] the phrase received fuller treatment from Tocqueville in 1852 when he addressed the Académie des sciences morales et politiques as its president. Here he presented "political science" as "[t]he science that treats of the conduct of societies" covering "an immense space extending from philosophy through the elementary studies of civil law." Within this space Tocqueville gave as examples, beside the canonical Plato, Aristotle, Machiavelli, Montesquieu, and Rousseau, the works of Grotius and Puffendorf on international law, Beccaria on criminal justice, Adam Smith on political economy, as well as works by jurists and legal commentators.[108] Tocqueville hence sketched a wide political science that—like Lieber's earlier "Politics" and the German *Staatswissenschaften*—encompassed both the theoretical and the practical, reached from domestic governance to international relations, and included political economy and public law as two of its multiple branches.[109]

But there were also notable differences. Tocqueville's overview of wide political science made no use of the concept of the state. Moreover, he surveyed its content largely by referencing well-known authors, while making no use of technical field labels tightly tied to academic usage.

These differences exemplified broader contrasts between the German *Staatswissenschaften* and the French *sciences politiques.* The *Staatswissenschaften* were based in the universities and had as a major aim the training of state officials who, ideally, would combine theoretical knowledge of principles of governance with technical skills in areas like police, statistics, and diplomacy. By contrast, the *sciences politiques* were centered in Lieber's day on the writing and discussion of

---

[106] Lieber to Tocqueville, May 30, 1857. Quoted from Craiutu and Jennings, *Tocqueville after 1840,* 232.

[107] Tocqueville, *Democracy in America,* 7.

[108] Alexis de Tocqueville, "Speech Given to the Annual Public Meeting of the Academy of Moral and Political Sciences on April 3, 1852," in *Alexis de Tocqueville and the Art of Democratic Statesmanship,* ed. Brian Danoff and L. Joseph Hebert Jr. (Lanham, MD: Lexington Books, 2011), 19.

[109] For examples of efforts to recover Tocqueville's conception of political science, as presented in this address, and reflect on how it compares with social science today, see Wilhelm Hennis, "Tocqueville's 'New Political Science,'" in *Politics as a Practical Science,* trans. Keith Tribe (New York: Palgrave Macmillan, 2009), chap. 5; Richard Swedberg, *Tocqueville's Political Economy* (Princeton, NJ: Princeton University Press, 2009), 226–30.

works aimed to engage and inform public opinion. Their ideal was, as Tocqueville put it in his 1852 address, to forge in "society something like a sort of intellectual atmosphere where the spirit of the governed and the governors breathes, and where the former and latter draw, often without knowing it, sometimes without wanting it, the principles of their conduct."[110]

Just as Tocqueville's conception of political science was most fully stated in his address to the Académie des sciences morales et politiques, so Lieber's conception was best conveyed in the inaugural address he gave during his first year at Columbia.[111] In this 1858 address, Lieber identified his faculty post as a "professorship of political science," and proceeded to treat history, political economy, and political philosophy, in turn, as three "branches" within its broad domain. Employing the concept of *society* to demarcate this domain, he described his chair as devoted to "the sciences which treat of man in his social relations, of humanity in all its phases in society." And looking beyond the academy, he praised these sciences as "important... for every one, whatever his pursuits in practical life may be."[112] Through the first half of his address, Lieber spoke in terms more akin to the *sciences politiques* than the *Staatswissenschaften*.

Yet just over halfway through his address, when Lieber turned from history and political economy to political philosophy, the concept of the state came to center stage as "the greatest of institutions" developed as "men and society advance."[113] In a fashion now more reminiscent of his 1832 "Politics" entry, Lieber laid out a series of particular areas as all parts of "a complete course of political philosophy." Starting from "the twin ideas of Right and Duty," his overview of this "course" proceeded through "Political Ethics," to "the science of government, and a knowledge of governments which exist and have existed," "a survey of all political literature as represented by its prominent authors," and concluded with America's "own polity and political existence... a manly discussion of Civil Liberty and Self-Government," and "that branch which is the glory of our race in modern history... International Law."[114] As compared with his earlier encyclopedia entry, Lieber's "course" here adds terms advanced in his own scholarship, such as "jural," while certain technical areas he earlier noted disappear, such as the "science of police." Though the later half of Lieber's address showed continuing

---

[110] Tocqueville, "Speech Given to the Academy," 20. The idea of political science having broad societal influence had been evident earlier in *Democracy in America* when Tocqueville praised America as a country "in which political science has descended to the last ranks of society." Tocqueville, *Democracy in America*, 156.

[111] Lieber delivered his inaugural at Columbia College on February 17, 1858. I draw on the address in its somewhat elaborated and revised published form. Lieber, "History and Political Science Necessary Studies," in Gilman, *Miscellaneous Writings of Lieber*, 1: 329–68.

[112] Lieber, "History and Political Science," 330, 336.

[113] Lieber, "History and Political Science," 357.

[114] Lieber, "History and Political Science," 355–67.

debts to the *Staatswissenschaften*, it also testified to the fact that Lieber had come to interpret and teach the sciences of the state in a manner marked with his own personal stamp.

Taking both halves of the inaugural together, and situating its overall presentation of political science in transatlantic perspective, we find in Lieber more than a passive reception of continental European models into America's antebellum academy. Lieber had crafted a hybrid that creatively drew from the distinct currents of the *Staatswissenschaften* and *sciences politiques* as he adapted transatlantic intellectual inheritances to the context of the American college. Both a symbol and a medium of Lieber's dual engagement with French and German thought is found in his extended correspondence of over a quarter-century with both Tocqueville and Mittermaier. As these old friends passed away, his engagement was extended via new interlocutors. From the early 1860s on, Lieber corresponded with Edouard Laboulaye, a prominent critic of Napoleon III and professor at the Collège de France, who carried forward Tocqueville's legacy of looking to America to clarify the character and challenge of liberty in a democratic age.[115] During the mid-1860s, Lieber also entered into correspondence with Bluntschli of the University of Heidelberg, whom we introduced in chapter 2. Their exchanges picked up as Lieber's older Hiedelberg friend Mittermaier died in 1867. Bluntschli later fondly recalled,

> Francis Lieber, in New York, Edward Laboulaye, in Paris, and I in Heidelberg, formed what Lieber used to call a "scientific clover-leaf," in which three men, devoting themselves especially to political science, and at the same time uniting the historical and philosophical methods, combining theory with practical politics, and belonging to three different nationalities, to three states, and to three peoples, found themselves growing together by ties of common sympathy, and thus figuratively speaking, representing also the community of Anglo-American, French, and German culture and science.[116]

This "scientific clover-leaf" existed for only a few years. But if we see Laboulaye as succeeding Tocqueville, and Bluntschli Mittermaier, then Lieber had been part of

---

[115] Laboulaye's admiration for America was most perhaps famously captured in his proposal—first made at a dinner party in 1865 when he and other liberal opponents of Napoleon's III Second Empire were celebrating the North's victory in the American Civil War—that the French should fund by popular subscription a monument to American independence and liberty. The proposal led to the design of the Statue of Liberty and its eventual erection in New York Harbor. For more on Laboulaye, see Walter D. Gray, *Interpreting American Democracy in France: The Career of Edouard Laboulaye, 1811–1883* (Newark: University of Delaware Press, 1994).

[116] Johann Caspar Bluntschli, "Lieber's Service to Political Science and International Law," in Gilman, *Miscellaneous Writings of Lieber*, 2: 13.

a transatlantic triad since the early 1830s, before he had any academic post. The entry of "political science" into America's academy was a transatlantic event, not only because it was led by a Prussian political émigré, but also because Lieber was in conversation throughout with European friends. It was, moreover, the very plurality of Lieber's transatlantic engagements that helped give the nascent political science of America's academy its own character, not entirely mapping the earlier political science of any single European country.

WIDE POLITICAL SCIENCE AND LIBERALISM IN THE GILDED AGE

CHAPTER 4

Political Science and Political Economy in the Age of Academic Reform

ANDREW D. WHITE AND WILLIAM GRAHAM SUMNER

At the end of Part I, we saw "political science" garner its earliest formal recognition in the American academy in the title that Lieber requested when he moved to Columbia College in 1857. Yet Lieber's cherished Chair of History and Political Science existed for less than a decade. In 1865 Columbia's Board of Trustees, responding to a new president's request, voted to eliminate the chair and consolidate its duties with those of the chair of English and philosophy. Lieber himself was shuffled off to a Chair of Constitutional History and Public Law that his supporters arranged for him in Columbia's Law School.[1] Over a decade would pass, and Lieber would die, before a second initiative to push political science at Columbia ultimately succeeded in giving rise to the School of Political Science, founded there in 1880.

The immediate post–Civil War years were, however, far from a fallow period for political science in the wide sense Lieber embodied. Though the Chair of History and Political Science was gone at Columbia, before the end of the 1860s a College of History and Political Science was founded in the new Cornell University. Lieber's *Civil Liberty and Self-Government* was, moreover, being taught in multiple American colleges, with a new third edition needed by the mid-1870s. That edition was prepared by Yale's recently retired president, Theodore Dwight Woolsey, whose 1871 retirement was followed by the creation of a new Yale Chair of Political and Social Science to carry forward his instruction in Lieberian political science.

To turn to the head of Cornell's College of History and Political Science, and the holder of Yale's Chair of Political and Social Science, is to move to a new

---

[1] Frank Freidel, *Francis Lieber: Nineteenth-Century Liberal* (Baton Rouge: Louisiana State University Press, 1947), 363–68.

academic generation. Whereas Lieber had been born in 1800, the college's head—
none less than Cornell's founding president, Andrew D. White—was born in
1832. Whereas Woolsey had been born in 1801, the Yale chair—William Graham
Sumner, on his way to becoming a seminal polarizing intellectual of America's
Gilded Age—was born in 1840. I turn to White and Sumner in this chapter to
introduce and illuminate the post–Civil War onset of major institutional changes
in America's academy, as well as new departures and divergences in the nascent
domain of wide political science. My first goal is to elucidate just what "political
science" meant for its academic proponents and practitioners from the 1860s into
the 1880s. By examining how White and Sumner used this phrase, I stress their
initial continuity with Lieber's wide political science, and then chart the differing ways in which each, during the 1870s, departed from this common starting
point. Then, I step back from White and Sumner to show how the post-Lieberian
directions in political science they had taken up in the 1870s were both further
articulated, and awkwardly mingled, at the School of Political Science founded in
1880 at Columbia.

The breadth that political science retained into the 1880s and the prominence
of political economy within it are pivotal to situating political science in relation
to the history of liberalism. In the second half of this chapter, I focus on White's
and Sumner's views on political economy. I show first how the divide, introduced in chapter 3, between moderate and uncompromising variants of classical
political economy was articulated during the 1860s and 1870s in discussions of
free trade and laissez-faire. Then, as the current chapter ends, we see both sides
of this divide shift character abruptly in the early 1880s, thereby setting a stage
for the controversy, recounted in chapter 5, that flared while progressive liberalism and disenchanted classical liberalism crystallized as competing late-century
liberal visions.

The Lieberian Moment: The Transatlantic Wide Political Science of White and Sumner

As the founding president of Cornell University, Andrew D. White is a vanguard
figure in histories of American higher education. The 1868 opening of Cornell was
a crucial starting point in the rise of university ideals and institutions, which, in
the last third of the nineteenth century, shifted the center of gravity in America's
academy away from the older model of small colleges with a fixed curriculum.[2]

---

[2] A classic synthetic study of this transformation is Laurence R. Veysey, *The Emergence of the
American University* (Chicago: University of Chicago Press, 1965). The transformation began in
earnest, not only with the 1868 opening of Cornell under White, but also the 1869 appointment of

White stands out for our purposes due to his advocacy of a prominent position for wide political science in the new university environment. Yet, while White gave a boost to wide political science by incorporating it into his university ideal, he had himself been introduced to it by the traditional mode of senior-year instruction by his college president. The inroads that Lieberian wide political science made in America's academy around the time of the Civil War were hence advanced in both the new university and older collegiate sides of that academy.

My pairing of White with Sumner illuminates both sides of this development. Each began his higher education as a midcentury Yale college student, and received senior-year instruction there from Yale's president, Woolsey, in such areas of wide political science as political economy, history of civilization, and international law. Like many other intellectuals in nineteenth-century America, White and Sumner each followed up their college education with graduate studies in Europe, and both remained engaged with European intellectual currents after they returned to make their careers in America's academy. But Woolsey's teaching had changed in the years between White's time at Yale in the 1850s and Sumner's undergraduate days in the 1860s, and the two went to different places in Europe to study different subjects. When paired together they suggest both more general, and more personally distinct, aspects of the process by which a young midcentury American could be introduced to wide political science and become its proponent and practitioner, whether in a university or a college setting.

WHITE: FROM YALE TO CORNELL

As a Yale student in the early 1850s, White received his instruction from Woolsey before Lieber's *Civil Liberty and Self-Government* had assumed its later central place in the president's teaching. The work White was assigned that grabbed his attention was, rather, an older blend of liberalism and developmental historicism: Guizot's *History of Civilization in Europe*. Inspired by that work, White then choose to spend the first year of his European studies in Paris in 1853–1854, where he attended lectures at the Sorbonne and Collège de France. He embraced French historical scholarship as exemplary, and inaugurated his research interests in modern France and its interaction with America.[3] Although White also went on to study at the University of Berlin later in his European sojourn, it was the politically liberal and unapologetically philosophical French historicist scholarship

---

reformer Charles W. Eliot as president of Harvard. While I highlight White in this chapter, intellectual developments at the reforming Harvard will move to the center of my narrative during subsequent chapters, especially in connection with the political scientist A. Lawrence Lowell, who would, after helping create the Department of Government, then succeed Eliot as Harvard president.

[3] Andrew D. White, *Autobiography of Andrew Dickson White*, 2 vols. (New York: Century, 1905), chap. 2.

exemplified by Guizot that left the biggest mark upon him. As a fellow American scholar would put it, when sketching White's intellectual temper in the 1880s:

> While thoroughly appreciating German scholarship and profoundly admiring German character, Mr. White represents French training rather than Teutonic. He was brought up, so to speak, at the feet of D'Aubigné, Guizot, Thierry, Mignet, Theirs, and Laboulaye. There is a certain largeness of view, a certain clearness, directness, and force of style—a certain passion for general results and positive conclusions, which mark the French habit of mind.… It is a quality which in political science can still be best acquired in Paris, a fact which American students are in danger of forgetting.[4]

White was soon able to bring his experiences to bear in teaching American students. He returned from Europe in 1856 and the next year was appointed as professor of history at the University of Michigan. There he taught General History and Philosophy of History, along with "original investigation and close criticism of important periods and noted characters," and saw both kinds of historical study as together serving to *"lay the foundation for a thorough study of the political and constitutional history of our country."*[5]

During the Civil War White was drawn away from academic life. In 1862 he went back to Europe to advocate for the North's cause, and after returning from this endeavor in 1863 was elected to New York's state senate. From there White soon moved back to the academy when he became Cornell University's founding president. Thus began a movement between the academy, government service, and party politics that became the leitmotif of White's career. In addition to his role as Cornell's president, he also, as we shall note later in this chapter, advocated for civil service reform in intra-Republican Party debates, and served as a prominent American diplomat, most extensively in Berlin. White's movement back and forth between America and Europe, and between academic and political life, would inform and update his view of political science and its role in the new university environment that he helped inaugurate in post–Civil War America.

White's prominence in the movement of the American academy toward university ideals and institutions developed directly from his service in the New York State Senate. As education committee chairman he fought to consolidate federal land grants for higher education accruing to New York under the 1862 Morrill Act, and to dedicate them to a school his fellow state senator Ezra Cornell intended to found and personally fund. This White-Cornell alliance secured the combination

[4] Herbert Baxter Adams, *The Study of History in American Colleges and Universities*, Bureau of Education Circular of Information no. 2 (Washington, DC: Government Printing Office, 1887), 96.

[5] H. B. Adams, *Study of History*, 98–100. Italics in original. The quotes are from the university catalog descriptions of White's instruction.

of public and private funds that made a new university viable. Charter New York state in 1865, it opened to students in 1868. Most significantly fc purposes, in the plan of organization he drafted for Cornell in 1866, and aga... in his presidential address at the university's opening, White explicitly advocated education in political science.[6]

One of the innovations that set Cornell apart from the colleges that previously dominated American higher education was its rejection of a uniform curriculum. There was to be "no single course... insisted upon for all alike." Instead "education in various *special* departments" was to be promoted.[7] Of the nine departments outlined in the 1866 plan that White drafted for Cornell's organization committee, one stood out as sufficiently unusual to warrant further justification: the "Department of Jurisprudence, Political Science, and History." White's plan declared that "great numbers of the most active young men long for such a department," and were "not attracted to the existing colleges" since instruction in the area was sparse. It then argued that the department would also serve ends beyond the university by helping to improve decision-making in state and national level politics. Appealing in part to his own experience as a legislator, White argued:

> We believe that the State and nation are constantly injured by their cho-
> sen servants, who lack the simplest rudiments of knowledge which such
> a department could supply. No one can stand in any legislative position
> and not be struck with the frequent want in men otherwise strong and
> keen, of the simplest knowledge of principles essential to public welfare.
> Of technical knowledge of law, and or practical acquaintance with busi-
> ness, the supply is always plentiful, but it is very common that in decid-
> ing great public questions, exploded errors in political and social science
> are revamped, fundamental principles of law disregarded, and the plain-
> est teachings of history ignored.[8]

White here advances a democratized classical liberal view that democracy can, but must, be educated if it is to have good political decision-making. Liberals who

---

[6] My treatment below is based on the lengthier discussion in the 1866 plan of organization. For White's presentation of political science in his inaugural address, see Andrew D. White, "Inaugural Address," in *Builders of American Universities*, vol. 1, ed. David Andrew Weaver (Alton, IL: Shurtleff College Press, 1950), 259–61, 264–66.

[7] Andrew D. White, *Report of the Committee on Organization, presented to the Trustees of the Cornell University, October 21st, 1866* (Albany, NY: C. Van Benthuysen & Sons, 1867), 3–4, italics in original. Among the approaches to the undergraduate curriculum at play during the post–Civil War remaking of American higher education, the department model took up a middle ground between the old college model of a fixed curriculum for all students and the model of free choice among course electives introduced at Harvard by Eliot.

[8] White, *Report of the Committee on Organization*, 6.

we introduced during Part I were, moreover, central to the education White called for. He envisioned a department that would teach its students through "large and hearty study and comparison of the views and methods of Guizot, and Mill, and Lieber, and Woolsey, and Bastiat, and Carey, and Maine, and others."[9] Courses in the proposed department were to be given by professors with various areas of expertise. White projected roles for professors of moral and mental philosophy, history, political economy, municipal law, and constitutional law.[10] As Cornell became a reality during the late 1860s, what the plan of organization had labeled a "department" came into being as the College of History and Political Science, led by White himself. Courses were also given by Goldwin Smith, a British academic who had extolled American democracy to British liberals in debates leading up to the 1867 suffrage extension in Britain,[11] and whom White drew away from Oxford to Cornell; and, on a visiting basis, by Columbia Law School's Theodore Dwight.[12]

Dwight's role at Cornell highlights the relation of developments there to higher education elsewhere in New York, specifically at Columbia. Dwight had recently helped Lieber find a new home in Columbia's Law School when the émigré's cherished chair in Columbia's College was eliminated in 1865. That event perhaps stood in the background of White's argument in the 1866 Cornell plan that "existing colleges" were not meeting educational needs of students in political science. Certainly, within a few years of Columbia eliminating its Chair of History and Political Science, the same phrasing reappeared at Cornell in the College of History and Political Science led by White. Lieber had himself, moreover, personally written to White in 1867 bemoaning the elimination of his chair, and sending along a copy of his 1858 inaugural address. Stressing the inaugural's arguments for "the necessity of teaching history and political economy," Lieber told White that he wrote "to stir you and incite you the more not to forget these noble and necessary branches." For Lieber, like White, the justification for giving these studies a prominent place in higher education looked beyond the academy to democratic politics. In his letter to White, Lieber declared: "Nowhere is it so necessary to hold before the eyes of young men a mirror of the sacredness and

---

[9] White, *Report of the Committee on Organization*, 6. I follow H. B. Adams, *Study of History*, 133, in reading "Mayne" in the 1866 report as a mistake and silently correcting it to "Maine."

[10] See White, *Report of the Committee on Organization*, 11–14, for the list of projected professorships, whose relations to the projected "Departments" is made a bit confusing by the fact that certain professors were expected to teach across multiple departments.

[11] Goldwin Smith, "The Experience of the American Commonwealth," in *Essays on Reform* (London: Macmillan, 1867), 217–37.

[12] The department (aka college), the faculty who taught in it, and the character of their instruction are surveyed at length in H. B. Adams, *Study of History*, chap. 5. The facts I report here draw specifically on 133–34.

gravity of political duties or the obligations of the citizen, as in a country in which his rights and privileges are almost unlimited."[13]

Looking across the Atlantic, we can also locate White's moves at Cornell in relation to the liberal tradition more broadly. They had striking contemporary parallels in J. S. Mill's 1867 inaugural address as rector of the University of St. Andrews. The "outline of a complete scientific education" Mill sketched there concluded with "instruction in that which it is the chief of all ends of intellectual education to qualify us for—the exercise of thought on the great interests of mankind as moral and social beings—ethics and politics, in the largest sense."[14] Mill identified four branches of specialized instruction within this grand domain. First, the "Professor of History" would teach the "stages of civilization" to help students distinguish "what is the same in all ages and what is progressive," and thus acquire a "conception of the causes and laws of progress."[15] Political economy was the second area that Mill noted, and the third "what is called Jurisprudence," of which he singled out Maine's *Ancient Law* as exemplary. Finally, he hailed international law as a subject that "should be taught in all universities, and should form part of all liberal education."[16] International law was the only subject identified in Mill's 1867 address that was not explicitly paralleled in White's 1866 Cornell plan. Such extensive parallels testify to a common conception of the content and importance of wide political science that was shared among midcentury democratized classical liberals on both sides of the Atlantic. This conception remained essentially the same as that we have noted earlier in Tocqueville's 1852 address to the Académie des sciences morales et politiques and Lieber's 1858 inaugural at Columbia.

TEACHING LIEBER AT YALE: FROM WOOLSEY TO SUMNER

While White was promoting the wide political science of Lieber and other democratized classical liberals in connection with new university institutions, it also continued to advance in existing colleges. In the mid-1850s, President Woolsey of Yale had started assigning Lieber's 1853 *Civil Liberty and Self-Government*, and

---

[13] Lieber letter to Andrew D. White, April 15, 1867. In Thomas Sergeant Perry, ed., *The Life and Letters of Francis Lieber* (Boston: Osgood, 1882), 372–73.

[14] John Stuart Mill, "Inaugural Address Delivered to the University of St. Andrews," in *Essays on Equality, Law, and Education*, ed. John M. Robson, *Collected Works of John Stuart Mill*, vol. 21 (Toronto: University of Toronto Press, 1984), 243.

[15] J. S. Mill, "Inaugural Address," 244. Here Mill—who, like White, admired Guizot—parallels the praise in White's Cornell plan of those "noble studies" that "give material for thought and suggestions for thought upon the great field of the history of civilization." White, *Report of the Committee on Organization*, 10.

[16] J. S. Mill, "Inaugural Address," 245–47.

he subsequently dedicated his own international law text to Lieber "as a token of respect for his services in the field of political science."[17] After retiring in 1871, Woolsey devoted much of the decade to promoting Lieberian political science. In addition to preparing a 1874 new edition of *Civil Liberty and Self-Government* after Lieber's death in 1872, Woolsey turned notes he had developed over his decades of teaching Yale seniors into his 1877 *Political Science: or, The State Theoretically and Practically Considered*, which is in large respects organized like an updated version of Lieber's 1830s work *Political Ethics*.[18]

After Woolsey's retirement, the task of carrying on his teaching in wide political science at Yale was made the province of a new faculty position, titled the Chair of Political and Social Science. In 1872 the chair was offered to William Graham Sumner, who had himself been a Yale student in the early 1860s, after Woolsey had made *Civil Liberty and Self-Government* central to his teaching. As Sumner took up the Yale chair he followed Woolsey's lead closely, assigning Lieber's *Civil Liberty and Self-Government* and teaching international law with Woolsey's 1860 textbook.[19] Sumner hence entered his Yale chair as a direct inheritor of the mid-century political science of Lieber and his disciple Woolsey.

That said, Sumner was shaped by further intellectual influences of his own. His graduate studies in Europe had immersed him in both midcentury German historicist science and British liberalism. He had spent two years studying with biblical scholars at the University of Göttingen. Especially struck by their method, he credited it as the laudable kin of the methods in philology and classics that were paradigmatic for German historicism. He judged the method to be "nobly scientific" and "worthy to rank, both for its results and its discipline, with the best of the natural science methods." After this immersion in specialized historicist research, Sumner had also more briefly studied Anglican theology at Oxford. There his "love for political science" was first "reawakened" by Hooker's *Ecclesiastical Polity* with its "doctrines of liberty under law," and then "intensified" by reading and discussing with other students Buckle's effort in *History of Civilization in England* to base a classical liberal account of progress on scientific induction from history.[20]

---

[17] Theodore Dwight Woolsey, *Introduction to the Study of International Law* (Boston: Munroe, 1860), title page.

[18] Theodore Dwight Woolsey, *Political Science: or, The State Theoretically and Practically Considered*, 2 vols. (New York: Scribner, Armstrong, 1877).

[19] Anna Haddow, *Political Science in American Colleges and Universities, 1636–1900* (New York: Appleton-Century, 1939), 177–78.

[20] I quote from Sumner's recollection of his European studies as reported in "Sketch of William Graham Sumner," *Popular Science Monthly* 35 (June 1889), 261–68. Sumner's admiration of German scholarship when he entered his Yale chair is evident in an 1873 talk where he held: "In Germany liberty attaches to thought and science. These are more free from dogmatical or traditional restraint there than anywhere else on earth. The scientific method is more perfectly understood and more rigidly applied there than elsewhere and it meets with few or no barriers from Church or State." William

After returning from Europe it took Sumner longer than White to secure a professorship. He spent time, back at Yale as a tutor in 1866–1869, and then as an Episcopalian minister. But he left the ministry without looking back when his alma mater offered him its new Chair of Political and Social Science. In fall 1873 Sumner began what became almost four decades in the chair. He would also serve in extra-academic posts—as an elected Republican alderman of New Haven in 1873–1876, and an appointed member of Connecticut's State Board of Education from 1882 till his death in 1910—but these were undertaken in addition to his Yale duties.[21]

One of Sumner's earliest endeavors in his new position was to explicate the "political science" so prominent in his title. He began an 1873 lecture, in which he presented his view of the remit of his chair and surveyed courses he would offer, by observing that there was only "the most vague notion in the popular mind of what is meant by political science." Sumner proposed distinguishing between "its narrower and its wider significance."[22] In "its narrower use" political science was "the science of government and the theory of the state." But far more was covered by "its widest sense." Sumner here presented a familiar array much of which we have, by now, heard in multiple liberal voices on both sides of the Atlantic: "political economy, or the science of wealth, as well as comparative politics, jurisprudence, international law, the theory of the state, the theory of government, and the history of all these." He explained that these studies came together as elements of an integrative effort to "learn what principles of the social order are *true*, that is, conform to human nature and to the conditions of human society." This effort called for a "turn away from tradition and prescription to re-examine the data," and it became scientific "by virtue of the methods it used."[23]

Sumner's view of scientific methods at this time was continuous with Lieber's. Earlier in 1873 he explained that he saw "science in its true sense, not merely as natural science, but as the methodical operation of the human reason in the investigation of truth." The "office" of science in this "true sense" was "to train men" to a "habit of mind in which they close their ears to all national, sectional, and personal rivalry." Among the "prejudices" Sumner believed that science could and should combat, it is especially telling that he included "partisan" prejudices.[24] Here he sounded a theme Lieber had also sounded almost four decades earlier. During his

---

Graham Sumner, "Solidarity of the Human Race," in *On Liberty, Society, and Politics: The Essential Essays of William Graham Sumner*, ed. Robert C. Bannister (Indianapolis, IN: Liberty Fund, 1992), 33.

[21] Harris E. Starr, *William Graham Sumner* (New York: Holt, 1925), chaps. 8–10.

[22] William Graham Sumner, "Introductory Lecture to Courses in Political and Social Science," in *The Challenge of Facts and Other Essays*, ed. Albert Galloway Keller (New Haven, CT: Yale University Press, 1914), 391.

[23] Sumner, "Introductory Lecture," 395, 401–402, italics in original.

[24] Sumner, "Solidarity," 34.

1835 inaugural address at South Carolina College Lieber had declared: "Let us learn one of the greatest acts of wisdom, to anticipate the judgment of time, and divest ourselves of partial and party views, and assume a loftier station from which we may contemplate our friends as well as our opponents with greater justice."[25]

Sumner's activities in his new chair exemplified both the encompassing scope of political science "in its widest sense" and a focused research agenda suggestive of the scientific standards of German historicist scholarship. In teaching Sumner strove (at least before he had colleagues to help him) to cover the full scope he attributed to his chair. Of six courses he taught across three terms in 1873–1874, one was on political science in "its narrower use," one on international law, two on political economy, one "on the history of politics and finance in the United States," and one introduced political science in the encyclopedic sense that encompassed his other courses.[26] At the same time, Sumner's German-informed conception of scientific research at the start of his career favored pursuing a focused agenda of primary-source-based inquiry. He turned to "the history of American finance and politics as a department which lies as yet almost untouched," with sources "all in the rough," and which would hence "require very long time and extensive research to do any justice to."[27] Sumner published his first book from this research agenda, *A History of American Currency*, in 1874, and his last, *A History of Banking in the United States*, in 1896.[28] Pursuing this agenda over more than two decades gave him a close knowledge of economic policymaking in America before, during, and after the democratization of its political ideals, institutions, and practices.

Sumner also directly engaged contemporary public policy debates. Believing political science to be of "immediate, practical, and specific importance," Sumner held that his scientific "obligation to truth" required him "to speak fully and boldly in regard to our national affairs at the present moment."[29] His historical research focused on policy areas in which he thought the public most needed to be educated, and he declared in his 1873 lecture: "There is no field of activity which now calls so urgently for the activity of honest and conscientious men as the enlightenment of the American public on the nature and inevitable results of the financial and industrial errors to which they are committed."[30]

---

[25] Francis Lieber, "On History and Political Economy, as Necessary Branches of Superior Education in Free States," in *Miscellaneous Writings of Francis Lieber*, 2 vols., ed. Daniel C. Gilman (Philadelphia: J. B. Lippincott, 1881), 1: 188.

[26] Sumner, "Introductory Lecture," 401–2.

[27] William Graham Sumner, *A History of American Currency* (New York: Holt, 1874), iv.

[28] William Graham Sumner, *History of Banking in the United States* (New York: Journal of Commerce and Commercial Bulletin, 1896). For Sumner's research in this area, see also William Graham Sumner, *The Financier and the Finances of the American Revolution*, 2 vols. (New York: Dodd, Mead, 1891).

[29] Sumner, "Introductory Lecture," 396.

[30] Sumner, "Introductory Lecture," 399.

Like Lieber before him, Sumner thus sought in part a nonacademic audience.[31] He drew on his historical research to write popularly oriented books about American statesman who had been especially prominent in economic policy: Andrew Jackson, Alexander Hamilton, and Robert Morris.[32] And Sumner is best known to posterity for his vigorous promotion of classical liberal ideas and policies in public lectures, newspaper and magazine articles, and most famously of all, his 1883 book *What Social Classes Owe to Each Other.*[33] By the time of that work, Sumner had been at Yale for a decade, during which period his political science had changed significantly in method and substance. It is time to consider the alternate ways in which Sumner and White each departed from their shared wide political science starting point.

Toward a Post-Lieberian "Political Science": White, Sumner, and the Columbia School

Political science as embodied in Sumner's Yale chair when he first took it up was a close cousin of political science as promoted by White as Cornell's founding president. Both were essentially continuous with Lieber's wide political science. From the mid-1870s into the mid-1880s, however, "political science" in America began to accrue post-Lieberian content. Novel departures are first evident in the alternative ways that White and Sumner each reworked their shared inheritance in the 1870s. On one hand, White further stretched the already wide reach of this inheritance as he wed the cause of political science in the academy to the rising agenda of civil service reform in the government. Sumner, by contrast, came to prefer a newer, *narrower* sense of political science that relocated it as a special field on par with political economy, rather than as an encompassing general field. Neither of these departures was idiosyncratic to either figure. To the contrary, each was informed by major developments in European intellectual life in the 1870s, and these were equally available to influence other American academics, as can be seen in the later independent rearticulation of each departure at the Columbia School of Political Science, founded in 1880.

---

[31] The continuity here is especially evident if one compares Lieber's late *Notes on Fallacies Peculiar to American Protectionists, or Chiefly Resorted to America*, published in 1869 by the American Free Trade League, to Sumner's early lectures, given less than a decade later in 1876, to the International Free Trade Alliance. See William Graham Sumner, *Lectures on the History of Protection in the United States* (New York: Putnam's Sons, 1877).

[32] William Graham Sumner, *Andrew Jackson as a Public Man* (Boston: Houghton Mifflin, 1882); William Graham Sumner, *Alexander Hamilton* (New York: Dodd, Mead, 1890); William Graham Sumner, *Robert Morris* (New York: Dodd, Mead, 1892).

[33] William Graham Sumner, *What Social Classes Owe to Each Other* (Caldwell, ID: Caxton, 1989; published first by Harper & Brothers, 1883).

THE AMERICAN RECEPTION OF SCIENCES PO:
FROM WHITE TO THE COLUMBIA SCHOOL

After leading the new Cornell University for a decade, White took leave in 1876 to travel in Europe. During his extended visit White served as US commissioner to the Paris Universal Exposition of 1878. In this official capacity, he prepared a report titled "The Provision for Higher Instruction in Subjects Bearing Directly upon Public Affairs" that surveyed courses in European universities and made recommendations for the United States.[34] White then drew on this report for his early 1879 address "Education in Political Science," which he delivered at the recently opened Johns Hopkins University while he was briefly back in America before his appointment as US minister to Prussia took him to Berlin for most of 1879–1881.

In "Education in Political Science," White elaborated on arguments he had made during Cornell's founding. Again he stressed that instruction in political science served "the interests of State and national legislation." In doing so he added a new temporal emphasis. Using a sweeping developmental framing to suggest that such instruction was becoming ever more essential, White declared: "[M]ore and more, as civilization advances, social and political questions become more complex; more and more the men who are to take part in public affairs need to be trained in the best political thinking of the world." He also invoked a looming threat, which we might relate to the heightening of economic tensions and debates during the persistent depression inaugurated by the crash of 1873. He warned that the time was coming in America, as in Europe, "when disheartened populations will hear brilliant preaching subversive of the whole system of social order." In the face of this threat "the only safeguard" was "provision for the checking of popular unreason, and for the spreading of right reason." Education in political science promised for White, among other things, to help provide just such a safeguard.[35]

White also refined details of the education he advocated. For example, he now explicitly highlighted international law as an area of instruction.[36] Moreover, in titling his address, he gave "political science" an even broader remit than he had when founding Cornell. In the College of History and Political Science he created at Cornell, the part of the college called the School of Political Science had grouped together courses in constitutional law and political economy.[37] In

---

[34] Andrew D. White, "The Provision for Higher Instruction in Subjects Bearing Directly on Public Affairs," in *Reports of the United States Commissioners to the Paris Universal Exposition, 1878*, vol. 2 (Washington, DC: Government Printing Office, 1880), 349–81.

[35] Andrew D. White, *Education in Political Science* (Baltimore: John Murphy, 1879), 44, 7, 34–35.

[36] White, *Education in Political Science*, 17–18.

[37] H. B. Adams, *Study of History*, 134. Adams notes this as the first use of the phrase "School of Political Science" in the American academy.

"Education in Political Science," White's "political science" traversed a family of uses, all wide in that all included political economy, and at times now also expanding to encompass history.

A new transatlantic influence illuminates the widest use of "political science" in White's address. This use had recently received a new institutional embodiment with the founding of the École Libre des Sciences Politiques (hereafter referred to, as it is commonly discussed today, as Sciences Po). Founded in 1872 after French defeat in the Franco-Prussian War and the collapse of the Second Empire, Sciences Po aimed to educate a political and administrative elite for the new Third Republic. It offered advanced education in a wide array of areas: history, public law, administration, political economy and finance, diplomacy, and colonial policy. When White was in Europe during the mid-1870s he visited Sciences Po, and the school received more space than any other in his report, "Provision for Higher Instruction in Subjects Bearing Directly upon Public Affairs." White heralded Sciences Po as "perhaps the most interesting creation of the last 25 years, as regards the preparation of young men for the service of the state," and presented it as a crucial supplement to the political science education earlier available in Paris:

> If in the lecture-room of the College of France, at various visits during the last quarter century, I have admired the impulse given to general political thinking, I have admired not the less in this newly founded school of political science the directness with which the best thought is applied to the immediate needs of the nation.

White accompanied his praise of Sciences Po with attention to how it was able to affect French governance. He stressed specifically the success of its graduates in winning "leading positions under the French Government" via "public competitive examinations."[38]

White's support for exam-based appointment of civil servants had been a prominent part of his political life for some time. In the late 1860s he was already advocating for civil service reform in intra–Republican Party debates on the issue.[39] However, it was only during the 1870s, and in the shadow of European models, that White wove his support for civil service reform into his promotion

---

[38] White, "Provision for Higher Instruction," 356–59.

[39] On White's recurrent promotion of civil-service reform over multiple decades of involvement in Republican Party politics, see White, *Autobiography*, 1: 171, 194–97, 224–28. He also vigorously spelled out his support for this reform as part of the public discussion leading up to the 1883 Pendleton Act. See Andrew D. White, "Do the Spoils Belong to the Victor?" *North American Review* 134, No. 303 (Feb. 1882), 111–33.

of political science in America's academy.[40] In doing he extended the scope of his long-standing liberal argument for education in political science. This education now came to be promoted as improving the views and judgment, not only of students who might later be elected political decision-makers, but also students who could enter government administrative service through competitive exams if these supplanted the spoils system in America's democracy.

American admiration for Sciences Po was not limited to the Francophile White. The Germanophile Columbia professor John W. Burgess also viewed the school as a model in light of which he also tied political science's academic cause to civil service reform.[41] After earning his PhD in Germany, Burgess in 1873 had returned to his alma mater, Amherst, as Professor of History and Political Science, and then moved to Columbia in 1876 as Professor of Political Science, History, and International Law. This appointment was championed by Dwight at the Law School and by trustees seeking someone to inherit the mantle of wide political science left vacated by Lieber's death in 1872. Burgess was ambitious to improve political science's standing at Columbia, and in 1880 would get to do so as he was empowered to found "a school designed to prepare young men for the duties of public life, to be entitled a School of Political Science."[42]

Both the success and substance of this initiative at Columbia drew on Sciences Po as a model. Burgess had learned about the French school in 1878 from a former student studying in Europe, and found its agenda of training civil servants to offer a key to promoting institutional changes aiding political science. Presenting his plans to Columbia's President Barnard, Burgess interwove an expansion of political science with predictions about national civil service reform:

It seems evident to me that the time has now fairly arrived both in the history of this nation and of this University, when a decisive step forward in the development of the political sciences is positively and specially demanded.

In the history of the nation it is so, not only because the Republic has now reached those mighty proportions demanding the finest training, as well as the finest talent, for the successful management of its affairs, but

[40] In arguing that university education of future civil servants encourages greater "excellence" and "efficiency" in administration, White appealed to "the experience of contemporary nations," especially France, but also Germany. White, *Education in Political Science*, 20–24.

[41] My account here of Burgess and the founding of the School of Political Science is based on R. Gordon Hoxie, *A History of the Faculty of Political Science* (New York: Columbia University Press, 1955), chap. 1.

[42] Wording from resolution to found the school proposed May 3, 1880, to Columbia's trustees, as quoted in Hoxie, *Faculty of Political Science*, 15.

because the Government itself has recognized this fact, and in its Civil Service reforms, which, I think, are now fairly planted and destined, under the proper influences to a noble growth, has opened the way for an honorable career to the young men of the nation in the governmental service, which may be successfully pursued by the best intelligence, skill, and fidelity, offering itself without any reference to political influence or patronage.

In the history of the University it is so, not only because it is the bounden duty of a university, worthy of the name to teach all that has been gathered by the world's experience in this as well as other departments of superior knowledge, and to add continually thereto, but because, also of its metropolitan situation, which fits better than any other in the nation, both to place its students in immediate connection with the Civil Service examinations, so far as they now exist, and to exert its influence with greatest efficiency for the extension of the same throughout every branch of that service, as the indispensable condition of appointment to governmental office, and because, I think I may assert, that the foundation is now already fairly laid in our University for the development which I now propose.[43]

As Burgess's initiative was debated among the trustees, its supporters emphasized that a "school of a character similar to this has for several years been in successful operation in Paris."[44] Even before final approval was won, Burgess set sail for France to examine his model in person. He spent two months in Paris discussing Sciences Po with its director Émile Boutmy, and returned again in 1881 and 1882.[45]

Columbia's School of Political Science opened in October 1880 with Burgess as its head. He had three faculty colleagues—Munroe Smith, Clifford Bateman, and Richard Mayo-Smith—who had all previously been his students at Amherst, and who had been in Europe with him that summer. In the new school's name "Political Science" was employed, as at Sciences Po and in White's 1879 "Education in Political Science" address, in a wide sense encompassing multiple areas of study. While not a direct copy, courses at Columbia's School of Political Science bore extensive parallels to their Parisian precursor. They covered the historical development and compared the contemporary character—in Britain, the United

---

[43] Letter from Burgess to Barnard, February 20, 1880, as quoted in Hoxie, *Faculty of Political Science*, 11–12.

[44] Hoxie, *Faculty of Political Science*, 13.

[45] John W. Burgess, *Reminiscences of an American Scholar: The Beginnings of Columbia University* (New York: Columbia University Press, 1934), 189–94, 219.

States, and the major states of continental Europe—of public law, political and administrative institutions, political and social thought, economic institutions and policies, and diplomacy and international law.[46]

FROM WIDE TO NARROW POLITICAL SCIENCE: SUMNER AND THE INFLUENCE OF SOCIOLOGY

In the same year that Sciences Po was established in Paris, Yale offered its new Chair of Political and Social Science to Sumner. As we have noted, he started the post in 1873 as a direct inheritor of the midcentury wide political science of Lieber as diffused by Woolsey. But, by the end of the 1870s, Sumner was breaking from the old wide sense of "political science" to adopt a novel, narrow sense. Just as White's 1870s trajectory showcased a new transatlantic influence, so does Sumner's. His inspiration was the sociology of British classical liberal Herbert Spencer.

Before Sumner became a lightning rod for debate about laissez-faire during the 1880s, he had earlier earned a reputation as a controversial figure due to a conflict with Yale's president Noah Porter in 1879–1881 that garnered national press attention. Porter had supported Sumner's hiring at Yale in the early 1870s, but became disturbed later in the decade as Sumner adapted his teaching to reflect his growing belief in the promise of Spencerian sociology. In an 1881 letter to Yale trustees and faculty, Sumner summed up his side of the conflict as follows:

> I am a professor of political and social science. Four or five years ago my studies led me to the conviction that sociology was about to do for the social sciences what scientific method has done for natural and physical science, viz.: rescue them from arbitrary dogmatism and confusion. It seemed to me that it belonged to me to give my students the advantage of the new standpoint and method just as fast as I could win command of it myself, just as every competent professor aims to set before his students all the speculations, anticipations, efforts, extensions, reconstructions, etc., etc., which mark the growth of the sciences.[47]

The conflict turned on a disagreement about Spencer's recent sociological works. In his early 1870s *Study of Sociology* Spencer argued for a naturalistic science of society; the volumes of his *Descriptive Sociology* offered an inductive foundation for this science with tables of data about societies, from all history

---

[46] From 1880 to 1887 Columbia's new school offered a fixed three-year curriculum of courses that is presented in Hoxie, *Faculty of Political Science*, Appendix A.

[47] Quoted from Starr, *William Graham Sumner*, 358.

and all across the globe; and Spencer presented his conclusions in his *Principles of Sociology*, the first volume of which appeared in 1876.[48] Eager to introduce students to what he saw as a crucial advance in the study of human societies, Sumner retitled his general overview course "Sociology" and beginning in 1879 assigned *Study of Sociology* to Yale students. For Porter, this constituted an unacceptable break from the teaching Sumner was meant to offer in "philosophy of history, and the history of human progress in institutions, art, industry, manners, and morals."[49] Philosophy of history allowed for, or indeed actively saw, God at work in the march of progress. But Spencer approached sociology as a science without any room for a causally active God. To Porter, assigning Spencer's *Study of Sociology* might imply endorsement of this naturalistic standpoint, and threatened thereby, as he complained in a late 1879 personal letter to Sumner, to "bring intellectual and moral harm to the students" and "work serious havoc to the reputation of the college."[50]

For our purposes, what matters particularly about Sumner's embrace of sociology is how it changed his conception of political science. Sociology replaced what Sumner had, at the start of his career, called political science "in its widest sense." He continued to talk of, and write on, political science in a narrow sense, but sociology now became the broader whole that integrated his more specialized studies. Hence in his 1880 "The Theory and Practice of Elections" Sumner presented the "science of politics" as concerned with a particular subset of "those laws of social forces which it is the province of sociology to investigate."[51] This paralleled Spencer, who would publish his "Political Institutions" in 1882 as Part V of his multivolume *Principles of Sociology*. Sumner's reframing limited political science to a narrow sense in which, rather than encompass political economy, the two stood alongside one another as special areas both falling "within the wider scope of sociology."[52]

---

[48] Herbert Spencer, *The Study of Sociology* (New York: Appleton, 1874); Herbert Spencer, *Descriptive Sociology; or, Groups of Sociological Facts, Classified and Arranged by Herbert Spencer*, 8 vols. (London: Williams and Norgate, 1873–81); Herbert Spencer, *Principles of Sociology*, vol. 1 (London: Williams and Norgate, 1876). Spencer's *Principles of Sociology* was published in parts over two decades, being finally completed in 1896.

[49] Porter as quoted by Burton J. Bledstein, "Noah Porter versus William Graham Sumner," *Church History* 43, no. 3 (1974), 348.

[50] Porter as quoted by Starr, *William Graham Sumner*, 347.

[51] "The Theory and Practice of Elections" originally appeared in two parts in *The Princeton Review* in 1880. These were reprinted along with a series of Sumner's other essays from the *Review* as chapters in the volume *Collected Essays in Political and Social Science* (New York: Holt, 1885). I quote here from p. 101 of the 1885 volume.

[52] Sumner located political economy as "the first branch of sociology which was pursued by man as a science" in his 1881 article "Sociology" in *The Princeton Review*, later reprinted in *Collected Essays in Political and Social Science*. For that move and the quoted phrase "within the wider scope of sociology,"

The significance of Sumner's reformulation can be illuminated by returning to the School of Political Science at Columbia. In looking at this school's founding in 1880 we have seen how it was informed by Sciences Po. Indeed, its head Burgess used the plural "political sciences" (as in the French *sciences politiques*) in an 1882 overview titled "The Study of the Political Sciences in Columbia College." When Burgess's faculty founded the journal *Political Science Quarterly* in 1886, its content covered, unsurprisingly, the full array of areas they taught. Yet, at the same time that the journal's title invoked political science in its wide sense, its subtitle discordantly *differentiated* "study of politics, economics, and public law."[53] This move was explicated in the journal's first article, "The Domain of Political Science," by its managing editor, Munroe Smith.

Smith sought here to clarify "political science." He complained that the term was "used vaguely, not by the laity alone but by professed experts" who spoke "sometimes of a 'political science,' at other times of 'political sciences.'" In response Smith advocated "endeavoring to distinguish political science from the so-called political sciences." He preferred "to recognize but one political science" located alongside "the sciences of economics and law" as only one of a set of "particular social sciences." Unlike Sumner, however, while noting that the general domain into which "political science" and "economics" together fell could be called "sociology," Smith himself preferred the plural "social sciences."[54]

Introducing Smith's 1886 article against the backdrop of Sumner's conceptual trajectory in the 1870s serves two purposes. First, we can locate the new narrower sense of political science as part of a broader flux in the relations between fields. The structure of the "social sciences" we are familiar with today developed rather fitfully through the late nineteenth century, and it did so alongside continuing usage of the older conception of a wide political science that encompassed political economy, and discordant blends of both patterns. Such a blend was evident, not only in *Political Science Quarterly* at its 1886 founding, but also a decade later in an organization that Midwestern scholars founded in 1895, the Political Science

see pp. 87–89. Sumner's view as to what political economy might gain from reframing within sociology is interesting. He suggested that, by studying "the industrial organization of society" in abstraction "from the organism of which it forms a part," political economy opened the door to "endless wrangling." Since sociology was an encompassing whole, it could study "the industrial organization in combination with the other organizations of society" and, in doing so, would carry forward "essential elements of political economy" while also rejuvenating them as "corollaries or special cases of sociological principles." Sumner saw, more specifically, the "Malthusian law of population and the Ricardian law of rent" as "cases in which by rare and most admirable acumen powerful thinkers perceived two great laws in particular phases of their action."

[53] The title page of the new journal read "Political Science Quarterly: A Review devoted to the Historical, Statistical, and Comparative Study of Politics, Economics, and Law."

[54] Munroe Smith, "Introduction: The Domain of Political Science," *Political Science Quarterly* 1, no. 1 (1886), 1–5.

Association of the Central States. Even as the name of this short-lived association used political science in an encompassing way, its statement of purpose located "political science" narrowly as one of the four fields—"history, political science, economics and sociology"—together making up the association's remit.[55]

The second point Sumner helps spotlight is the relation between the new narrower sense of political science and the transatlantic reception of sociology. Although Smith's 1886 article preferred "social sciences" over "sociology" as a general label that encompassed narrow political science and other fields, he conceived the overall process of transformative historical change in which he situated his era and its thought in notably sociological terms. Smith spoke of "social evolution" seen as "a constant tendency from the simple to the complex, a constantly increasing differentiation of form and specialization of function."[56] The reception of sociology in America's academy in the closing decades of the nineteenth century is contemporaneous with the rise of a newer, narrower sense of political science. The American Sociological Society (ASS) would be founded in 1905, shortly after the 1903 founding of APSA as a national institutional home for political science conceived as a special professional field distinguishable from economics or history. In situating the ASS and APSA together we see two sides of the American reception of sociological thought, and the working through of its ramifications in the new "social sciences" framework that supplanted the nineteenth-century pattern of what Sumner had initially, back in 1873, called political science "in its widest sense."

In the post–Civil War era, however, the older pattern, inherited from Europe, of political science "in its widest sense" continued to prevail in America. Although there was never exact uniformity in just how far the boundary of wide political science reached, political economy was consistently located as a core area of specialized scholarship *within* it. It is on this once central aspect of a once wide political science that we must concentrate attention if we are to follow how the liberal visions articulated in the domain of political science first moved beyond the classical liberal parameters within which they remained until the late 1870s.

From Divide to Divergence: Liberal Political Economy between the 1860s and 1880s

White and Sumner illustrate a two-stage dynamic in liberal views in political economy espoused during the second generation of wide political science in America.

[55] George W. Knight, "The Political Science Association of the Central States," *Annals of the American Academy of Political and Social Science* 5 (March 1895), 144–45.

[56] Smith, "Domain of Political Science," 5–8.

First, in the 1860s and 1870s, the divide among liberals between moderate and uncompromising interpretations of classical political economy was articulated in connection with contemporary policy debates. In the early 1880s, however, this older *divide* gave way to a new and more fractious *divergence* as one side of the conversation departed beyond the parameters of classical political economy, and in doing so, beyond the classical liberalism that, until that time, had been a common ground of wide political science in the American academy. In particular, the moderate classical liberalism White earlier expounded now gave way to the novel progressive liberal claim that laissez-faire had become entirely outdated. On the other side, Sumner remained wedded to classical political economy in its most uncompromising interpretation, but became increasingly disenchanted as contemporary trends in political economy scholarship and policy departed ever further from the classical liberal principles he championed.[57]

Let us turn to Andrew D. White's most developed work of political economy. In April 1876 the politically well-connected Cornell president read a paper in Washington, DC, to a gathering of US senators and representatives from both parties. Later that year the paper was published as the short book *Paper-Money Inflation in France*. National politics at this time was riled by contention over whether the paper money greenbacks, initially issued by the federal government during exigencies of the Civil War, should be made redeemable in specie, thereby returning the nation to the hard money stance of prewar decades.[58] White deployed his expertise in French history to contend that the introduction of irredeemable paper money during the French Revolution had spurred rampant inflation with disastrous economic and ultimately moral effects. The historical course of these events showcased, White contended, the "natural laws" of political economy, and should teach America to put its own money back on a specie-basis.[59]

---

[57] My narrative of a *divide* followed by a *divergence* relies on giving particular content to the "classical." For me it refers to a set of general policy principles—prominently including hard money, free trade, and laissez-faire—along with assumptions about the content and trajectory of liberal progress that tend to integrate these policy commitments into a set. Different intellectual moves in different countries at different times could each be portrayed in light of this ideal type as departures from the "classical." I locate a departure in which certain American liberals moved beyond the "classical" during the early 1880s. Another political scientist studying the history of political economy for other purposes may treat in the same terms a change in thought in the later context of the Great Depression, as does Mark Blyth in his *Great Transformations: Economic Ideas and Institutional Change in the Twentieth Century* (New York: Cambridge University Press, 2002). Both are possible, and far from incompatible, if classical political economy is conceptualized as an ideal type. What matters is to be clear *which* element of the ideal type is used when narrating a particular intellectual move as a change within, without, or crossing the boundary of, "classical" political economy.

[58] For an overview of the post–Civil War monetary policy debate, see Joseph Dorfman, *The Economic Mind in American Civilization*, vol. 3 (New York: Viking Press, 1949), 3–20.

[59] Andrew D. White, *Paper-Money Inflation in France* (New York: Appleton, 1876).

Advocacy of hard money was one major principle of classical political economy. It was, moreover, a policy on which White agreed with his fellow Yale graduate Sumner. Indeed, White used Sumner's 1874 *History of American Currency* to contend that America was, like any other nation, subject to the same "natural laws" by referencing Sumner's account of how irredeemable paper money produced ruinous consequences at various earlier periods in American history.[60] If we consider only these mid-1870s works, White and Sumner appear to be fighting hand in hand, wielding vivid historical examples to advocate for classical liberal economic policy. In doing so, moreover, they would seem to extend Lieber's uncompromising approach to political economy.

The problem with such a narrative is that it leaps from views on monetary policy alone to a general intellectual characterization. If we look past monetary policy to other pressing issues of their day, we find that White and Sumner were, in fact, on different trajectories in their political economy. They had a common midcentury starting point in uncompromising classical political economy, and this was still evident in their works on monetary policy. But over time their views were becoming increasingly discrepant. This was particularly true with regard to issues of free trade and laissez-faire.[61]

DEBATING FREE TRADE AND LAISSEZ-FAIRE WITHIN CLASSICAL POLITICAL ECONOMY

As midcentury Yale students, White and Sumner both heard their president, Woolsey, propound what White would recall in his *Autobiography* as "the Manchester view" in political economy. White's retrospective use of this

---

[60] White, *Paper-Money Inflation*, 33, 59–64, 67.

[61] To keep my main text as accessible as possible I leave out a nuance notable for scholars of political economy. The "hard money" side in American monetary policy debates in the 1870s had its own internal division between those who held that the specie basis of the currency should be the gold standard, and those open to a bimetallic basis involving gold and silver. This distinction maps well the divide between uncompromising and moderate variants of classical political economy that I unpack in the main text with reference to views on trade and laissez-faire. My exemplar of an uncompromising variant of classical political economy, Sumner, attacked bimetallism as well as any and all forms of soft money. By contrast, White, as my exemplar (at this point in his intellectual evolution) of a moderate classical stance, promoted a specie basis without committing specifically either to the gold standard or to the bimetallic alternative. The policy outcome of the 1870s debates in America was to put the dollar back on a bimetallic specie-basis, as it had been before the Civil War. The dollar was not put upon a purely gold standard until the 1900 Gold Standard Act. The gold standard is thus one example of a hard-money policy position, but other examples were also prominent in the theory and practice of nineteenth-century classical political economy. What examples of a hard-money policy position have in common is anxiety about inflation and thus advocacy of a monetary policy (whatever its specific details) that restrains inflation.

commonly pejorative phrase—first made popular by German critics of classical political economy—reflects the endpoint of a multistage rethinking that led
him, between the early 1860s and mid-1880s, far away from the uncompromising
views in political economy with which he began his career. As a faculty member
at Michigan in the late 1850s White had fought hard against protectionism. But
during the Civil War he began to question his once firm belief that free trade was
universally desirable. His earlier commitment had been intertwined with a belief
that "Great Britain was our best friend," which received a shock when British
elites registered sympathy for the South. White also had to consider the economic
policy turn of the 1861 Morrill Tariff, which, followed by further tariff raises in
1862 and 1864, reversed the low tariff trend of the late 1840s through 1850s to put
America on a firmly protectionist path (and fed some of the British hostility to the
North). After returning from advocating the North's cause in Europe and entering
New York's senate as a Republican in 1863, White came to accept his party's protariff
policy and sought intellectual support for his new stance.[62]

White did not exchange unwavering free trade views for staunch protectionism.
Instead he took a compromise position, acknowledging both sides to have informed
arguments, with the best policy differing for different nations at different times. He
found support in J. S. Mill's granting, in his *Principles of Political Economy*, that protection of infant industries could justify an exception to the general classical liberal
principle of free trade. Additional support was drawn from the midcentury German
economist Roscher, whose "Historical System" White understood as teaching that it
was for "statesmen to determine" how policy lessons of political economy are to be
"adapted to the circumstances of any nation at any time." The position White came to
with the help of these European intellectual influences remained classical liberal in
that it favored free trade as the "ultimate" goal. But it opened up, at the level of means,
to the possibility to accept protection as aiding, or even "the only road" for, countries
to develop industries to a point at which free trade became viable and beneficial in
these sectors of the economy.[63]

White carried this stance into Cornell University. When his 1866 plan of organization proposed a Department of Jurisprudence, Political Science and History,
it favored "large and hearty study and comparison of the views and methods" of

[62] White, *Autobiography*, 1: 29, 269–71, 379–80. On tariff increases of the early 1860s and
their departure from preceding trends, see F. W. Taussig, *The Tariff History of the United States*
(New York: Putnam's, 1888), 155–70.

[63] White, *Autobiography*, 1: 380. For an overview of Roscher's political economy that highlights
the contrast between what Roscher did when first introducing "historical method" into political
economy in midcentury, and how this methodological agenda was transformed and made the basis
for an anticlassical "ethical economy" by later German "historical school" political economists, see
Birger P. Priddat, "Intention and Failure of W. Roscher's Historical Method of National Economics,"
in *The Theory of Ethical Economy in the Historical School*, ed. Peter Kolowski (Berlin: Springer-Verlag,
1995), 15–34.

different thinkers, and it made this pedagogical principle concrete by pairing French free trader Bastiat with the leading American protectionist Carey as political economists whose work should be taught. During his inaugural address at Cornell's 1868 opening, White declared it his goal to "have both the great schools in political economy represented here by their ablest lecturers." He framed this goal as embodying a core commitment that "historical studies and studies in social and political science" at Cornell would "not be pursued in the interest of any party." "On points where honest and earnest men differ," he wished to "have courses of lectures presented on both sides."[64]

White here tied "science" to nonpartisanship, but did so in a manner distinctively suited to one side of the divide among liberals over moderate versus uncompromising interpretations of classical political economy. Whereas White viewed having lectures "on both sides" as a means to avoid partisanship on the tariff issue, such an approach was inimical to Sumner's commitment to uncompromising application of general policy principles of classical political economy. Sumner thought that science called for an embrace of free trade stronger than *either* major political party in America favored. If on this issue the Democratic Party was nearer to the stance Sumner saw science as endorsing, neither party was reliably closer across multiple economic policy domains. As White enacted one conception of nonpartisanship when inviting lectures "on both sides" of the trade issue, so Sumner enacted a different notion when, in the 1876 election, he publicly endorsed the Democratic presidential candidate, Tilden. Although he was, at the time, serving as a Republican alderman in New Haven, Sumner avowed himself "an 'Independent'" who was free, indeed duty-bound, to support whichever presidential candidate appeared more likely to act in ways closer to the uncompromising economic policies he saw science as teaching.[65]

White's equation of science with hearing "both sides" illustrated a form of liberalism that rejected uncompromising economic policy views. Having moved toward this moderate position during the Civil War in regard to free trade, White further pursued its potential in an 1874 speech defending public funding of universities. His starting point was the argument, which we already saw in White's promotion of political science, that higher education serves general public interests. He argued that *"regular and thorough public provision for advanced education,"* in addition to serving *"our highest political interests"* via education in political science and cognate fields, would also promote *"the material prosperity of the nation"*

---

[64] White, *Report of the Committee on Organization*, 5–6; "Inaugural Address," 259–60. The pedagogical principle White appealed to has parallels in Mill. In his University of St. Andrew's inaugural, Mill contended that training students to think "in a scientific spirit" about political issues required teaching "the best speculations on the subject, taken from different points of view." J. S. Mill, "Inaugural Address," 243–44.

[65] William Graham Sumner, "For President?" in *Challenge of Facts*, 365–79.

as scientific and engineering education helped America to compete in the "*indus-trial warfare*" of the international economy.[66]

From a classical liberal perspective, arguing that institutions of advanced education serve general public interests was necessary, but not sufficient, to justify government funding. To meet the burden of the laissez-faire principle, it also had to be argued that these institutions cannot be as well, or even better, developed by civil society acting autonomously. Clearly cognizant of the challenge, White held that "to leave the building up of such institutions entirely to private hands" was "an undue extension of the *laissez-faire* argument." He did not challenge laissez-faire as a general principle. Instead he differentiated a moderate reading of the principle from the strident stance of "those whose whole system of public action consists... in sighing over or screaming at everything supposed to contravene ultra doctrines of non-interference and the ultra *laissez-faire* policy."[67] To support his reading, White invoked Mill's *Principles of Political Economy*:

> The *laissez-faire* argument is good against government provision for those things which private persons may be fairly expected to establish and maintain from expectation of gain; but all history shows that advanced education is not one of those things. The greatest modern apostle of the *laissez-faire* principle—John Stuart Mill—on this and other grounds, especially excludes education, in all its grades, from the operation of the *laissez-faire* principle. He demonstrates that no nation has the right to leave education to the laws of supply and demand, or to the sums dribbled and doled out by ill-considered philanthropy.[68]

In defending public funding of universities as a justified exception to a general principle of laissez-faire, rather than a challenge to the principle itself, White was still arguing in classical liberal terms. The policy stances he charted from the mid-1860s to mid-1870s departed from the "Manchester" political economy of his youth. But his shifts articulated a divide, *within* classical liberalism, between moderate and uncompromising interpretations of how general principles of classical political economy inform the practical choice of specific policies in specific contexts.

The character of this divide is illuminated by differences between White's arguments and the mode and conclusions of Sumner's treatments of trade and the role of government.[69] Sumner wrote with the belief that his uncompromising

---

[66] Andrew D. White, "The Relation of National and State Governments to Advanced Education," *Journal of Social Science* 7 (Sept. 1874), 309–10. Italics in original.

[67] White, "Relation," 311, 316.

[68] White, "Relation," 313.

[69] In identifying this divide and concretely unpacking it through a comparison between White and Sumner I build on its presentation specifically in relation to laissez-faire by Henry C. Adams

classical liberalism had robust scientific authority, and that it was his duty to do all he could to educate an American public ill-informed, or indeed actively misled, with regard to economic policy. Just as Lieber had done previously, so Sumner rejected modes of argument that could allow for practical exceptions to the general principles of classical political economy. His mid-1870s *Lectures on the History of Protection* paralleled the stance of Lieber's 1869 *Fallacies of Protection* by declaring it "a radical absurdity" to "say that a thing is true in theory but bad in practice." Sumner's ire was raised here by precisely the same argument about infant industries on which White had drawn, in looking to Mill for support, in changing his views about trade.[70] The mode of reasoning characteristic of moderate classical liberalism was, for the uncompromising Sumner, an evasion of what he took to be a logically dichotomous and fundamental political choice: "You either want a paternal Government or you want a Government which is merely a reserved force in behalf of peace, justice, and security, and which is at its best when it has the least occasion to act."[71]

Sumner's dismissal of the logical plausibility of practical exceptions to general classical liberal principles provides the philosophical backdrop to the reading of laissez-faire he would famously offer in his *What Social Classes Owe to One Another*. Avowing unapologetically a stance that White had dismissively called "ultra *laissez-faire*," Sumner there declared:

> [W]e are, then, once more back at the old doctrine—*Laissez faire*. Let us translate it into blunt English, and it will read, Mind your own business. It is nothing but the doctrine of liberty. Let every man be happy in his own way. If his sphere of action and interest impinges on that of any other man, there will have to be compromise and adjustment. Wait for

in the 1880s, and the recent secondary reading by Andrew Jewett of contours of post–Civil War debates about political economy in the American academy. See Henry C. Adams, "Relation of the State to Industrial Action," *Publications of the American Economic Association* 1, no. 6 (1887), 14–27; Andrew Jewett, *Science, Democracy, and the American University: From the Civil War to the Cold War* (Cambridge: Cambridge University Press, 2012), chap. 2.

[70] Sumner, *Lectures on the History of Protection*, 37. The objection Sumner stated here in the mid-1870s was more fully expounded later, with explicit reference to Mill, in his 1881 *Princeton Review* essay "The Argument against Protective Taxes." That essay is reprinted in Sumner, *Collected Essays in Political and Social Science*, 58–76.

[71] Sumner, *Lectures on the History of Protection*, 31. The immediate context of this quote is Sumner's expression of admiration for the "good faith" of Hamilton who, rather than seeking a middle ground, followed through "the whole system of interference" as "one consistent theory" entailing a whole set of policies both restricting trade and giving government an expansive role in the domestic economy. Sumner thought Hamilton wrong, but admired his having "treated his subject philosophically" in a way that "logically carried out" principles, and therefore put issues "squarely."

the occasion. Do not attempt to generalize those interferences or to plan for them *a priori*.[72]

Read beside White's 1874 comments on laissez-faire, Sumner's comments show-case the range of interpretations of general principles taught by classical political economy. But so long as the principles themselves were accepted in general terms such alternate interpretations remained within classical liberal parameters.

DEPARTING FROM VERSUS DEFENDING CLASSICAL LIBERALISM

In the early 1880s, however, discussions within the wide political science of America's academy began to push unreservedly *beyond* the parameters of classi-cal liberalism. The turning point came when the midcentury moderate classical liberal conception of a laissez-faire open to practical exceptions gave way to a new progressive liberal argument that rejected the principle itself, on the grounds that it had been superseded by qualitative changes in the economy. Mill had died in 1873, just before the panic of that year was to plunge both sides of the Atlantic into economic hard times. As economic strains lasted into the late 1870s—and, by certain measures, the "Long Depression" in some countries lasted into the mid-1890s—the stage was set for some liberals to seek a postclassical liberalism.

This critical transition can be seen within the thought of White, who did not persist in his moderate classical liberalism of the 1860s and 1870s. Just as White's earlier shift away from the "Manchester" views of his youth was mediated by a combination of specific political shocks and exposure to alternative perspec-tives in political economy, so the second key shift in his political economy also unfolded, around 1880, in a context that combined exposure to surprising events with new ideas. White's service in 1879–1881 as US minister to Prussia gave him a front-row view of a dramatic economic policy reorientation in Germany, the most prominent rising great power of the era. In 1879 Germany broke from its previous free-trade policy to raise tariffs in an unapologetically protectionist fashion. In 1880 the railways in Prussia were nationalized. Then, in 1881, Bismarck proposed the state-mandated social insurance for sickness, workplace injury, and old-age pensions whose enactment later in the 1880s would become a landmark in the

---

[72] Sumner, *What Social Classes Owe*, 104. A fuller consideration of Sumner's interpretation of laissez-faire should consider if he simply clarified the reading stated in *Social Classes* or revised it in a moderate direction in the unpublished fragment that Robert Bannister dated to 1886. See "Laissez-Faire," *Liberty, Society, and Politics*, 227–33. For my narrative what matters is that Sumner was seen at the time as a major intellectual proponent of uncompromising laissez-faire. It is this that made him a primary target during the founding of the American Economics Association.

history of the welfare state.[73] White's own interest in the policy reorientation that was gathering steam while he was in Berlin is suggested by the fact that, as minister, he commissioned a report for the US Department of State on the nationalization of Prussia's railways.

White found both an author for the report and an introduction to newer views in political economy in a young American, Richard T. Ely, who was then pursuing further studies in Berlin after earning his PhD from Heidelberg in 1879 under the historical economist Karl Knies. Ely in his autobiography would later pick out his Heidelberg advisor "more than any other man, as *My Master*," and also gratefully acknowledge "the friendship of Andrew D. White" as "invaluable." Ely attributed the interest that White took in him when they met in Berlin to "the new ideas I had in relation to economics." He recalled White as "greatly pleased to hear" him expound on these ideas, which combined "contempt for the dogmatic English economics" with advocacy of the "fundamentally scientific approach" that Knies had introduced Ely to, "in which relativity and evolution played a large role."[74] Knies's political economy exemplified a newer historicism whose stress on change over continuity facilitated conceiving industrialization as a revolutionary shift. We will show in chapter 5 how this transformative historicist view of industrialization helped Ely to consign laissez-faire to the past as a once useful, but now outdated, principle. White's own shift toward this new progressive liberal political economy is suggested by an 1885 letter that he wrote supporting Ely's effort to found the American Economic Association (AEA) on an anti-laissez-faire platform. Whereas in 1874 White had espoused a moderate interpretation of laissez-faire, his views by 1885 were such that he emphatically declared to Ely: "[T]he *laissez-faire* theory is entirely inadequate to the needs of modern states."[75]

The early to mid-1880s were, in sum, a turning point for the character of the liberalisms articulated among American academic proponents and practitioners of wide political science. A contained divide within classical liberalism gave way to a more fractious divergence between a nascent progressive liberalism and scholars who retained allegiance to general policy principles taught by classical political economy. As moderate liberals, like White, departed from classical liberalism, the

[73] Presenting this as if it were a single policy turn that occurred almost completely in just a few years simplifies a drawn-out back-and-forth process. For my purposes what matters, however, is how the process was perceived by Americans. The sense that a grand turn had been made in Germany was common by the early 1880s, both among Americans who viewed German economic policy departures with sympathetic interest and those who looked on them with dismay.

[74] Richard T. Ely, *Ground under Our Feet: An Autobiography* (New York: Macmillan, 1938), 43–45, 56–63.

[75] Letter dating from 1885 from Andrew D. White to Richard T. Ely, quoted in Richard T. Ely, "Report of the Organization of the American Economic Association," *Publications of the American Economics Association* 1, no. 1 (1886), 9.

interpretation of its principles was left in the hands of their most uncompromising proponents, such as Sumner.

When Sumner began his academic career, his writings on political economy expressed a confidence that the long-term trend of history was, ultimately, in tune with his uncompromising classical liberalism. His *Lectures on the History of Protection*, for example, boldly asserted: "The time will come, in the advance of enlightenment, when men will demand to be allowed to conduct their business in entire freedom." Sumner concluded these lectures by optimistically declaring it "impossible that a system of legislation so shameful and ignorant as our present tariff legislation can long disgrace a free country." The means for advance were at hand in "study of the science of economy, and a more correct adjustment of our arrangements to the laws which it teaches." This adjustment could, moreover, be promoted by the democratized classical liberal means of bringing individuals together to "meet and discuss" and thereby "gain and propagate sound ideas." Sumner believed at this time that, as a "sound and true doctrine," free trade could, if "fairly and plainly taught," persuade enough of the American public to bring about the policy change he both prescribed and predicted.[76]

However, the years following the 1877 publication of Sumner's *Lectures* showed no sign of the policy shift he advocated for. Instead of America turning to free trade, Germany joined the protectionist path America had been on since the 1860s. Sumner appears to have been caught off guard by Germany's policy reorientation, as indicated by an abrupt shift in his judgments about that nation's economists. His antiprotection *Lectures* had brusquely dismissed as "utterly unjust and untrue" the belief that German economists offered intellectual support for a protective tariff. Even as he recognized that German scholars held "every variety of opinion, from extreme willingness to entrust the state with judgment in the application of economical prescriptions to the greatest conservatism in that regard," Sumner had sweepingly declared that it was "not true that any of them are protectionists."[77] After the 1879 German tariff rise, Sumner abruptly shifted his claims. When he returned to antiprotection writing in an 1881 article his targets prominently now came to include the view "cultivated now by the learned protectionists of Germany," whom Sumner charged with producing "some of the most remarkable curiosities of economic literature which have ever been produced either by the learned or the unlearned."[78]

---

[76] Sumner, *Lectures on the History of Protection*, 57, 64, 52. Sumner served on the executive committee of the Society for Political Education, which described itself as "organized by citizens who believe that the success of our methods of government depends on the active political influence of educated intelligence." Quoted from the back material of pamphlet on recommended readings, *Political Economy and Political Science*, compiled by W. G. Sumner, David A. Wells, W. E. Foster, R. I. Dugdale, and G. H. Putnam (New York: Society for Political Education, 1881).

[77] Sumner, *Lectures on the History of Protection*, 7.

[78] Sumner, "Argument against Protective Taxes," 59.

The redirection of Sumner's ire became especially clear in his late 1882 "Wages" article. At the start of his career he had understood political economy to be a science with settled general principles, and took as his main task in public writing and speaking to teach the American people these classical liberal principles and their uncompromising policy applications. Sumner's later recognition that economists were, in fact, increasingly at odds with one another complicated his public education agenda. In the rising belief of fellow scholars "that political economy is going through a transition phase," Sumner saw an ominous indicator that "those who call themselves economists are busy in turning economic science to scorn." His disenchantment led him to worry that "conflicting and baseless notions" had achieved "standing in the science," and to charge that political economy was therefore failing to be a "progressive science." What it needed to get back on track was "competent criticism" of newer ideas. Sumner confessed that "for some years the writers of the new school imposed on me not a little by their airs of confidence and superiority." But now he had decided to make pugnacious public criticism of other scholars a key plank of his own writings.

> The men of the new school have scarcely met with any contradiction for the last ten years. They have had things all their own way. The effects of their teachings are to be met with in newspaper and popular writings. I am, however, one of those who believe that all of this activity of the new school has been in the way of confusion and mischief.[79]

In highlighting "the last ten years" Sumner called attention to the decade since 1872. For readers with a transatlantic awareness of recent intellectual trends, 1872 might have stood out as the year in which a coalition of German academic political economists convened the conference on "the social question" that led, in turn, to their 1873 founding of the Verein für Sozialpolitik. This organizing effort helped give new public prominence in Germany to criticisms of classical liberal political economy and associated efforts to formulate and promote policies that aimed to directly improve the condition of the industrial working classes.[80] These German scholars—who during the 1870s came to be known as the "socialists of the chair"—were an obvious target of Sumner's argument that there was "no 'social question'" and his assault on the "socialist and semi-socialist teaching" telling laborers "not to avail themselves by their own energy of the chances which

---

[79] Sumner's "Wages" was first published in the *Princeton Review* in November 1882 and then reprinted in his 1885 *Collected Essays in Political and Social Science*. Quotes are from the 1885 volume, pp. 36–38.

[80] On this organizing move in Germany see Erik Grimmer-Solem, *The Rise of Historical Economics and Social Reform in Germany, 1864–1894* (Oxford: Clarendon Press, 2003), chap. 5.

are open to them, but to stay where they are and expect somebody else to make them happy there."[81]

Even as Sumner trained his sights on this German scholarly movement, it was gaining a more favorable hearing elsewhere in the American academy. In fall 1881 the German-trained Ely was hired onto the faculty of the young John Hopkins University, while his friend White returned from Germany to again take up the reins of Cornell. White invited Ely to present at Cornell the lectures on socialism he was giving at Hopkins, and encouraged Ely to turn them into a book, which Ely published in 1883 as *French and German Socialism in Modern Times* and dedicated to White. Ely's chapter "Socialism of the Chair" presented policy departures in Germany as reflecting the power of new ideas. He characterized Bismarck as a convert who had intellectually broken free from classical liberal political economy to chart innovative policies informed by the advice of German scholars associated with the Verein.[82]

The interactions of Americans with German scholarship and policy thus set a stage for conflict in America's own academy. In late 1882 Sumner's "Wages" fired a first shot in the American version of what Ely's soon-to-be PhD student, Woodrow Wilson, would call a "war among the political economists."[83] In chapter 5, after first introducing the Hopkins context in which Ely educated Wilson and others, we will recount how this transatlantic intellectual war informed the 1885 founding of the AEA.

[81] Sumner, "Wages," 56, 43.

[82] Richard T. Ely, *French and German Socialism in Modern Times* (New York: Harper, 1883), chap. 15. Grimmer-Solem's penetrating historical study of the *Verein* highlights intellectual differences—specifically between Adolph Wagner's state socialism and Gustav Schmoller's social liberalism—among its members that make any one-to-one mapping onto Bismarck's policies too simplistic. Grimmer-Solem, *Rise of Historical Economics*, chaps. 5–6. What matters for my study, however, is not the complexities of the scholarship-policy nexus as it existed in Germany, but how that nexus was perceived in American debates. Figures like Sumner and Ely overlapped in the simplicity of the nexus they perceived even as they disagreed over whether to assault or praise its substance.

[83] Woodrow Wilson, "Of the Study of Politics," *New Princeton Review* 3, no. 2 (1887), 188. The transatlantic parallels in this war can be seen by observing that Sumner took his first shots at the "new school" among German political economists and its American offspring, just as the famous *Methodenstreit* in German-language scholarship was about to be sparked by Carl Menger's criticism of that school in a methodological work published in 1883. For a recent English-language translation, see Carl Menger, *Investigations into the Method of the Social Sciences with Special Reference to Economics*, trans. Francis J. Nock (New York: New York University Press, 1985).

CHAPTER 5

Historical and Political Science at the Johns Hopkins University

HISTORICIST SCIENCE, LIBERALISM, AND THE FOUNDING OF NATIONAL ASSOCIATIONS

The American university as we know it today is multifaceted. It houses, at the same time, undergraduates taking courses structured by their choice of major, aspiring civil servants in professional programs, PhD students being initiated into the rigors and rituals of specialized research, and faculty writing for and editing journals that publish such research. None of these activities was part of the antebellum American college. All were initiated in the American setting by the reforming university movement of the post–Civil War decades.

In his canonical survey *The Emergence of the American University*, Laurence Veysey synthesized the many changes in American higher education during this era in terms of the ideals informing various conceptions of the university.[1] Andrew D. White and Cornell exemplified for Veysey the ideal of utility. In the previous chapter we saw White extol the political benefits of giving political science a prominent place in the nascent American university. In this chapter we turn to the Johns Hopkins University, which innovatively prioritized PhD over undergraduate education when it opened in 1876. Hopkins embodied for Veysey a second ideal of the university movement: the ideal of research. During its youthful heyday, from the late 1870s through the 1880s, Hopkins pioneered multiple features of America's academy that we still spotlight today when we speak

---

[1] Laurence R. Veysey, *The Emergence of the American University* (Chicago: University of Chicago Press, 1965), Part I. The ideals of utility and research discussed in this paragraph are presented in chapters 2 and 3 of Veysey's study. In chapter 1 he presents the ideals of discipline and piety that informed the antebellum college, and in chapter 4 he presents an additional ideal, the ideal of liberal culture, found within the university movement. This ideal especially affected reforms of student living arrangements.

specifically of *research* universities. It set the pace for a surge in American production of PhDs and academic research in the 1880s. By the 1890s, however, Hopkins was in financial disarray and its best practices copied elsewhere. It had spread the research ideal, but was then supplanted as a center of research by Harvard and other schools.[2]

I show in this chapter how the place of Hopkins at the research frontier of wide political science in the 1880s supported the articulation and diffusion of progressive liberalism as a new liberal vision. By examining the multiple currents of historicist science brought together in the intellectual hothouse of Hopkins's department of historical and political science, I highlight the way in which the methodological difference between developmental and a new transformative historicism informed the political difference between democratized classical liberalism and the new progressive liberal vision. These differences were not sources of conflict in the department. Rather cooperation between its leading faculty, Herbert Baxter Adams and Richard T. Ely—who stood on either side of these interwoven differences—suggests, as did the friendship of Ely with Andrew D. White in the prior chapter, that the 1880s transition between democratized classical liberalism and progressive liberalism was facilitated by friendly relations connecting the older liberal vision to one of its late-century successors.

When conflict flared it arose specifically between the nascent progressive liberalism and the disenchanted classical liberalism that competed with it as an alternative successor to midcentury democratized classical liberalism. Such conflict started, as we have seen, expressly in political economy in the early 1880s. In the second half of this chapter I argue that this conflict illuminates why the mid-1880s founding of the American Historical Association (AHA) and the American Economic Association (AEA) contrasted so notably in tenor, with charged tensions in and about the AEA a world apart from the consensual AHA founding. Both associations were created—with central roles played, respectively, by H. B. Adams and Ely of Hopkins—to bring academics and nonacademics together in meetings to promote research, and diffuse publicly useful lessons of it, in areas of scholarly specialization understood at the time to be closely allied with, or aspects of, political science in its then prevalent wide science. But the contentiousness of the first years of the AEA was the proverbial canary in the gold mine of wide political science. It showcased the onset of conflict between

---

[2] Hugh Hawkins, *Pioneer: A History of the Johns Hopkins University, 1874–1889* (Ithaca, NY: Cornell University Press, 1960). On the supplanting of Hopkins, see also Veysey, *Emergence*, 164–65, 174–76. The dynamic here was highlighted by Charles W. Eliot, Harvard's reforming president from 1869 into the early twentieth century, when he spoke at the twenty-fifth anniversary of Hopkins. Eliot generously declared: "I want to testify that the graduate school of Harvard University, started feebly in 1870 and 1871, did not thrive, until the example of Johns Hopkins forced our faculty to put their strength into the development of instruction for graduates." Quoted in Hawkins, *Pioneer*, 77.

divergent late-century liberal visions that was raging in political economy. Pairing the founding of the AHA and the AEA spotlights where within wide political science, when, and how, the synthesis of historicist science and classical liberalism that Lieber had advanced in midcentury first came apart.

The Hopkins Department of Historical and Political Science

The new Hopkins played a pivotal role in the development of political science in the American academy. Continuing a path earlier identified with Cornell's White and Columbia's Burgess, Hopkins's department of historical and political science brought wide political science into the emerging American university.[3] But, whereas wide political science at Cornell primarily informed a reformed undergraduate education, and at Columbia's School of Political Science (initially at least) it was tied to a mission of educating potential civil servants, at Hopkins it shaped the training of PhDs.[4] Here I examine the Hopkins department in its heyday. I survey its transatlantic intellectual inheritances, explicate and compare the historicist science and liberal visions of H. B. Adams and Ely, under whom it blossomed in the 1880s, and examine the influence of these faculty on PhD students as seen in the case of Albert Shaw.

The founding president of the Johns Hopkins University was Daniel Coit Gilman. He had been a student at Yale in the early 1850s, where he was taught wide political science by Woolsey and became friends with Andrew D. White. Fellow members of Yale's famous Skull and Bones society, Gilman and White traveled together for a considerable part of the time they each spent in Europe

---

[3] The phrase "historical and political science" prevailed at Hopkins up through the 1880s, but later gave way to talk of the "Department of History, Politics, and Economics," as used in *Herbert B. Adams: Tributes of Friends, with a Bibliography of the Department of History, Politics and Economics, 1876–1901* (Baltimore, MD: Johns Hopkins Press, 1902). The later phrasing suggests proto-disciplinary distinctions sharper than had existed in the department's 1880s heyday. In the opening years of the twentieth century this shift received institutional recognition in the forming of departments of political science and economics independent of history. See John C. French, *A History of the University Founded by Johns Hopkins* (Baltimore: Johns Hopkins Press, 1946), 48–49. At the head of the new political science department was Westel W. Willoughby, who soon thereafter helped found the American Political Science Association (APSA) as similarly autonomous of the AHA.

[4] Looking ahead to the early-twentieth-century founding of the APSA we see the import of Hopkins's training of PhDs dramatically among early APSA presidents. The majority of APSA's first ten presidents had legal, but not PhD, training. Of the four PhDs, one had been earned in Germany at Freiburg University (by Albert Bushnell Hart of Harvard). The other three were *all* from Hopkins. Albert Shaw, Woodrow Wilson, and W. W. Willoughby had each trained in the Hopkins's department of historical and political science.

in the mid-1850s, and remained friends long thereafter. As White had at Cornell, Gilman strove to give wide political science a home at the new Hopkins. But whereas White led and taught in Cornell's College of History and Political Science, Gilman preferred the model of a nonteaching president devoted fully to his administrative work.[5] He thus had to find others to take the lead in building the department he envisioned "for the education of publicists, with history, political economy, &c, as leading subjects."[6]

Gilman's initial efforts had only limited success. He looked first to Francis A. Walker, who had won a national reputation when superintending the 1870 federal census, and since 1872 had been Professor of Political Economy in Yale's Sheffield Scientific School.[7] Walker declined the invitation but did assist Gilman on a visiting basis, giving lectures at Hopkins in 1877–1879. History was also taught at first only on a visiting basis. Once a week Austin Scott traveled from Washington, DC, to lead the "Historical Seminary" at Hopkins. Under his guidance from 1876 to 1881, the seminary taught the critical use of primary sources with materials from the formative period of the US Constitution.[8]

Historical and political science began to blossom as a department at Hopkins beginning in 1881, when H. B. Adams took over the seminary (after which point it came to be known as the Historical and Political Science Seminary) and Ely joined the faculty. Because the department lagged developments elsewhere at Hopkins, it was able to replicate research-promoting strategies already advanced by faculty in other departments, who had founded specialized journals such as the *American Journal of Mathematics* in 1878, and founded the Modern Language Association in 1883. With such strategies on hand to extend, the ambitious young Adams and Ely were able to rapidly build a vibrant department and give it national-level academic prominence.

---

[5] While Gilman did not teach, he did pursue limited scholarly activities that highlighted his commitment to wide political science. He served as president of the Hopkins Historical and Political Science Association, founded in December 1877. The association's once-monthly public meetings brought together graduate students and faculty from across the university, and Baltimore lawyers, with shared interest in wide political science. At early association meetings Gilman presented on Woolsey and Lieber, and he also edited Lieber's *Miscellaneous Writings*. On the association and its early meetings, see Herbert Baxter Adams, "New Methods of Study in History," *Johns Hopkins University Studies in Historical and Political Science* 2, nos. 1–2 (1884), 131–36.

[6] Gilman as quoted in Hawkins, *Pioneer*, 55.

[7] On Walker and his contributions as a political economist see Joseph Dorfman, *The Economic Mind in American Civilization*, vol. 3, *1865–1918* (New York: Viking, 1949), 101–10. The faculty spot at the Sheffield School that Walker occupied had been opened up when Gilman himself left that school in 1872 after he failed in his ambition to be appointed Yale's president following Woolsey's retirement in 1871.

[8] On Scott's seminar, see H. B. Adams, "New Methods," 97–100.

TRANSATLANTIC HISTORICIST INHERITANCES

The department that Adams and Ely built was intellectually rich in the depth and breadth of its transatlantic engagement across several currents in wide political science informed by historicist conceptions of science and research practices. Adams and Ely had each followed the established transatlantic path from American colleges—Adams graduated from Amherst in 1872, and Ely from Columbia in 1876—to further studies in Europe. Both had earned PhDs in the *Staatswissenschaften* at Heidelberg University, while also spending time at the University of Berlin. Adams earned his PhD in 1876 under Bluntschli, just as the latter's *Lehre vom modernen Stat* was being published, with the historical economist Knies also serving on his examination committee. Adams then returned to America to enter Hopkins that fall as a postdoctoral fellow aspiring "to become a professor of historical and political science."[9] Two years later he began teaching classes, and he became the lead figure in the historical and political science department when he took over seminary instruction in 1881, the same year Ely was hired to teach political economy. Ely, as previously noted, had earned his doctorate under Knies in 1879, and also had Bluntschli on his examination committee. Bluntschli died soon after his American students were brought together at Hopkins, but his legacy was rounded out posthumously as German citizens of Baltimore purchased his personal library for the university. On its arrival it almost doubled the size of the library Adams was organizing for the historical and political science department.[10]

The heritage of the Hopkins department reached beyond Heidelberg. Adams's interest in historicist political science had been kindled as a student at Amherst, where he (like Columbia's Burgess before him) studied Lieber under the college's president, Julius Seelye.[11] Admiration for Lieber also provided a tie between Adams and Hopkins's President Gilman, whom Adams helped to edit Lieber's *Miscellaneous Writings*, published in 1881.[12] Lieber's papers were soon donated to Hopkins by his widow, and arrived in early 1884 to fanfare noted by Woodrow Wilson, then a first-year graduate student in the department.[13] Adams celebrated the collecting together of the publications and papers of Lieber and Bluntschli by

[9] Adams stated this career aim in his Hopkins fellowship application. Quoted in Raymond J. Cunningham, "The German Historical World of Herbert Baxter Adams: 1874–1876," *Journal of American History* 68, no. 2 (1981), 271.

[10] H. B. Adams, "New Methods," 109–110.

[11] Dorothy Ross, *The Origins of American Social Science* (Cambridge: Cambridge University Press, 1991), 68.

[12] Francis Lieber, *The Miscellaneous Writings of Francis Lieber*, 2 vols., ed. Daniel C. Gilman (Philadelphia: Lippincott, 1881).

[13] Woodrow Wilson, "Newsletter from Johns Hopkins," in *The Papers of Woodrow Wilson*, ed. Arthur S. Link, vol. 3 (Princeton, NJ: Princeton University Press, 1967), 124.

housing this "most cherished part" of his department's library in a special case under a bust of Lieber and a portrait of Bluntschli.[14]

Alongside its Bluntschli-Lieber legacy the Hopkins department also drew upon British developmental historicist scholars like Arnold, Maine, and Freeman. Adams viewed the "science of institutional history" as a "modern growth" that began in Germany, and then inspired a "new school of English historians," with both currents now inspiring Americans.[15] The British legacy was personalized when Freeman, coiner of the phrase "comparative politics," visited Hopkins in 1881 and endorsed Adams's efforts. That endorsement took published form when Freeman wrote a glowing introduction for the opening issue of the journal *Johns Hopkins University Studies in Historical and Political Science,* which Adams founded in 1882. Adams had Freeman's motto "History is past Politics and Politics present History" emblazoned on the wall of his seminary room and the title page of every issue of *Studies in Historical and Political Science.*[16] He would later summarize, in a letter to Gilman, his transatlantic view of his intellectual commitments and department in the following terms:

> What I really represent in this University is the practical union of History and Politics. That combination is the main strength of my department. The spirit of my work and of our University Studies in History and Politics has been commended in this country and in Germany because it illustrates precisely that blending of historical and political science which Bluntschli and Lieber, Arnold and Freeman regarded as inseparable. The term "Institutional History" or "Historical Politics" fairly expresses the spirit of the motto printed upon our University Studies and Seminary Wall.[17]

[14] H. B. Adams, "New Methods," 111–12.

[15] Herbert Baxter Adams, "Saxon Tithingmen in America," *Johns Hopkins University Studies in Historical and Political Science* 1, no. 4 (1883), 17, and "Norman Constables in America," *Johns Hopkins University Studies in Historical and Political Science* 1, no. 8 (1883), 4. Adams saw the reception of this legacy at Hopkins as part of a broader American reception, also encompassing work by Henry Adams and Oliver Wendell Holmes. See Henry Adams, Henry Cabot Lodge, Ernest Young, and J. Laurence Laughlin, *Essays in Anglo-Saxon Law* (Boston: Little, Brown, 1876); Oliver Wendell Holmes, *The Common Law* (Boston: Little, Brown, 1881).

[16] Edward Freeman, "An Introduction to American Institutional History," *Johns Hopkins University Studies in Historical and Political Science* 1, no. 1 (1882), 13–39. After Adams died in 1901 his successors as editors of the *Studies* quickly dropped Freeman's motto from its title page, symbolizing in doing so the ending of the predisciplinary perspective of Adams's wide political science.

[17] Letter from Adams to Gilman, December 19, 1890. Quoted in Dorothy Ross, "On the Misunderstanding of Ranke and the Origins of the Historical Profession in America," in *Leopold von Ranke and the Shaping of the Historical Discipline,* ed. Georg G. Iggers and James M. Powell (Syracuse, NY: Syracuse University Press, 1990), 158.

When surveying the "union of History and Politics" at Hopkins in the 1880s we should also recall that the then-prevalent wide sense of political science included political economy. As editor of Lieber's *Miscellaneous Writings*, Gilman placed the pro-free trade work "Fallacies of Protection" among "Contributions to Political Science."[18] Adams likewise carried the wide sense into his leadership of the Hopkins department. He explained that his Historical and Political Science Seminary taught graduate students "to investigate in a systematic way...Institutional or Economic History," and that he sought, in doing so, to foster "a generation of economists and practical historians, who realize that History is past Politics and Politics present History."[19] The Hopkins department that blossomed in the 1880s was, in sum, indebted to and engaged across multiple currents in wide political science that had developed as scholars had applied historicist conceptions of science and research practices, first to political and legal institutions, and later to political economy.

HERBERT BAXTER ADAMS: DEVELOPMENTAL HISTORICISM AS A SCIENTIFIC RESEARCH PROGRAM

The Hopkins department strove to do more than transmit ideas. Adams wanted to jump-start American production of research that would make internationally recognized contributions to historicist science. He saw opportunities in bringing research agendas developed in Europe to bear on the "vast tracts of American Institutional and Economic History," which lay "almost as unbroken as were once the forests of America, her coal measures and prairies, her mines of iron, silver, and gold."[20] Just as the application of technologies that had been pioneered in Europe to American natural resources was helping fuel the industrial expansion raising America to a new position in the international economy, so the application of historicist techniques to American experience held out the promise of advancing America to a new international position in wide political science scholarship.

Adams first honed this research strategy during his postdoctoral years, while participating in Scott's seminary at Hopkins on the formation of the US Constitution. Adams's research was informed by a theory of the state that he drew from Bluntschli and other recent German scholars, whom he cited to support the position that

> Political Science no longer defends the Social Contract as the basis of government. The best writers of our day reject those atomistic theories

---

[18] Lieber, *Miscellaneous Writings*, vol. 2.

[19] Herbert Baxter Adams, "Cooperation in University Work," *Johns Hopkins University Studies in Historical and Political Science* 1, no. 2 (1882), 47–49.

[20] H. B. Adams, "Cooperation," 51.

of State that would derive national sovereignty from compact, or arithmetical majorities, and not from the commonwealth, or the solidarity of public interest.

Government is derived from the living necessities and united interests of a people. The State does not rest upon compact or written constitutions. There is something more fundamental than delegated powers or chartered sovereignty. The State is grounded upon that continuity of material interests which arises from the *permanent* relation of a people to some fixed territory.[21]

Adams's theoretical position spotlighted an opening for research. "Although a free and sovereign people is undoubtedly the animating life of the American Republic, yet that life has a *material basis* of which writers on American constitutional history have taken too little cognizance."[22] Adams argued that, after the War of Independence ended, the American colonies were no longer united by "external pressure." Their interests remained intertwined, however, due to their claims on lands west of the original colonies, and revenues from sales of those lands. The material basis for permanent political union was secured when, during the 1780s, the individual colonies ceded their land claims to the United States. This created "a truly national sovereignty" exercised "on the grandest scale" in the 1787 Northwest Ordinance *before* the national Constitution went into force. Constitutional ratification in 1789 had not created America's national state. Rather it had constitutionalized a national state that already existed in actual political practice.[23]

---

[21] Herbert Baxter Adams, "Maryland's Influence upon Land Cessions to the United States," *Johns Hopkins University Studies in Historical and Political Science* 3, no. 1 (1885), 49. Italics in original. The paper had first appeared in 1877 under the aegis of the Maryland Historical Society.

[22] H. B. Adams, "Maryland's Influence," 50–51. Italics in original.

[23] H. B. Adams, "Maryland's Influence," 40–49. This research led Adams to document "the vast extent of Washington's landed interests." He proudly held that, in his work, these interests were "for the first time brought into systematic shape and historic connection." Interpreting this finding as refining rather than threatening the usual veneration of Washington, Adams held: "Public spirit and private enterprise are the leading traits of the American people. This dualism of character constitutes the healthful vigor of our state life. The coexistence in George Washington of the most earnest zeal for the public good and the most active spirit of business enterprise, is but the prototype of the life of our nation." Herbert Baxter Adams, "Washington's Interest in Western Lands," *Johns Hopkins University Studies in Historical and Political Science* 3, no. 1 (1885), 74–75. While landownership was the core of Adams's material interests research, he also attended to capital investment, especially in company stocks. His study of Washington's land interests was paired with a study of Washington's investment in a company seeking to build a transportation link to the western lands. Herbert Baxter Adams, "Washington's Interest in the Potomac Company," *Johns Hopkins University Studies in Historical and Political Science* 3, no. 1 (1885), 79–91.

Adams next applied this approach on the local level in his home region of New England. The intellectual backdrop to this research was the American Whig view—famously reiterated by Tocqueville in *Democracy in America*—that celebrated New England's self-governing towns as the seedbed of democratic governance in America.[24] Adams warmly endorsed the received belief that "these little communes" had been "the germs of our state and national life."[25] But he saw an opportunity to rework the older view in a new scientific manner by researching the early history of landholding in Plymouth, Salem, and other towns. In "territorial history" he saw a key with which to unlock "the material foundations upon which the town rests as an abiding institution."[26]

Adams's research documented the extent, and expounded the significance, of communal landholding and control over agricultural practices in early New England. Plymouth had been, Adams argued, settled "upon communal principles of the strictest character." Likewise, in Salem, the "communal spirit" had been "implanted and fostered" by "acquisition and administration of common land."[27] Subsequently, as the population and economy grew, the common lands were largely divided into individual landholdings, with this shift essential to "economic evolution."[28] But institutions used to manage common lands outlasted the division of those lands to become the admired institutions of township self-government. Adams extended this admiration even as he advanced his new material account of "the *genesis* of the town."[29]

When studying New England towns Adams drew on the latest historicist scholarship in order to place his primary source-based economic-political reconstruction of town histories in comparative perspective. His history of Salem's shift from communal to individual landholding was presented as, in effect, a case study of a general process Sir Henry Maine had found at work in the history of property across multiple times and places. Drawing on Maine's studies and authority enabled Adams to interpret historical events in Salem as embodying the "natural and underlying laws" earlier seen in the "economic history of Old Rome."[30] In her

---

[24] Adams later documented a key influence on Tocqueville's view of New England towns by publishing a report on the topic that Jared Sparks, later president of Harvard, prepared for Tocqueville. Herbert Baxter Adams, "Jared Sparks and Alexis de Tocqueville," *Johns Hopkins University Studies in Historical and Political Science* 16, no. 12 (1898), 1–49.

[25] Herbert Baxter Adams, "The Germanic Origin of New England Towns," *Johns Hopkins University Studies in Historical and Political Science* 1, no. 2 (1882), 5.

[26] Herbert Baxter Adams, "Village Communities of Cape Anne and Salem," *Johns Hopkins University Studies in Historical and Political Science* 1, nos. 9–10 (1883), 29–30.

[27] H. B. Adams, "Germanic Origin," 33; "Village Communities," 64.

[28] H. B. Adams, "Village Communities," 64–77.

[29] H. B. Adams, "Germanic Origin," 8. Italics in original.

[30] H. B. Adams, "Village Communities," 64. "Village Communities" in Adams's article title echoes Maine's 1876 *Village-Communities in the East and West*, which Adams assigned to students at Hopkins while pursuing his New England research. On Adams's use of Maine, see Adams, "New Methods," 101.

book on Maine, Karuna Mantena has shown that studies of the move from communal to private property were a lightning rod in European debates on property at this time, with thinkers interpreting this shift in politically competing ways.[31] By interpreting historical changes in property in Salem as essential to economic advance, and implemented by well-timed reforms enacted in a framework of stable institutions, Adams extended the blend of developmental historicist science with classical liberal substance exemplified in Maine.

Adams's use of comparative perspective relied not only on a law of economic evolution, but also, even more centrally, on transatlantic inheritances. He used his findings about communal landholding and agrarian practices as evidence that "town institutions were propagated in New England by old English and German ideas, brought over by Pilgrims and Puritans." To support this claim Adams compared his New England findings with details of Tacitus's classical account of ancient Germans, and recent Teutonist histories of ancient Germany and medieval England. He interpreted the parallels that he saw as the products of historical inheritance. In the Dark Ages "the village community system and agrarian customs" had been brought with the Saxons "from ancient Germany to the eastern part of England," and from England it had, centuries later, been "transferred across another and broader sea" to take "root in the eastern parts of New England."[32] These links across oceans and centuries led Adams to his grand conclusion that "a vast and wide-ranging commonwealth... of law and customs, of race and kinship" extended "under the dividing sea of Revolutionary History itself, uniting the New World inseparably with the Old."[33]

As envisioned by Adams, this transatlantic Teutonic commonwealth was largely a blank canvas whose details he invited future researchers to flesh out. He did, however, venture some broader brushstrokes of economic and political substance. On the economic side, "[T]he Yankee disposition to truck and trade, to hunt and fish, was inherited from a nation [England] of traders and adventurers, and by them from their Germanic forefathers." The economic history of New England was thus a history in which the "spirit of Saxon and Norman enterprise dawned upon New England from shores beyond the ocean," with "English capital, and the spirit of corporate association for economic purposes" combined with

---

Although H. B. Adams drew on Maine in thinking in these terms, the basic framework of this view of historical changes in property had long been part of the classical liberal tradition. Lieber, for example, had earlier identified it as a "law of mankind exhibited by the course of history" that "[w]ith every onward step which culture makes, some land, until then held in common, as waste land, huge forests, or common pasture, is parceled out to private ownership, in order to receive the fertilizing culture of private industry." Francis Lieber, *Essays on Property and Labor* (New York: Harper & Brothers, 1841), 153.

[31] Karuna Mantena, *Alibis of Empire: Henry Maine and the Ends of Liberal Imperialism* (Princeton, NJ: Princeton University Press, 2010), 127–37.

[32] H. B. Adams, "Germanic Origins," 8, 23.

[33] H. B. Adams, "Germanic Origins," 38.

the labor of those who faced "a struggle for existence" that demanded their "patient industry."[34] In politics, Adams celebrated the "sturdy growth of popular institutions" and "the sovereignty of the people." He therefore outlined the transatlantic history "of the great Teutonic race" as a democratized classical liberal narrative of "germs of liberty" developing into the "tree of liberty."[35]

By embedding America in a transatlantic narrative with democratized classical liberal contours, Adams carried forward a major feature of Lieber's antebellum political science. But by extending the temporal and cross-national scope of inheritances he portrayed a "Teutonic" liberty older and broader than the "Anglican Liberty" of Lieber's *Civil Liberty and Self-Government*. In his 1853 work, Lieber had elaborately expounded the view that core American institutions grew from ideas and practices brought over by English settlers, but also rejected tying this "Anglican liberty" further back to the ancient Teutons.[36] While Lieber thus ran a line of contrast along the English Channel, Adams instead invited Americans to see their nation, not simply as a "newer England across the Atlantic," but also a "younger Germany."[37] In doing so he extended a recent upsurge of Teutonist scholarship in both Germany and Britain.

Although Adams would have seen the shift from Lieber's Anglican liberty to his Teutonic narrative as a scientific advance, the change might be viewed as much, if not more, as a product of the way that dramatic political events of the 1860s had remade the transatlantic imagination of democratized classical liberals. The North's hard-won victory in America's Civil War had been heralded on both sides of the Atlantic as validating democracy and was, as such, connected to suffrage expansions that followed rapidly on its heels in both Germany and Britain.[38] The Civil War hence appeared as starting a transatlantic leap forward for

---

[34] H. B. Adams, "Village Communities," 66, 4. Adams recurrently spoke in evolutionary language about the "struggle for existence," the process of "natural selection" it spurred, and the resulting "survival of the fittest." For an economic example regarding transportation improvements, see Herbert Baxter Adams, "Origin of the Baltimore and Ohio Railroad," *Johns Hopkins University Studies in Historical and Political Science* 3, no. 1 (1885), 100. On selection of the fittest as a dynamic of representative government and higher education at their best, see Herbert Baxter Adams, *The College of William and Mary: A Contribution to the History of Higher Education, with Suggestions for its National Promotion*, Circulars of Information of the Bureau of Education, no. 1 (Washington, DC: Government Printing Office, 1887), 69.

[35] Adams, "Germanic Origins," 33, 23.

[36] Francis Lieber, *On Civil Liberty and Self-Government*, ed. Theodore D. Woolsey, 3rd ed. (Philadelphia: Lippincott, 1874), 53.

[37] H. B. Adams, "Germanic Origins," 11.

[38] To talk of "Germany" in this period is to talk about a moving target. Universal male suffrage was introduced by the 1867 constitution of the new North German Confederation for elections to its national parliament, the Reichstag. Subsequently, after Prussia's victory in the 1870 Franco-Prussian War, the new German Empire was founded in 1871. While it encompassed more territory, its constitution was largely carried over from the constitution of the prior North German Confederation, including universal suffrage in Reichstag elections.

democracy continued in 1867 as universal manhood suffrage was introduced for parliamentary elections in the new North German Confederation (founded following Prussia's 1866 defeat of Austria) and the Second Reform Act extended suffrage in Britain into the working classes for the first time.[39] Adams was in his late teens when broad suffrage, as pioneered in antebellum America, was introduced to Germany and Britain. In the 1870s he studied in the new German empire, and then returned to apply the cutting edge of its, and British, historicist scholarship to American materials. If he looked to inheritances on a millennial scale as the basis of a transatlantic Teutonic commonwealth, in weaving together America, Britain, and Germany Adams also refracted their apparent political convergence in the post–Civil War years. The basic outline of Adams's transatlantic narrative of New England towns had been laid down in 1877,[40] *before* economic policy shifts in Germany deflated the post–Civil War confidence of democratized classical liberals that the world was moving toward their ideal. Adams's connecting of America with both Britain and Germany should, I suggest, be seen as a product of the same fleeting transatlantic moment in which a youthful William Graham Sumner could assert in 1872 "that in the three leading nations [Germany, Britain, and America] of the present time, the amount of liberty is equal."[41]

[39] It is perhaps worth stressing that it is not my purpose to endorse *or* reject the interpretation of events of this period as victories for "democracy." For example, while it was widely believed in Britain at the time that the 1867 Reform Act ushered in democracy, from the perspective of how that concept is often used in political science today it did not because the suffrage remained far from universal. Similarly, Germany in this period is often seen today as having had only some forms, not the substance, of democracy. We might see in shifting conceptions of democracy over time within political science a telling register of changes in the character of the liberal visions it articulates. Thus, when in chapter 8 we see A. Lawrence Lowell arguing in the mid-1890s that the German political system was not, and never had been, properly democratic, I will treat this, not as a step of intellectual "progress" toward how political scientists today use the concept and interpret Bismarckian Germany, but as an expression of the disillusioned classical liberalism taking shape in the last decades of the nineteenth century, and which stood in contrast to, and competition with, a progressive liberalism that was far more sympathetic toward Germany. Lowell's characterization was, at the time, criticized by the older scholar Burgess for failing to do justice to how democratic the "true spirit of the German revolution of 1866" had been. This criticism reflected, on my reading, Burgess's own earlier intellectual formation during the era of the post–Civil War democratized classical liberalism enthusiasm I am flagging here. See John W. Burgess, "Review of *Government and Parties in Continental Europe* by A. Lawrence Lowell," *Political Science Quarterly* 12, no. 1 (1897), 161–63.

[40] On the genesis of H. B. Adams's New England research agenda, see "New Methods," 103. By the end of 1877 he had developed his ideas enough to present at the inaugural December 17 meeting of the Hopkins Historical and Political Science Association (on the association see n. 6 in this chapter) "The Village Communities of Ancient Germany and Medieval England: An Introduction to the Study of New England Towns and the Institutions of Local Self-Government in America." Adams, "New Methods," 134.

[41] William Graham Sumner, "Solidarity of the Human Race," in *On Liberty, Society, and Politics: The Essential Essays of William Graham Sumner*, ed. Robert C. Bannister (Indianapolis, IN: Liberty Fund, 1992), 32.

RICHARD T. ELY: TRANSFORMATIVE HISTORICISM, INDUSTRIAL SOCIETY, AND PROGRESSIVE LIBERALISM

Adams's developmental weaving together of past and present was not the only mode of historicism practiced in the Hopkins department of historical and political science. Ely was just as wedded to the basic historicist idea that studies of the economic and political present must put them in historical perspective. But Ely was a few years younger than Adams and had forged his own mode of historicist science while studying in Germany in 1877–1880, just as that ascending nation was dramatically turning its economic policy away from classical liberal teachings. When Ely historicized the present, this move had a different character and consequence. Whereas Adams sought inheritances and recurrences to bind past and present in a narrative of centuries-spanning continuity and development, Ely contrasted past and present in a narrative of transformation that centered on contemporary changes in the economy. Ely's distinctively transformative historicism provided, in turn, the intellectual basis upon which he set aside as historically superseded central principles of classical political economy, and articulated instead a new progressive liberal vision.

Ely's transformative historicism is exemplified in "The Past and the Present of Political Economy," published in *Studies in Historical and Political Science* in early 1884. This manifesto for "the Historical School" articulated a combative contrast that Ely had imported from German debates involving the Verein für Sozialpolitik. That contrast tied the method, policy, and national origin of political economists together in simplified portraits of two competing "schools"—the English ("Manchester") versus the German ("Historical"). Ely ascribed to each school a method—deductive (a priori) versus inductive—and argued that differences in method underwrote differences in policy conclusions. Deduction from general premises was held to lead the "English school" to laissez-faire, while induction led the "German school" to avoid any such "*doctrinaire* extremes" in favor of basing policy on an extensive gathering of facts from "experience," with prescriptions expected to vary across times and places.[42]

The mode of historicism employed by Ely requires careful unpacking. His transformative historicism comes to fore, not in his conception of English and German "schools,"[43] but when he employs his contrast between them to structure

---

[42] Richard T. Ely, "The Past and the Present of Political Economy," *Johns Hopkins University Studies in Historical and Political Science* 2, no. 3 (1884), 5–64. Italics in original. Ely lays out his deductive versus inductive starting point on pp. 7–9, and proceeds from this to his portrait of the English school on pp. 9–23, and the Historical School on pp. 43–60. On the use of this polemical contrast among German scholars of political economy and its intertwining with debates in and around the Verein für Sozialpolitik, see Erik Grimmer-Solem, *The Rise of Historical Economics and Social Reform in Germany, 1864–1894* (Oxford: Clarendon Press, 2003), chap. 1.

[43] Even though Ely's contrast of schools promoted the "Historical School," it was itself articulated in an essentially deductive manner. Ely ascribed to each school a simplified premise about method,

claims about intellectual advance. Ely introduced his English versus German contrast as a contrast between "the older school" and "the newer school." This temporal contrast was then characterized as a competitive dynamic in which the "historical school" had been "continually gaining ground." Ely presented the "historical school" as having first "carried the day" in Germany, as now coming to the fore in English scholarship, and on the rise in the American academy as "younger men" abandoned "the dry bones of orthodox English political economy for the live methods of the German school." As Ely's phrases "dry" and "live" suggest, his framing of an "entire change in the spirit of political economy" relied on organic and evolutionary metaphors to portray this change as a scientific advance achieved via international intellectual exchange and competition.[44]

Ely's transformative historicism was more than a way to approach intellectual change in political economy. It also structured a general account of contemporary economic transformation that subsumed these intellectual shifts. In "The Past and the Present" Ely looked to changes in the economy to suggest how English classical political economy "broke down as a scientific system and as a political guide." The "older school" broke down, he argued, as it was found to have "nothing to say when industrial progress and new economic formations brought to the front fresh problems for solution."[45] Ely assumed that economic change is and should be accompanied by change in economic thought, and this premise linked his studies of thought in and beyond the academy to his belief that the contemporary economy was in the midst of a transformation. Ely's endeavor to remake political economy in America's academy was tied to his beliefs that his own era was "one in which the evolution of society is proceeding with more than its usual rapidity," and that the "true economist is a guide who always keeps in advance, who marks out new paths of social progress."[46]

The centerpiece of Ely's view of his late-nineteenth-century present was his interpretation of industrialization as fundamentally transformative. He spoke of "the industrial revolution" and skipped over the early history of American industrialization to portray this revolution as occurring so recently in America that he could illustrate it with changes since his childhood (he was born in 1854), and

and took each premise as a given from which he reasoned to other features of a portrait that was, in effect, an ideal type. It is, as a result, easy to find examples that do not fit either of Ely's portraits, such as Sumner's blend of uncompromising laissez-faire views with methodological celebration of induction from historical experience. Identifying such exceptions is a problem to the extent we assume—as both Ely and Sumner alike tended to in treating classical political economy—that concepts and theories should be approached as if they are intended to be applied in practice across all empirical cases without any qualifications.

[44] Ely, "Past and Present," 5–6, 62–64.

[45] Ely, "Past and Present," 23.

[46] Richard T. Ely, "Political Economy in America," *North American Review* 144, no. 363 (February 1887), 115–16.

document it with statistics about economic trends from 1870 to the mid-1880s. At the same time that Ely's view of industrialization located America's present in contrast to its past, it situated that present comparatively as exemplifying economic shifts that he held to be advancing in parallel on both sides of the Atlantic. He presented contemporary changes in the American economy, including prominently the "concentration of business" and creation of "trusts," as illustrating "general features of industrial society... very similar in all modern countries."[47]

In treating "industrial society" as part and parcel of modernity, Ely built on the classical liberal celebration of economic growth, while historically relativizing, and thereby casting aside as outdated, much of the policy content of classical political economy. We can see this move in Ely's adaptation of the four-stage model of socioeconomic development—(1) hunting-gathering, (2) shepherding, (3) agricultural, (4) commercial—used by classical political economists from the Scottish Enlightenment through J. S. Mill. Rather than interpret industrialization as part of the commercial stage, as Mill had done, Ely set it apart from the commercial stage as a new fifth stage. Whereas classical liberals treated "commercial society" as the leading edge and agent of the modern, Ely relocated it to the past, where it functioned as a historical contrast against which the late-nineteenth-century industrial present was to be interpreted as new and reformed accordingly. For Ely, "modern economic life" began properly only with "the industrial revolution"—which he located in his own day, and saw as giving rise to "industrial society," whose "new and heretofore unknown conditions" required "new laws, new institutions, and new ideals in legislation."[48]

Ely's progressive liberal interpretation of contemporary America as an industrial society deployed a sense of contrast far different from the sense of continuity H. B. Adams used to locate America in a democratized classical liberal Teutonic commonwealth developed over centuries. At Hopkins historicist research in wide political science was, to use a metaphor, a coin that came up continuity when Adams flipped it and contrast when Ely flipped it. It was, however, the same coin. Adams and Ely agreed that scientific research situates political and economic phenomena historically. Moreover, even as the details of their transatlantic comparisons differed, both tied America to Germany, the other rising great power of the day.

In sum, the historicist practices and liberal visions alternately articulated by Adams and Ely were more complementary than competitive in the 1880s context of the Hopkins department of historical and political science. The success of Adams and Ely in working together suggests, like the White-Ely friendship introduced earlier, that the 1880s transition between democratized classical liberalism

---

[47] Richard, T. Ely, *An Introduction to Political Economy* (New York: Chautauqua Press, 1889), 55–61.
[48] Ely, *Introduction to Political Economy*, 40–50, 61.

and progressive liberalism was marked by friendly interaction that facilitated the new liberal vision's advance. Students in the Hopkins department did not find in Adams and Ely two conflicting approaches between which they had to choose. They were free to work with both. Yet this cooperative environment makes it only more telling that it was Ely who tended to leave a more lasting intellectual imprint on students.

ALBERT SHAW: THE INFLUENCE OF HOPKINS

Although Woodrow Wilson is the most famous political scientist trained at Hopkins, his classmate, Albert Shaw, who would later become the American Political Science Association's second president, lies at the opposite pole of relative obscurity. He slightly preceded Wilson at Hopkins, and the two became friends while both were students in the department during 1883–1884. The discrepancy in their retrospective recognition among political scientists today is largely due to the fame that Wilson accrued in his later political career. But it may also reflect the fact that Shaw never became a professor. He was, and chose to remain, a media man. His time at Hopkins in the spring term of 1882 and the 1883–1884 academic year was squeezed into respites in his newspaper work. While he was offered and seriously considered academic posts, Shaw's career path was settled in 1890–1891 when he turned down a Cornell chair in political and municipal institutions to become the founding editor of an American edition of the *Review of Reviews*, a successful Progressive Era magazine that would be under his stewardship for over four decades.[49] I examine Shaw's mid-1880s works here in order to showcase how he was influenced by his studies under Adams and Ely. Doing so closes this section's sketch of the intellectual character of the Hopkins department in its heyday, and also sets a stage for chapter 7's recounting of its impact on the more famous Wilson.

Shaw brought to Hopkins a journalist's ability to write quickly and engagingly. This soon combined with the intellectual stimulation he received there to produce notable results. During his first semester in spring 1882 Shaw studied extensively with Adams, writing two papers that were published within a year. The first drew on Tocqueville and on Adams's research to portray Illinois local governments as "transplanted scions from older growths of Anglo-Saxon communal life." This developmental historicist framing was, as usual, combined with a veneration of "local self-government" as "the training-school for popular rule and representative institutions." Shaw heartily pronounced that the "township

---

[49] Lloyd J. Graybar, *Albert Shaw of the "Review of Reviews": An Intellectual Biography* (Lexington: University Press of Kentucky, 1974). Shaw pondered his decision about the Cornell chair in 1890 letter exchanges with Wilson. See *Papers of Woodrow Wilson*, vol. 6 (1969), 640–41, vol. 7 (1969), 62–63, 71–74.

system, Old England's best gift to the nation, has always been the groundwork and basis of democracy in America." [50] The paper pleased Adams so much that he published it in *Studies in Historical and Political Science* in the issue following the one in which the first of Adams's articles on New England local government appeared.

If Shaw's first paper illustrates the impact of Adams's research, the second testifies to the broader reach of Adams as a teacher. Entitled "The Growth of Internationalism," this paper was written for Adams's course International Law, which was, as Wilson observed when taking it soon thereafter, "really a history of international relations."[51] In the paper Shaw again deployed "[t]hat great contribution of our time to legal and political science, the historical and comparative method," applying it now to the "processes of development" shaping "international institutions" and "international organization." Sketching selected events from the Thirty Years War up to the treaties, diplomatic congresses, and international law societies of the 1870s, Shaw portrayed a set of trends, at varied stages of fulfillment, toward codification of international law, an international judiciary, and ultimately, an international legislative body. In doing so he sought to show that a liberal confidence "that the world is making strong and tangible progress toward union, law, and perpetual peace" rested "not alone upon sentiments of benevolent optimism, but also upon the facts of history and society."[52]

The Hopkins influence of greatest importance for Shaw, however, was Ely, who recruited Shaw into his endeavor to remake political economy. If Shaw's 1883 articles exemplified the developmental historicism of Adams, his next works showed Shaw becoming, as he later put it, a "confirmed Elyite."[53] Shaw studied political economy with Ely during spring 1882 and then developed his dissertation from field research he did in 1883 to assist Ely's *French and German Socialism in Modern Times*. Ely asked Shaw, who was in Iowa at the time working for a newspaper,

---

[50] Albert Shaw, "Local Government in Illinois," *Johns Hopkins University Studies in Historical and Political Science* 1, no. 3 (January 1883), 3, 19.

[51] *Papers of Woodrow Wilson*, vol. 2 (1967), 448. For H. B. Adams's own overview of his "instruction upon the Historical Development of International Law," see "New Methods," 48–49.

[52] Albert Shaw, "The Growth of Internationalism," *International Review* 14 (April 1883), 267–83. Shaw's interest in, and liberal hopes for, international relations would persist in his later thought and actions. In response to an 1899 request from Adams, he gave Hopkins funds to establish the Albert Shaw Lectures on Diplomatic History. Graybar, *Albert Shaw*, 196. Shaw's liberal faith in progress toward peace through international organization would resonate again as, with World War I coming to a close, he edited *President Wilson's State Papers and Addresses*, and in his introduction declared of his Hopkins friend: "His sentences and paragraphs, in their discussion of world affairs, have helped to crystallize the vague longings of right-thinking men in all nations into something like definite policies for permanent peace on the basis of democracy and international justice." Albert Shaw, "Introduction," in *President Wilson's State Papers and Addresses*, ed. Albert Shaw (New York: Doran, 1918).

[53] Quoted in Hawkins, *Pioneer*, 181.

to visit an agricultural commune founded by followers of the French thinker Étienne Cabet.[54] Ely then included Shaw's long letter describing the community in his book.[55] Extending this research, Shaw wrote his dissertation on communes founded by Cabet's followers in Texas, Iowa, and California. Finished in 1884, it was published that year as *Icaria: A Chapter in the History of Communism*. Just as Ely saw it as the goal of his 1883 book "to give a perfectly fair, impartial presentation of modern communism and socialism in their two strongholds, France and Germany," so Shaw saw himself as striving "scrupulously to avoid all preaching for or against communism." This attitude was, he declared in his preface, essential for a study "conducted in the true historical spirit."[56]

While impartiality was an ideal common to the wide political science of both Adams and Ely, Shaw's book was framed in terms more suggestive of Ely's transformative historicism, with its break between past and present. He presented *Icaria* as the study of a completed "experiment" whose results had proven "feeble and disappointing," and which he interpreted as a phenomenon of the past, not the developmental germ of anything vibrant in the present or with promise for the future.[57] When Ely wrote on "Recent American Socialism" the next year in *Studies in Historical and Political Science*, he would, in turn, rush past the "antiquated" agricultural era in "American communism" with a passing reference to Shaw's book, and focus instead on the "revolutionary socialism" of the late-nineteenth-century industrial present.[58]

Yet Ely was far from a revolutionary socialist, but rather a progressive liberal whose own hopes centered during the mid-1880s on workers cooperatives.[59] Shaw became one of the first of multiple Ely students to research cooperatives.[60] He found his examples in Minneapolis, where he had moved post-PhD to edit the *Tribune* newspaper. He published his results as "Coöperation in a Western City," an 1886 study that Ely would later recall as a "joy to me, for it was not only

[54] Graybar, *Albert Shaw*, 25.

[55] Richard T. Ely, *French and German Socialism in Modern Times* (New York: Harper, 1883), 42–48.

[56] Ely, *French and German Socialism*, prefatory note; Albert Shaw, *Icaria: A Chapter in the History of Communism* (New York: Putnam's, 1884), vi.

[57] Shaw, *Icaria*, preface.

[58] Richard T. Ely, "Recent American Socialism," *Johns Hopkins University Studies in Historical and Political Science* 3, no. 4 (1885), 12, 16.

[59] See Richard T. Ely, *The Labor Movement in America* (New York: Crowell, 1886). On the broader interest in the cooperative movement among young American progressive liberal political economists at this time, see Dorothy Ross, "Socialism and American Liberalism: Academic Social Thought in the 1880s," *Perspectives in American History* 11 (1977–78), 5–80.

[60] The extent of these efforts is shown in the five hundred-plus pages of vol. 6 of *Studies in Historical and Political Science*, which was entirely devoted to research on examples of cooperation around the United States. The 1886 Shaw study I discuss was reprinted there, with added material on cooperatives elsewhere in the Northwest, as "Coöperation in the Northwest," *Johns Hopkins University Studies in Historical and Political Science* 6, no. 4–6 (1888), 195–359.

a good economic monograph, it was literature."[61] The work was set up, like *Icaria*, as a study of an "experiment." But this study was framed in contemporary and forward-looking terms. Shaw saw in cooperation, not simply an experiment, but nascent progress to be furthered for the future by drawing lessons impartially from existing experience. His ideal of impartiality pointed here to a goal of offering "a painstaking and unbiased record" of "facts about coöperative enterprises" that would treat "[u]nsuccessful as well as successful ventures." Shaw thus tempered his introductory comments about the "immediate applicability" and "great remedial virtue" of cooperation with a warning that it was no "panacea for all the present ills of labor." However after almost a hundred pages of presenting facts, Shaw felt able, as he ended his study, to celebrate cooperation as "the most admirable form of self-help because each man is helping his fellows to climb as rapidly as he climbs himself," and to propose that successes by the cooperatives in a city be recognized as a "mark of true progress in that community."[62]

Further developing the potential of applying Ely's progressive liberalism to the world in which he was immersed as a Minneapolis editor, Shaw next studied the activity of Minnesota's legislature in his 1887 "The American State and the American Man." His goal was to question the "view of the comparative prevalence of *laissez-faire* as a practical rule in the United States." Shaw suggested that this view prevailed for two reasons. First, the "average American" lived "in one world of theory and in another world of practice," and observers mistook what Americans thought for what they did. Second, the federal government distracted the attention of observers away from the activity of state and local governments. By flagging these oversights Shaw set up the importance of his own attempt "to describe impartially the legislation of the Northwest." He spotlighted the number and variety of recent Minnesota laws at odds with the "non-interference theory," and extended this argument with supporting examples from other states in the region.[63]

Shaw's descriptive survey of legislative acts was, by itself, politically ambivalent. It was a standard move among disenchanted classical liberals—whose late-century political vision was crystallizing alongside, and competing with, progressive liberalism—to survey recent legislation. But disenchanted classical liberals did so to condemn recent legislative trends and prescribe laissez-faire.[64] Shaw was clearly

---

[61] Richard T. Ely, *Ground under Our Feet: An Autobiography* (New York: Macmillan, 1938), 106.

[62] Albert Shaw, "Coöperation in a Western City," *Publications of the American Economic Association* 1, no. 4 (1886), 10, 106.

[63] Albert Shaw, "The American State and the American Man," *Contemporary Review* 51 (May, 1887), 695–711.

[64] The classic example is Herbert Spencer's 1884 *The Man versus the State*. Herbert Spencer, *The Man versus the State, with Six Essays on Government, Society, and Freedom* (Indianapolis, IN: Liberty Fund, 1992).

aware of this move, and perhaps actively trying to subvert it. After concluding his own survey he stressed that it had "not been made in a spirit of hostility to Government regulation." Yet he did allow that there was a "deplorable tendency to reckless, selfish, and strained employments of the State prerogative." Only after he had hereby positioned himself in a kind of middle ground, did Shaw then criticize laissez-faire prescriptions. He did so, moreover, on their own terms, by provocatively holding that these prescriptions were "to a considerable degree responsible for the reckless and ill-considered applications of the State power." Shaw contended that laissez-faire left legislators "without rudder or compass" in their decision-making since it was "grotesquely foreign to the facts and conditions" of the practical choices they actually had to make. As a "homeopathic" alternative, Shaw suggested, "nothing else could have so wholesome and so restraining an effect upon these Western legislators as a thorough-going conversion to the doctrines which radically oppose the *laissez-faire* school." In terms echoing Ely's manifesto for "the Historical School," Shaw characterized these doctrines as favoring "more careful and scientific law-making" that would draw on insights from "statistical and comparative study" and judge each legislative proposal "on its own merits."[65]

Shaw's criticism of laissez-faire in the name of careful lawmaking is rhetorically adept. Just as worthy of attention is what it takes for granted. Shaw assumes that laissez-faire uniformly favors non-interference, rather than, more moderately, placing the burden of argument on advocates of new government activities, without prejudging where the argument may lead in a given policy area. Shaw, in sum, gives laissez-faire the content it had in Sumner's *What Social Classes Owe to One Another*, rather than in J. S. Mill's *Principles of Political Economy*. The limiting of laissez-faire to only its uncompromising interpretation was a common ground of Sumner, Ely, Shaw, and indeed, most liberal thought since. This delimitation facilitated common agreement that recent legislative trends were at odds with laissez-faire and focused debate onto competing evaluations of those trends. But this common framing of debate elided the possibility of a moderate interpretation of laissez-faire. Figures who, like Shaw, intellectually came of age in the 1880s showed little or no awareness that such an interpretation was possible, even though it had retained active proponents, as we saw in chapter 4, into the mid-1870s.

Founding the AHA and the AEA: Continuities and Controversy in Wide Political Science

I ended Part I with the wide political science articulated in antebellum America by Francis Lieber. In ending Part II with the mid-1880s creation of the AHA and the

---

[65] Shaw, "American State," 710–11.

AEA, I use the founding of these associations to assess how Lieber's combination of democratized classical liberalism and developmental historicism was faring a half a century after he entered America's academy as Professor of History and Political Economy. The associations founded in the mid-1880s promoted scholarship in areas allied to, or indeed branches of, political science in Lieber's wide sense. In this and the prior chapter we have followed the spread and institutionalization of that sense during the post–Civil War development of the American university. I thus work within the conceptual standpoint of the era in treating the founding of the AHA and AEA as events that participated in the wide political science Lieber had advanced in America's academy. This was, for example, how Shaw framed the two associations when in 1888 he located them together as developments in a "movement" giving "the study of political science so remarkable an impetus in this country."[66]

A comparison of the two new associations highlights the contrasting fate of Lieberian standpoints in history and political economy by the mid-1880s. The AHA founding promoted the developmental historicist study of political institutions much as Lieber had pursued it. But the AEA founding highlighted a new political economy pitted in opposition to the classical liberal political economy that we earlier saw Lieber espouse. Pairing the establishment of the AHA and the AEA shows where within wide political science, when, and how, Lieber's synthesis began to fall apart. It broke down first in political economy, and it did so as classical liberal prescriptions and historicist science were reconstructed within this area of scholarship to become competitors, rather than the complements they had been for Lieber.

THE AMERICAN HISTORICAL ASSOCIATION: CONNECTIONS AND CONTINUITY

The founding of the AHA in 1884 drew upon an academic network radiating out from the university leaders and friends Andrew D. White and Daniel Gilman. Gilman proposed White as the association's first president, but the bulk of the organizing labor was done by younger faculty tied to the more senior figures: H. B. Adams (of Gilman's Hopkins), Moses Coit Tyler (of White's Cornell), and Charles Kendall Adams (White's early protégé at Michigan, who became in 1885 his chosen successor as Cornell president). These three issued the call for a convention to

---

[66] Shaw saw this movement as one in which "history and economics have been closely allied,—so closely, indeed, that their teaching and investigation have been inseparably blended," and went on to praise the new AHA and AEA for showing "remarkable vigor" and being "more successful in fostering original and scientific research than the most sanguine of their founders had dared to expect." Albert Shaw, "Introductory," in *The National Revenues: A Collection of Papers by American Economists*, ed. Albert Shaw (Chicago: McClurg, 1888), 28–30.

found the AHA in June 1884, played lead roles in the convention that September, and received posts on the new association's board.[67] Among the three, H. B. Adams stands out especially for his outreach to older centers of historical inquiry, which gave the AHA the character, as much as possible, of a development that built on existing American historical inquiry and supporting institutions.

In reaching beyond the network centered on White, Gilman, and their young universities, Adams moved in two directions. First, he drew upon nonacademic ties he had cultivated (in conjunction with his studies on western lands and New England towns) with historical societies along the Eastern Seaboard. Second, he encouraged figures at America's most venerable home of higher education, Harvard, to join in creating the AHA. The success of his outreach efforts is suggested by the roll call of people involved in the founding: there were around twenty-five to thirty-five attendees at sessions of the founding convention, at the close of which forty members were enrolled in the new AHA. This roster was closely balanced between nonacademics and academics. Among the former, the largest group were representatives of state historical societies. Among the academics three groups stood out: five individuals were current or recent affiliates of Hopkins, five were current or soon-to-be Cornell affiliates, and five were Harvard affiliates. These four groups dominated the first AHA board of officers, holding between them eight of its nine posts, with the last going to a New York newspaperman.[68] Adams's efforts in bringing the groups together probably made him an obvious choice for the organizationally pivotal post of AHA secretary, which he occupied from the association's founding until he died in 1901.

If Adams's outreach testified to his skills as an institution builder, it also expressed his developmental historicist commitments. His scholarship, teaching, and institutional service all stressed "the vital connection between the past and present" as foundational for "the essential idea of history, which is the growing self-knowledge of a living, progressive age."[69] During the AHA founding, he advanced this connection by encouraging his fellow founders to see their association as building progressively

[67] The call was also signed by officers of the American Social Science Association (ASSA), under whose auspices the founding meeting was to be held. Against the objections of these officials, the first step taken in the meeting was a decision to create the AHA as an independent association, rather than a section of the ASSA. The sidelining of the ASSA officials in the AHA founding process is further evident in their absence from the new association's board of officers. For a history of the ASSA and interpretation of the significance of the AHA's founding in relation to it, see Thomas L. Haskell, *The Emergence of Professional Social Science: The American Social Science Association and the Nineteenth-Century Crisis of Authority* (Baltimore, MD: Johns Hopkins University Press, 2000).

[68] Facts about the AHA founding stated here are taken from H. B. Adams, "Secretary's Report of the Organization and Proceedings," *Papers of the American Historical Association* 1, no. 1 (1885), 5–44, supplemented with further details on the activities of Gilman and Adams from Haskell, *Emergence*, 168–72.

[69] H. B. Adams, "Special Methods of Historical Study," *Johns Hopkins University Studies in Historical and Political Science* 2, no. 1 (1884), 22.

on precursors. Making the theme concrete, he recalled that an American Historical Society had been founded in Washington, DC, in 1836 with John Quincy Adams as its president, and noted how the AHA might extend and improve on this precursor.[70]

In linking the AHA to a precursor headed by a storied American statesman, Adams also spoke to the ties that, at this time, bound historical inquiry to wide political science. These were evident in the prevalence among the association's founders of a substantive focus upon political history and a belief in the political utility of such inquiry. Ties between historical scholarship and political life were, moreover, personally embodied in the AHA's first president, White. We saw in chapter 4 how White's academic labors as a professor and university president were interspliced with his activity as a state legislator, advocate of civil service reform in intra–Republican Party debates, and leading American diplomat in Europe. The political utility of historical studies was, moreover, a major theme propounded in White's address at the AHA founding. Looking out upon contemporary American politics, he declared to his fellow founders:

> Not one of us reads the current discussions of public affairs in Congress, in the State Legislatures, or in the newspapers, who does not see that strong and keen as many of these are, a vast deal of valuable light is shut out by ignorance of turning-points in the history of human civilization thus far.

Such ignorance provided White a backdrop against which to reaffirm well-worn liberal beliefs in knowledge and association as agents of political progress. In America's "little band of historical scholars" White saw taking shape "a means for the greater enlightenment of their country and the better development of mankind." By bringing this once "scattered" band into an association "of historical scholars from all parts of the country, stimulating each other to new activity" the AHA would "elicit most valuable work" in history, and in doing so, "contribute powerfully… to the opening up of a better political and social future for the nation at large."[71] The research ideal was here wedded to the ideal of utility, which White had advanced at Cornell almost two decades earlier when helping to launch the university movement and secure wide political science a place in that movement.

In emphasizing political education White reasserted a cherished liberal agenda that had, by now, informed wide political science through some half a century. Continuities in White's address also extended to the persons and practices of historicist science. He argued that political education would be ably served if

[70] Adams, "Organization and Proceedings," 34–35.
[71] Andrew D. White, "Studies in General History and the History of Civilization," *Papers of the American Historical Association* 1, no. 2 (1885), 24, 28.

American scholars looked as a model to Guizot, the statesman-scholar he had admired for over three decades. The title of White's address, "Studies in General History and the History of Civilization," carried echoes of Guizot's *History of Civilization in Europe*, which White had earlier held up in his 1866 plan for Cornell as "[t]he greatest course of lectures ever delivered before an University,—the one which remodeled the science of history, and which is felt to-day in every historical treatise of repute."[72] Guizot modeled, specifically, the combination of "general and special investigation," and, White declared, as "it was in Guizot's case; so it should be in all cases." The "special" work of "critical analysis" of primary sources was crucial, but not alone sufficient, if historical study was to advance liberal political education and progress. The "highest effort and the noblest result" of "special historical investigations" was to inform a "philosophical synthesis of human affairs" offering politically relevant teachings like Guizot's "profound and fruitful generalizations as to the laws governing and consequences flowing from national development in civilization."[73]

Along with his veneration of Guizot, White also noted negative models to avoid. Though philosophical synthesis was needed to correct the "danger of pettiness and triviality" in specialist historical studies, not all philosophy was welcome. White warned fellow AHA founders to be on guard against the "danger of looseness and vagueness" displayed in "Hegel's shadowy results." The methods dispute that, as we saw in chapter 2, flared within historicist science over a half-century earlier at the University of Berlin hence still echoed into the mid-1880s. But White also took up a more contemporary challenge presented to narrative history by sociology. The negative model here was Spencer, whose works, as we saw previously, had recently drawn Sumner away from historicist wide political science toward a naturalistic sociology. Even as he granted that the general collection of social data from across all times and places that Spencer championed might occasionally illuminate, White warned that, if overly relied on, it would undermine political education. Facts and lessons of grave political importance were best taught using vivid historical narratives. To attempt to meet "our ethical necessity for historical knowledge with statistics and tabulated sociology entirely or mainly" would, White dismissively declared, be "like meeting our want of food by the perpetual administration of concentrated essence of beef."[74]

White's AHA address hence marked out a mission—combining primary source analysis, philosophical synthesis, and historical narrative in the service of the liberal political education of American democracy—and differentiated it

---

[72] Andrew D. White, *Report of the Committee on Organization, presented to the Trustees of the Cornell University, October 21st, 1866* (Albany, NY: C. Van Benthuysen & Sons, 1867), 19.

[73] White, "Studies in General History," 6–10.

[74] White, "Studies in General History," 13–22; quote specifically from 18–19.

against intellectual alternatives. This mission was continuous with that which Lieber had pursued. Such continuity was widespread among the founders of the AHA, who carried forward the tradition of developmental historicist study of institutions we have followed from European exemplars across the Atlantic. The common faith of this tradition had been expressed eloquently by White's protégé C. K. Adams in the preface of his *Democracy and Monarchy in France*, where he declared that "every genuine student of history must feel that there is no more potent political truth than this, that the present has its roots running far back into the past, and that it draws its life from the ideas and institutions that have gone before."[75]

The 1884 AHA founding was, in sum, characterized by a consensus on long-established premises and practices. This consensus did not eliminate debate, but focused it onto substantive questions. A spirited discussion during the founding meeting arose, for example, in response to a paper arguing that New England town institutions developed from sixteenth-century English parish institutions. One respondent contended that what was brought across the Atlantic were "not English institutions, but English principles" that only later "entered into and unfolded themselves in" institutions. By contrast, H. B. Adams proposed that parish institutions themselves descended from earlier Germanic institutions.[76] This lively, but contained, discussion puts into clear relief the different tenor of the AEA founding one year later. No substantive papers were given at that 1885 meeting, which was dominated instead by tense discussions about the character of political economy scholarship and the association being founded.

THE AMERICAN ECONOMIC ASSOCIATION: CONTROVERSY, SCIENTIFIC BOUNDARY DRAWING, AND THE STATE

The AEA founding followed closely upon the successful creation of the AHA. The AEA was established during the second AHA meeting in September 1885, with the majority of figures involved being AHA members. The academic network that extended from Hopkins and Cornell was again central. Francis A. Walker, who had taught at Hopkins on a visiting basis in the late 1870s and had since become MIT's president in 1881 and president of the American Statistical Association in 1882, was honored with the AEA presidency. Again the organizing labor was done by younger faculty, including Henry Carter Adams, who had earned the first Hopkins PhD in 1878, then pursued additional studies in Germany, and since

---

[75] Charles Kendall Adams, *Democracy and Monarchy in France: From the Inception of the Great Revolution to the Overthrow of the Second Empire* (New York: Holt, 1874), vii.

[76] H. B. Adams, "Secretary's Report," 23–29.

the early 1880s had taught jointly at Cornell and Michigan.[77] And again, it was a young Hopkins faculty member who led outreach beyond the Hopkins-Cornell network, with Ely playing this role and becoming AEA secretary, as had H. B. Adams for the AHA. Ely's nonacademic outreach centered around his ties to the social gospel movement, and twenty of the fifty AEA members enrolled at its founding were former or current ministers.[78] Inside the academy Ely reached out to other young political economists who had trained in Germany, including Edmund J. James of the University of Pennsylvania, John B. Clark of Smith College, and Edwin R. A. Seligman of the Columbia School of Political Science. Along with Ely, H. C. Adams, and Walker, these men made up the initial board of AEA officers.

There was, however, a major difference between the academic coalition pulled together in the AEA founding and that involved in the AHA. Whereas H. B. Adams tied Harvard's prestige to the AHA by persuading Harvard historians to be a lead group in the new association, Harvard's political economists were notably absent from the AEA founding. They were missing because they, along with Yale faculty, actively boycotted it.[79] Whereas the AHA founding was a decidedly consensual affair, the AEA was founded in an area of scholarship that was in the midst of tense, at times acrimonious, contention over its character and future direction. The new association had potential to be employed to advance one side within that contention. During its founding and first years, the AEA was thus a site of sharp discussion and shifting power plays that spotlighted the recent outbreak of conflict between diverging liberal visions.

In chapter 4 we traced how liberal political economy in the post–Civil War American academy became fractured by politically charged policy shifts and responses to them. The years after Lieber's 1872 death had seen dramatic changes in the global economy, political economy scholarship, and the policy intersections between them, during which the uncompromising mode of classical liberal political economy expounded by Lieber had faltered. Yet no single successor had replaced it. Uncompromising classical liberal policies were still being advocated by

[77] On H. C. Adams see A. W. Coats, "Henry Carter Adams: A Case Study in the Emergence of the Social Sciences in the United States, 1850–1900," *Journal of American Studies* 2, no. 2 (1868), 177–97. To distinguish Henry Carter Adams from Herbert Baxter Adams and Charles Kendall Adams, I refer to them, respectively, as H. C. Adams, H. B. Adams, and C. K. Adams, when "Adams" alone might not be a clear referent.

[78] Mary O. Furner, *Advocacy & Objectivity: A Crisis in the Professionalization of American Social Science, 1865–1905* (Lexington: University Press of Kentucky, 1975), 74. While the AEA enrolled a large group of ministers, unlike the historical society nonacademics in the AHA, none of them received officer positions. The AEA pursued a slightly different organizational model than the AHA. It paired a smaller core set of officers with a larger council, and ministers were given council but not officer positions.

[79] On Harvard's, as well as Yale's, initial boycott of the AEA, see Furner, *Advocacy*, 77–80.

Sumner, but in an increasingly disenchanted manner as he launched his assault on the "new school" he associated with Germany's "socialists of the chair." His 1882 and 1883 publications had helped ignite a conflict, which intensified as Ely joined the fray from the opposing side in 1884 with his combative contrast between "old" and "new" schools in "The Past and the Present of Political Economy." Ely next personalized the alternatives by juxtaposing his own work to Sumner's. The same press had, in 1883, published Ely's *French and German Socialism in Modern Times* and Sumner's *What Social Classes Owe to Each Other*. Ely opened the conclusion of an 1885 article by contrasting the "spirit" in which these two books "treated social problems." Ely characterized the books without naming authors and titles. But few if any people engaged with wide political science in the American academy could have missed that it was Sumner who was being charged with "treating the discontented with irritating impatience and stinging harshness."[80]

The contrast Ely drew between himself and Sumner fed directly into his work organizing the AEA in the following months of 1885. In a May letter to Shaw, his recent PhD student, Ely explained that he was aiming to create a national association that could unite younger political economists against Sumner. Ely continued to flag this anti-Sumner agenda in June letters he wrote inviting non-Hopkins figures, such as Columbia's Seligman, to join him in founding the AEA.[81] While Ely was privately organizing, Shaw was wielding the Ely versus Sumner contrast publicly and polemically. In a July review titled "New Studies in Political and Social Science," Shaw praised Ely's "Recent American Socialism" for being "scrupulously impartial" at the same time that he proclaimed, "*Laissez-faire* politics does not conform with those ethical standards which are an economic requirement of the times; and Dr. Ely advocates a higher and truer view of the State and its functions." After thus extolling Ely, Shaw invoked Sumner as a negative foil:

> Professor Sumner's economic methods are precisely the reverse of Professor Ely's. Two or three years ago it happened that the same publishing house, at about the same time, issued in uniform binding a small book by each of these gentlemen. Dr. Ely's was a painstaking historical presentation of modern European socialism replete with valuable statements of fact and doctrine. Mr. Sumner's book had also to do with social relations; and it was a captious, off-hand essay, containing a great deal of flippant sarcasm at the expense of social reformers and economic scholars of the modern school, and presenting *laissez-faire* doctrines in a balder and cruder form than the most extreme English writer of the Manchester school ever suggested.

[80] Ely, "Recent American Socialism," 70.

[81] On Ely's May 7, 1885, letter to Shaw, see Hawkins, *Pioneer*, 181; on his June 9 and June 23 letters to Seligman, see Furner, *Advocacy*, 69.

Turning next to Sumner's just-published *Collected Essays in Political and Social Science*, Shaw declared that its political economy essays

> have no value as contributions to the science of economics. Mr. Sumner seems to have no conception of political economy as a modern and pro-gressive science.... He has of late contributed nothing whatever to eco-nomic literature excepting dogmatic and sneering depreciation of the work which the scientific students of the new economic school at home and abroad are accomplishing.[82]

The cutting thrusts of Shaw's review testify to the heat of the conflict in political economy in the months immediately preceding the September 1885 meeting that would found the AEA.

The AEA, like the AHA, was founded with twin aims to promote research and to educate public opinion, integrated by a belief that the former activity would serve the latter.[83] But whereas White's AHA presidential address prof-fered well-worn liberal platitudes about diffusing a nonspecified politically use-ful knowledge to a public and political class that lacked it, Ely intended the AEA to take a more combative role in the public sphere. As he saw it, the problem in regard to political economy was less ignorance in the sense of lack of informa-tion, than in the sense that views were being publicly propagated as scientific that he considered fallacious. In his speech opening the AEA founding, Ely declared, "In no other science is there so much quackery," and held that "it must be in our province to expose it and bring it into merited contempt."[84] While he refrained from giving an example of "quackery," since major meeting participants had been told by Ely in private letters that the association would take aim at Sumner, we might assume that, for a significant subset of his audience, Ely's comments called Sumner to mind.

If the AEA was to play a public role bringing some figures, and more partic-ularly a Yale professor, "into merited contempt," the new association needed a more substantive foundation of public commitments than the AHA. Whereas the AHA constitution simply and noncontroversially stated that the association's "object shall be the promotion of historical studies,"[85] Ely drafted a page-long platform of commitments he proposed the AEA adopt. This platform sought a

---

[82] Albert Shaw, "New Studies in Political and Social Science," *The Dial* 6 (July 1885), 72–73.

[83] In his AEA report on the association's organization Ely declares: "This association intends to com-bine two ends. It proposes to influence public opinion; also to investigate and study." Richard T. Ely, "Report of the Organization of the American Economic Association," *Publications of the American Economic Association* 1, no. 1 (1886), 18.

[84] Ely, "Report of the Organization," 15.

[85] The AHA Constitution appears in H. B. Adams, "Secretary's Report," 20.

middle ground between the models of the brief AHA constitution and the constitution proposed for the Society for the Study of the National Economy, which two younger German-trained political economists, Simon Patten and Edmund James, hoped to create. The long platform they had prepared for that society, which they modeled on the Verein für Sozialpolitik, expounded upon economic trends and called for expanded state functions. With his platform Ely sought to get Patten and James onboard as AEA founders, while also securing for the new association broader backing than their proposed society had.[86] But Ely's platform proved controversial, and the statement of principles actually adopted in the AEA's founding constitution was a notably trimmed and tempered revision of what he had proposed. Two components of Ely's platform and the adopted principles warrant attention in light of themes of this book: first, their exclusion of the partisan, and second, the view they took of the state.

In this and the previous chapter we highlighted claims that scientific studies of politically charged topics can and should be "impartial" and transcend the "partisan." While we have seen Sumner himself make this claim in the early 1870s, it was brought into the AEA founding as part of Ely's anti-Sumner agenda. Ely was forthright about the scientific boundary he hoped the AEA would endorse and enforce. In his speech at the association founding Ely held that "fundamental differences between economists are so radical that they cannot all work profitably together," and he proposed to his fellow founders that it was "essential that intelligent men and women should distinguish between us and certain economists in whom there is little faith." The distinction Ely favored would draw a boundary to "scientific work in economics" excluding the "advocates of any political opinion or set of political opinions, as for example, free-trade or protection." Such "advocates" acted in a political "sphere" that, while "legitimate" in its own terms, "lay outside the realm of science."[87] Ely's choice of example perfectly fit Sumner, so prominent in the public discourse of the day as a caustic critic of America's tariffs.

Ely's proposed platform included language that would formally put the authority of the AEA behind the boundary he advocated. As part of its final clause, his platform stated:

> In the study of the policy of government, especially with respect to restrictions on trade and to protection of domestic manufactures, we take no partisan attitude. We are convinced that one of the chief reasons why greater harmony has not been attained, is because economists have been too ready to assert themselves as advocates.[88]

---

[86] Ely, *Ground*, 121–42.

[87] Ely, "Report of the Organization," 19, 5.

[88] Ely, "Report of the Organization," 7.

This treatment of free trade versus protection echoed White's approach in founding Cornell almost two decades earlier. Indeed, when White himself spoke at the AEA founding, he flagged this parallel while more generally endorsing Ely's entire platform. Such unqualified support was, however, unusual. The AEA's actual statement of principles would tone down the style, though not really the substance, of Ely's language in this clause. His negative sentence criticizing "advocates" was cut, while the commitment to nonpartisanship was restated in more general terms in the actually adopted principle: "In the study of the industrial and commercial policy of governments we take no partisan attitude."[89] Formal exclusion of the partisan was without any precedent in the AHA constitution. Its language was soon to be used, as Ely surely intended, to portray Sumner as beyond the boundary of "science." Reviewing Sumner's *Protectionism—the -Ism Which Teaches That Waste Makes Wealth* in December 1885, Ely's trusty swordsman Shaw would declare:

> [T]his book's appearance is fortunate for the cause of political economy in the United States. It has been the misfortune of the science that persons claiming to speak authoritatively in its name have made no other use of it than to drag it perpetually into their exchange of epithets and sarcasms on the tariff question. Professor Sumner has, fortunately, carried the thing so far that everybody can see that he has stepped out of the economic and into the merely partisan sphere.[90]

There was ample historical irony here. Sumner, who had himself set science against the "partisan," did not, of course, see his antiprotection writings as partisan. They were, moreover, not "partisan" in the sense of being written to promote, or with the support of, either major American political party of the day. Finally, the conception of objectivity as ethical neutrality, which would later often be read into scientific exclusion of the partisan, was entirely at odds with the beliefs of Ely, the originator of the "no partisan attitude" AEA language. Indeed, Ely stressed that political economy should, as he put it in 1887, be a "distinctively ethical science."[91] For him, homage to the ethical and hostility to the partisan were complementary, not competing, stances.[92] Both featured in the platform he proposed for

---

[89] Ely, "Report of the Organization," 24, 29–30; "Constitution, By-Laws and Resolutions of the American Economic Association," *Publications of the American Economic Association* 1, no. 1 (1886), 36.

[90] Albert Shaw, "Recent Economic Works," *The Dial* 6 (December 1885), 212.

[91] Ely, "Political Economy in America," 119.

[92] Ely's stance here was not idiosyncratic. Commitment to a political economy that was, at once, "ethical" and not "partisan," was characteristic of leading scholars of the Verein für Sozialpolitik. See, for example, the close account of the stance Gustav Schmoller developed in the 1860s in Grimmer-Solem, *Rise of Historical Economics*, 136–49.

the AEA. Even as the final clause of that platform excluded the "partisan," its first clause embraced a characterization of the state as an "ethical" agent of progress:

> We regard the state as an educational and ethical agency whose positive aid is an indispensable condition of human progress. While we recognize the necessity of individual initiative in industrial life, we hold that the doctrine of *laissez-faire* is unsafe in politics and unsound in morals; and that it suggests an inadequate explanation of the relations between the state and the citizens.[93]

Whereas Ely's nonpartisanship clause elicited only limited discussion and revision during the AEA founding, this clause about laissez-faire was the centerpiece of extensive sharp debate. Rising as the first speaker after Ely's opening speech, H. C. Adams worried that "a formal denial of the claims of laissez-faire might be construed to mean the acceptance of what is popularly known as the German view of social relations." Advancing what would later become a common framing of progressive liberalism as a moderate middle ground, he proposed that the "path" to be sought had to avoid two "equally erroneous" opposing views: on one hand, "the English political philosophy (or what goes by that name) which regards the state as a necessary evil," and "on the other hand, German political philosophy, which presents the state as the final analysis of human relations." Multiple subsequent speakers further challenged Ely's proposed first clause, some from within the nascent progressive liberalism, which Ely and H. C. Adams were each, in their own way, seeking the best formulation of; but others, like Alexander Johnston of Princeton, from the older declining stance of moderate classical liberalism. As discussion of the platform ended, Clark of Smith summarized what had been learned: "the point upon which individuals will be unable to unite is, especially, the strong condemnation of the *laissez-faire* doctrine."[94]

The discussion made it clear that Ely's platform needed revision if the AEA's founders were to reach accord. An initial proposal by Ely's colleague H. B. Adams to address the impasse with a footnote stating that the platform did not bind individual members proved insufficient. The search for resolution was then handed to a small committee, excluding Ely, but including Adams and diverse figures, from Princeton's classical liberal Johnston to the University of Pennsylvania's Verein-admiring James. In trimming and tempering Ely's proposed platform, the committee strove for "a positive rather than a negative statement in every practicable instance."[95]

[93] Ely, "Report of the Organization," 6–7.
[94] Ely, "Report of the Organization," 21–29.
[95] Ely, "Report of the Organization," 29–30.

The revised language the committee crafted was the basis of the statement of principles adopted the next day as Article III of the AEA constitution. The revision process cut the second negative sentence of Ely's first clause, with its explicit rejection of laissez-faire, just as it did the sentence in his final clause criticizing "advocates." Meanwhile, although Ely's "no partisan attitude" phrasing was carried directly into the statement of principles, more substantive changes were made to his language about the state. Whereas Ely's platform declared, "We regard the state as an educational and ethical agency whose positive aid is an indispensable condition of human progress," the AEA statement of principles dropped talk of the "ethical" to begin, "We regard the state as an agency whose positive assistance is one of the indispensable conditions of human progress." A footnote, as H. B. Adams had suggested, was also added to make explicit that "[t]his statement was proposed and accepted as a general indication of the views and the purposes of those who founded the American Economic Association, but is not to be regarded as binding upon individual members."[96]

THE AEA COMPROMISE OF 1887 AND THE BOUNDARY OF "SCIENTIFIC" SCHOLARSHIP

The revision of Ely's platform during the September 1885 AEA founding sufficiently conciliated the tensions among those present to bring the new association into being. But the AEA's character quickly proved to be, as yet, unsettled. Its council included Princeton's Johnston, who had announced at the founding, "He would not care to live in a state of society in which the popular sense of reliance on the true principle of *laissez-faire* was dulled or destroyed."[97] Yet in May 1887, we find the Hopkins PhD Shaw claiming the AEA to be "a new body" that "frankly repudiates *laissez-faire*."[98] This claim may be attributed to the fact that Shaw had not been at the AEA founding and thus had not seen firsthand the mediation that took place there. But it was also in line with the public face Ely had since given the association. As AEA secretary he controlled the *Publications of the American Economic Association*. Its first issues appeared from early 1886 on and consisted in monographs with a clear progressive liberal orientation, including Shaw's "Coöperation in a Western City," as well as "Coöperation in New England" by another Ely student, Edward W. Bemis. Considered beside the sympathetic picture Ely himself offered in an 1886 book, *The Labor Movement in America*, early issues of the *Publications* made it plausible to believe that the AEA was turning out to be a vehicle for the articulation and diffusion of a new progressive liberalism.

[96] "Constitution, By-Laws and Resolutions of the American Economic Association," 35–36.
[97] Ely, "Report of the Organization," 22.
[98] Shaw, "American State," 711.

If Shaw welcomed this outcome, others did not, and it soon became evident that Ely had overplayed his hand. A corrective reaction set in to produce compromise. In June 1887 the AEA council voted to extend a special membership invitation to Harvard's senior political economist, the classical liberal Charles Franklin Dunbar, who accepted and would later become the AEA's second president. Then, in December 1887, the council voted to recommend to the membership removing the statement of principles from the AEA constitution. The details and import of these 1887 moves are compellingly recounted in the core "Compromise" chapter of Furner's *Advocacy & Objectivity*,[99] a classic study whose impact on my own account of the AEA will be obvious to anyone familiar with the intellectual history canon on American social science. The compromise of 1887 would settle the character of the AEA in a way its 1885 founding had failed to.

Two aspects of the 1887 compromise are of special import for us. First is the fate of the formal exclusion of the "partisan" that Ely had promoted as part of his anti-Sumner agenda. The council-recommended removal of the statement of principles—approved by the membership at the December 1888 annual meeting—did not eliminate all traces of that statement. The "no partisan attitude" language drawn from Ely's initial platform proposal was retained, as was the language H. B. Adams had proposed about not committing members. This was accomplished, at the same time the principles were removed, by adding a sentence to the statement of "Objects" of the AEA. The third object—"The encouragement of perfect freedom of economic discussion"—was extended with the following sentence: "The Association, as such, will take no partisan attitude, nor will it commit its members to any position on practical economic questions." Thus, while formal endorsement of the state as an agent of progress was eliminated, exclusion of the "partisan" was retained in the AEA constitution.[100] Later, we shall see this language carried with only minimal alteration into the 1903 founding constitution of the American Political Science Association.

A second crucial aspect of the 1887 compromise is the extent of its base of support. The compromise made the AEA into an association in which classical liberals like Harvard's Dunbar were comfortable. This broadening occurred with support from figures, prominent in the AEA from its founding, whose own scholarship was critical of classical liberal political economy. The AEA's president, Walker, for example, noted in an April 1887 letter to Columbia's Seligman that the statement of principles was a "stumbling block" that "should never have been adopted" and "should be repealed." H. C. Adams, in turn, participated in the outreach to Harvard's Dunbar, who graciously responded in July 1887, "Your own purpose to let nothing stand in the way of making the Association broad enough

---

[99] Furner, *Advocacy*, chap. 5.

[100] "Constitution, By-Laws and Resolutions of the American Economic Association with List of Officers and Members," *Publications of the American Economic Association* 4, Supplement (July 1889), 3.

to include all schools and to save it from being the propaganda of any one is so clear to me as to enlist all my sympathies."[101] The 1887 compromise, therefore, as Furner's classic history established, "represented a renunciation of extremes and a merging of interests from both conservative and revisionist sides, not a conservative victory."[102]

These two thrusts of the 1887 compromise had come to mutually inform one another in 1886 in a series of criticisms of Ely. The scientific boundary drawing that Ely had advocated in organizing the AEA had quickly been turned back against him following the appearance of his *Labor Movement in America*. Published at a time when American elites were frightened by the rapid growth of the Knights of Labor, a large wave of strikes, and the anarchist bomb that killed Chicago policemen dispersing the Haymarket demonstration, Ely's sympathetic treatment of labor leaders and their organizations produced a barrage of criticism. Ely feared the furor would cost him a promotion at Hopkins, and perhaps even his position. His fellow, if more moderate, progressive liberal H. C. Adams saw Ely's problem, however, as a matter less of his politics than of his scholarship. Writing to fellow German-trained AEA founder Clark in late 1886, Adams noted: "To speak frankly... I think it is lack of scholarly analysis, and a tendency to depend too much on exhortation, that stands in the way of Ely's promotion, rather than his view on social questions."[103]

In a telling parallel to the manner in which Ely's student Shaw had applied scientific boundary policing against Sumner, Sumner's Yale junior faculty colleague Henry W. Farnam chastised Ely in the *Political Science Quarterly*. Farnam's December 1886 review of Ely's *Labor Movement* credited the book with giving "a great deal of valuable information," but complained that

> [I]n many of the discussions the author seems to have given the arguments in favor of the various phases of the labor movement from the point of view of those engaged in it, rather than to have supplied an impartial criticism from the point of view of the economist.

Lack of impartiality was tied, in turn, as Ely and Shaw had tied it, to bounding the "scientific." Farnam carefully quoted Ely's contention that the Knights of Labor "was established on truly scientific principles," in order to question Ely's scientific credentials by observing:

---

[101] April 25, 1887, letter from Walker to Seligman, and July 1, 1887, letter from Dunbar to H. C. Adams, as quoted in Furner, *Advocacy & Objectivity*, 116 and 118.

[102] Furner, *Advocacy & Objectivity*, 119.

[103] December 16, 1886, letter from H. C. Adams to Clark quoted from Furner, *Advocacy & Objectivity*, 91. On the furor raised more generally by Ely's book, and the political-economic context in which it arose, see Furner, *Advocacy & Objectivity*, 84–92.

To say that a society is founded on scientific principles is the highest praise that a scientific man can bestow. In view of the killing of engines, the destruction of property, and the virulent persecution of "scabs," which the Knights of Labor were carrying on at the very time which Dr. Ely must have been writing his book, is it unfair to expect him to explain what particular science has lent its principles to the establishment of this order? To many people the Knights of Labor seem to have furnished quite as striking an exhibition of some of the vulgar weaknesses of human nature, such as envy, hatred, and uncharitableness, as of the principles of science.[104]

In sum, just as the linkage between the "scientific" and the "impartial" (or "nonpartisan") drawn by Sumner had come to be used by Shaw to challenge Sumner's own scientific credentials, so in turn had the very same linkage been deployed against Shaw's mentor Ely.

The 1887 compromise that broadened the AEA across the divide between classical and progressive liberalism institutionalized a desire to temper the controversy in political economy. This tempering was aided by the working out of a new sense of the boundary to what, and how, scholars could write if they were to recognize one another as "scientific." In advancing their own liberal visions, Sumner and Ely had each promulgated conceptual connections between science, impartiality, and nonpartisanship. Yet, during the cut and thrust of the mid-1880s, each had then had these connections turned against him. Their conflict decisively reshaped the contours of the "scientific" among scholars of political economy, and in the process, both were relegated to the margins of a field they taught, by negative example, to become wary of entering too forcefully into issues of contemporary political debate.

---

[104] Henry W. Farnam, "Review of *The Labor Movement in America*," *Political Science Quarterly* 1, no. 4 (1886), 684, 685.

LATE-CENTURY LIBERALISMS AND THE NEW POLITICAL SCIENCE

CHAPTER 6

Disenchanted Classical Liberalism as a Political Vision

WILLIAM GRAHAM SUMNER AND A. LAWRENCE LOWELL

From the Chair of Political and Social Science William Graham Sumner took up at Yale in 1873 and Andrew D. White's 1879 "Education in Political Science" address, to the School of Political Science established at Columbia in 1880 and the department of historical and political science that blossomed at Hopkins during the 1880s, "political science" in America's academy retained characteristically European-informed content. That content exemplified the continuing legacies of Francis Lieber's wide political science. Lieber had won the antebellum beachhead in America's academy from which teaching and research in "political science" had advanced during the post–Civil War emergence of the American university. Yet by the time this phrase was used a generation later to name the American Political Science Association (APSA), founded in 1903, it had shed much of its earlier Lieberian content. Part III of this book studies the late-nineteenth-century transformations that gave shape to American political science in the newer and narrower sense institutionalized in the APSA at the dawn of the twentieth century.

One central dynamic of this transformation was the changing character of liberal beliefs, hopes, and fears among American political scientists in the last two decades of the century. The midcentury democratized classical liberalism in which I situated Lieber's wide political science had fractured to give way to two competing late-century successors: progressive liberalism and disenchanted classical liberalism. More specifically, as we saw during Part II, the once broad support for principles of classical political economy had been ruptured by contrasting responses to transatlantic shifts in policy and scholarship in political economy. As the divergence that had first came to the fore in political economy subsequently diffused throughout other areas of wide political science, its political content was fleshed out into competing liberal visions that advanced alternative analyses of mass suffrage political systems. By late century such systems had come to Europe as well as America, and transatlantic comparisons provided a concrete medium via which disenchanted classical liberal and progressive liberal political analyses were each developed.

I structure Part III around these alternative liberal analyses of mass suffrage political systems. This chapter examines the political vision of disenchanted classical liberalism. The next chapter explores the alternative political vision of progressive liberalism as articulated in works that Woodrow Wilson wrote as a student and young professor of political science. Then Chapter 8 shows how both of these currents of liberal political analysis subsequently put to use the posthistorical method pioneered by British scholar, Liberal Party politician, and later diplomat James Bryce in his 1888 *The American Commonwealth*.

My elucidation in the current chapter of the political substance of disenchanted classical liberalism proceeds as follows. First, I argue that changes in Sumner's political writings between the mid-1870s and late 1880s chart how contemporary American political events drew him away from Lieberian notions of the state and democracy to articulate, instead, a disenchanted classical liberal political vision. I then set out to pinpoint broader commonalities, and differences within, disenchanted classical liberal political analyses by exploring the more moderate analysis offered by Harvard's pioneering political scientist, A. Lawrence Lowell. Finally, by locating Sumner and Lowell in light of transatlantic intellectual exchanges, I argue that these Americans were part of a transatlantic disenchanted classical liberal political conversation, mediated by the British figures of Herbert Spencer and Sir Henry Maine, and divided on the issue of American exceptionalism.

Sumner's Political Science: From Democratized to Disenchanted Classical Liberalism

For almost four decades (1873–1909) Sumner served as Yale's Professor of Political and Social Science, a chair whose remit he understood, as we saw previously, in encompassing and evolving terms. Writing throughout his career, Sumner produced a huge corpus of works diverse in both substantive focus and style. Contributions to political science in the narrower sense he identified in 1873 make up a relatively small, but notable portion of his corpus, especially during the first decades of Sumner's career, when he repeatedly addressed political institutions, ideas, and practices, particularly but not only in America.

These works derive special importance for my book from their relationship to the democratized classical liberal political science of Lieber. Sumner's political science had a key starting point in his study and teaching of Lieber. The concept of "civil liberty," construed in the developmental institutional sense Lieber had favored, was a consistent cornerstone of Sumner's political writings. He used the concept prominently from early works through a series of essays on liberty in 1887–1890.[1] Even as Sumner held onto this Lieberian conceptual core, however, he began, from the late 1870s on, to break step by step away from other parts of Lieber's political science. Sumner first cast aside the theory of the state with which Lieber had reconciled classical liberal fear about government and the democratic principle of popular sovereignty. Later Sumner came to view America's political system itself as deteriorating, with economic policies made in the name of "democracy" unwittingly putting America onto a path to "plutocracy." His political science had thus, by the late 1880s, left behind the more hopeful side of Lieber's democratized classical liberalism to advance a cutting critique of politics in a changing America. What we can see with Sumner is, therefore, how a late-century disenchanted classical liberal political analysis could develop from a starting point in midcentury democratized classical liberalism.

LIEBER'S LEGACY: CIVIL LIBERTY, RIGHTS, AND DEMOCRACY

Civil liberty was for Sumner, like Lieber, a modern achievement born in the exceptional history of the Anglo-American people. Civil liberty was the "great end for which modern states exist."[2] It was the "status of a freeman in a modern jural state" as "embodied in" and "guaranteed by institutions" that had developed over centuries. It hence had to be understood "in terms drawn from history and law."[3] This developmental historicist approach presented civil liberty as crafted in England through centuries of struggle and growth. From there it was, in turn, "inherited by all the English-speaking nations, who have made liberty real because they have inherited it, not as a notion, but as a body of institutions." By contrast, efforts to create it on the European continent "realized it only imperfectly" since, without support from "local institutions or traditions," civil liberty was simply "a matter of 'declarations,'" not something "positive, practical, and actual."[4]

---

[1] The concept slips into the background of Sumner's thought only in the last and most sociological period of his scholarship, but it never disappeared entirely. For examples of its lingering presence see William Graham Sumner, *Folkways: A Study of the Sociological Importance of Usages, Manners, Customs, Mores, and Morals* (New York: Mentor Book, 1960; first published in 1907), 58, 154.

[2] William Graham Sumner, "Republican Government," in *On Liberty, Society, and Politics: The Essential Essays of William Graham Sumner*, ed. Robert C. Bannister (Indianapolis, IN: Liberty Fund, 1992), 91.

[3] William Graham Sumner, *Earth-Hunger and Other Essays*, ed. Albert Galloway Keller (New Haven, CT: Yale University Press, 1913), 160. Cites to this collection in the current subsection all draw on a pamphlet and series of essays first published in 1887–1890, and reprinted together as the "Liberty" section in *Earth-Hunger*, 109–203.

[4] William Graham Sumner, *What Social Classes Owe to Each Other* (Caldwell, ID: Caxton Printers, 1989; published first by Harper & Brothers, 1883), 26, 29–30.

Sumner's own particularly uncompromising variant of classical liberalism was evident in the way he interpreted the concept of civil liberty he inherited. In an 1880 essay, he spelled out his understanding of the equality before the law, which was a central element of civil liberty:

> The object of equality before the law is to make the state entirely neutral. The state, under that theory, takes no cognizance of persons. It surrounds all, without distinctions, with the same conditions and guarantees. If it educates one, it educates all—black, white, red or yellow; Jew or Gentile; native or alien. If it taxes one, it taxes all, by the same system and under the same conditions. If it exempts one from police regulations in home, church, and occupation, it exempts all.

Sumner recognized that perfect realization of this neutrality was "impossible." But by appealing to it as an ideal he spotlighted the granting of "exceptions and special cases" as an activity rife with "chance for abuse."[5] Defenders of civil liberty should limit the extent of all such activity—by, for example, favoring a uniform rule of free trade over the discretionary decisions involved in politicians deciding which goods would and would not be part of a system of protective tariffs.

A second element of civil liberty for Sumner was its tie to personal liberty, understood in terms of a socioeconomic order that centered on self-reliance and self-improvement. Laws and institutions embodying civil liberty secured the "personal liberty of individuals" by guaranteeing a free man "that, in doing his best to learn the laws of right living and to obey them, to the end that his life may be a success, no one else shall be allowed to interfere with him or to demand a share in the product of his efforts."[6] If a state offered its citizens less, or indeed more, than this, it did so at a cost. Granting that the "Prussian bureaucracy can do a score of things for the citizen which no governmental organ in the United States can do," Sumner contended that if Americans wanted "to be taken care of as Prussians and Frenchmen are," to achieve this would require them sacrificing some of their personal liberty, which he held to be so precious.[7]

In addition to equality before the law and personal liberty, Sumner's conception of civil liberty also highlighted, as Lieber had done, connections between rights and duties. He stressed that no individual can enjoy a right as a positive reality without others having correlative duties to respect and sustain that right. Any person whose rights exceed his duties therefore enjoys a privileged status that can exist only if other members of the society are in a status of servitude in which their duties exceed their rights. But between these positions there lay a "middle

---

[5] William Graham Sumner, "Socialism," in *Liberty, Society, and Politics*, 177.

[6] Sumner, *Earth-Hunger*, 169–70.

[7] Sumner, "The Forgotten Man," in *Liberty, Society, and Politics*, 212.

point or neutral point, where there is neither privilege nor servitude, but where the rights and duties are in equilibrium, and that status is civil liberty." The mission of "the modern jural state, at least of the Anglo-American type," was to realize and sustain this status by rejecting both "privileges and servitudes." This dual rejection maintained a balance of rights and duties along with equality before the law and personal liberty. Each of the three elements in Sumner's conception of civil liberty was thus an intertwined part of a classical liberalism that, he declared to Americans, "fills our institutions at their best, and... forms the stem of our best civil and social ideals."[8]

If American institutions and ideals at their best were infused with classical liberalism, this was not, for Sumner, the only major feature of American politics. In the rising historical tide of democracy he saw a second feature, one that potentially threatened civil liberty. Sumner took pains to remind his fellow Americans that the "framers of the Constitution... knew well that it differed from a democracy." They crafted a "constitutional republic" that was only democratized later, and thence became a "democratic republic." In this hybrid the "element of democracy" was "the aggressive element... all the time trying to subjugate the institutions of the constitutional republic" and thereby "establish democratic absolutism."[9] In a democratic age, sustaining civil liberty required clear recognition that its "institutions and laws" did "not consist in majority rule or in universal suffrage or in elective systems at all." Such democratic "devices" were not to be valued themselves, but judged "good or better just in the degree to which they secure liberty."[10]

In analyzing the relation of civil liberty to an extended suffrage and majority rule Sumner applied his Lieberian stress on balancing rights and duties. To be given political rights was to be given a share in the power to alter laws and institutions, and hence shift arrangements of positive rights and duties. The "danger of democracy" lay in the possibility of lower classes using their political power to acquire rights and alter duties in ways inconsistent with civil liberty. But that outcome was not inevitable. Sumner could extol the "free man in a free democracy" at the same time that he expounded the demanding prerequisites of this combination. Democracy could be "a sound working system" if and only if those it gave political rights would "oppose the same cold resistance to any claims for

---

[8] Sumner, *Earth-Hunger*, 126–28.

[9] William Graham Sumner, "Politics in America, 1776–1876," *North American Review* 122, no. 250 (January 1876), 51–53; William Graham Sumner, "The Theory and Practice of Elections," *Collected Essays in Political and Social Science* (New York: Holt, 1885), 137. I quote here from articles first published in 1876 and 1880 respectively, but the persistence in Sumner's thought of this way of conceptualizing the arc of American political history is testified to some two decades later in an unpublished manuscript dated by Albert Galloway Keller to 1896 or 1897. William Graham Sumner, "Advancing Social and Political Organization in American History," in *The Challenge of Facts and Other Essays*, ed. Albert Galloway Keller (New Haven, CT: Yale University Press, 1914), 334–36.

[10] Sumner, "Forgotten Man," 204–07.

favor on the grounds of poverty, as on the ground of birth and rank."[11] The sound-ness of wide suffrage depended on the extent to which holders of political rights were committed to self-reliance. It was, in sum, essential to recognize that "the only man who is fit to help govern the community is the man who can govern himself."[12]

By highlighting potential tension between classical liberal civil liberty and wide suffrage, Sumner's political science presented a classical liberal-democratic hybrid regime as exceptional. If America's "democratic republic" instantiated democracy in a manner attractive for classical liberals, this was so just to the extent that civil liberty survived democratization. But to study the rise of democracy as a more general trend in modern nations—and thereby better elucidate the poten-tial threat of democratic doctrines to civil liberty—it was crucial to recognize that illiberal regimes had also instantiated democracy. Sumner, like Lieber, found a motley parade of these displayed in the history of modern France: "Jacobinism," "sansculottism," and the plebiscitary appeals of Napoleon III's Second Empire were all examples of democracy's dark side and had to be addressed in an analysis of democracy as a rising general trend of the modern world.[13]

Sumner's general analysis of democracy was concerned not only to differenti-ate between the varied political forms it took, but also to explain the general trend itself. As had Tocqueville and Lieber, Sumner saw democracy as a transatlantic trend, but he explained it more exclusively in the terms of nineteenth-century political economy: both actual features of the economy, and its "laws" as dis-cerned by classical political economists, especially Malthus and Ricardo. As a core dictum, stated in his 1881 essay "Sociology," but used throughout his life, Sumner declared:

> The law of population, therefore, combined with the law of diminishing returns constitutes the great underlying condition of society. Emigration, improvements in the arts, in morals, in education, in political organiza-tion, are only stages in the struggle of man to meet these conditions, to break their force for a time, and to win room under them for ease and enlargement.... Let him, therefore, who desires to study social phenom-ena first learn the transcendent importance for the whole social organi-zation, industrial, political, and civil, of the ratio of population to land.

---

[11] Sumner, *What Social Classes Owe*, 32–34.

[12] Sumner, "Republican Government," 85.

[13] Sumner specifically discussed Napoleon III in 1877 in "Republican Government," 83. I draw the phrases "jacobinism" and "sansculottism" from Sumner's unpublished manuscript of 1896 or 1897, which shows the persistence some two decades later of a continuing tendency to look to France for examples of democracy in a "degenerate form." Sumner, "Advancing Social and Political Organization," 305–6.

The import of this ratio centered on its relationship to the "struggle for existence." Maintaining human life required struggle against nature to acquire and work upon materials to meet human needs. The struggle for existence also involved, however, struggles that men wage against one another for control over materials. The ratio of a society's population to the supply of materials available to meet needs of its members was a key factor shaping the character of social relations.

> If the actual number present is very much less than the number who might be supported, the condition of all must be ample and easy. Freedom and facility mark all social relations under such a state of things. If the number is larger than that which can be supplied, the condition of all must be one of want and distress, or else a few must be well provided, the others beings proportionally still worse off. Constraint, anxiety, possibly tyranny and repression, mark social relations.[14]

Sumner's commitment to this general outlook involved more than presenting laws drawn from reading classical political economists. He also used the outlook when explaining particular political changes. In an 1876 historical survey of the first century of American politics since the 1776 Declaration of Independence, Sumner looked to "physical and economic circumstances" to explain why "constitutional barriers" the founding fathers set up against democracy had "proven feeble and vain." Given America's character as "a new country…with unlimited land" it was, he argued, "inevitable" that there would develop "substantial equality of the people in property, culture, and social position." From social equality, "political equality" had followed "naturally." Sumner more specifically tied the

---

[14] This analysis is in Sumner's "Sociology" article, which first appeared in *The Princeton Review* in 1881, and was reprinted with a series of Sumner's other essays from the *Review* in his 1885 *Collected Essays*. I quote here from pp. 82–84 of the 1885 collected essays. Sumner labels the denominator in his ratio variously both "land" and "the supply of materials." He was, moreover, attentive to how the materials available to sustain a given population on a given amount of land is affected by technology. His comments on land are thus best read as a placeholder and starting point for what is, in substance, a broad analysis of factors shaping the supply of materials available for consumption within a society. In "Sociology" and other early 1880s writings Sumner notoriously employs the phrase "survival-of-the-fittest" in connection with the struggle for existence in a loose way that attracted criticism at the time, and did much, over the longer term, to earn him his reputation as America's premier social Darwinist. After trying in 1884 to clarify this phrase, Sumner himself would subsequently drop it. What was persistent and unaffected by the fleeting rise and fall in Sumner's writings of the "survival of the fittest" phrase was his concern with the relationship population and resources had to the intensity of struggle in society, and thereby the character of social relations. This concern was drawn from classical political economy, while the "survival-of-the-fittest" was an easily dispensed with flourish Sumner probably picked up from Spencer. On Sumner and the phrase, see the essay "Survival of the Fittest" and accompanying information given by the editor Robert Bannister in Sumner, *Liberty, Society, and Politics*, 223–26.

surge of democratization during the Jacksonian era to the "great series of inven-
tions" in transportation that was then opening up the "continent to mankind"
to an extent not previously possible. Based in material circumstances, the democratic tide in American politics would last as long as these circumstances did.
Efforts to advance "political aristocracy" would be able to succeed "only when
the pressure of population, and the development of a more complex social organization" led to "inequality in the circumstances of individuals" and, in turn, a
concomitant "social aristocracy" upon which such a political system could rest.[15]

The material explanation that Sumner offered of American political history
could also, he believed, be extended to explain the rise of democracy as a more
general transatlantic trend. How did an explanation that connected America's
democracy to its open frontier explain democratic tendencies in Europe?
Sumner's general analysis related the material situation in Europe to that in
America and other outposts of European settlement, such as Australia and South
Africa. He noted that "advances in the arts and sciences" improved "transportation and communication" that facilitated emigration from Europe and the import
into Europe of staple goods, such as meat and grain. As emigration kept down
Europe's population, while staple imports decreased the cost of living there, both
acted in tandem to "relieve" the intensity of "social pressure and competition" in
the "great centers of population." It was this relief that then underpinned "the general tendency towards equality, the decline of aristocratic institutions, the rise of
proletariat, and the ambitious expansion," which were all characteristic of "modern civilized society."[16]

DEPARTING FROM LIEBER: DEMOCRACY
AND THE THEORY OF THE STATE

Sumner offered a more materialist and contemporary-focused explanation of
democracy than the grand developmental historicist narratives of democracy's
rise preferred by Tocqueville and Lieber. But Sumner followed their lead in conceiving democracy as a general phenomenon instantiated, for better and worse,
in varied modern examples. We saw in chapter 1 that one of Lieber's seminal contributions had been to make this conceptualization part of a democratized classical liberal theory of the state. Lieber's acceptance of popular sovereignty was
interwoven with his distinction between the state and the government: his theory spotlighted democracy as a form of *state* that could be combined with varied

[15] Sumner, "Politics in America," 52–53, 64–65, 78. What Sumner argued more specifically about
America in this earlier essay is restated as general claims about economics, society, and politics in
"under-populated" countries in his "Sociology." See Sumner, "Sociology," 89–90.
[16] Sumner, "Sociology," 93–95.

forms of *government*, some of which he judged better, and some worse, in light of his classical liberal beliefs.

Sumner's exposure to Lieber provides the intellectual context relative to which we might best interpret the specific identification, in his 1873 introductory lecture, of "political science in its narrower use" with "the science of government and the theory of the state."[17] The keystone of Lieber's theory of the state was its locating of sovereign power in society. This enabled Lieber to identify the will of the state with the will of the people as expressed in elections and public opinion. In line with Lieber's theory, Sumner's 1873 lecture characterized the "nation" as "a vast organism" whose members freely undertake "independent enterprises," form "combinations," and develop opinions, and in doing so, find themselves "inextricably entangled with each other" in a "[s]ociety...solidified and bound together by these numerous bonds." Sumner presented the members of society as agreeing "by common consent...upon what we will do, what concessions we will make to the common interest, what efforts we will contribute to the general welfare." He then distinguished society from the government into whose hands society "lodged" the "[p]ower of control." Government was necessary, but also problematic since "those who are clothed with this power undergo an inevitable temptation to abuse it." Hence society's members should, in their collective capacity, decide both "what powers we will give to the officers of government" and "what restrictions we will put upon them."[18]

This Lieberian democratized classical liberal notion of the people acting collectively as a society to authorize and constrain their government informed Sumner's political works into the mid–1870s. For example, when concluding his "Politics in America, 1776-1876," he invoked the "distinction between the administration of the government, or the methods of party politics, and the general political morale of the people." Sumner used this "obvious distinction" in responding to "lamentations" that "we are degenerating." His response argued that, while the administration of government had indeed "deteriorated" and party methods "become worse and worse," to pass judgment on America's political system it was also crucial to look "behind all this" to the "public will." Doing so would reveal that, Sumner optimistically claimed, "the political will of the nation never was purer than it is to-day." With "instruction and guidance" this will might be roused in support of reforms "to recover that of which the people" were robbed by "political machinery" as it had developed during recent decades.[19] It was in the manner of providing

---

[17] Sumner, "Introductory Lecture to Courses in Political and Social Science," in *Challenge of Facts*, 402.

[18] Sumner, "Introductory Lecture," 392–93. In an address the year before that similarly treated the nation as "a unit with an organic life" Sumner credited the experience of the Civil War with having taught the American people the "idea of a nation and its value as a unit and as a commonwealth." William Graham Sumner, "Memorial Day Address," in *Challenge of Facts*, 353–54.

[19] Sumner, "Politics in America," 87.

such "instruction and guidance" that Sumner, later in 1876, explained in a long letter to a New Haven paper (reprinted subsequently by Democratic papers elsewhere) the reasoning that led him, even though he was a Republican alderman at the time, to prefer the Democratic presidential candidate Tilden in the upcoming election. Sumner appealed again here to the people as the fulcrum for improvement as he contended that "any reform which shall be real...must begin and spread far in the minds and consciences of the sovereign people."[20]

Yet, far from affirming any such hopeful appeal to "the sovereign people," events during the following months would instead turn Sumner away from his initial Lieberian conception of democracy. He was harshly criticized in Republican publications for endorsing Tilden, and the New Haven party declined to renominate him for alderman, thereby abruptly ending his brief time as an elected politician.[21] Meanwhile, the presidential election turned into a national political firestorm when the Republican, Rutherford B. Hayes, while losing the popular vote, still won the presidency due to decisions by Republican-dominated electoral boards in three southern states. Appealing to their Reconstruction mandate to counteract fraud and voter intimidation, the boards disqualified enough Democratic ballots to award Hayes victory in these states, and along with them, the presidency. In the aftermath of the election, as the parties jockeyed to shape the outcome of the controversial situation, Sumner traveled to New Orleans at the behest of the Democratic national committee as part of a team to investigate how the election had been conducted, and therefore if reassignment of Louisiana's electoral votes to Hayes was justified. He came away from his visit supporting the Democratic view that the Republicans had effectively stolen the election.[22]

By the time Sumner returned from New Orleans in early 1877, immersion in the practical power plays of contemporary America politics had shifted his political science onto a new track. In endorsing Tilden before the election Sumner sought to publicly model the action of "rational beings, making a selection on rational grounds" assumed by "the theory of our political system" to be what voting should involve. By contrast, when speaking in Chicago shortly after his return from New Orleans, he now declared that the 1876 election had highlighted the need to critically "re-examine the whole plan and idea of elections."[23] Where Sumner previously concentrated his public writings and speeches on instructing and motivating fellow citizens in light of the high-minded ideals built into the

[20] William Graham Sumner, "For President?" in *Challenge of Facts*, 370.

[21] Sumner was then nominated by New Haven's Democrats, but lost the election to the Republican nominated in his stead. See Harris E. Starr, *William Graham Sumner* (New York: Holt, 1925), 192–94.

[22] Starr, *William Graham Sumner*, 192–94. For a historical overview and statistical reassessment of decisions made by the Louisiana electoral board see Ronald F. King, "A Most Corrupt Election: Louisiana in 1876," *Studies in American Political Development* 15 (Fall 2001), 123–37.

[23] Sumner, "For President?" 369; Sumner, "Republican Government," 86.

Lieberian theory of a democratic republic, he now took up a new agenda of critically questioning and discrediting central components of that theory.

Sumner undertook this critical activity in a sustained fashion in his two-part 1880 article "The Theory and Practice of Elections." Here he subjected the "theory of elections as they are employed in the democratic-republican state" to a withering assault. Taking it as his goal "to test that theory by experience and practice," he unpacked the "theory" as a set of ideal assumptions regarding, for example, how voters reach and express their "will," and the ability of the "ballot with majority rule" to function as a "mechanism for getting a clear expression of the public will." Sumner then argued for each assumption that "in practice" it did "not hold true." Observing that practices fail to live up to a theory based on democratic ideals about the capabilities of common men and balloting was, however, less pivotal (ideals are after all, *ideals*, not descriptions) than Sumner's belief that the fitting intellectual response to this gap between theory and practice was to "attack" the theory as "superstitious." He argued that the theory was a "superstition" since in presenting democratic elections as the "guarantee of good government" it attributed to elections a "causative force which they do not possess." This misattribution was, in turn, "dangerous and hostile to constitutional liberty" because it drew "people's attention and respect away from the institutions of civil liberty which deserve and need reverence, support, and protection."[24]

The late 1870s shift in Sumner's political science was reflected in his changing treatment of the principle of popular sovereignty. Shortly before the 1876 election, he had explained in a Lieberian manner that democracy was

> not a system of government for a state with any but the narrowest limits. On a wider field it is a theory as to the depository of sovereignty. It seizes upon majority rule, which is the only practical expedient for getting a decision where something must be done, and a unanimous judgment as to what ought to be done is impossible, and it makes this majority the depositary of sovereignty, under the name of the sovereignty of the people.

Sumner had gone on to emphasize that a democratic sovereign was "as likely as any despot to aggrandize itself."[25] Yet in doing so he did not discredit the sovereignty of the people in general terms. Like Lieber he simply warned against democracy's potential dark side. In his 1880 article, by contrast, Sumner did discredit popular sovereignty more generally. Democracy was, he now declared, "a set of dogmas about political rights and who ought to rule." He went on to expound the

---

[24] Sumner, "Theory and Practice of Elections," 102, 113–21, 133–36.
[25] Sumner, "Politics in America," 51–52.

pernicious tendency of the "dogma of the 'sovereignty of the people'" to promote a fallacious faith that replacing "divine right of kings" with the "divine right of the majority" had finally put power in its "true seat."[26] In redescribing this principle of democratic theory as a "dogma," and democratic "theory" in general as "a set of dogmas," Sumner departed decisively from his pre-1876 election image of the nation's "political will" and appeal to the "sovereign people."

By the early 1880s Sumner thus saw the democratic conception of "the people" having a collective "will" that could and should be sovereign as a dogma that obscured the realities of political power. Approached from a more practical standpoint, the "will" of "the State" called to mind, not the people as a whole valorized as a collective actor, but those who actually held and wielded the power of government. In the introduction to his 1883 *What Social Classes Owe to Each Other* Sumner summed up how he had rethought the state:

> My notion of the State has dwindled with growing experience of life. As an abstraction, the State is to me only All-of-us. In practice—that is, when it exercises will or adopts a line of action—it is only a little group of men chosen in a very haphazard way by the majority of us to perform certain services for all of us. The majority do not go about their selection rationally, and they are almost always disappointed by the results of their own operation.... Furthermore, it often turns out in practice that "the State" is not even the known and accredited servants of the State, but, as has been well said, is only some obscure clerk, hidden in the recesses of a Government bureau, into whose power the chance has fallen for the moment to pull one of the stops which control the Government machine.[27]

Sumner here unapologetically collapses Lieber's distinction between state and government. The weight of that distinction rested upon the conception of "the people" as collectively exercising a sovereign will, which stands outside of, authorizes, and limits government. When Sumner had turned against that conception as a "dogma" to discredit, he removed the keystone of Lieber's theory of the state, and without it, the distinction between state and government collapsed.

---

[26] Sumner, "Theory and Practice of Elections," 103–4. While Sumner had earlier spoken of democratic doctrines as "dogmas," when he did so he had qualified the implication of the term by also holding that these dogmas "were not without truth." Sumner, "Politics in America," 58. His "Elections" article dropped this qualification.

[27] Sumner, *What Social Classes Owe*, 9.

SUMNER ON PLUTOCRACY: CRAFTING A
DISENCHANTED CLASSICAL LIBERAL CRITIQUE
OF A CHANGING AMERICA

Sumner's collapsing of Lieber's distinction between the state and government embodied a push to leave theory aside as an obfuscating abstraction and focus instead on where power lies "in practice." As his political science further developed that push, it gave growing prominence to a new dynamic, the rise of plutocracy, which reworked Sumner's analysis of American politics.

The concept of plutocracy came to the forefront of Sumner's political science during the 1880s. He had used it earlier, even before the 1876 election, but its role in this thinking was then more limited. For example, in his 1876 survey "Politics in America," which treated the century since the Declaration of Independence, Sumner noted that Hamilton's solicitude for "the interest of the wealthy class" was "a theory which would have changed" America "into a plutocracy." But this threat then disappeared from Sumner's historical survey with the 1800 election victory of Jefferson and his Democratic Republicans, which he interpreted as "the first triumph of the tendency towards democracy,—a triumph which has never yet been reversed."[28] By 1880, however, Sumner began to nuance this interpretation with more attention to plutocracy in his "Theory and Practice of Elections." Here he introduced a suggestion that "[m]odern democracy seems fated to fall under the dominion of plutocracy." The background of this suggestion was the way in which a "modern industrial system" created conditions under which "those who can dispose of political power can serve their own interests with an almost immeasurable advantage." The counterpart of nineteenth-century industrialization was hence "the plutocrats of all countries aiming to control the political power, either directly by getting seats in the legislature, or indirectly through the lobby."[29]

Sumner carried this new line of argument into *What Social Classes Owe to Each Other*. After noting that recent history showed "a plain tendency of all civilized governments toward plutocracy," Sumner argued that this "danger" was most "formidable" in America. In Europe the lingering social prestige of aristocracy helped to temper the ways in which wealth was employed. But in America democracy stood alone as "the opponent of plutocracy," which had its "army" in the lobby, and found the political machinery of "caucus, convention, and committee" all too well suited "to serve" its purpose. At stake, Sumner proposed, was "nothing less" than the question of whether "free self-government under the forms of a democratic republic" was still possible. To recognize and meet the plutocratic threat Americans had to escape "the notion that we are better than other nations."

---

[28] Sumner, "Politics in America," 56, 60.
[29] Sumner, "Theory and Practice," 104, 117.

It was, at the same time, also essential not to be misled by "denunciations and complainings about the power of chartered corporations and aggregated capital." Elected legislatures had passed the laws and charters that supported this power, and nothing good would come from turning to those same legislatures to "heap law upon law." The "ground for hope" lay instead in "constitutional guarantees and the independent action of self-governing freemen."[30]

The vague note of hope with which Sumner's closed his 1883 discussion of plutocracy would disappear, later in the decade, as he refined his analysis and it became both clearer and more disenchanted. This refinement took place in light of a concrete example. Since the 1870s state legislatures had been passing laws to regulate railroad practices and prices in response to popular discontent. In 1886 the issue was catapulted to the federal level after the Supreme Court ruled that state laws regulating railway business across state lines violated the commerce clause of the Constitution. Within less than six months, the Interstate Commerce Act was enacted in early 1887. One of the law's innovations was to set up the first federal regulatory agency, the Interstate Commerce Commission, to interpret and enforce its regulatory provisions.

An active participant in public debates over what should be done in the aftermath of the Court's 1886 decision, Sumner was bitterly disappointed at the result. He had joined the debate with a January 1887 article titled "Federal Legislation on Railroads," which argued that "the notion that something must be done" was insufficient to justify immediate legislation regulating a large and swiftly changing sector of the economy. Sumner was willing to grant "that legislation might ultimately prove necessary or expedient," but he proposed that what was essential first was "a commission to study railroads" with the powers needed to gather information, and personnel capable of investigating the issues "impartially from the standpoint of justice to all interests."[31]

While Sumner was prescribing patience and study, legislation was itself racing through Congress, to be signed by President Cleveland in February 1887. Dropping the calmer tone of his earlier article, Sumner responded by taking up critical cudgels in his next article, "Legislation by Clamor." He charged that the new act was "the latest case of legislation by clamor," a broader contemporary trend in which democracies on both sides of the Atlantic were coming to "abandon all sound traditions as to the method of legislative activity." The Congress had "set all reason and common sense at defiance" in hastily producing a bill with vague provisions that would not be clarified until the Interstate Commerce Commission was itself up and running.[32] In May 1887 Sumner returned to print to denounce the act as a "remarkable case of speculative legislation... opposed to the spirit of

---

[30] Sumner, *What Social Classes Owe*, 90–96.

[31] William Graham Sumner, "Federal Legislation on Railroads," in *Challenge of Facts*, 179, 182.

[32] William Graham Sumner, "Legislation by Clamor," in *Challenge of Facts*, 185, 189.

our institutions, wrong in principle, and sure to produce evil effects." It carried, he suggested, the foreign spirit of German *Sozialpolitik*, and the commission it created was a confused hybrid that mixed German and Anglo-American "systems of jurisprudence and administration" in a manner that created great uncertainty about what was to be allowed, what not, and how these decisions would be made, by whom, and when.[33]

The Interstate Commerce Act was a turning point for Sumner. By August 1887 he was declaring in general terms that, under democracy, it was "rapidly becoming the chief art of the legislator to devise measures which shall sound as if they satisfied clamor while they only cheat it."[34] As late as 1883 the darker side of Sumner's political science was still leavened by a rallying cry of a "free man in a free democracy." But now his writings came to display a more uniformly disenchanted critical analysis of democracy. In fleshing out this analysis Sumner returned, in a set of essays in 1888 and 1889, to refine his treatment of the theme he had pondered all decade: the conflict between democracy and plutocracy.

The disenchanted Sumner of the late 1880s continued to see plutocracy as the "really new and really threatening" phenomenon of the late century, but he now, more gravely, pronounced its conflict with democracy "destined to dispel the dreams which have been cherished, that we were on the eve of a millennium." His refined analysis found its focus and clarity in an argument that democracy itself was spurring, albeit unknowingly, the rise of plutocracy. Sumner now stressed more clearly that plutocracy should not be equated with the "power of capital." Capitalists only become plutocrats when they used the power capital gave them "not industrially, but politically," to operate "upon the market by legislation" to create jobs and businesses "half political and half industrial." The unintended consequence of "uncritical denunciations of capital, and monopoly, and trust" was, however, "to help forward plutocracy" by drawing more capitalists into active involvement with politics. Denunciations fueled popular clamor for politicians to legislate more government control over the economy. But if threatened by legislation, capital would mobilize to "defend itself" and in doing so would inevitably resort "to all the vices of plutocracy." Pointing as an example to the Interstate Commerce Law, Sumner stated it as a maxim that "[i]f legislation is applied to the control of interests, especially when the latter are favored by the facts of the situation, the only effect is to impose on the interests more crafty and secret modes of action."[35]

Once battle was joined between democracy and plutocracy, it was the latter that would, Sumner suggested, win out. Reformers proposing regulation in the

---

[33] William Graham Sumner, "Speculative Legislation." In *Challenge of Facts*, 215–16, 218.

[34] William Graham Sumner, "State Interference," *North American Review* 145, no. 369 (August 1887), 117.

[35] William Graham Sumner, "Democracy and Plutocracy," in *Liberty, Society, and Politics*, 140–47.

name of democracy were "a large and unorganized body, without discipline, with its ideas undefined, its interests illy [sic] understood, with an indefinite good intention." Meanwhile, on the other side, plutocracy came "into the contest with a small body, strong organization, a powerful motive, a definite purpose, and a strict discipline." In a democratic system "the contest between numbers and wealth," once provoked, would come down, in practice, to "a contest between two sets of lawyers, one drawing Acts on behalf of the state, and the other devising means of defeating those Acts on behalf of their clients." Success in this contest would go to the lawyers "better paid in consideration, in security, and in money"—who worked for the plutocrats.[36] In sum, pushing to extend government regulatory control would, in practice, only promote plutocracy. Or, as Sumner pithily stated his warning in an 1894 essay, in pursuing "social reformation" Americans "may find that instead of democratizing capitalism we have capitalized democracy— that is, have brought in plutocracy."[37]

As Sumner forged and refined his increasingly disenchanted political analysis, he stayed throughout a classical liberal believer in laissez-faire of a firmly uncom- promising variety. His late 1880s essays on democracy and plutocracy concluded that the "wise policy" in regard to the conflict between these twin forces was "to minimize to the utmost the relations of the state to industry." Well aware how divergent such views were from the progressive liberal analysis then on the rise elsewhere in the American academy, Sumner proudly avowed: "*Laissez-faire*, instead of being what it appears to be in most of the current discussions, cuts to the very bottom of the morals, the politics, and the political economy of the most important public questions of our time."[38] If progressive liberals (as we will see further with Woodrow Wilson in the next chapter) interpreted America's industrialization as making laissez-faire anachronistic, Sumner offered a starkly competing vision. For him, the problems of late-century America could not be explained as a consequence of laissez-faire, or overcome by relegating that clas- sical liberal policy principle to the past, because America had never lived up to the principle. For Sumner, American history repeatedly showed—from the pro- tective tariff, to banks and the currency, to corporate charters and government contracts—political actors who knew little about classical political economy and civil liberty making flawed decisions. The late-century plutocratic dynamic of capital increasing its control over politics would only be promoted by new devia- tions from laissez-faire, and hence the old policy principle remained, for the dis- enchanted Sumner, as relevant as it had been when he began his career as a young scholar teaching a democratized classical liberal political science.

---

[36] Sumner, "Democracy and Plutocracy," 147–48.

[37] William Graham Sumner, "The Absurd Effort to Make the World Over," in *Liberty, Society, and Politics*, 259.

[38] Sumner, "Democracy and Plutocracy," 148.

A. Lawrence Lowell: Disenchanted Classical Liberal Political Analysis in a Different Key

Sumner's critical analysis of contemporary America as at the forefront of a transatlantic rise of "plutocracy" was only one form that disenchanted classical liberal political analysis could take. Turning from Sumner to the figure of A. Lawrence Lowell pinpoints for us both a broader commonality of, and the room for variety within, the political substance of disenchanted classical liberalism as a late-nineteenth-century liberal vision. Lowell shared with Sumner a disenchanted sense of living in a time in which the political tide was turning away from classical liberal beliefs and hopes he cherished. For Lowell the tide was one of movement toward "paternalism." But his disenchantment was moderated by a belief that America was less susceptible to this tide than the political systems of contemporary Europe.

Viewed retrospectively from the perspective of American political science's twentieth-century development, Lowell is a more familiar "political scientist" than Sumner. Beginning in the 1890s, Lowell would, as we will explore in chapter 8, make seminal contributions to the comparative empirical study of modern mass suffrage politics. He was hired at Harvard in 1897, and once there worked with his colleague Albert Bushnell Hart to create Harvard's celebrated Department of Government.[39] In the same year, 1909, that he served as an early APSA president, Lowell also become Harvard's president, and during his long administration (1909–1933), the department he earlier helped create prospered to become, by the mid-1920s, the nationally best-ranked department of political science, as it remains to this day.[40]

Lowell was, however, over forty when he first became a political science professor. He had a prior career as a lawyer, and no less importantly, he had been born a *Lowell*. Generations of his storied Boston family had attended Harvard on their way to prominence in law, politics, and business, or cultural prominence as pastors, poets, professors, or assorted combinations of these. The Lowell who stands out for political scientists as a pioneer of the field at Harvard, had been a Harvard College student in the 1870s, graduated Harvard's Law School in 1880, and

---

[39] There was a single department of history and government at Harvard until 1911, but from 1892 the course catalog separated courses under these two headings. Lowell was hired to teach under the government heading, and did much to further the emphasis on "the actual performance of government in modern countries" stressed by Albert Bushnell Hart in his later retrospective on the department's history. Albert Bushnell Hart, "Government," in *Development of Harvard University*, ed. Samuel Eliot Morison (Cambridge, MA: Harvard University Press, 1930), 181–82.

[40] Harvard was first ranked the leading department in 1925. Albert Somit and Joseph Tanenhaus, *The Development of American Political Science: From Burgess to Behavioralism* (Boston: Allyn and Bacon, 1967), 105–6.

practiced law in Boston in partnership with his cousin, Francis C. Lowell, for almost two decades before his turn to political science brought him back to Harvard.[41] Locating Lowell in light of his family and his legal career is helpful if we are to see him, not only as a pioneering practitioner of political science in its narrow sense, but as a scholar whose empirical research developed against a background of classical liberal beliefs. As Bernard Crick astutely noted in his classic study of political science in America, Lowell's political science consisted in a "happy balance of research into new processes and reiteration of old principles to young men."[42]

A. LAWRENCE LOWELL AS A CLASSICAL LIBERAL: ENTERPRISE, PERSONAL LIBERTY, RIGHTS, AND CONTRACTS

Since Lowell, unlike Sumner, did not make scholarly contributions to political economy, the *classical* liberal character of the beliefs informing his political science is not as immediately manifest. If Lowell was no political economist, he was, however, well exposed to economics in a practical sense. His father, Augustus Lowell, was a successful businessman, and more generally, business was one of multiple domains in which his family had long been prominent. The family name had been given to the Massachusetts textile mill town of Lowell, founded in the 1820s, and the neighboring industrial town of Lawrence, founded in the 1840s, was named for Lowell's own maternal grandfather and namesake, Abbott Lawrence. The town of Lowell was, we saw in Part I, named for Francis Cabot Lowell, who had founded the Boston Manufacturing Company, and in doing so helped pioneer the shareholder corporation as a model for American business organization. Francis Cabot Lowell's grandson, also named Francis Cabot Lowell, was A. Lawrence Lowell's cousin, legal partner, and the coauthor of his first book, *The Transfer of Stock in Private Corporations*.[43] This 1884 legal work and the family history in business offers a backdrop against which to take up A. Lawrence's Lowell 1889 *Essays on Government*, which collected together his first forays into political science.[44]

---

[41] For a biography of Lowell, see Henry Aaron Yeomans, *Abbot Lawrence Lowell, 1856–1943* (Cambridge, MA: Harvard University Press, 1948).

[42] Bernard Crick, *The American Science of Politics: Its Origins and Conditions* (Berkeley: University of California Press, 1957), 105.

[43] A. Lawrence Lowell and Francis C. Lowell, *The Transfer of Stock in Private Corporations* (Boston: Little, Brown, 1884).

[44] A. Lawrence Lowell, *Essays on Government* (Boston: Houghton, Mifflin, 1889). The *Essays* collected together five pieces Lowell wrote in the later half of the 1880s, two of which had first appeared in the *Harvard Law Review*. See A. Lawrence Lowell, "The Responsibilities of American Lawyers," *Harvard Law Review* 1, no. 5 (1887), 232–40; A. Lawrence Lowell, "The Limits of Sovereignty," *Harvard Law Review* 2, no. 2 (1888), 70–87. As the volume numbers here suggest, the *Harvard Law*

Lowell's *Essays* perched on the boundary of the "scientific." On one hand, in introducing the collection, Lowell emphasized: "Throughout these essays I have tried to preserve a scientific spirit, and to study different political systems, without weighing their respective advantages, or expressing a preference for any of them." On the other hand, he also held that it did "not seem improper to assume a different tone" and "speak freely" within his introduction itself. Lowell then devoted the remainder of his introduction to expounding the "merits of that belief in the sacredness of personal liberty and private rights on which the American constitutions are in large measure based."[45]

Lowell began by aligning himself philosophically as a utilitarian:

> Discarding the exploded doctrine of the natural rights of man, and assuming on the contrary that the system of government which most promotes the moral and material welfare of the community is best, let us examine the principles of utility on which the protection of personal liberty and private right depends.

Avowing next that the "chief of these [principles] is the encouragement of individual enterprise and exertion," he went on to argue that "for the effective development of enterprise, three things are requisite."[46] Lowell devoted multiple pages to unpacking these requisites. In examining his discussion, we may bear in mind that, by the end of his introduction, Lowell would include under the concept of "enterprise," not only the activities of individuals ("natural persons"), but also of corporations (in legal terms, "imaginary persons").[47] Characterizing corporations as based upon "voluntary" cooperation, Lowell saw in such cooperation "no discouragement to enterprise, but, on the contrary, a striking manifestation of it." This set up his take-home claim that "[e]nterprise has indeed been immensely helped in the United States by that class of coöperation which takes the form of corporations."[48]

Identification and praise of "coöperation" as a key feature in the contemporary economy was not novel to Lowell. We met the very same term earlier in the mid-1880s progressive liberal writing of Albert Shaw. But Lowell's focus on the "class of coöperation which takes the form of corporations" carried a markedly different political valence from Shaw's Ely-inspired focus on worker's cooperatives.

Review had just been founded in 1887. It created the model of a law student-edited review whose later replication across the nation made it a standard journal form in legal academe.

[45] Lowell, *Essays*, 8.

[46] Lowell, *Essays*, 9–10.

[47] Lowell used the legal terms "natural persons" and "imaginary persons" in explaining what a corporation is on the opening pages of his 1884 legal treatise. Lowell and Lowell, *Transfer of Stock*, 3–4.

[48] Lowell, *Essays*, 17–18.

At midcentury J. S. Mill's democratized classical liberal *Principles of Political Economy* had heralded *both* of these forms of cooperation; now, by the latter half of the 1880s, we find them heralded in *isolation* by two future APSA presidents. There could, perhaps, be no better indicator of the divergence that had opened up in liberal political economy in the first half of the 1880s and that, as it spread across the substantive domain of wide political science, came in the latter half of the decade to inform alternative analyses of contemporary politics.

Lowell's three "requisites" for the "effective development of enterprise" were as follows. First, "absence of restraint to the greatest extent that is possible." Giving pointed classical liberal political content to the kind of "restraint" he had in mind, Lowell contended:

> A bureaucratic system where everything is regulated by the state is certain to be a stationary system; and if enterprises had to be submitted to the public authorities for approval before they were put in operation, there would soon cease to be any great enterprises at all.[49]

His second requisite was "confidence on the part of the individual that he will be able to enjoy unmolested the fruits of his labor." Hailing this confidence as "the chief stimulus to exertion," Lowell specified that "the prospect of moderate gains alone" would be insufficient since "[i]t is the fact that one man in a thousand wins an enormous prize which induces others to struggle on in neglect and poverty." "The prospect of large returns" was, in addition, necessary "to induce capital to embark in hazardous ventures," and, Lowell suggested, justifiable in utilitarian terms. As an example, he noted, "It has been truly said that the millions which Vanderbilt made were a cheap price to pay for the railroad facilities which he gave to the city of New York."[50]

Lowell's final requisite highlighted the consequences of law when it functions to clarify and predictably enforce private rights. The flourishing of enterprise required "the possibility of calculating the result of a course of conduct so that the projector of an enterprise can foresee the consequences of his actions and lay plans accordingly." Law could facilitate this calculability. More specifically, "amid the complicated relations of modern life," it was the law of contracts that provided "the chief means of determining the future actions of men." Arguing in utilitarian fashion along a chain of consequences, Lowell contended that "confidence that the obligation of contracts will not be violated, together with a belief in the permanence of vested rights," was "a necessary condition of the ability to calculate

[49] Lowell, *Essays*, 10–11.
[50] Lowell, *Essays*, 12–13.

upon the future conduct of men," and this, in turn, was "essential to the existence of individual enterprise and to the prosperity of the community."[51]

By highlighting contracts, viewed in terms of the predictable consequences law attached to them, Lowell's third requisite echoed a central theme of Oliver Wendell Holmes's 1881 *The Common Law*.[52] Lowell's *Essays* show that he was conversant with Holmes's then recent legal classic.[53] This is unsurprising given that Lowell at this time was an intellectually engaged Boston lawyer. But there was also a more intimate connection. Holmes's work grew out of lectures he gave under the auspices of the Lowell Institute. Based on an endowment bequeathed by one of A. Lawrence Lowell's ancestors, the institute funded a series of free prestigious public lectures in Boston every year, with the lecturers chosen by a contemporary Lowell, who served as the institute's trustee.[54] A. Lawrence Lowell would be that trustee from 1900 on, replacing his businessman father, Augustus Lowell, who had held this position during the prior two decades.

Holmes's *The Common Law* proved the most lasting product of what was, at the time, a broad reception among Cambridge-Boston intellectuals of the historicist scholarship of Sir Henry Maine.[55] This reception had, in turn, a significant influence on Lowell's political science. As a Harvard undergraduate Lowell had found in Henry Adams, another scion of a storied Boston family, one of his most (and few) inspiring teachers.[56] During Adams's brief professorship (1870–1877), his engagement with historicist research on law and institutions, especially Maine's works, and his introduction of the seminar as a mode of teaching had a

---

[51] Lowell, *Essays*, 10, 13–15.

[52] Oliver Wendell Holmes, *The Common Law* (Boston: Little, Brown, 1881), esp. lectures 6–9.

[53] For example, see the invocation of Holmes by Lowell, *Essays*, 173.

[54] On the history of the institute and its prominent role in the intellectual life of nineteenth-century Boston, along with details of its many, often illustrious, lecturers, and books that came out of institute lectures, see Harriette Knight Smith, *The History of the Lowell Institute* (Boston: Lamson, Wolffe, 1898).

[55] In addition to Holmes and Henry Adams, whom I mention in the main text, a full historical account of this reception would also include the popular historian John Fiske, who gave multiple Lowell Institute lectures in the 1880s and 1890s. For examples of Fiske's works in this vein, see John Fiske, *American Political Ideas: Viewed from the Standpoint of Universal History* (New York: Harper & Brothers, 1885), John Fiske, *The Beginnings of New England, or The Puritan Theocracy in Its Relation to Civil and Religious Liberty* (Boston: Houghton, Mifflin, 1889).

[56] Yeomans, *Abbot Lawrence Lowell, 1856–1943*, chap. 3. Henry Adams left the academy in 1877, never to return. In his famous autobiography he would dismiss his teaching at Harvard in a chapter pointedly entitled "Failure." But others saw his efforts very differently. Faculty who followed in his footsteps at Harvard looked back upon Adams's labors there in the 1870s as a founding moment in developments leading up to the later departments of both history and government. Henry Adams, *The Education of Henry Adams* (New York: Oxford University Press, 1999), chap. 20; Ephraim Emerton, "History," in *Development of Harvard University* ed. Samuel Eliot Morison (Cambridge, MA: Harvard University Press, 1930), 150–77; Albert Bushnell Hart, "Government," in *Development of Harvard*, 178–86.

major influence. A collection of his and his students' studies of law and institutions in England after the Germanic invasions of the late fifth century, *Essays in Anglo-Saxon Law*, published in 1876, was credited on both sides of the Atlantic as a contribution to historicist scholarship.[57] Extending this lead, Holmes's *The Common Law* offered a developmental historicist study that charted slow progressive advance in the law through many centuries, from origins among the early Germans, via medieval England, to contemporary America.[58] Lowell's own familiarity with the transatlantic historicist tradition Adams and Holmes extended is evident in his 1891 review of a book, *A Short History of Anglo-Saxon Freedom*, popularizing the tradition's findings. Lowell there noted,

> Scholars have long been telling us that the real stream of our social and political forces is to be traced through the whole course of English history to a tiny spring that flowed out of the darkness of the German forests. This idea can easily be exaggerated... but in the main it is sound.[59]

In chapter 8, when we examine Lowell's later empirical analyses of mass suffrage politics, we will see the legacy of this transatlantic historicist tradition.

What matters for now, as we recount the classical liberal backdrop to Lowell's works, is to recognize the place of Maine's concepts and concerns in Lowell's earliest forays into political science. In introducing his 1889 *Essays* Lowell used the normatively loaded distinction between "stationary" societies (which were "stagnant") and "progressive" societies (with "a flexible state of society"). In terms even more distinctively Maine's, Lowell treated progress as embodied in, and promoted by, a grand historical development of social relations away from "status" toward "contract" that was assisted by, and articulated in, the law. Far from inevitable, this progressive movement could all too easily be stopped or reversed, and "any serious weakening of the bonds of contract, or in fact any general distrust in the strength of those bonds, would not only prevent any further progress, but would soon cause the social fabric to decay."[60]

---

[57] Henry Adams, Henry Cabot Lodge, Ernest Young, and J. Laurence Laughlin, *Essays in Anglo-Saxon Law* (Boston: Little, Brown, 1876). On this book and its reception, see Herbert Baxter Adams, "New Methods of Study in History," *Johns Hopkins University Studies in Historical and Political Science* 2, nos. 1–2 (1884), 87–89. In the late 1870s, H. B. Adams consulted personally with Henry Adams as he began his Maine-informed research agenda on New England towns.

[58] On the influence of Maine, and Holmes's friend and Harvard colleague Henry Adams, on *The Common Law*, see Mark DeWolfe Howe, "Introduction," to Oliver Wendell Holmes, *The Common Law* (Little, Brown, 1963), xiv–xvi.

[59] A. Lawrence Lowell, "Review of James K. Hosmer, *A Short History of Anglo-Saxon Freedom. The Polity of the English-Speaking Race: Outlined in its Inception, Development, Diffusion, and Present Condition," Annals of the American Academy* 1 (January 1891), 493.

[60] Lowell, *Essays*, 11–12, 14.

In anxiously suggesting that progress, even social order itself, was on the line in the way "bonds of contract" were treated, Lowell combined his classical liberal beliefs with a specifically disenchanted classical liberal fear. He deployed the commonplace classical liberal dichotomy of "paternal government" versus "a social organization in which the success of each man depends entirely upon his own exertions" to frame a disenchanted classical liberal fear that contemporary political attitudes and trends were turning back toward "paternalism." Interweaving this fear with Maine's account of progress as movement from status to contract, Lowell ended the introduction of his 1889 *Essays* ringing an alarm for the future: "We are placed to-day between individualism and paternal government, which deals with men as rigid masses; and to accept the latter would be a step backward from contract toward status, not an advance in the direction which the world has followed hitherto."[61]

CLASSICAL LIBERAL ANXIETIES AND POLITICAL ANALYSIS: LOWELL ON "PATERNALISM" AND "CLASS LEGISLATION"

Anxiety about political movement from classical liberal beliefs and hopes back toward a revival of paternal government was the common concern of the disenchanted classical liberalism of late century. This concern could, however, be engaged in multiple ways, and thus gave rise to a variety of particular analyses of contemporary politics. In the late 1880s, as Sumner critically analyzed contemporary America as at the forefront of a transatlantic rise of plutocracy, Lowell offered a less provocative (for Americans, at least) analysis, which he would, in turn, further moderate in the years ahead.

Lowell's disenchanted classical liberal fear of reviving paternalism, explicitly expressed in the introduction to his 1889 *Essays*, set up for the substantive interest in the "limitation of political power" pursued in each of the collection's essays.[62] But in line with the bounds on the "scientific spirit" also announced in the introduction, the essays themselves were more tempered in tone. For example, while Lowell in his introduction treated "paternal government" in frankly moralizing terms as striving "to treat the citizens as children, and keep them forever in leading-strings," when he took it up in his longest essay, "Democracy and the Constitution," he presented it as a view of government which holds that "it is the duty of the sovereign to provide directly for the well-being of his subjects."[63]

---

[61] Lowell, *Essays*, 15, 19.

[62] For Lowell's identification of the substantive "point of view" and "standpoint" of his essays as one of concern with the limitation of power, see Lowell, *Essays*, 4, 7.

[63] Lowell, *Essays*, 15, 61. On p. 74 Lowell similarly described "paternal government" as holding it to be "the mission of the state to provide for the welfare and to promote directly the progress of society."

Lowell noted, in a matter-of-fact way, that the "paternal theory of government has of late years been gaining ground rapidly in all countries, and especially in England," and then made it the focus of his own analysis "to examine the various political institutions in democratic countries, and to inquire how far they are adapted to promote or to check this tendency." Lowell did not hide his anxiety about the tendency. But his analysis of what promoted or checked it was set up as an empirical exercise with a degree of remove from that anxiety.

As Lowell in his 1889 *Essays* opened space between anxiety and analysis, his analysis in turn advanced substantive claims about America very different from Sumner's. The plutocracy writings of Sumner wedded provocative style and substance in a decline narrative that was more than informed by classical liberal anxiety. It was infused by, and indeed intensified, such anxiety. By contrast, Lowell delivered, in a matter-of-fact style, a substantive analysis that could soothe classical liberal anxiety, at least with regard to America. Lowell argued that America and Britain, while both now democracies, had very different institutions. America's institutional division of powers, high barriers to constitutional change, and the ability of courts to rule laws unconstitutional, offered as much hindrance as possible (within a democratic political system) to the translation of rising public support for the "paternal theory" into major changes in law and government.[64] Britain's parliamentary system was, by contrast, "developing" toward a combination of mass suffrage—in 1884 the Third Reform Bill had further expanded the suffrage beyond the prior 1867 Reform Bill—with institutionally concentrated power. This combination was, Lowell held, the most "appropriate" *if* "paternal government is the object to be sought."[65] To support this comparative claim about how institutions related to the rising tide of paternalism, he ended his "Democracy and the Constitution" essay by reviewing the prior decade and half of British legislation to show that "England although only beginning to be a democracy, has already gone further in the direction of socialism than the communities on this side of the ocean."[66]

This early foray into comparative study in Lowell's 1889 *Essays* anticipates the far more extensive and systematic empirical inquiries that came to characterize his later political science. The increasing empirical sophistication of Lowell's political science never displaced his view of the present as an era of revived paternalism. His 1896 *Governments and Parties in Continental Europe* treated efforts "to restrain the liberty of the individual and subject him to governmental supervision and control" as a "general tendency" in all modern countries, while observing that

---

[64] Lowell, *Essays*, 83–106. These themes were further developed in Lowell's next essay, "The Responsibility of American Lawyers," which charged lawyers with explicating and defending the "excellence of the principles" of the US Constitution (*Essays*, 125, 127–28).

[65] Lowell, *Essays*, 74–76.

[66] Lowell, *Essays*, 117. For Lowell's review of recent British legislation, see pp. 110–16.

it had gone further in some countries than others.[67] Similarly Lowell's 1898 article "Oscillations in Politics" offered—in addition to multiple pages of times series charts documenting the repeated ebb and flow in major parties' electoral fortunes in different nations and in different American states—comments about the "drift toward paternal government" seen in the "great increase in the functions of the state, and the widespread faith in the possibility of regenerating the world by legislation." In closing, Lowell drew from his technically pioneering empirical documentation of "rapid alternations of party" the political lesson that "the desire of a mere party majority cannot be said to express the lasting popular will," and thus "[t]he tendency to political oscillations in a democracy teaches, therefore, the ever growing value of constitutional limitations."[68]

The persistence in Lowell's work of disenchanted classical liberal concepts and concerns did not mean that his liberal political vision was immune to any updating of details. His classical liberalism was moderate in the sense, introduced in earlier chapters, that it could allow justified exceptions. This is most evident in the "Reflections" chapters ending Lowell's 1908 *Government of England*. In the chapter "The Growth of Paternalism" Lowell kept his long-standing concept, but updated his views in light of results in practice. He granted that a good part of the "paternal, perhaps even grandmotherly, legislation" of recent decades in England had turned out to be beneficial. Indeed, he noted that the paternal turn "to some extent might have been expected, for unless one adopts the principles of *laissez-faire* in their most absolute form, more or less regulation of economic and social relations is always necessary."[69] While Lowell's distancing of himself from uncompromising laissez-faire parallels the moderate classical liberalism J. S. Mill had articulated in midcentury, he himself had lumped together "Adam Smith, John Stuart Mill, and the English political economists of the earlier school" as preachers of "extreme *laissez-faire* doctrines."[70] Lowell's own obscuring of past nuances in the liberal tradition should not, however, obscure for us the parallel between his moderate stance and earlier moments in that tradition.[71]

---

[67] A. Lawrence Lowell, *Governments and Parties in Continental Europe*, 2 vols. (Boston: Houghton, Mifflin, 1896), 1: 34.

[68] A. Lawrence Lowell, "Oscillations in Politics," *Annals of the American Academy of Political and Social Science* 12 (July 1898), 95–97.

[69] A. Lawrence Lowell, *The Government of England*, 2 vols. (New York: Macmillan, 1908), 2: 526.

[70] Lowell, *Governments and Parties*, 1: 34.

[71] The parallels extend beyond the domain of laissez-faire to trade policy also. Just as John Stuart Mill had, Lowell combined general admiration for free trade with the exception that protection might be justified "in developing the industries of a new land." Lowell, *Government of England*, 2: 516. Lowell's openness to this caveat is perhaps not surprising given that the textile mills of Lowell, Massachusetts, had been developed, and produced windfall profits, in the context of American protective tariffs actively lobbied for by the Boston Manufacturing Company.

When treating paternalism in *Government of England*, Lowell tempered the anxiety about this tendency that had centrally informed his *Essays* two decades earlier. But he still remained a disenchanted classical liberal. His anxiety had simply become more focused. In his 1889 *Essays* Lowell's distrust of paternalism (which overlapped in his usage with "socialism") overshadowed another more specific worry. He had held that Britain's Parliament was "not only more inclined to socialistic measures than our [American] legislatures," but also "far more ready to pass laws for the benefit of one class in the community at the expense of others."[72] As Lowell moderated his view of paternalism, his dislike of laws conferring "special rights" on selected classes came to the fore. After his chapter titled "The Growth of Paternalism," he turned to "Party and Class Legislation." Lowell saw "class legislation" as exemplified by the Trade Disputes Act of 1906, which exempted trade unions from major legal liabilities. The act showed the "peril" of political parties "bidding for support of whole classes of voters by legislation for their benefit," which was "probably the most serious menace to which British institutions are exposed."[73]

Disenchanted Classical Liberalism as a Transatlantic Political Vision

Disenchanted classical liberal analyses of contemporary politics advanced a transatlantic political vision. Disenchanted classical liberals articulated fears about broad late-century political tendencies and anxiously analyzed, with varying results, the extent to which particular countries partook in those tendencies, or were exceptional relative to them. Such transatlantic comparisons were, moreover, informed by transatlantic intellectual exchanges. The two Americans we have examined, Sumner and Lowell, were not directly in conversation with one another. What made them fellow participants in a common conversation was that both engaged concepts and concerns of prominent British classical liberal intellectuals who, as midcentury became late century, had lost trust in contemporary political trends and become disenchanted critics. By situating Sumner and Lowell alongside two such British figures—Herbert Spencer and Sir Henry Maine—I

---

[72] Lowell, *Essays*, 110.

[73] Lowell, *Government of England*, 2: 531–35. In Lowell's fear it is easy to hear in advance the later liberalism of Hayek, for whom the 1906 act was "the most fateful law in Britain's modern history," marking for him the moment when British Liberals left behind the principle of a social order without special privileges for short-term political gain, with negative longer-run economic consequences. See Friedrich A. Hayek, *Law, Legislation, and Liberty*, vol. 3: *The Political Order of a Free People* (Chicago: University of Chicago Press, 1979), 31–32.

seek, in conclusion, to pinpoint both commonalities of disenchanted classical liberal political analysis and a key difference within it.

Anxiety about the tide of the times came to the fore in Spencer's writings in the 1870s, as his mature sociology (whose influence on Sumner we noted in chapter 4) took shape. In the first volume of *The Principles of Sociology*, published in 1876, after Spencer presented his basic typological contrast of "military" versus "industrial" societies, he quickly put the contrast to work to critique contemporary politics.[74] He charged the British Liberal Party with going astray when it pursued policies that forgot that "in essence Liberalism stands for the freedom of the individual *versus* control of the State." Where the party had earlier promoted "individual liberty" by "abolishing religious disabilities, establishing free-trade, removing impediments from the press, etc," it now "vied with the opposite party in multiplying State-administrations which diminish individual liberty." Applying his sociological concepts to interpret this change, Spencer contended that a retrograde move away from traits of "industrial" society toward those of "military" society was developing in tandem in Britain and on the European continent. He thus provocatively proposed to British readers that the "changes of late undergone by our own society" were "kindred" to contemporary tendencies in Bismarck's Germany.[75]

Spencer here articulated a disenchanted classical liberal stance that, in the 1880s, became the centerpiece of a full-fledged political vision developed and debated by liberal intellectuals on both sides of the Atlantic. At first Spencer's fear had been idiosyncratic. But by the early 1880s it was instead coming to appear prescient to other classical liberals. In chapter 4 we stressed the onset of pivotal departures in German economic and social policy in its 1879 tariff rise, and showed how this shocked Sumner and reshaped his polemics. In Britain, meanwhile, intellectual moves to rework liberal concepts to support Liberal Party legislation regulating the economy had been inaugurated by T. H. Green's famous 1881 "Lecture on Liberal Legislation and Freedom of Contract."[76] Alongside the policy and intellectual shifts of 1879–1881, Spencer had also adapted how he framed his anxiety in a way that facilitated its broader reception. In his 1882 "Political Institutions" (Part V of *Principles of Sociology*), Spencer began to

---

[74] The importance of supplementing the popularizing *The Man versus the State* with Spencer's sociological writings to understand his political thought is extensively and compellingly shown in Mark Francis's recent biography. Mark Francis, *Herbert Spencer and the Invention of Modern Life* (Stocksfield, UK: Acumen, 2007), part 4.

[75] Herbert Spencer, *The Principles of Sociology*, 3 vols. (New York: Appleton, 1898; vol. 1 first published in 1876), 1: 585 (italics in original), 580.

[76] Thomas Hill Green, "Lecture on Liberal Legislation and Freedom of Contract," in *The Works of Thomas Hill Green*, vol. 3, *Miscellanies and Memoir*, ed. Richard Lewis Nettleship (London: Longmans, Green, 1888), 365–86.

use Maine's famous "status" versus "contract" contrast to elucidate his own "military" versus "industrial" contrast, with reversion toward military society now identified as a retreat from contract toward status.[77] Both Green's effort to delimit and downgrade the place of freedom of contract in liberalism, and Spencer's use of Maine to frame any such move as inimical to progress, highlighted contracts as a focal point of concrete political significance. Debate over the role of law in enforcing, or via new legislation limiting, the terms of contracts helped to crystallize the divergence of British liberalism between figures reconstructing it to support the Liberal Party's contemporary agenda, and those wielding older classical liberal arguments to criticize that agenda. Spencer gave the disenchanted classical liberal side of this split probably its most famous articulation with the political essays of his 1884 *The Man versus the State*.

The twists and turns of British liberalism matter for us because they informed American discussions. Even before Spencer's 1884 essays put the combination of his and Maine's language to their most polemical political effect, that combination had already been used by Sumner in his 1883 *What Social Classes Owe to Each Other*.[78] The two had met when Spencer visited America in 1882, and Sumner paid gracious public homage to Spencer at the large farewell banquet given for him in New York that November.[79] In 1883 Sumner sent *Social Classes* fresh from the press to Spencer, who read it that winter, while working on *The Man versus the State* essays, which appeared in February to July of 1884. In a November 1883 letter acknowledging his receipt of Sumner's book, Spencer had spelled out to Sumner his disenchantment with the present, and how he saw both their efforts:

> I fear very much, however, that little can now be done in resisting the communistic tendencies which are daily growing stronger in civilized societies. The wave has become too vast.... However, we can but severally do what in us lies toward checking this disastrous tendency; and it is very satisfactory to me to find that you have issued what I am quite sure will be a telling exposition of rational views.[80]

The "we" Spencer spoke of in 1883 turned out to encompass more than just himself and Sumner. Spencer's move to bring Maine's concepts to bear in the

---

[77] Spencer, *Principles of Sociology*, 2: part 5 (first published 1882).

[78] Sumner, *What Social Classes Owe*. For an example of Sumner's use of the status/contract contrast Maine had originated, see 23–24. For an example of his use of the military/industrial contrast from Spencer, see 29–30.

[79] William Graham Sumner, "Professor Sumner's Speech," in *Herbert Spencer on the Americans and the Americans on Herbert Spencer*, ed. E. L. Youmans (New York: Appleton, 1883), 35–40.

[80] Letter from Spencer to Sumner, October 4, 1883. Reprinted in Starr, *William Graham Sumner*, 503–4.

fraught debate in the fracturing liberal tradition did more than help his analysis win a wider audience. It won Maine's approval. The year after *The Man versus the State* appeared, Maine published a set of political essays of his own in 1885, which were then subsequently collected as *Popular Government*. Tipping his hat to Spencer, Maine declared: "It is perfectly possible, I think, as Mr. Herbert Spencer has shown in a recent admirable volume, to revive even in our day the fiscal tyranny which once left European populations in doubt whether it was worth while preserving life by thrift and toil."[81] For Maine, like Spencer, disenchantment with the changing politics of a democratizing Britain fueled fear that the rise of democracy threatened the motors of liberal progress. As he put it:

> [O]ne of the strangest of vulgar ideas is that a very wide suffrage could or would promote progress, new ideas, new discoveries and inventions, new arts of life.... but the chances are that, in the long-run, it would produce a mischievous form of Conservatism... [and] arrest everything which has ever been associated with Liberalism.[82]

Maine thus could, in his darker passages, match Spencer in the forcefulness with which he gave voice to disenchanted classical liberal fears.

The substance of Maine's *Popular Government* was, however, moderated by a belief in American exceptionalism foreign to Spencer. When Spencer, in an 1871 essay, first diagnosed British politics as undergoing a retrograde turn from "industrial" toward "military" society, he had seen the same turn—from "assertion of the individuality of the citizen" toward "centralized control"—also occurring in America.[83] Maine, by contrast, used the embedded exceptionalism of the historicist scholarly tradition that he (unlike the extra-academic Spencer) worked within, to lighten his dark framing of contemporary trends by presenting America as an exception. In the pages of *Popular Government* he repeatedly looked across the Atlantic to interpret "American experience" as a demonstration "that, by wise constitutional provisions thoroughly thought out beforehand, Democracy may be made tolerable."[84]

The contrast Lowell drew between America's constitutionally constrained democracy and democracy as it was taking shape in late-century Britain had thus been offered earlier by Maine. The preface, first essay, and second essay of *Popular*

[81] Henry Sumner Maine, *Popular Government* (Indianapolis, IN: Liberty Fund, 1976; first published 1885), 69.

[82] Maine, *Popular Government*, 57. On Spencer's views in this regard, see Francis, *Spencer*, chap. 19.

[83] Herbert Spencer, "Specialized Administration," in *The Man versus the State, with Six Essays on Government, Society, and Freedom*, 435–86 (Indianapolis, IN: Liberty Fund, 1992; essay first published 1871). See especially 451–54.

[84] Maine, *Popular Government*, 122.

Government all closed with this contrast, which Maine then developed fully in his final essay, "The Constitution of the United States."[85] After endorsing Spencer's fears with regard to "European populations," Maine turned his eyes westward in his next pages to admiringly declare, "Americans are still of opinion that more is to be got for human happiness by private energy than by public legislation," and to argue that America's "beneficent prosperity" rested "on the sacredness of contract and the stability of private property."[86] Alongside his general contrast between "all the infirmities of our [British] constitution in its decay" and America's "securities against hasty innovation," Maine stressed, more specifically, that there was "no more important provision in the whole Constitution" than the "rule which denies to the several states the power to make laws impairing the obligation of contracts." The rule was "the bulwark of American individualism against democratic impatience and Socialistic fantasy."[87]

The back-to-back appearance, in 1884 and 1885 respectively, of Spencer's and Maine's books of critical political essays provides an essential intellectual context for the *Essays* Lowell composed in the middle to late 1880s and published together in 1889. When Lowell observed that the "paternal theory of government" was on the rise, he turned for authority to Spencer's book, holding that Spencer's review of "recent English legislation...shows very forcibly its paternal character." He did, however, reject Spencer's language of a "militant" turn, and Lowell's larger debt was clearly to Maine. Alongside the contrast between America's and Britain's democracies used by Lowell in his *Essays*, Maine's *Popular Government* had also called attention to two sets of phenomena—the referendum as used in Switzerland, and mass political parties—to which, we will see in chapter 8, Lowell would devote empirical research in the 1890s.[88] When Lowell later, after finishing his 1908 *Government of England*, started work on a general political science textbook, he explained to a Harvard colleague that he was writing "something in the way that Sir Henry Maine treated popular government, putting it, however, in a more systematic form."[89] The resulting text, *Public Opinion and Popular Government*, signaled debts to Maine, both in its title and by opening with a direct quote from Maine's *Popular Government*.[90]

By locating Sumner and Lowell in light of transatlantic intellectual exchanges we can see these Americans as engaged in a common disenchanted classical liberal

---

[85] Maine, *Popular Government*, 25–26, 70–74, 122–36, 199–247.

[86] Maine, *Popular Government*, 71.

[87] Maine, *Popular Government*, 236, 239, 242–43.

[88] For Maine on referendum see *Popular Government*, 60–62, 110–11; on parties see 112–19.

[89] Lowell to Albert Bushnell Hart, November 27, 1908, in letterpress book (Jan. 31, 1906–Feb. 27, 1911), box 22, Abbott Lawrence Lowell Papers, Harvard University Archives. Quoted courtesy of the Harvard University Archives.

[90] A. Lawrence Lowell, *Public Opinion and Popular Government* (New York: Longmans, 1913), 3.

conversation mediated by the British figures of Spencer and Maine. That conversation received a common content from the disillusionment of Maine, Spencer, and other British classical liberals, when Britain's Liberal Party moved, in the democratizing Britain of late century, toward the "New Liberalism" (akin to what I, in an American context, call "progressive liberalism"). They found a concrete common concern in defending the priority classical liberalism put on freedom of contract. This concern was, in turn, easily carried across the Atlantic, where it appears as a central disenchanted classical liberal theme in the 1880s writings of Sumner and Lowell.

A major difference within disenchanted classical liberal political analysis is highlighted, however, when we look, not only at transatlantic intellectual exchanges, but also at transatlantic comparisons. Lowell followed Maine in characterizing America as exceptional in the height of the hurdles facing reforms at odds with classical liberal prescriptions. Disenchanted classical liberal anxiety was, as a result, moderated in reference to America in Lowell's 1889 *Essays* in a way that contrasts with Sumner's late 1880s analysis of American politics. The uncompromising classical liberal Sumner had, by this time, joined Spencer in portraying the late century in terms of transatlantic trends from which America had no special relief. Indeed, Sumner's analysis of the rise of plutocracy saw America's democracy as, if anything, leading a descent into darker political times.

CHAPTER 7

Progressive Liberalism as a Political Vision

WOODROW WILSON'S POLITICAL SCIENCE

In Part II we were introduced to Richard T. Ely's progressive liberal interpretation of industrialization as a transformative process superseding earlier liberal commitments to laissez-faire. It is now time to elucidate more fully the content of progressive liberalism as a specifically *political* vision by connecting this interpretation of industrialization to claims about democracy and the administrative state. I do so in this chapter through a close examination of the writings of Woodrow Wilson as a student and young professor of political science during the 1880s. Wilson offers us the opportunity to chart within the works of a single political scientist the content of a move *from* democratized classical liberalism *to* progressive liberalism.

In 1883 Wilson began graduate study in the historical and political science department at Hopkins. He came into the department as a twenty-six year-old lawyer who had been publicly propounding democratized classical liberal views since his years as a Princeton undergraduate in the 1870s. In speech and print he had celebrated the principles and practices of British liberal politicians (specifically, Cobden, Bright, and Gladstone) who had fought and won midcentury battles for free trade and other classical liberal reforms.[1] I devote the first part of this chapter to the Britain-venerating ideal of representative government, and accompanying criticism of the American Constitution, that Wilson brought with him to Hopkins. I argue that the early work in which Wilson most fully expressed these youthful views—his *Congressional Government*—was identifiably liberal, but unlike his later works, not a distinctively progressive liberal work.

---

[1] See the long lionizing character sketches of these leaders of liberalism that Wilson presented while studying law at the University of Virginia in spring 1880. Woodrow Wilson, "John Bright," in *The Papers of Woodrow Wilson*, edited by Arthur S. Link, vol. 1 (Princeton, NJ: Princeton University Press, 1966), 608–21; Woodrow Wilson, "Mr Gladstone, A Character Sketch," in *Papers of Woodrow Wilson*, 1: 624–42.

It was only in the middle to late 1880s, when the influence of the Hopkins department, and specifically of Wilson's studies with Ely, becomes evident that Wilson's developing political science moved in directions unambiguously divergent from classical liberalism. The second and third parts of this chapter pinpoint the timing and substance of Wilson's departure from classical liberalism by documenting changes in his views of administration and political economy. I show Wilson refashioning his use of transatlantic comparisons to replace Britain with Germany and France as a paradigmatic model of good administration, and also shifting from firmly espousing classical political economy to embracing Ely's view of the "historical school" in economics as a scientific advance. These twin changes were directly connected through Wilson's adoption of a progressive liberal argument linking expansion of the administrative state to the transformative impact of industrialization on government. Finally, I showcase how Wilson's 1889 *The State* and other contemporaneous writings and speeches rounded out his progressive liberal political science by using the concept of the "modern" to revisit issues of freedom and self-government that had engaged him ever since his democratized classical liberal youth. By the end of 1880s Wilson had articulated a full-fledged political vision of the "modern Democratic State" as the progressive liberal end of history.

Representative Government and the Constitution: Comparing America and England

At Princeton in the late 1870s Wilson read multiple works by Lieber and Freeman and embraced a liberal developmental historicism. In 1878 he wrote in the *Princetonian* of "the German forests in which the English race was cradled," expressing gratitude that the American people were "a lusty branch" of that "noble race," and exhorting his readers to cherish "the grand principles of liberty in whose development nine centuries have been consumed."[2] Five years or so later, when Wilson put aside a post-Princeton foray into law to pursue an academic career, he identified his special research interest as "Constitutional History" in applying to graduate study at Hopkins.[3]

Wilson thus arrived at Hopkins in 1883 imbued with a liberal developmental historicism that situated American politics in light of transatlantic lineages. More specifically he wanted to apply this liberal historicism to America's constitution and national government. Since the late 1870s he had been working

---

[2] *Papers of Woodrow Wilson*, 1: 374–75.
[3] *Papers of Woodrow Wilson*, vol. 2 (1967), 430.

out an argument that America fell distressingly short of liberal ideals of representative government, along with a diagnosis of the executive-legislative divide in the Constitution as the root of this problem.[4] Within a month of arriving at Hopkins, Wilson asked if he could develop this line of thought as a dissertation. H. B. Adams welcomed the proposal, and by the end of his first year Wilson was already presenting chapters to the Seminary of Historical and Political Science. In fall 1884 Wilson finished a full manuscript, which was soon published. He had thus been at Hopkins under eighteen months when, in early 1885, *Congressional Government: A Study in American Politics* appeared. While it would serve as Wilson's dissertation, the book was less a Hopkins product than a culmination of self-guided "studies in comparative politics" that, as Wilson put it, had been his "delight during leisure hours for the last five or six years" before graduate school.[5]

Congressional Government applied a comparative developmental approach to American institutions. Wilson cast contemporary glances at the Reichstag of "our cousin Germans" and the Assembly of France's Third Republic.[6] But his main comparison was to England. Wilson treated America's political system as a historical growth from centuries-old English rootstock that had then branched onto its own national developmental path during the founding. Eighteenth-century England therefore offered a shared historical departure point to frame comparison of more recent developments in representative government in both England and America. In using a historicist Anglo-American comparison, Wilson paralleled Lieber's antebellum *Civil Liberty and Self-Government*. But *Congressional Government* used the comparison to markedly new effect. Wilson contended that representative government had been hamstrung in America by a written constitution whose veneration protected even its flaws. By contrast, representative government had been flourishing in the more flexible constitutional context of England, where the successive waves of nineteenth-century parliamentary reform had now created a "House of Commons truly representative of the nation." The Commons was at the center of a "system of self-government" that had, as Wilson judged it, become "superior" to America's variant of self-government.[7]

Wilson's interpretation of England was heavily indebted to the classical liberal Bagehot's *The English Constitution* and the contrast it popularized between

---

[4] Wilson had first published a version of this argument in the summer after his 1879 graduation from Princeton. See "Cabinet Government in the United States," in *Papers of Woodrow Wilson*, 1: 493–510.

[5] The composition of *Congressional Government* and its relation to Wilson's reading and writing in this topic area since the late 1870s is summarized in an editorial note in *Papers of Woodrow Wilson*, vol. 4 (1968), 6–13. Wilson describes the interest he brought with him to Hopkins, and securing Adams's approval to develop it in his dissertation, in a letter to his fiancée. See Wilson to Ellen Louise Axson, October 13, 1883, in *Papers of Woodrow Wilson*, 2: 478–80.

[6] Wilson, *Congressional Government: A Study in American Politics* (Boston: Houghton, Mifflin, 1885), 304, 123–29.

[7] Wilson, *Congressional Government*, 306–15.

parliamentary and presidential government. Wilson took up the English content and positive valuation Bagehot had given to the parliamentary side of this contrast. But he thought Bagehot's presidential concept overlooked key features of contemporary American politics, and he sought to provide for America the kind of exploration into how power works in actual practice that Bagehot had pioneered for the case of England. Writing to his fiancée as he began drafting *Congressional Government*, Wilson explained his goal for the book:

> My desire and ambition are to treat the American constitution as Mr. Bagehot (do you remember Mr. Bagehot, about whom I spoke to you one night on the veranda at Asheville?—) has treated the English Constitution. His book has inspired my whole study of our government. He brings to the work a fresh and original method which has made the British system much more intelligible to ordinary men than it ever was before, and which, if it could be successfully applied to the exposition of our federal constitution, would result in something like a revelation to those who are still reading the Federalist as an authoritative constitutional manual.[8]

Wilson aimed to identify the "real depositaries and the essential machinery of power" in American politics, and thereby to highlight, as Bagehot had done for England, how this "'living reality'" differed from "the 'literary theory' of the Constitution" presented in legal treatises and celebratory accounts. He contended that the century since the adoption of the federal Constitution had seen transformative political change in America. The powers of the states and the presidency had waned to the point that balances highlighted in the text and theory of the Constitution now obscured more than they reflected the "actual form of our present government." A student of American politics hence had to "escape from theories and attach himself to facts." Doing so revealed, Wilson argued, that political power in contemporary America was not centered in the presidency, as the label "presidential government" suggested. What America had, in practice, was not presidential but rather "congressional government," in which "the predominant and controlling force, the centre and source of all motive and of all regulative power, is Congress."[9]

Having identified what he took to be a historical trend toward concentrating power in Congress, Wilson interpreted this trend in transatlantic perspective. It paralleled, he suggested, the increase in power of the House of Commons. These trends taken together testified to "the inevitable tendency of every system of

---

[8] Wilson to Ellen Louise Axson, January 1, 1884, in *Papers of Woodrow Wilson*, 2: 641.
[9] Wilson, *Congressional Government*, chap. 1. Specific quotes are drawn from pp. 6 and 10–12.

self-government like our own and the British to exalt the representative body, the people's parliament, to a position of absolute supremacy."[10] For today's readers this grand developmental generalization may appear ironic in light of the later growth in the power of America's president, in which Wilson's own presidency played a notable role. But the assertion was not idiosyncratic at the time. Sumner, for example, had declared in 1881: "The legislatures of modern times are the real depositaries of the power and will of the State. The centre of gravity of our system tends all the time to settle more firmly in the House of Representatives."[11]

Where Wilson struck his most original note was in his comparative analysis of changes in the *internal* working of Congress and Commons that accompanied their growth in power. Wilson suggested that these changes could be seen as "experiments in the direction of the realization of an idea best expressed...by John Stuart Mill" in Mill's legislative commission proposal, which expressed the "necessity of setting apart a small body, or bodies, of legislative guides through whom a 'big meeting' may get laws made."[12] Before Mill registered it in liberal thought, this "necessity" had already prompted changes in political practice. It was here that Wilson saw a pivotal divergence between America and England. In America, as Congress grew in power, it proliferated committees that parceled out the power of lawmaking. This led to "government by the chairmen of the Standing Committees of Congress," who employed their power in ways uncoordinated with, or even antagonistic to, other chairmen and the executive branch. In England, by contrast, a cabinet composed of the leaders of the party that had a Commons majority evolved to function as "a single standing committee" for originating legislation, and as "a device for bringing the executive and legislative branches into harmony and cooperation."[13] For Wilson, analyzing the who and how of power showed that congressional government was hence in practice "Committee Government," while parliamentary government was in practice, as Bagehot taught, "Cabinet Government."[14]

[10] Wilson, *Congressional Government*, 311.

[11] William Graham Sumner, "Presidential Elections and Civil-Service Reform," *Collected Essays in Political and Social Science* (New York: Holt, 1885), 157. This article had first been published in the *Princeton Review* in 1881.

[12] Wilson, *Congressional Government*, 115. See John Stuart Mill, *Considerations on Representative Government*, in *Essays on Politics and Society*, ed. John M. Robson, *Collected Works of John Stuart Mill*, vol. 19 (Toronto: University of Toronto Press, 1977), 428–32.

[13] This contrast is developed in Wilson, *Congressional Government*, chap. 2. Quotes from pp. 102 and 117–18.

[14] Wilson moved back and forth in the terms he emphasized within his twin equations Congressional Government = Committee Government, and Parliamentary Government = Cabinet Government. While *Congressional Government* highlighted in its title the first side of these equations, their second side was highlighted, for example, in the title of Wilson's 1884 essay "Committee or Cabinet Government?" in *Papers of Woodrow Wilson*, 2: 614–40.

This Anglo-American comparison was charged with theoretical import for Wilson. He saw England and America as developing from the same historical lineage of self-government via representatives, but believed this liberal inheritance had, more recently, been adapted to flourish better in England. In an 1879 essay Wilson had decried America's "committee government" as "utterly at variance with the true principles of representative government as understood by our English fore-fathers."[15] That same year, in terms notably similar to Mill's democratized classical liberal *Considerations on Representative Government*, Wilson had spelled out the ideal content he ascribed to representative government:

> At its highest development, *representative* government is that form which best enables a free people to govern themselves. The main object of a representative assembly, therefore, should be the discussion of public business. They should legislate as if in the presence of the whole country, because they come under the closest scrutiny and fullest criticism of all the representatives of the country speaking in open and free debate. Only in such an assembly, only in such an atmosphere of publicity, only by means of such a vast investigating machine, can the different sections of a great country learn each other's feelings and interests.... *debate* is the essential function of a popular representative body. In the severe, distinct, and sharp enunciation of underlying principles, the unsparing examination and telling criticism of opposite positions, the careful, painstaking unraveling of all the issues involved, which are incident to the free discussion of questions of public policy, we see the best, the only effective, means of educating public opinion.... The educational influences of such discussions is two-fold, and operates in two directions,—upon the members of the legislature themselves, and upon the people whom they represent.[16]

After thus expounding his ideal, Wilson had then directly declared "this matter of a full and free discussion" to be the "hinge" on which he judged the merits of the contemporary American and English political systems, to the decided advantage of the latter.[17]

When Wilson elaborated his Anglo-American comparison during 1883–1884 to produce *Congressional Government*, he offered more empirical detail but stepped back from enunciating his political ideal explicitly as he had in his 1879 essays. Explaining this move to a friend from his Princeton days, Wilson declared that he had "abandoned the evangelical for the exegetical."[18] Yet a strong deliberative

---

[15] Wilson, *Congressional Government*, 557.
[16] Wilson, "Cabinet Government," 494, 500–501. Italics in original.
[17] Wilson, "Cabinet Government," 501.
[18] Wilson to Robert Bridges, November 19, 1884, in *Papers of Woodrow Wilson*, vol. 3 (1967), 465.

and educational ideal still gave a firmly liberal thrust to Wilson's book. Hence, for example, in the midst of his description of standing committees, Wilson asserted that the "chief, and unquestionably the most essential, object of all discussion of public business is the enlightenment of public opinion." He then used this claim to develop his observation that the meetings of committees were "private and their discussions unpublished" into a complaint that they did not help to instruct the "nation." Indeed, the absence from Congress's legislative process of "searching, critical, illuminating" public debates involving a politically consequential "contest of principles"—which he saw as occurring in Britain's Parliament—struck Wilson so strongly that he declared that America's political system lacked "essential conditions of intelligent self-government."[19]

The belief that representative bodies can and should be deliberative spaces of principled debate in dynamic interaction with public opinion is a persistent substratum of Wilson's liberal political thought. It is in light of this ideal that we can best interpret his criticism of the American Constitution in *Congressional Government*. In opening the book Wilson provocatively presented himself as a member of a new generation challenging the "unquestioned prerogative of the Constitution to receive universal homage."[20] He then put this challenge into action by arguing that the problematic practices of committee government grew out of a flaw in the Constitution itself. For Wilson, the rise of the committee system showed that the way the Constitution "parcels out power" had turned out, in practice, to be "a radical defect" since it "confuses responsibility." Specifically, the separation of legislative and executive power was "the defect which interprets all the rest."[21] In Britain, by contrast, the rise of cabinet government interwove these powers. The cabinet was the clear center of power whose actions the British public could follow through its decisions, and through the explanations that ministers gave of these decisions in Parliament. The contrast between contemporary practices of representative government in America and England showed, Wilson argued, that interweaving executive and legislative power is a prerequisite of a system in which the actions of power holders are visible and responsible to public opinion.

Wilson's constitutional criticism was, as such, premised on an ideal of representative government that we have seen to be a major theme in the liberal tradition.

---

[19] Wilson, *Congressional Government*, 83–86. A hundred pages or so later Wilson's deliberative educational ideal is again evident when he observes that the public "cannot watch or understand forty odd Standing Committees, each of which goes its own way in doing what it can" and argues that "Congress evades judgment by avoiding all coherency of plan in its action." These more specific points are part and parcel of a general critical charge that "we lack in our political life the conditions most essential for the formation of an active and effective public opinion." See 185–89.

[20] Wilson, *Congressional Government*, 4.

[21] Wilson, *Congressional Government*, 283–86, 318–19.

Locating Wilson's criticism as a criticism from *within* the evolving liberal tradition helps us to comprehend his belief that he was updating, not rejecting, the spirit of America's Constitution. He suggested that the wisdom of the framers lay, not in every feature of the Constitution they crafted, but in their practical ability to learn from experience—an ability such that, if they could now be reconvened to study "the work of their hands in the light of the century that has tested it, they would be the first to admit that the only fruit of dividing power had been to make it irresponsible."[22]

Wilson's proposal that America's eighteenth-century founders would themselves, if alive in his day, share his criticism assumed, however, reading back into the founders the midcentury democratization of classical liberalism. He was, moreover, advancing this suggestion at exactly the same time that some prominent classical liberals were expounding their disenchantment with that democratization. In the same year *Congressional Government* was published so also was Sir Henry Maine's *Popular Government*. As noted in the conclusion of chapter 6, Maine's 1885 book venerated America's Constitution and institutions. When hailing America's political system as a "success," Maine forcefully declared, moreover, that its success arose "rather from skillfully applying the curb to popular impulses than from giving them free rein."[23] Like Wilson, Maine saw Britain's parliamentary reforms as having produced a political system now more responsive to public opinion than America's. But for Maine that transatlantic contrast spoke to the merit, not the detriment, of the American system.

Wilson's *Congressional Government* was, moreover, quickly criticized in America for its claims about the nation's institutions. The critic here was none other than A. Lawrence Lowell. Lowell's first published foray into political science was an 1886 *Atlantic Monthly* article (later republished as chapter 1 of his 1889 *Essays on Government*) that criticized Wilson's book.[24] Lowell suggested that Wilson's sweeping claims about a historical transformation in America's institutions overstated the facts. The states, presidency, and especially the judiciary remained stronger than Wilson recognized.[25] Lowell framed his criticism as an empirical matter of getting the facts right. But he made the criticism against a backdrop of evaluative disagreement. Whereas Wilson questioned the division of power (or, more specifically, certain aspects of it) as an ideal, for Lowell, like Maine, division of power was a salutary curb against a too rapid and unreflective translation of shifts in public opinion into institutional and legal change. Against Wilson's praise for present-day Britain, Lowell stressed that its political system

[22] Wilson, *Congressional Government*, 284. See also 332–33.

[23] Henry Sumner Maine, *Popular Government* (Indianapolis, IN: Liberty Fund, 1976), 26.

[24] A. Lawrence Lowell, "Ministerial Responsibility and the Constitution," *Atlantic Monthly* 57 (February 1886), 180–93.

[25] A. Lawrence Lowell, *Essays on Government* (Boston: Houghton, Mifflin, 1889), 46–57.

had both "merits" and "faults," and suggested that neither system could, on balance, be judged superior in general terms. Lowell instead simply, and perhaps proudly, avowed that "our system is still the best for us."[26]

Wilson soon recognized the force of the challenges to *Congressional Government* arising from Maine's *Popular Government* and Lowell's article. Just a few months after Lowell's article appeared, Wilson engaged both works in an *Atlantic Monthly* article of his own. His response is especially telling for establishing that Wilson was a less radical critic of America's Constitution than might be supposed based on some of the bolder statements in *Congressional Government*. Wilson's embrace in the book of criticism of the Constitution was moderated by an expectation that critics would find flaws in specific features of the Constitution, not reject it more generally. In responding to Maine and Lowell, Wilson clarified his own views by stressing that there were major features of the Constitution he agreed did warrant veneration. He singled out "the distinct division of powers between the state and federal governments, the slow and solemn formalities of constitutional change, and interpretative functions of the federal courts" as features "of our Constitution... to which our national pride properly attaches."[27]

Wilson's constitutional criticism was hence actually quite limited. There was, moreover, nothing especially novel or radical about his taking specific aim at the separation of executive and legislative powers. After all, Sumner had shot at the same target a few years earlier in his 1881 article, when he complained that "the Constitution very mistakenly endeavored to sunder" the "bond between the executive and the legislative." In sum, though the willingness to criticize the

---

[26] Lowell, *Essays on Government*, 58. When returning to US-UK comparisons in his later work Lowell would again strike a note of equanimity, suggesting each system had its pros and cons and emphasizing that it was not his concern to pass a general judgment on their relative merit. A. Lawrence Lowell, "Oscillations in Politics," *Annals of the American Academy of Political and Social Science* 12 (July 1898), 96–97; A. Lawrence Lowell, "The Influence of Party upon Legislation in England and America," in *Annual Report of the American Historical Association for the Year 1901*, vol. 1 (Washington, DC: Government Printing Office, 1902), 350.

[27] Woodrow Wilson, "Responsible Government under the Constitution," *Papers of Woodrow Wilson*, vol. 5 (1968), 123. Even as they differed about democracy and the executive/legislative relation, Wilson and Lowell partook in a broader shared tradition of liberal interests and concern, and developed good personal relations. In April 1886, the same month Wilson's response to Lowell's article appeared, he personally called on Lowell to introduce himself, and wrote of their first meeting afterwards to his wife: "We were very glad to see each other. I found him really delightful. He is a young lawyer of just my age (we compared ages, quite like two boys).... He is full of matter of the right sort: and our hour's conversation ran off as if it were a tenth part so long." Wilson to Ellen Louise Wilson, April 24, 1886, in *Papers of Woodrow Wilson*, 5: 169. Decades later, when Lowell became president of Harvard, he would draw inspiration from efforts to reform undergraduate life Wilson had pursued at Princeton. Veysey's classic study of American higher education identified Wilson and Lowell together as exemplifying the reform ideal of "liberal culture." Laurence R. Veysey, *The Emergence of the American University* (Chicago: University of Chicago Press, 1965), chap. 4.

Constitution exemplified in *Congressional Government* would become a recurrent trait of American progressive liberalism, that willingness was not in itself sufficient to constitute a progressive liberal political vision. We must look to Wilson's later writings to find arguments that decisively depart from the democratized classical liberalism of his youth.

Administration: Continental Europe, Convergence, and the Expansion of Government

Only in the middle to late 1880s, when the influence of the Hopkins department, and Ely especially, becomes evident, did Wilson's writings move in directions unambiguously divergent from classical liberalism. The impact of Ely registers clearly in two of Wilson's 1887 articles: "The Study of Politics" and "The Study of Administration." The "Politics" article flags Wilson's introduction to the "war among the political economists" in which "John Stuart Mill no longer receives universal homage, but has to bear much irreverent criticism."[28] In chapter 5 we saw Ely recruit Wilson's classmate and friend Albert Shaw into this war, and in the next section we will see how Ely also drew Wilson into battle. First, I take up Wilson's "Administration" article, which vividly captures the post–*Congressional Government* turn in his thought. Administration and its reform had been a sub-theme in Wilson's first book. But when he returned to this issue in 1887 Wilson treated it using a new transatlantic framework that registered his introduction, via Ely, to the continental European science of administration.[29]

Wilson had arrived at Hopkins with strong views about administration. A firm advocate of civil service reform, he had looked forward in early 1881 to "a great organized agitation" for reform modeled on Cobden and Bright's democratized classical liberal Anti–Corn Law League.[30] Later that year, a disgruntled office seeker assassinated President Garfield, and the National Civil Service Reform League was established to coordinate local reform leagues that had sprung up in recent years. Following on from these events, a surge of public support helped lead to the 1883 enactment of the Pendleton Civil Service Reform Act.[31] The

---

[28] Woodrow Wilson, "The Study of Politics," *New Princeton Review* 3, no. 2 (1887), 188.

[29] In his autobiography Ely saw administration as the area in which his teaching most clearly influenced Wilson, and explained that he taught "the idea that in matters of administration the United States lags far behind other countries with which we would like to rank." Richard T. Ely, *Ground under Our Feet: An Autobiography* (New York: Macmillan, 1938), 114.

[30] Woodrow Wilson, "What Can be Done for Constitutional Liberty," in *Papers of Woodrow Wilson*, 2: 38.

[31] On the act, and especially the role of public opinion in its success, see Sean M. Theriault, "Patronage, the Pendleton Act, and the Power of the People," *Journal of Politics* 65, no. 1 (2003), 50–68.

promise of the act's introduction of competitive exams for selected government offices was made especially tangible for Wilson in 1884, when his own former law partner qualified by exam for a Treasury position, from which he provided Wilson material for the "Revenue and Supply" chapter in *Congressional Government*.[32]

Wilson's treatment of administration in *Congressional Government* trumpeted the "recent movements in the direction of a radical reform of the civil service" as the beginning of a process pointing toward a "consummation devoutly to be wished!" More specifically, he contended that "real and lasting reform" required drawing "a sharp line between those offices which are political and those which are *non*-political." In exploring this line Wilson offered an expansive reading of the reach of nonpolitical offices, questioning if even the secretary of the Treasury and other cabinet members had "properly political" duties.[33] The Pendleton Act had put only an initial 10.5 percent of federal positions onto a merit-selection basis and Wilson's comments reflected his support for extending that percentage, as happened step by step through subsequent decades to reach 70 percent during Wilson's own presidency.[34]

In addition to exploring the proper extent of the domain of nonpolitical offices, Wilson also considered the standard by which operation of those offices should be judged. He identified "efficiency" as "the only just foundation for confidence in a public officer" with a nonpolitical position. To convey this standard Wilson deployed business analogies on the grounds that "the executive duties of government constitute just an exalted kind of business."[35] Nonpolitical posts should be characterized, he held, by the "strictest rules of business discipline" as well as "merit-tenure and earned promotion."[36] But business was not Wilson's only model. He also valorized Britain as having "achieved the reform for which we are striving" via the civil service reform it began in the 1850s, and as having "the most advanced" system in the area of financial policy and administration.[37] The view of America lagging midcentury classical liberal Britain that framed the political central theme of *Congressional Government* thus extended to its administrative subtheme also.

To put it simply, nothing that Wilson said about administration up through his *Congressional Government* was incompatible with classical liberalism. Sumner

---

[32] Edward Ireland Renick to Wilson, February 14, February 28, and March 2, 1884, in *Papers of Woodrow Wilson*, 3: 22, 52, 54–55.

[33] Wilson, *Congressional Government*, 236, 290, 261–65. Italics in original.

[34] *Biography of an Ideal: A History of the Federal Civil Service* (Washington, DC: Government Printing Office, 2003). Accessed at http://www.opm.gov/biographyofanideal/ on June 24, 2011. The steps of this trend are described on pp. 207–19 of the downloaded pdf of this history.

[35] Wilson, *Congressional Government*, 255–56.

[36] Wilson, *Congressional Government*, 290.

[37] Wilson, *Congressional Government*, 285–89, 180.

and Lowell also supported civil service reform, which had been developing in America since the Civil War, and now had its first national-level victory in the Pendleton Act. Sumner registered his support, for example, in an as-ever uncompromisingly classical liberal fashion, when in his 1883 *What Social Classes Owe to Each Other*, he provocatively held: "Civil service reform would be a greater gain to the laborers than innumerable factory acts and eight-hour laws."[38] Lowell's support introduced a key nuance into his 1886 article engaging Wilson's book. He argued there that Wilson's hope that American politics might be improved by introducing elements of parliamentary government failed to see that America and Britain had alternative *systems*, each with complex interrelated parts. Adjusting one aspect of a system could set off hard-to-predict consequences that might, on balance, produce more harm than good. Yet Lowell had one key caveat. Analysts could identify "abuses" lacking a "necessary connection" to the political system, and these should be reformed. His example was America's party-based distribution of spoils. Lowell, like Wilson and Sumner, looked forward to America following midcentury Britain's lead in implementing civil service reform.[39]

Against this common backdrop, it appears as a pivotal turn in Wilson's liberalism when, during 1885, soon after *Congressional Government* appeared in print, he abruptly reworked his transatlantic comparisons to replace Britain with Germany and France as his paradigmatic model of good administration. In spring of that year Wilson took a course on administration with Ely, who used Bluntschli's *Lehre vom modernen Staat* in lectures and provided students bibliographic introductions to continental European literature on administration more broadly. Wilson would draw on these sources extensively in following years as he made administration into one of his own academic specializations.[40] It was through Ely that Wilson therefore came, during 1885, to believe that "[n]either the practice nor the theory of administration has ever been reduced to a science either in this country or in England.... The Germans and the French have done most in developing a

[38] William Graham Sumner, *What Social Classes Owe to Each Other* (Caldwell, ID: Caxton Printers, 1989), 139.

[39] Terence Ball has argued that political scientists favored civil service reform as a way to tame democracy. I would suggest that this was a widely shared inheritance from democratized classical liberalism's anxiety about the illiberal potential of democracy. See Terence Ball, "An Ambivalent Alliance: Political Science and American Democracy," in *Political Science in History: Research Programs and Political Traditions*, ed. James Farr, John S. Dryzek, and Stephen T. Leonard (Cambridge: Cambridge University Press, 1995), 41–65.

[40] On Ely's course see editorial notes, *Papers of Woodrow Wilson*, 3: 335 and 5: 43. While Ely drew on the third *Politik als Wissenschaft* volume of Bluntschli's *Lehre*—which Wilson, in turn, cites in "Study of Administration"—Wilson was also introduced to other parts of Bluntschli's work in fall 1884 and spring 1885 in Adams's "History of Politics" lectures. In fall 1885 Wilson read for himself and took notes on the first *Allgemeine Statslehre* volume. See editorial notes, *Papers of Woodrow Wilson*, 5: 56 and vol. 6 (1969), 154.

science of administration." This belief, in turn, spurred him to craft a transnational intellectual agenda: adapting the science "developed by German and French professors" to make it of "use to us in the solution of our own problems of administration in town, city, county, State, and nation."[41] In advocating this agenda in his 1887 article and developing it in an increasingly sophisticated fashion in lectures he gave at Hopkins from 1888 to 1896, Wilson helped inaugurate administration as a specialized subject within the evolving remit of American political science.[42]

Coming into his new agenda from a liberal historicism that celebrated Anglo-American exceptionalism, Wilson was acutely aware that some Americans might be skeptical of a science from continental Europe. He accordingly stressed that it was essential that this "foreign science... be Americanized, not in language only, but in thought, in principle, in aim as well." He found aid in overcoming "obstacles to its domestication" in recent political changes making continental Europe less unpalatable to Americans. Subsuming his earlier liberal exceptionalist narrative into a broad transatlantic convergence, Wilson began to "discern a tendency, long operative but only of late days predominant, towards the adoption of the same general principles of government everywhere."[43] The convergence narrative that took shape in his thought in 1885–1886 would appear in print in "Study of Administration" in 1887.

Wilson's article revisited a core comparison in the history of government: the comparison between the path of institutional development followed since the early-modern era in continental Europe versus that in England and America. Wilson shifted his transatlantic perspective away from that of classical liberals like Sumner, for whom continental European governments offered only negative warnings. On the one hand, Wilson retained a belief that the exceptional history of England and America led to "vast advantages in point of political liberty, and above all in point of practical political skill and sagacity." Yet he moved in a new

[41] Woodrow Wilson, "Three Essays on Administration," in *Papers of Woodrow Wilson*, 5: 49, 52, italics in original.

[42] As Wilson pursued the agenda that took shape with the 1885 shift in his transatlantic administrative comparisons he would adapt his views. For example, while the attraction to business as a model derived from his early classical liberalism lingered into "Study of Administration," Wilson would step away from it in his Hopkins lectures of 1888. Assessing the belief that "organs of a government" are "best tested by the same standards of propriety and efficiency by which we test the organs of a great commercial corporation," he now contended that, while there is an "important element of truth" here, "little but confusion can result from its adoption as a guiding view." Woodrow Wilson, "Lecture II. The Functions of Government," in *Papers of Woodrow Wilson*, 5: 689–90. Wilson's refining of his views points toward later lectures as the best source for study of his mature position on administration. I focus on middle to late 1880s texts because my goal is, by contrast, to show a critical juncture in the trajectory of his thought and the role that transatlantic comparison played at this juncture. A detailed study of Wilson's mature position, as developed through a decade of reading, reflection, and teaching on administration, lies beyond the scope of this book.

[43] Wilson, "Three Essays," 52–53.

direction by also holding that the "English race" had neglected "the art of perfecting executive methods," with progress in this aspect of government instead charted on the European continent, where especially Prussia, but also France, led the way "in administrative organization and administrative skill."[44] Paralleling Bluntschli's placement of the onset of the "modern" at the time of Prussia's eighteenth-century administrative reforms, Wilson declared:

> Those governments are now in the lead in administrative practice which had rulers still absolute but also enlightened when those modern days of political illumination came in which it was made evident to all but the blind that governors are properly only servants of the governed. In such governments administration has been organized to subserve the general weal with the simplicity and effectiveness vouchsafed only to the undertakings of a single will.
>
> Such was the case in Prussia, for instance, where administration has been the most studied and most nearly perfected. Frederic the Great, stern and masterful as was his rule, still sincerely professed to regard himself as only the chief servant of the state, to consider his great office a public trust; and it was he who, building upon the foundation as laid by his father, began to organize the public service of Prussia as in very earnest a service of the public.[45]

There had thus been two historical paths of modern progress in government, one charted in England and America, the other in France and Germany. The present era was characterized, in turn, by reforms that attempted to bring these two paths together. On the European continent institutions of representative democracy had recently been established. The challenge there was to develop a public opinion that was effectively sovereign and thereby make the new institutions democratic in actual practice.[46] In America, which had long ago "enthroned public opinion," it was professional administrative institutions that had only

---

[44] Woodrow Wilson, "The Study of Administration," *Political Science Quarterly* 2, no. 2 (1887), 206. The idea that Germany, while lagging politically, displayed an admirable excellence in administration had previously been stated, though less fully explored, by Andrew D. White in his 1879 address at Hopkins. See Andrew D. White, *Education in Political Science: An Address* (Baltimore, MD: John Murphy, 1879), 21.

[45] Wilson, "Study of Administration," 204.

[46] Wilson was franker in his preliminary drafts than he was in print about his view that France and Germany had not as yet met this challenge. He contended there that the "essential difference between free governments and unfree governments lies in the *authority* which public opinion invariably has in the former and often or always lacks in the former," and then observed that "when judged by this radical test" Germany and France remained "examples of the unfree." Italics in original. Wilson, "Three Essays," 53.

just been introduced. The challenge on this side of the Atlantic was to develop "a corps of civil servants prepared by special schooling and drilled, after appointment, into a perfected organization, with appropriate hierarchy and characteristic discipline," while keeping that corps "sensitive to public opinion" so as to ensure that there was not "anything un-American" about it.[47] Wilson's new grand historical narrative thus highlighted the promise of transatlantic convergence in recent reforms *and* the contrasting challenges to realization of that promise that arose in continental Europe and America from the legacy of their previously exceptional historical paths.

This convergence narrative brings us right to the borderline of progressive liberalism as a political vision. H. B. Adams, on the one hand, stayed shy of the progressive vision by interpreting increasing American attention to administration as a welcome return to concerns of the founding fathers.[48] Wilson, by contrast, moved decisively into progressive liberal terrain in the course of the argument of "Study of Administration." In opening the article he identified it as "the object of administrative study to discover, first, what government can properly and successfully do, and, secondly, how it can do these proper things with the utmost possible efficiency and at the least possible cost either of money or of energy."[49] The stress on efficiency in the second object echoes Wilson's stance in *Congressional Government* and is perfectly compatible with classical liberalism. But when we turn to Wilson's treatment of the preceding object—"what government can properly and successfully do"—we find him articulating a new liberal vision.

Wilson took it as his first task to explain why the science of administration was, as he (in contrast to Adams) saw it, "a birth of our own century, almost of our own generation." He went on to portray his age as one in which "the functions of government" were "everyday becoming more complex and difficult" and "vastly multiplying in number," with administration therefore "everywhere putting its hands

---

[47] Wilson, "Study of Administration," 207, 216.

[48] In 1887, the year that Wilson published "Study of Administration," Adams held that the "professorship of law and police" Jefferson had established at the College of William and Mary over a century earlier "was much the same as the modern science of administration, which is just beginning anew to creep into our university courses in America." Adams also contended that the "schools of administration now flourishing in Paris and Berlin are based upon precisely the same idea as that proposed by Washington in his plan for a national university in the Federal City." Herbert Baxter Adams, *The College of William and Mary: A Contribution to the History of Higher Education,* Circulars of Information of the Bureau of Education no. 1 (Washington, DC: Government Printing Office), 39, 48. These claims show the possibility of supportively interpreting American attention to administration without using the progressive liberal idea of a new era with new tasks for government that Wilson, building on Ely, uses. A return-to-the-founders frame was an alternative also already applied to administration by, for example, Henry Adams, who argued for civil service reform in terms drawing on the 1780 Massachusetts Bill of Rights, authored by his great-grandfather John Adams. Henry Adams, "Civil Service Reform," *North American Review* 109, no. 225 (October 1869), 443–75.

[49] Wilson, "Study of Administration," 197.

to new undertakings." Alongside this trend in government practice the "idea of the state and the consequent ideal of its duty" was "undergoing noteworthy change" to embrace "every day new things which the state ought to do."[50] Wilson's sense of being in the midst of a transformative moment in practice and theory parallels Sumner's sense of the same time period. But whereas Sumner criticized the transformation as a falling away from classical liberal verities, Wilson presented it as a given to be observed, accepted, and indeed welcomed.

The divergence between Wilson and Sumner was concretely displayed in their reaction to contemporary American legislation. In the midst of his grand interpretation of the age Wilson put flesh on his claims by pointing, as an example of new government undertakings, to the "creation of national commissioners of railroads."[51] Readers in 1887 would have seen reference here to the Interstate Commerce Act signed a few months before Wilson's article was published (and indeed the subject of the article that followed Wilson's in that issue of *Political Science Quarterly*). As we noted in chapter 6 when discussing Sumner's criticism of the act, this landmark law made railroads the first industry subject to federal regulation. In indicating support of the act, Wilson's comment enables us to date quite precisely the divergence between his and Sumner's liberalism. Both had supported the 1883 Civil Service Act, expected to make government more *efficient*, but they disagreed about the 1887 Interstate Commerce Act, which would *expand* government's role. Wilson was now developing a progressive liberal vision that could welcome this, and additional future expansions, while Sumner was charting a disenchanted classical liberal political path that criticized such expansion with anxious foreboding. However we judge their disagreement, both grasped the same trend. During the next two decades federal government positions would expand to reach almost 370,000 by the end of Theodore Roosevelt's presidency. There had, by contrast, been just over 130,000 positions when the 1883 Civil Service Act introduced merit selection into the federal workforce.[52]

The progressive liberal turn in Wilson's political science may be unpacked in alternative ways. There is, on the one hand, a hint of Hegel in the "Administration" article. In setting up his interpretation of his era, Wilson quotes Hegel—whom he heard lectures about in a Philosophy of History course at Hopkins in fall 1884— on the relation of philosophy to its own time.[53] But this performance of academic erudition concerned historicist method, not political beliefs. It must be considered beside Wilson's ringing embrace of popular sovereignty, which made his article a far cry from Hegel's antidemocratic views about sovereignty. Moreover,

---

[50] Wilson, "Study of Administration," 198–201.

[51] Wilson, "Study of Administration," 201.

[52] These figures on federal positions are drawn from *Biography of an Ideal*, 207–19.

[53] The lecturer was George S. Morris. Wilson's notes from lectures in November 1884 in which Morris contrasted Spencer and Hegel are reproduced in *Papers of Woodrow Wilson*, 3: 426–28, 457–58.

whereas Hegel's political vision assumed a preindustrial society, Wilson's new progressive liberal political vision turned to America's industrializing economy to support its account of expanding government.

Industrialization was, in Wilson's invocation of it, a recent transformation creating novel problems. It gave rise to "giant monopolies" and "ominous" labor tensions in light of which "no one can doubt" the need for government to pursue new tasks such as to "make itself the master of masterful corporations." Of course, Wilson's "no one can doubt" was a rhetorical flourish, and as we have seen, a disenchanted classical liberal political vision was being fleshed out precisely by questioning such claims. Lowell, for example, when extolling corporations in the introduction to his 1889 *Essays on Government*, granted in a footnote that "[s]ome of the more gigantic of these bodies have used their power oppressively," only to then propose that this was "unfortunately a danger which is inseparable from all coöperation on a very large scale."[54] It was a central trait of the progressive liberal political vision Wilson was now articulating to take it as given that "the needs of this industrial and trading age" produced "fast accumulating" and "enormous" "burdens of administration" that made not only administrative reform, but also the expansion of government roles, imperative.[55] The pivot of the progressive turn in Wilson's liberal political science was not a dose of Hegel, but an economically centered transformative historicism. Specifically, it was the view, which we saw earlier in Ely, of industrialization as a transformative change creating a new kind of society in need of new laws and institutions.

Political Economy: From Classical Liberal Principles to the Progressive "Middle Ground"

Wilson's concern with political economy, like his interest in administration, predated his entry to Hopkins. Here again the substance of his views shifted while he was at Hopkins and did so even more dramatically. Wilson's views about administration and economics were more than connected, with the latter providing support for the former. They also changed in tandem, at the same time, and both under the influence of Ely.[56] This change is a centerpiece of the move from democratized classical liberalism to progressive liberalism in Wilson's political science.

As a Princeton undergraduate awed by the ability of Bright and Gladstone "to control and direct the current of public feeling and conviction" in midcentury

---

[54] Lowell, *Essays*, 17–18.

[55] Lowell, *Essays*, 199–201, 218.

[56] The contemporary shifts in Wilson's thinking about administration and political economy have been connected by Niels Thorsen. See Niels Thorsen, "The Origins of Woodrow Wilson's 'The Study of Administration,'" *American Studies in Scandinavia* 21 (1989), 16–29.

Britain, Wilson longed to see his fellow American college students aspire to emulate his democratized classical liberal heroes. In 1878 he expressed a hope that students would "thoroughly study the interests of the country" so they could "go forth prepared to lift the people to the comprehension of the great principles of political economy: raising the masses to the level of each great principle rather than lowering the principle to the level of the masses and thus degrading both."[57] After graduating from Princeton and attending law school at the University of Virginia, Wilson tried out this edifying role himself in newspaper articles and public testimony to a Tariff Commission established by Congress. His 1881–1882 public pronouncements show that the pre-Hopkins Wilson held classical liberal views in political economy. Writing about the southern economy, he took as given that "true principles of political economy" favored "free agricultural labor" and concluded from this that the "unnatural system of slave labor" hindered the pre–Civil War economy. With slavery ended, the South now, by contrast, had a "natural division of labor" on the basis of which agriculture, commerce, and manufacturing with a characteristic "naturalness" were all growing. Speaking as a southerner as well as a classical liberal, Wilson proudly pointed to this new South, which "needs and asks no 'protection' even for the infancy of her manufactures," as a positive lesson for the North in "the healthy principles of free trade."[58]

Wilson's political economy at this time was not simply classical liberal but stridently so. In his 1882 Tariff Commission testimony Wilson criticized John Stuart Mill for tempering free trade principles to allow that it might be expedient in practice for new countries to use a tariff to temporarily protect infant industries. He asserted that, to the contrary, "manufacturers are made better manufacturers whenever they are thrown upon their own resources and left to the natural competition of trade."[59] The "whenever" in Wilson's claim exemplifies a dogmatic tendency to treat classical liberal economic principles as always applying in practice without qualification. This tendency was again displayed as Wilson confidently predicted future capital investment in the South on the grounds that capital was "certain to come soon where it can find its most facile, and therefore most profitable, employment."[60] Future movement of skilled labor to the South was, likewise, "a simple question of supply and demand.... Labor will flow to the best market as surely as will molasses or any other marketable commodity."[61]

[57] Woodrow Wilson, "Some Thoughts on the Current State of Public Affairs," in *Papers of Woodrow Wilson*, 1: 352–54.

[58] Woodrow Wilson, "Stray Thoughts from the South," in *Papers of Woodrow Wilson*, 2: 19–25.

[59] Woodrow Wilson, "Testimony before the Tariff Commission," in *Papers of Woodrow Wilson*, 2: 142–43.

[60] Wilson, "Stray Thoughts," 24.

[61] Woodrow Wilson, "New Southern Industries," in *Papers of Woodrow Wilson*, 2: 125.

The young Wilson's dogmatic application to the concrete case of the South of classical liberal economic principles about the free flow of trade, capital, and labor exemplifies a mode of argument John Stuart Mill had warned against. As we saw earlier in comparing Mill with Lieber, Mill's political economy asserted a fundamental methodological point:

> It is not pretended that the facts of any concrete case conform with absolute precision to this or any other scientific principle. We must never forget that the truths of political economy are truths only in the rough... it is impossible in political economy to obtain general theorems embracing the complications of circumstances which may affect the result in an individual case.[62]

Failure to grasp this point, Mill went on to observe, "led to improper applications of the abstract principles of political economy, and still oftener to an undue discrediting of those principles."[63] Mill here, in effect, foresees the trajectory of Wilson's political economy, which would abruptly shift from its dogmatic starting point in "improper applications of the abstract principles" to the "discrediting of those principles" after Ely introduced him to the historical school in economics.

Wilson began to study political economy with Ely as soon as he arrived at Hopkins. In fall 1883 lectures he heard Ely present his classification of political economy, which separated socialists from scholars, and subdivided scholars into dueling schools: the "Historical" school versus the "a priori school of England."[64] In Wilson's second semester Ely's manifesto "The Past and Present of Political Economy," which we discussed earlier, appeared, and Ely asked Wilson to collaborate with him on a book titled *History of Political Economy in the United States*. Late in 1884 Wilson began the research he was assigned into American thinkers and works since the late 1830s. In spring 1885 he finished the research, summarized his findings for the Seminary of Historical and Political Science, and drafted his part of the book.[65]

Although the book project was never completed, Wilson's draft makes evident the extent to which he had internalized Ely's conception of dueling schools in which the "historical school" constituted a scientific advance beyond classical

---

[62] John Stuart Mill, *The Principles of Political Economy with Some of Their Applications to Social Philosophy*, ed. John M. Robson, *Collected Works of John Stuart Mill*, vols. 2–3 (Toronto: University of Toronto Press, 1965), 2: 422.

[63] Mill, *Principles of Political Economy*, 3: 461.

[64] Woodrow Wilson, "Notes Taken in Dr. Ely's Minor Course in Political Economy," in *Papers of Woodrow Wilson*, 2: 506.

[65] On Wilson's courses in 1884–1885, see *Papers of Woodrow Wilson*, 3: 335. On his project with Ely, see editorial notes, *Papers of Woodrow Wilson*, 3: 447–48 and 4: 628–31.

political economy.[66] What Wilson did, in effect, was to apply Ely's contrast to structure a chronological survey in which older American thinkers expressed "orthodoxy" and "rigid *laissez-faire*," but there was advance over time toward the "historical" approach, culminating with the "essentially modern" Francis A. Walker.[67] Summing up his research for the Seminary of Historical and Political Science, Wilson contended that the "progress of the science [political economy]" was marked by "a general tendency to use less and less the strictly and exclusively deductive method and to adopt more and more exclusively the opposite, the inductive, method."[68] Ely's satisfaction with Wilson's changed views on political economy is suggested by his consulting with Wilson about the organization of the American Economics Association (AEA), and Wilson's election, alongside his friend and fellow Ely-student Albert Shaw, to the large council of the new association at its founding meeting in September 1885.[69]

The interpretation of the "progress of the science" offered in Wilson's draft contribution for a *History of Political Economy in the United States* is a key moment in his progressive liberal turn. The view of scientific method informing this interpretation shows that Wilson inherited the standpoint from which Ely was then striving to give scientific authority to founding the AEA as explicitly anti-laissez-faire in economic policy. This move was, I argued in Part II, pivotal for liberal visions in political science. The field's Lieberian precursors in the midcentury American academy understood "political science" to encompass political economy, and working with this wide conception, they combined advocacy of liberal government and of principles of classical political economy. In propounding "the historical school" as a methodological advance beyond classical political economy, Ely and his allies, who now included Wilson,[70] were clearing ground for their progressive liberalism. They used transformative historicism to reinterpret the historical

---

[66] In his autobiography half a century later Ely recalled Wilson's draft fondly, saying that it had "expressed what were then somewhat new and modern ideas in this country, namely, an appreciation of the evolution of thought and the relativity of economic doctrines" and noting that "I still have [the manuscript] and treasure it as a precious possession." Ely, *Ground under Our Feet*, 112–13.

[67] Woodrow Wilson, "Wilson's Section for a *History of Political Economy in the United States*," in *Papers of Woodrow Wilson*, 4: 632, 634, 639, 653. We met Walker in chapter 5, in connection with his visiting teaching at Hopkins in the late 1870s, and his enlistment by Ely and fellow founders of the American Economic Association as the new association's first president, a position Walker held from 1885 until 1892.

[68] Woodrow Wilson, "Draft of a Report to the Historical Seminary," in *Papers of Woodrow Wilson*, 4: 424.

[69] Richard T. Ely, "Report of the Organization of the American Economic Association," *Publications of the American Economic Association* 1, no. 1 (March, 1886), 7, 40.

[70] Further evidence for locating Wilson within this scholarly network is provided by his choice to assign Francis A. Walker's *Political Economy* and Ely's *French and German Socialism in Modern Times* as his two textbooks when teaching political economy at the recently opened Bryn Mawr, where he held his first professorship from 1885 to 1888. *Papers of Woodrow Wilson*, 5: 733.

overlaps between liberal commitment to representative government and commit-ment to laissez-faire in economic policy, as a contingent juxtaposition outdated by industrialization, rather than a constitutive feature of liberalism itself.

The foundations for progressive liberalism laid during the mid-1880s organiz-ing of the AEA were subsequently preached for a broader audience in textbooks Ely and Wilson authored. Wilson gave Ely feedback on his *Introduction to Political Economy*, which was completed just before Wilson's *The State*, with both appear-ing in 1889.[71] Their shared interpretation of laissez-faire was concisely summed up when Ely stated, as if it were an uncontestable matter-of-fact, that

> *laissez-faire*... has generally been abolished both by science and practice in all civilized lands. It is thought that it performed good service at the time it became powerful, but that it is no longer suited to the needs of the modern world.[72]

Wilson, in turn, made rejection of laissez-faire central to the final chapter of *The State*. Here he presented the "controversy" about "the proper objects of govern-ment" by framing two "extreme views" and propounding "the middle ground" between them. One extreme was laissez-faire. In presenting the view as a dogma—rather than, as Mill had favored, a practical maxim about the burden of arguments for government action—Wilson took Ely's interpretation of it as given. He then identified the extreme "in the opposite direction" as the view that "would have society lean fondly upon government for guidance and assistance in every affair of life." This second extreme was attributed, among others, to the "fathers of Socialism" who were presented as believing "the state can be made a wise foster-mother to every member of the family politic."[73] This reading of socialism was, of course, no less contestable than Wilson's presentation of laissez-faire. These inter-pretations enabled Wilson, however, to use the frame of opposing "extremes" to open up a "middle ground" that positioned progressive liberalism as embodying the kind of deliberative moderation many liberals had long venerated.[74]

Wilson's discussion took as its starting point the Ely-echoing premise that the "birth and development of the modern industrial system was changing every aspect" of matters such as the relations of the state to labor. He stated it as a "rule" that "in proportion as the world's industries grow must the state

---

[71] Richard T. Ely, *Introduction to Political Economy* (New York: Chautauqua Press, 1889), 6.

[72] Ely, *Introduction to Political Economy*, 125.

[73] Woodrow Wilson, *The State: Elements of Historical and Practical Politics, a Sketch of Institutional History and Administration* (Boston: Heath, 1889), 656–57.

[74] The frame of seeking the sensible middle ground is found likewise in Ely's promotion of "the golden mean" of "practicable social reform." Richard T. Ely, *Socialism: An Examination of its Nature, and its Weaknesses, with Suggestions for Social Reform* (New York: Crowell, 1894). As an example of how this framing works in relation to concrete policy consider the 1887 Interstate Commerce Act.

advance in its efforts to assist the industrious to advantageous relations with one another." Although Wilson did credit socialists with highlighting problems that accompanied industrialization, he argued that they went astray in blaming competition. It was not competition per se that gave rise to problems, but specifically "distorted" and "unfair competition." Problems calling for government action arose when "unconscientious" rivals drove principled businessmen to "the choice of denying their consciences or retiring from business." Government regulation was then justified in pursuit of the goal "of making competition equal between those who would rightfully conduct enterprise and those who would basely conduct it."[75] Wilson here parallels Ely's argument in *Introduction to Political Economy* for government regulation to raise "the moral level of competition."[76]

In laying grounds for government regulation in an industrial economy, Wilson pursued a pivotal move in liberal thought. Taking up a classical liberal economic principle—the aggregate benefits of competition—he reformulated its concrete content, by emphasizing *fair* and *equal* rather than *free* competition, and used it to justify expanding rather than limiting government action. The blend of inheritance and adaptation here is a recurring trait of Wilson's progressive liberalism. This was strikingly evident when, in the closing pages of *The State*, he stepped back from economic policy to address generally the "natural and imperative limits to state action." In using this language and declaring that no serious student of society can doubt that there are such limits, Wilson showed the classical liberal inheritance on which he drew. But in giving concrete content to his view, he exemplified his progressive liberal adaptation of that inheritance. Wilson declared state action to be legitimate when

> it is indispensable to the equalization of the conditions of endeavor, indispensable to the maintenance of uniform rules of individual rights and relationships, indispensable because to omit it would inevitably be

---

Applying Wilson's framing would position the act as seeking the "middle ground" between "extremes" of no national regulation versus having government buy, build, and run railroads (as was being done on the European continent). The "middle ground" policy of the act and the Interstate Commerce Commission it set up was to introduce federal regulation while retaining private ownership and operation. More generally, on the centrality to progressive political theory of the search for a "via media" between laissez-faire and socialism, see James T. Kloppenberg, *Uncertain Victory: Social Democracy and Progressivism in European and American Thought, 1870–1920* (Oxford: Oxford University Press, 1986).

[75] Wilson, *The State*, 653–64.

[76] Ely, *Introduction to Political Economy*, 83–85. If I point from Wilson to Ely's textbook for more on this argument, Ely in turn points his readers to Henry Carter Adams for "undoubtedly one of the best treatises ever written in the English language on the functions of the State." Ely, *Introduction to Political Economy*, 93; referring to Henry C. Adams, "Relation of the State to Industrial Action," *Publications of the American Economic Association* 1, no. 6 (1887), 7–85.

to hamper or degrade some for the advancement of others in the scale of wealth and social standing.[77]

The emphasis on uniform rules in the second clause of this statement carried forward a core tenet of classical liberalism. The first and third clauses, by contrast, offered egalitarian goals that could justify expanding roles for government. Such expansions had the potential, moreover, to become antithetical to classical liberalism to the extent that pursuing these egalitarian goals might require government to act through means beyond the promulgation and enforcement of uniform rules.

Political Development: The Modern Democratic State as the Liberal End of History

Writing about his ongoing projects in 1887 to Albert Shaw, Wilson noted that alongside his textbook *The State* he was pursuing a grander ambition. He had begun "an extended study and analysis of Democracy" that he hoped "to fill with the best thoughts of my lifetime."[78] This project had been formulated at the end of 1885 with the working title *The Modern Democratic State*. Describing in May 1886 his projected study of the "nature, structure, ends and functions of the modern democratic state," Wilson had identified its "object" as

> a very ambitious one: no less than to answer Sir Henry Maine's "Popular Government" by treating modern democratic tendencies from a more truly historical point of view than he has taken; keeping very close to the concrete examples of popular govt. by means of careful comparative constitutional study.[79]

Subsequently retitled *The Philosophy of Politics* by 1891, Wilson's grand project never reached fruition. But major conceptual and historical moves he had made did appear scattered across *The State*, public addresses, and articles in 1889–1891.[80] Two interwoven intellectual initiatives were pursued: the "modern state" was wedded to individual freedom, and "modern democracy" was projected as its culminating form of government. In sum, Wilson offered a political vision that anointed the "modern Democratic State" as the progressive liberal end of history.

---

[77] Wilson, *The State*, 664–65.

[78] Wilson to Albert Shaw, May 29, 1887, in *Papers of Woodrow Wilson*, 5: 511.

[79] Wilson to Horace Elisha Scudder, May 12, 1886, in *Papers of Woodrow Wilson*, 5: 218.

[80] For more about Wilson's project and its fate, see the editorial note in *Papers of Woodrow Wilson*, 5: 54–58.

Throughout the evolution of his political science Wilson remained steadfastly committed to conceiving history in terms of liberal progress. He remained, moreover, committed to viewing individual freedom as the principal driver of progress in the modern world. Thus he forthrightly declared in *The State*:

> The hope of society lies in an infinite individual variety, in the freest possible play of individual forces: only in that can it find that wealth of resources which constitutes civilization, with all its appliances for satisfying human wants and mitigating human sufferings, all its incitements to thought and spurs to action.[81]

This passage may read in isolation like a classical liberal clarion call. But it appeared in the final chapter of Wilson's textbook in the middle of a progressive liberal argument about government's roles in the era of "modern industrial organization." The coherence of this chapter presupposed a prying apart of individual freedom from the limiting, or even diminishing, of government's roles to which it was tied in classical liberal narratives of progress. By propounding this separation, the preceding chapters of *The State* had laid the basis for the progressive liberal "middle ground" of the book's final chapter.

Building upon Freeman and other midcentury developmental historicists, Wilson in *The State* assumed that a grasp of the grand sweep of the past was essential to understand the present, and he located the most crucial developments for understanding the political present specifically in the history of Western "Aryan" peoples. *The State* started with a historical survey running from early "Aryan" institutions, through ancient Greece and Rome, to the medieval fusion of Roman and "Teutonic" institutions. This survey was followed with nation-by-nation presentations of the modern history and present character of government in continental Europe, England, and the United States. A perspective that reached from early Aryan institutions up to modern systems of government offered, for Wilson, the basis of "a thorough comparative and historical method" able both to identify "wide correspondences of organization and method in government" *and* to highlight differences and trace them "to their true sources in history and national character."[82] His approach hence attended to continuity and change, and the latter came especially to the fore in Wilson's closing chapters as he articulated a forceful challenge to classical liberal views.

In his penultimate chapter Wilson advocated distinguishing change in "conceptions of the nature and duty of the state" from change in the "functions" that governments perform. Taking up the historical advance of individual freedom

---

[81] Wilson, *The State*, 660.
[82] Wilson, *The State*, xxxv.

celebrated by classical liberals, he interpreted this development specifically as a change in the former respect, that is, in *conceptions* of the state.

> The modern idea is this: the state no longer absorbs the individual; it only serves him: the state, as it appears in its organ, the government, is the representative of the individual, and not his representative even, except within the definite commission of constitutions; while for the rest each man makes his own social relations.[83]

For Wilson, this "modern idea" was instantiated in constitutional and representative government. The distinctiveness of his own liberal vision came to the fore, however, in his argument that the historical advance of the liberal conception of the state had not been wedded to a reduction in the *functions* performed by government, such as the classical liberal John Stuart Mill assumed when declaring that "the proper functions of government are not a fixed thing, but different in different states of society; much more extensive in a backward than in an advanced state."[84] Wilson held, by contrast, that a comparative study of what governments do showed that "even under the most liberal of our modern constitutions we still meet government in every field of social endeavor."[85]

Classical liberals had failed, Wilson suggested, to grasp the nuance of the change that set the modern state apart as a progressive development beyond the ancient. The end of government in the modern state did "not stop with the protection of life, liberty, and property, as some have supposed." Its "ultimate standard of conduct" remained, as it had been in ancient states, to serve "social convenience and advancement." The heart of liberal progress lay in "new ideas as to what constitutes social convenience and advancement." Governments had learned to aspire "to aid the individual to the fullest and best possible realization of his individuality" by creating "the best and fairest opportunities," while rejecting "administration of the individual by the old-time futile methods of guardianship."[86] Wilson offered here a historicist account of political development in which the relation between government action and individual freedom was not fixed, but instead changed as part of progress, moving toward reconciliation and mutual support. *The State's* final chapter hence pictured a progressive liberal government that would leave "wide freedom to the individual to pursue his self-development" but also offer "mutual aid" to this self-development and guard it "against the competition that kills," and thereby reduce "antagonism between self-development and social development to a minimum."[87]

---

[83] Wilson, *The State*, 640, 645–46.
[84] J. S. Mill, *Considerations on Representative Government*, 383.
[85] Wilson, *The State*, 646.
[86] Wilson, *The State*, 646–47, emphasis in original.
[87] Wilson, *The State*, 660.

Wilson's vision of government in modern states shared much with Bluntschli's German liberal theory of the state. But Wilson's treatment of political development should not be seen as simply importing a German liberalism. When Bluntschli presented the modern *state* as the liberal end of political development, he also, as we saw in chapter 2, held that conditions in different nations suited them for either of two modern forms of *government*: "constitutional monarchy" or "representative democracy." Although Wilson did acknowledge that the modern state had taken more than one form of government historically, when looking forward he pronounced, "Democracy seems about universally to prevail." He declared that the tendencies of his age "promised to reduce politics to a single pure form by excluding all other governing forces and institutions but those of a wide suffrage and a democratic representation." The "modern State" Bluntschli presented as the liberal end of history was thus reformulated in Wilson's *The State* as finding its culmination specifically in "the modern Democratic State."[88]

In *The State* Wilson invoked a global democratizing trend as a given fact. To see better how he viewed that trend, we can turn to his 1889 "Nature of Democracy in the United States." Wilson devoted several pages of this public address to "the forces... bringing in democratic temper and methods the world over." The most important force was, he proposed, the "progress of popular education." But it did not act alone. "Steam and electricity... coöperated with systematic popular education" in "the diffusion of enlightenment among the people." These technologies were, in turn, reinforcing "the mighty influences of commerce and the press." For Wilson the overall dynamic of "the forces which have established the drift toward democracy" seemed clear: "when the world's thought and the world's news are scattered broadcast where the poorest can find them, the non-democratic forms of government find life a desperate venture."[89]

The forces Wilson highlighted were relatively new, some decidedly so. He dated the drift toward democracy from the mid-eighteenth century, and saw it as really gaining momentum in the next century, successively reinforced by further democratizing forces. He thus held in his 1890 public address "Leaders of Men" that it was "the Nineteenth Century" that "established the principle that public opinion *must* be truckled to... in the conduct of government."[90] To study this latest stage of political development it was essential to see that, just as the forces promoting democracy were distinctively modern, so the character of the democracy

---

[88] Wilson, *The State*, 603–5.

[89] Woodrow Wilson, "Nature of Democracy in the United States," in *Papers of Woodrow Wilson*, 6: 224–26. Given as a public address in May 1889, this work was published with small changes as "Character of Democracy in the United States," *Atlantic Monthly* 64 (November 1889), 577–88, and again after more small changes in Woodrow Wilson, *An Old Master and Other Political Essays* (New York: Scribner's, 1893), 99–138.

[90] Woodrow Wilson, "Leaders of Men," in *Papers of Woodrow Wilson*, 6: 658. Italics in original.

being promoted was itself novel. When initially formulating his democracy project, Wilson stated it as "a conception absolutely prerequisite to any competent study of the development of the modern state that the democracy which is now becoming dominant is a *new* democracy."[91] The outcome under study was to be conceived as "modern democracy," which Wilson contrasted to "ancient democracy" to convey its specific character. He viewed "modern democracy" as distinctive along multiple dimensions: it was representative rather than direct, rejected slavery and recognized personal rights, and saw the state as existing for the sake of the individual rather than vice versa.[92] Along each dimension "modern" served in effect as a synonym for liberal. Wilson hence made "modern democracy," by definition, liberal democracy.

Wilson's democracy project brought his evolving political science into a nuanced relation with the racialized developmental historicism he had embraced as a Princeton undergraduate. A clear Teutonist note was sounded in his 1889 "Nature of Democracy" when Wilson declared it

> a deeply significant fact... that only in the United States, in a few other governments begotten of the English race and in Switzerland where old Teutonic habit has had the same persistency as in England, have examples yet been furnished of successful democracy of the modern type.[93]

Long historical experience with local self-government had habituated these peoples in "adult self-reliance, self-knowledge, and self-control, adult-soberness and deliberateness of judgment, adult sagacity in self-government, adult vigilance of thought and quickness of insight." Now, in the modern era, this habituated "maturity" was proving key to success introducing and operating modern democratic government. The educational, economic, and technological forces sweeping the world were, Wilson qualified, "critical" forces with "little in them of *constructive* efficacy." They explained why nondemocratic forms of government were being generally undermined. But the very prevalence of these forces meant that they could not explain why modern democratic government took firm root and flourished in only some nations, while elsewhere socioeconomic modernity fed a turbulent politics of revolutions, confusion, and paralysis. Wilson appealed to the presence or absence "of the highest and steadiest political habit" in a nation's people to explain cross-national variety in success with modern democracy, and he turned to Teutonist historicism to explain differences in political habit (or, as twentieth-century political science would rename it, "political culture"). His

---

[91] Woodrow Wilson, "The Modern Democratic State," in *Papers of Woodrow Wilson*, 5: 80. Italics in original.

[92] Wilson, *The State*, 603–5.

[93] Wilson, "Nature of Democracy," 230.

response to Maine's argument that America's Constitution was key to its success, while Britain was starting to suffer from its lack of a similarly constraining constitution, was to see both nations as successful and attribute that success to habits shared by "the English race" in all its homes. He forcefully contended that Maine's *Popular Government* "utterly failed… to distinguish the democracy, or rather the popular government of the English race, which is bred by slow circumstance and founded upon habit, from the democracy of other peoples, which is bred by discontent and founded upon revolution."[94]

If Wilson's study of modern democracy gave major *explanatory* work to a developmental historicism reminiscent of midcentury, he at the same time practiced transformative historicism in his *conceptual* work. His penchant for conceptualizing "modern democracy" via contrast went beyond the ancient versus modern contrast commonplace in the liberal tradition. Taking up the self-government of Swiss villages and New England towns in his 1891 lecture "Democracy," Wilson now put them to use as another contrast against which to spotlight the transformed character of modern democracy:

> The democracy of the local assembly is not modern: it is as ancient, probably, as Aryan states.… It is not of this democracy that I would speak, but of quite another: that *modern* democracy in which the people who are said to govern are not the people of a commune or a township, but all the people of a great nation, a vast population which never musters into any single assembly, whose members never see each others' face or hear each others voices, but live, millions strong, up and down the reaches of continents.[95]

This transformation spurred Wilson to revisit the concept of popular sovereignty. While he had used this concept without qualms as recently as "Study of Administration," he now saw little more than "patriotic fervour" in Lieber's attribution of sovereignty to the nation. Asking what "we *mean* when we say that we have here in America *a sovereign people*, a nation *governed by itself*," Wilson contended that "[w]e cannot mean that the people themselves *originate measures* and *shape policies*, as those little groups do that meet from season to season in townhalls and in Swiss market places."[96] To carry over the concept of popular rule from local self-government to a modern nation obscured key practical differences in politics at these levels. The concept hence had to be reworked to study modern democracy:

---

[94] Wilson, "Nature of Democracy," 227–31.

[95] Woodrow Wilson, "A Lecture on Democracy," in *Papers of Woodrow Wilson*, vol. 7 (1969), 347. Italics in original.

[96] Wilson, "A Lecture on Democracy," 351, 353. Italics in original.

What we really mean when we say that the people govern is that they freely consent to be governed, on condition that *a certain part* of them *do* the governing,—that part which shall, by one process or another, be selected out of the mass and elevated to the places of rule:—and *that is the best democratic government* in which the processes of this selection are best.[97]

This reconception broke decisively from the democratized classical liberal treatment of democracy. The break is especially evident in relation to civil service reform, which informed Wilson's concern with selection processes. In mid-century John Stuart Mill had identified merit-selected civil servants as a valuable counterbalance to democracy's illiberal potential.[98] To see civil servants playing this role assumed that merit selection, advantaging as it does the better educated, was not itself democratic. Wilson, by contrast, reframed it in exactly these terms. He argued that, while a meritocratic civil service was "*not* democratic in the sense in which we have taught our politicians wrongly to understand democracy," it was "democratic in this sense, *that it draws all the governing material from the people.*" Selecting into government positions by merit "such *part* of the people as will fit themselves for the function" was "*but another process of representation.*" Wilson carried forward the midcentury liberal endorsement of merit selection of civil servants, but put that endorsement in new late-century progressive liberal terms when he conceptualized such selection as "*eminently democratic.*"[99]

We earlier saw Wilson build liberalism by definition into modern democracy. Now we have seen him read democracy into a prominent liberal reform. Whereas democratized classical liberals saw liberal commitments and reforms in potential tension with democracy and debated how to best manage this tension, Wilson eliminated the tension by reconceptualizing modern democracy as liberal, and contemporary liberalism as democratic. His progressive vision allowed that there had historically been tensions between liberalism and democracy, and that traces of that past lingered on among, for example, opponents of civil service reform. But these tensions were now, Wilson taught, to be superseded in the forward march of political development toward his progressive liberal end of history: the modern democratic state. After first envisioning this end in his political science, Wilson later strove to lead America toward it in his political career as a progressive liberal reformer.

---

[97] Wilson, "A Lecture on Democracy," 357. Italics in original.

[98] Mill's view of the relationship between professional civil servants and democracy has been connected to recent political theory discussions of "antagonism" by Brandon Turner. See Brandon P. Turner, "John Stuart Mill and the Antagonistic Foundation of Liberal Politics," *Review of Politics* 72, no. 1 (2010), 31–34.

[99] Wilson, "Lecture on Democracy," 351, 356. Italics in original.

Democracy and the Divided Legacy of Democratized Classical Liberalism

We have followed through the interwoven elements of Wilson's turn in the middle to late 1880s away from the democratized classical liberalism of his youth. This turn took place in the same decade, and departed from the same starting point, as the shift in Sumner's thought that we examined previously. I have compared these figures at several points in this chapter. To conclude both the chapter and comparison, I elucidate here the divergence in their treatment of democracy, which is especially significant for their political science. Sumner and Wilson each developed his own analysis of democracy starting out from the same midcentury democratized classical liberal political vision that had framed political science as pursued by Lieber. In separately developing different sides of this preceding liberal vision, Sumner and Wilson divided its legacy into two alternative, indeed conceptually incompatible, late-century liberal analyses of democracy.

Midcentury democratized classical liberal treatments of democracy derived a two-sided character from their emphasis on the *potential* compatibility of liberalism and democracy. When realized, this potential made liberal democracy viable. Hence, one side of democratized classical liberalism's political analyses explored the properties of this hybrid and the prerequisites for its successful functioning and maintenance. But liberalism and democracy were only potentially, not necessarily, compatible. There could be a nondemocratic liberal regime, as in midcentury England, or an illiberal democracy, as exemplified by Louis Napoleon's France. The dark second side of the democratized classical liberal treatment of democracy explored its illiberal forms.

Sumner and Wilson in the 1880s moved in divergent directions away from democratized classical liberalism's emphasis upon the potential compatibility of democracy and liberalism. As Sumner lost faith in his fellow Americans, he increasingly came to interpret democracy as simply inimical to classical liberalism. A hybrid "democratic republic" had seemed viable for a period in midcentury America, but for Sumner democracy was now failing the late-century test posed by the economic strains following from the Panic of 1873 through subsequent decades. Democratic reactions to these strains were undercutting classical liberal ideals and institutions. In doing so democracy did not triumph; rather it opened the door for plutocracy. Sumner here extended the democratized classical liberal fear of the dark side of democracy. But extending only this dark side of the prior midcentury liberal vision led Sumner toward presenting democracy as generally illiberal in its consequences.

In Wilson's treatment of democracy we see, by contrast, a hopeful exploration of liberal democracy as the main legacy of democratized classical liberalism. As a youth Wilson pursued both sides of the democratized classical liberal analysis of democracy. Worry about illiberal democracy was evident, for example, in his 1879 essay "Self-Government in France," which lingered over the "minutely-complete *centralization*" that focused the "powers of despotism" in France and enabled periods of "centralized democracy" that were "a virtual despotism."[100] Fear of illiberal democracy still remained part of Wilson's political science in late 1885 when he first formulated his study of modern democracy. In an early draft he anxiously suggested that, if the "democratic polity based on individual initiative" failed, modern nations would instead turn "in the doubtful light of Socialism, towards a democratic polity based on communal initiative."[101]

Yet, by 1887, Wilson's notes show him refocusing the "substantial correspondence" between socialism and democracy onto the "germinal conceptions of democracy"—that is, ancient democracy. The modern versus ancient contrast enabled him to propose that, under the influence of "a political philosophy radically individualistic," the "democracy of our own century" observed "individual rights" in a manner at odds with either ancient democracy or socialism.[102] By the time fragments of his democracy project appeared in *The State* and his articles and addresses in 1889–1891, Wilson had relegated the dark side of democracy to the past. He now consistently characterized "modern democracy" in terms that made it liberal by definition. No longer seen as just potentially compatible, liberalism and democracy were now indelibly tied through mutual redefinition. Wilson's interpretation of political development made this integration itself part and parcel of modern progress. In his late-century progressive vision, democracy had become liberal, and liberal reform agendas of the present, such as civil service reform, had come to be conceived as advancing democracy, rather than as tempering it.

---

[100] Woodrow Wilson, "Self-Government in France," in *Papers of Woodrow Wilson*, 1: 523. Italics in original.

[101] Wilson, "Modern Democratic State," 62.

[102] Woodrow Wilson, "Socialism and Democracy," in *Papers of Woodrow Wilson*, 5: 561–62.

CHAPTER 8

The Transatlantic Study of Modern Political Systems

THE NEW POLITICAL SCIENCE OF JAMES BRYCE, A. LAWRENCE LOWELL, AND FRANK GOODNOW

In the first two chapters of Part III we have seen the divergence between disenchanted classical liberalism and progressive liberalism develop into political visions offering alternative late-century conceptions of democracy and the nascent administrative state. These developments speak to the *political* in political science. In this final chapter I examine a late-century change in the *science* in political science. Specifically, I document the rise of a new more present-oriented method of relating a broad array of contemporary institutions and phenomena as interacting parts of a "political system." In a closing example of the transatlantic intellectual exchanges between European liberals and American political scientists identified throughout this book, I argue that the British liberal scholar-politician James Bryce's *The American Commonwealth* deserves to be hailed, or harangued, as *the* founding work of this new kind of political science.

Bryce was a quintessentially transatlantic figure. To survey the impressive network of American friends he built up through repeated transatlantic visits from 1870 onward would be to sweep across, and beyond, most of the academic institutions and figures I have discussed in Parts II and III.[1] Bryce's many months in America over repeated visits, and his many American friends, informed his multivolume account of the American political system in *The American Commonwealth*,

---

[1] On Bryce's American visits and their relation to his *American Commonwealth*, see Edmund Ions, *James Bryce and American Democracy, 1870–1922* (London: Macmillan, 1968), chaps. 4–10. In the acknowledgments of his book Bryce thanks past, present, or future presidents of Columbia, Cornell, Hopkins, and the University of Michigan, as well as four early presidents of the future American Political Science Association (of which he himself would serve as the fourth president while Britain's ambassador to the United States).

which ran through multiple editions, from its 1888 first publication into the early twentieth century. In the first part of this chapter I consider methodological reasons why Bryce's book was so well received among American political scientists, by contrasting it with the poorly received 1891 magnum opus, *Political Science and Comparative Constitutional Law*, of John Burgess, the head of Columbia's School of Political Science.

At the same time that *The American Commonwealth* modeled a new method for political science, its substantive portrait of America's democracy was one of the last great expressions of the democratized classical liberalism that had flourished during midcentury, when Bryce came intellectually of age. Standing at the point in the liberal tradition from which I have charted the divergent development of the alternative late-century political visions of disenchanted classical liberalism and progressive liberalism, Bryce's classic proved able to engage younger American political scientists on both sides of this divergence. The second and third parts of this chapter document this dual influence as seen in the disenchanted classical liberal A. L. Lowell's studies of political parties, and the progressive liberal Frank Goodnow's studies of local government. Finally, I compare how Bryce, Goodnow, and Lowell addressed a single topic—the power of political parties in America—to showcase the room *within* the methodological parameters of the new political science for substantive scientific debate between political scientists with different liberal political visions.

The "Science" in Political Science Revisited: Methods and Bryce's Posthistorical Turn

The distinction between "a priori" (philosophical, deductive) and "historical" methods was a recurring theme in the wide political science of midcentury. Turns of phrases we first saw used in Part I in T. B. Macaulay's criticism of James Mill's views on suffrage, and in the methodological conflict at the University of Berlin after Hegel's arrival, remained fighting words over a half-century later on the other side of the Atlantic. At the height of the 1880s conflict in political economy surveyed in Part II, even as Ely and Sumner disagreed sharply in the substance of their liberal visions, both claimed the authority of science, and in doing so, both cast aspersions on the a priori. This long-standing aversion continued to resonant among the next generation of scholars. Ely's student Woodrow Wilson, for example, opened the first lecture of the public law course he gave during his first semester at Princeton in 1890 by identifying the course as a "study in political science" and then stressing that he meant "the new, historical, political science," not "the old speculative, *a priori* political science."[2]

---

[2] Woodrow Wilson, "Notes for a Course in Public Law," in *The Papers of Woodrow Wilson*, ed. Arthur S. Link, vol. 7 (Princeton, NJ: Princeton University Press, 1969), 9.

Yet, even as habitual hostility to the a priori carried forward into the 1890s, a new way of doing political science was fracturing the coherence of "historical" as a banner under which more empirically minded scholars could march together. Bryce's *American Commonwealth* modeled a new approach of avowedly present-focused empirical study of mass suffrage politics. The work anticipated and informed a refocusing of attention toward the present among American political scientists that made Bryce, according to Lowell, "the master and guide of all students of modern political systems."[3] To understand how Bryce won such a standing we can situate his approach beside contemporary alternatives and compare how these fared as political scientists debated methods as the nineteenth century neared its close.

BURGESS: MISPLAYING THE METHOD CARD

Soon after Bryce's *American Commonwealth* appeared, the head of Columbia's School of Political Science, John Burgess, published his principal work, *Political Science and Comparative Constitutional Law*. The hefty 1891 book initiated a "Systematic Series edited by the University Faculty of Political Science" intended to advance the Columbia school.[4] In the shadow of the example set by Hopkins, the research ideal had gained ground at the school in the decade after its 1880 opening as an institution centered upon training potential civil servants. The school in 1886 began publishing *Political Science Quarterly*, which quickly supplanted the *Johns Hopkins University Studies in Historical and Political Science* as the most prominent American venue for articles in political science. In 1887 the *Columbia College Handbook* was updated to state as a goal of the School, in addition to civil service training, educating "teachers of political science."[5] The series Burgess's 1891 book began was meant to express and extend the Columbia school's challenge to the position Hopkins had won in the 1880s as the leading American academic center for political science. The grand ambition of the series was, Burgess would later recall, "to create a school of American political philosophy and a distinct American literature of these sciences."[6]

The rising standing of Columbia's School of Political Science ensured Burgess, as its leader, prominence among American scholars of politics. His book would be read. But its *reception* was another matter. As Bernard Crick incisively noted in his

---

[3] A. Lawrence Lowell, *The Government of England*, 2 vols. (New York: Macmillan, 1908), vii.

[4] John W. Burgess, *Political Science and Comparative Constitutional Law*, 2 vols. (Boston: Ginn, 1891). I quote the language about "Systematic Series" directly from the book's title page.

[5] R. Gordon Hoxie, *A History of the Faculty of Political Science* (New York: Columbia University Press, 1955), 29.

[6] John W. Burgess, *Reminiscences of an American Scholar: The Beginnings of Columbia University* (New York: Columbia University Press, 1934), 201–2.

pioneering study of American political science: "Burgess, for all his great influence as a university administrator and a founder of political science, left no intellectual disciples at all."[7] Thus at the very time the British Bryce's *American Commonwealth* was, as we will see, informing the works of multiple future American Political Science Association (APSA) presidents in the 1890s, the magnum opus of America's most institutionally prominent political scientist failed to inspire. Why?

Burgess himself stressed that his book stood out for "its method." Indeed, he confidently highlighted this as its trump card. His preface declared that "publication of a new book in the domain of Political Science is never justifiable unless it contains new facts; or a more rational interpretation, or a more scientific arrangement, of facts already known; or a new theory." Not claiming to offer new facts, Burgess instead proposed that, with his book, "some slight advance has been made in the development of the comparative method." He located his method as "the method chiefly followed by the German publicists." While acknowledging that Bryce, Wilson, and others had "broken the ground" in English-language scholarship for "comparative study," Burgess declared "the field capable of a much wider, and also a more minute, cultivation" and presented his book as an scientific "advance" on the grounds that it pursued this opportunity.[8]

Political Science and Comparative Constitutional Law was a transatlantic work in several senses. Burgess compared the United States with three other "Aryan" (and more specifically, "Teutonic") nations: Britain, Germany, and France.[9] In addition, he looked across the Atlantic for his method, venerating German scholars as "exact and scientific in their political and legal nomenclature." This model led Burgess to fastidiously define and explain his key terms, such as nation and state, and in treating the latter he deployed a Hegelian differentiation between the idea and the conception of the state.[10] But, while he saw his method following

---

[7] Bernard Crick, *The American Science of Politics: Its Origins and Conditions* (Berkeley: University of California Press, 1959), 31. See also Michael Frisch's similar judgment that Burgess "managed to dominate the field while, paradoxically, having almost no real intellectual influence and few dedicated disciples. In fact, his own work served more as a negative reference." Michael H. Frisch, "Urban Theorists, Urban Reform, and American Political Culture in the Progressive Period," *Political Science Quarterly* 97, no. 2 (1982), 299.

[8] Burgess, *Political Science*, 1: v–vi.

[9] Whereas Wilson's comparative survey of "Aryan" nations in *The State* was of broader scope (both in cross-sectional terms in the number of modern nations treated, and cross-temporally in its attention to ancient and medieval periods), Burgess aimed "to be systematic, not encyclopaedic." He explained his selection of four nations to compare on the grounds they were the "most important states of the world" and had constitutions that "represent substantially all the species of constitutionalism which have as yet been developed." Burgess argued that comparative studies seeking, as he did, "general principles of public law... will be more trustworthy if we exclude the less perfect systems from the generalization, disregard the less important states, and pass by those species which are not typical." *Political Science*, 1: 90–91.

[10] Burgess, *Political Science*, 1: 1–4, 49–58. Burgess's labors in the general theory of the state, undertaken in the "political science" section that opened his book, laid the analytical framework for the

a lead set by German theorists of the state, Burgess substantively critiqued them and other European scholars for not adequately distinguishing the state from the government. It was in America that this pivotal distinction had been most fully realized, and this was why "the public law of the United States" had "reached a far higher development than that of any state in Europe." Burgess credited Lieber and Woolsey with earlier noting the distinction due to their appreciation of American institutions, but charged they had not used it with a consistent clarity in the manner of German scholarship. The task for American political science was, as Burgess saw it, to use "European science...as a stepping-stone to a higher and more independent point of view" that would "win scientific appreciation of the distinctive lessons of our own institutions."[11] He exemplified how transatlantic exchange and comparison could inform an American exceptionalism that, in its substance, reaffirmed a midcentury democratized classical liberalism. Sounding substantively much like Lieber, Burgess proudly taught that "for a clearly defined and well secured civil liberty...Europe must come to us, and take lessons, in the school of our experience."[12]

In wielding a self-consciously Hegelian apparatus to facilitate "scientific appreciation" of American institutions, Burgess failed to heed the misfit between this endeavor and the sentiments about method commonplace within the American political science he strove to lead. Wedding Hegelian conceptual logic to Lieberian democratized classical liberal substance produced a work that would, at best, have confused the anti-Hegelian Lieber we met in chapter 3. It was also at odds with the more recent strictures of Andrew D. White, whom we previously saw warning his fellow American scholars against "attempts to approximate Hegel's shadowy results." In the hands of Lieber and White, and their disciples and students, the inclinations and insults about method articulated by the University of Berlin's historical school in its battle with Hegel had been passed down through over half a century of wide political science in America's academy.[13]

---

comparative study of the constitutional law of Britain, the United States, Germany, and France that then took up the bulk of his two volumes.

[11] Burgess, *Political Science*, 1: 57, 68–71.

[12] Burgess, *Political Science*, 1: 264. To follow through how Burgess's stress upon distinguishing the state from the government framed both a democratized classical liberal vision of constitutionally enshrined individual liberty and limited government, and a venerating interpretation of America as "in advance of all the rest in this line of progress" and "the great world organ for modern solution of the problem of government as well as liberty," see *Political Science*, 1: 174–252, 263–64, 2: 37–40.

[13] While I attribute the poor reception of Burgess's book to the mismatch between its Hegelian method and anti-Hegelian sentiments that had long informed political science in America's academy, an alternative explanation may suggest that the fault lay with a democratized classical liberal substance that was outdated relative to the contemporary shifts and divide in liberal visions being articulated among American scholars. *Political Science and Comparative Constitutional Law* often does read as if it dated from 1876, when Burgess was hired at Columbia. Only later did Burgess revise his thought, and when he did he became a disenchanted classical liberal. As Progressive Era reforms made headway in the

Legacies of that long-ago battle lived on among younger scholars. When Wilson identified the approach he planned to use in his never completed work on the modern democratic state, he announced "the 'historical school' furnishes me with *method*." At the same time, as a negative example, he pointed to the "logical" approach of Burgess's article in the first issue of *Political Science Quarterly*. These tastes and distastes were stated in letters to a friend who, when Burgess's major book appeared a few years later in 1891, asked Wilson to review it for *The Atlantic Monthly*. When Wilson noted that a review from him would reflect his position as a member of "an opposite school," he was encouraged to write as a "conscientious enemy" expected to be more than "equal to a whole House of Burgesses."[14]

Whereas Burgess saw his book's method as its scientific trump card, Wilson's review made it the object of cutting, almost derisive, criticism. After allowing that Burgess's conceptual labor produced "utmost clearness" and "perfect consistency everywhere," Wilson charged that these "excellences" came along with "irritating" faults: "a mechanical and incorrect style, a dogmatic spirit, and a lack of insight into institutions as detailed expressions of life, not readily consenting to be broadly and positively analyzed and classified." Respectful presentation of the "theoretical side" of Burgess's book only cast into relief the dismissive character of Wilson's commentary on how it treated "the actual facts of political life." When Burgess applied his theories to "complex national histories, like those of Germany, France, and England," he displayed, Wilson charged, "an extraordinary dogmatic readiness to force many intricate and diverse things to accommodate themselves to a few simple formulas." Even when using "forms and expressions of induction," Burgess tended to employ "in reality the processes of a very absolute deduction." He had "strong powers of reasoning," but "no gift of insight," and this was, Wilson claimed, "why he is so good at logical analysis, and so poor at the interpretation of history."[15]

---

years ahead, Burgess came to see the reforms as sacrificing individual liberty and limited government in a way that added up to a disastrous departure from the path of liberal progress in which America had earlier led the world. See the last chapter, "The New United States of America," in John W. Burgess, *The Reconciliation of Government with Liberty* (New York: Scribner's, 1915). By 1895 Burgess was already identifying a "socialistic movement toward paternalism in government," but initially he had expected it to make little headway in America. See John W. Burgess, "The Ideal of the American Commonwealth," *Political Science Quarterly* 10, no. 3 (1895), 411.

[14] Wilson to Horace Elisha Scudder, May 12 and July 10, 1886, in *Papers of Woodrow Wilson*, vol. 5 (1968), 218–20, 301–4; Wilson to Scudder, February 7, 1891, in *Papers of Woodrow Wilson*, 7: 165; Scudder to Wilson, February 4 and 13, 1891, in *Papers of Woodrow Wilson*, 7: 164, 166. The Burgess article Wilson addressed in his 1886 letter was John W. Burgess, "The American Commonwealth: Changes in Its Relation to the Nation," *Political Science Quarterly* 1, no. 1 (1886), 9–35. The methodological stance from which Wilson would come to assail Burgess in 1891 was already well developed by 1887. See Woodrow Wilson, "Of the Study of Politics," *New Princeton Review* 3, no. 2 (1887), 188–99.

[15] Woodrow Wilson, "Review of John W. Burgess, *Political Science and Comparative Constitutional Law*," in *Papers of Woodrow Wilson*, 7: 196, 199, 201.

The cutting character of Wilson's review was neither idiosyncratic nor an indirect way of expressing political differences between his own progressive liberalism and Burgess's classical liberalism.[16] Just as charged a disagreement soon arose between Burgess and the classical liberal Lowell. When Burgess reviewed Lowell's *Governments and Parties in Continental Europe* in 1897, he applied the model of method, drawn from German theorists of the state, that guided his own work. Failing to engage in any detail the empirical study of party systems, which was Lowell's central concern, Burgess offered instead a "general criticism" that the book lacked "any consistent and scientific nomenclature." He grumbled that terms he saw as essential to "political science, namely, sovereignty, state, government, rights and liberty" were "employed in more than one sense, sometimes even in connection with a single topic."[17]

Burgess's taste in matters of method was not widely shared among American scholars, and Lowell's comparative work was better received than Burgess's had been. It helped Lowell win appointment at Harvard in 1897 as Lecturer on Existing Political Systems. After he became permanent faculty, when he was named Professor of the Science of Government in 1900, Lowell pushed to develop Harvard's incipient program on methodological lines that contrasted directly with Burgess's Columbia.[18] Writing to Harvard's President Eliot in 1901, Lowell observed that, in "the subject of Government...we are decidedly behind the other large universities," and proposed a strategy to catch up. In terms reminiscent of Wilson's earlier review of Burgess, Lowell contended that Columbia's School of Political Science pursued "a program of work which is not really inductive." This left Harvard the chance "to fill a position which no other university in the country can fill." Lowell proposed that "we could build up a school which would profoundly influence thought in the future," by taking as a basis the

---

[16] To suggest that Wilson's dismissive review was but one reflection of a broader misfit between Burgess's method and prevailing tastes and distastes among American scholars, I draw out in my main text parallels between Wilson's opposition to Burgess's method and that of fellow future APSA president A. L. Lowell. I do so both because Lowell is, alongside Wilson, a major figure in my narrative, and because I have located Lowell and Wilson on opposite sides of the divergence in late-century liberalism. Parallels in their reactions to Burgess despite differences in their political visions support reading those reactions as rooted in methodological leanings. Looking beyond the future APSA presidents I center my narrative on, more evidence for the misfit character of Burgess's method, and the hostility from empirically minded scholars it could provoke, is found in the dismissive reactions Burgess received when he laid out his methodological views at the American Historical Association's 1896 annual meeting. See the remarks on 211–19 of John W. Burgess, "Political Science and History," *Annual Report of the American Historical Association for the Year 1896*, vol. 1 (1897), 203–19.

[17] John W. Burgess, "Review of *Government and Parties in Continental Europe* by A. Lawrence Lowell," *Political Science Quarterly* 12, no. 1 (1897), 161–63.

[18] On Lowell's hiring and promotion at Harvard, see Henry Aaron Yeomans, *Abbott Lawrence Lowell, 1856–1943* (Cambridge, MA: Harvard University Press, 1948), chap. 5.

"strongly inductive character" of the "tone of thought" of existing Harvard faculty, and extending this in hiring additional faculty.[19]

In other letters during the 1900–1901 academic year Lowell spelled out this proposal in terms of particular hiring priorities. He promoted hires in the growing, practical, and eminently present-focused areas of "Municipal Government" (which I examine later in this chapter) and "Colonies and Dependencies" (then flourishing in the aftermath of the war of 1898, as the United States became a colonial power).[20] Lowell specifically stressed to his colleague A. B. Hart that such hires "in the inductive line" should "take precedence" over bringing in someone to teach "political theories." If a theorist was to be hired, he favored a scholar who focused on the history of political theories, rather than on "the recent German contributions" that expounded such topics as "the relation of the Nation to the State, the Location of Sovereignty." Summing up his position to Hart, Lowell stated that he wanted Harvard to teach "the history of political theories through some man whose culture on the subject was not that of the modern German theorists."[21]

If Lowell was suspicious of certain, especially German, theoretical work, neither he nor Wilson was a naive empiricist. Just as Andrew D. White had when warning against Hegel, both could welcome "theory" or "philosophy" so long as they raised defenses against the kind of theoretical work they distrusted. They shared a pragmatist view that, as Lowell put it,

> theory and practice are in reality correlatives, each of which requires
> the aid of the other for its own proper development... a theory which

[19] Lowell to Eliot, February 10, 1901, in letterpress book (Feb. 1889–March 13, 1901), box 20, Abbott Lawrence Lowell Papers, Harvard University Archives. Quoted courtesy of the Harvard University Archives.

[20] Lowell to unidentified recipient ("Joe"), December 14, 1900, in letterpress book (Feb. 1889–March 13, 1901), box 20, Abbott Lawrence Lowell Papers, Harvard University Archives. Quoted courtesy of the Harvard University Archives. For examples of Lowell's own contribution to the study of colonies that blossomed after the war of 1898, see A. Lawrence Lowell, "The Colonial Expansion of the United States," *The Atlantic Monthly* 83 (February 1899), 145–54, and A. Lawrence Lowell, *Colonial Civil Service: The Selection and Training of Colonial Officials in England, Holland, and France* (New York: Macmillan, 1900). For historical studies of this literature, see Brian C. Schmidt, *The Political Discourse of Anarchy: A Disciplinary History of International Relations* (Albany: State University of New York Press, 1998), chap. 4, and Robert Vitalis, "The Noble American Science of Imperial Relations and Its Laws of Race Development," *Comparative Studies in Society and History* 52, no. 4 (2010), 909–38.

[21] Lowell to Hart, April 13, 1901, in letterpress book (March 18, 1901–Jan. 25, 1905), box 21, Abbott Lawrence Lowell Papers, Harvard University Archives. Quoted courtesy of the Harvard University Archives. On the impact of German theorists at Columbia, and their import for the character and development of the political theory subfield more generally, see John Gunnell, *The Descent of Political Theory: The Genealogy of an American Vocation* (Chicago: University of Chicago Press, 1993).

does not agree with the facts, or will not work in practice, is simply wrong. A practice, on the other hand, which is not guided and enlightened by abstract or theoretical study is short-sighted, unprogressive, and extremely likely to be based upon a blunder.[22]

Burgess exemplified what it meant to be on the wrong side of the line between the welcome and worrisome in matters theoretical. Neither Lowell nor Wilson could find attractive the Hegelian view of philosophy and its elevated role that resounds through Burgess's 1896 declaration:

> Political science... contains an element of philosophical speculation which, when true and correct, is the forerunner of history. When political facts and conclusions come into contact with political reason, they awaken in that reason a consciousness of political ideals not yet realized. Thrown into the form of propositions, these ideals become principles of political science, then articles of political creeds, and at last laws and institutions. Now, while this speculative element in political science must be kept in constant, truthful, and vital connection with the historical component, and must be, in a certain very important sense regulated by the historical component, it is, nevertheless, the most important element in political science, because it lights the way of progress and directs human experience toward its ultimate purpose.[23]

In the late nineteenth century and early years of the twentieth, when the phrase "political science" was informed by the preeminence of the Columbia School of Political Science led by Burgess, Lowell and Wilson both avoided the phrase when labeling the more empirically inclined programs they each helped create: Government at Harvard, Politics at Princeton. What was disconcerting about Burgess was not his talk of "ideals" and "progress," but the elevated role he, as a Hegelian, gave to "reason" as a vanguard agent articulating ideals and illuminating progress. This was a far cry from Wilson's declaring, "There are no parts of Burke upon which I more love to dwell than those in which he defends prejudice against the assaults of the rational," or Lowell's comment to Bryce that "man is in very small part rational, and mainly a suggestable animal."[24] It was Burgess's

---

[22] A. Lawrence Lowell, "The Responsibilities of American Lawyers," *Harvard Law Review* 1, 5 (1887), 237–38. On Wilson as a pragmatist, see Trygve Throntveit, "The Higher Education of Woodrow Wilson," in *The Educational Legacy of Woodrow Wilson: From College to Nation*, ed. James Axtell (Charlottesville: University of Virginia Press, 2012), 407–43.

[23] Burgess, "Political Science and History," 210.

[24] Wilson made this affirmation in an 1886 address to Princeton alumni propounding his vision of a "Professor of Politics" and stating his preference for "the Aristotelian word 'politics'" over "the broad but elegant 'umbrella' of political science." Woodrow Wilson, "An Address to the Princeton Alumni

veneration of reason that was liable to trigger anxieties about the a priori among other scholars of politics. If the *theoretical reason* of idealist philosophy worried them, Lowell and Wilson welcomed *practical insight*, which they trusted to better interpret the often far from rational dynamics of politics. Thus Wilson declared when reviewing Burgess:

> Politics can be successfully studied only as life; as the vital embodiment of opinions, prejudices, sentiments, the product of human endeavor, and therefore full of human characteristics, of whim and ignorance and half knowledge; as a process of circumstance and of interacting impulses, a thing growing with thought and habit and social development—a thing various, complex, subtle, defying all analysis save that of insight.[25]

BRYCE: ENGAGING, EXTENDING, AND REFOCUSING THE EMPIRICAL STUDY OF POLITICS

While Burgess's *Political Science and Comparative Constitutional Law* was at odds with methodological tastes common among American scholars of politics, Bryce and his *American Commonwealth* were well placed to win a far warmer reception. In addition to being a renowned institutional and legal historian, Bryce was, as Wilson stressed in reviewing his book, "a member of Parliament and an English constitutional statesman." Breathing "the air of practical politics in the country from which we get our habits of political action" enabled Bryce to supplement his "comprehensive mastery of the materials of comparative politics" with "great practical sagacity in interpreting them."[26] As Wilson's praise suggests, Bryce spoke to the proclivity of American scholars of politics for empirical and practically oriented studies. The ways that Bryce's work engaged, extended, and refocused American political science can each be elucidated in relation to Wilson.

Before starting to compose *The American Commonwealth*, Bryce took the measure of his famous predecessor Tocqueville's *Democracy in America*. But he did not do so alone. During his third visit to America in 1883, while lecturing on Roman law at Hopkins, Bryce led the Seminary of Historical and Political

of New York," in *Papers of Woodrow Wilson*, 5: 137–41. Almost two decades later, while Wilson was Princeton's president, this preference for "Politics" would be reflected in the labeling of Princeton's program in the field. For Lowell's comment in a letter to Bryce, see Lowell to Bryce, February 7, 1902, in letterpress book (March 19, 1901–Jan. 25, 1905), box 21, Abbott Lawrence Lowell Papers, Harvard University Archives. Quoted courtesy of the Harvard University Archives.

[25] Wilson, "Review of Burgess," 202.

[26] Woodrow Wilson, "Bryce's *American Commonwealth*," *Political Science Quarterly* 4, no. 1 (1889), 154–55.

Science in a discussion of Tocqueville's classic. He used the occasion to try out criticisms of Tocqueville, and to solicit from graduate students their assessment of how arguments of *Democracy in America* had held up in the half-century since its publication. For the graduate students at Hopkins, including Wilson, then in his first semester there, the session was an intellectual highlight amid the more mundane initiation into the rituals of specialized research that usually character-ized Seminary meetings.[27]

When *The American Commonwealth* appeared five years later, Tocqueville's classic was featured prominently in its introduction as the foil for Bryce's own method and aim. *Democracy in America* had been, Bryce suggested, "not so much a description of the country and people as a treatise, full of exquisite observa-tion and elevated thinking, upon democracy, a treatise whose conclusions are illustrated from America, but are in large measure founded, not so much on an analysis of American phenomena, as on general views of democracy which the circumstances of France had suggested." By contrast, Bryce sought in his book "to avoid the temptations of the deductive method, and to present simply the facts of the case, arranging and connecting them as best I can, but letting them speak for themselves rather than pressing upon the reader my own conclusions."[28] In using Tocqueville as a foil Bryce drew, in a tempered form, on arguments he had made in an article growing out of the 1883 Hopkins seminar. There he labeled Tocqueville's "method" as "*a priori,*" and went on to ascribe the "scholasticism we observe in him... partly to this deductive habit, partly to his want of familiarity with the actualities of politics."[29]

Bryce's *American Commonwealth* took up, as had Wilson's *Congressional Government*, the question of how American politics worked in actual practice, and conceived of this practice as potentially, indeed likely, to be at odds with theory. If Wilson's 1885 book had, as hailed by his friend Albert Shaw, "inaugurated the concrete and scientific study of our political system," then Bryce's 1888 book dra-matically extended that study.[30] In treating the national government in his book's

[27] Herbert Baxter Adams, "New Methods of Study in History," *Johns Hopkins University Studies in Historical and Political Science* 2, nos. 1–2 (1884), 105–6; Ions, *Bryce and American Democracy*, 118–21.

[28] James Bryce, *The American Commonwealth*, 3 vols. (London: Macmillan, 1888), 1: 5.

[29] James Bryce, "The Predictions of Hamilton and De Tocqueville," *Johns Hopkins University Studies in Historical and Political Science* 5, no. 9 (1887), 23–25. The contestability of Bryce's characterization of Tocqueville is captured in the fact that Wilson, in the same year, grouped his favored model of method, Bagehot, together with Tocqueville, as "*men of the world,* for whom the only acceptable philosophy of politics was a generalization from actual daily observation of men and things." Wilson, "Study of Politics," 190. What matters for my account is that, even as Bryce and Wilson disagreed in how they characterized Tocqueville, in doing so both used a methodological dualism tying the "actual" and "practical" together, and setting them over against the deductive "*a priori.*"

[30] Albert Shaw, "Review of *Congressional Government,*" in *Papers of Woodrow Wilson*, vol. 4 (1968), 315.

first part, Bryce built upon *Congressional Government*.[31] But that treatment was only one of six parts of a far longer work. Bryce's multiple volumes had the ambitious "aim of portraying the whole political system of the country in its practice as well as its theory, of explaining not only the National Government but the State Governments, not only the Constitution but the party system, not only the party system but the ideas, temper, habits of the sovereign people."[32]

The aim and achievement of *The American Commonwealth* is well captured in Wilson's praise of Bryce's treatment of parties. Bryce's detailed study of "The Party System" in America was unprecedented. He devoted three hundred pages to, as he put it, "the actual working of party government."[33] Wilson saw this part of Bryce's book as modeling "a new and vital conception of what it is to study constitutions in the life," and characterized the result as follows:

> Part III, on "The Party System," is the crowning achievement of the author's method. Here in a learned systematic treatise which will certainly for a long time be a standard authority on our institutions, a much used hand-book for the most serious students of politics, we have a careful, dispassionate, scientific description of the "machine," an accurately drawn picture of "bosses," a clear exposition of the way in which the machine works, an analysis of all the most practical methods of "practical politics," as well as what we should have expected, namely, a sketch of party history, an explanation of the main characteristics of the parties of to-day, a discussion of the conditions of public life in the United States, those conditions which help to keep the best men out of politics, and produce certain distinctively American types of politicians, and a complete study of the nominating convention.[34]

Yet, for all such praise, Wilson was struck and bothered by a shift in method that set *The American Commonwealth* apart from *Congressional Government*. Alongside foreswearing "the temptations of the deductive method," Bryce also

---

[31] In early 1888, when writing Wilson to solicit him, unsuccessfully, to contribute a chapter on women's suffrage (Wilson was then teaching at Bryn Mawr) to be included along with a couple of chapters by other Americans in *The American Commonwealth*, Bryce declared, "I know your *Congressional Government* so well and value it so highly that I seem to know you." Bryce to Wilson, February 25, 1888, in *Papers of Woodrow Wilson*, 5: 707. Early the next year, when discussing his *Political Science Quarterly* review of Bryce's work in a letter to the journal's editor Munroe Smith, Wilson noted: "How remorselessly 'Congressional Government' (a small volume by myself) is swallowed up in Part 1 of Bryce! Was I not 'nice' not to say anything about it?" Wilson to Smith, January 7, 1889, in *Papers of Woodrow Wilson*, vol. 6 (1969), 45.

[32] Bryce, *American Commonwealth*, 1: 3.

[33] Bryce, *American Commonwealth*, 2: 323.

[34] Wilson, "Bryce's *American Commonwealth*," 159.

held that he "had to resist another temptation, that of straying off into history."[35] As a scholar who had made his reputation over two decades earlier with a millennia-sweeping study *The Holy Roman Empire*, Bryce did not (and was not seen to) leave history aside due to lack of knowledge or interest.[36] His focus on the present in *The American Commonwealth* was, he explained, needed "to bring within reasonable compass a description of the facts of to-day."[37] The past was not entirely absent, but Bryce sketched historical changes on a scale of decades rather than centuries, and used such sketches sparingly to set up for far longer examinations of present-day phenomena.

This focus on the present called forth a vigorous protest from Wilson. He suggested that, even as Bryce's *American Commonwealth* offered "an invaluable store-house of observations in comparative politics," it failed to go beyond this to draw out "guiding principles of government inductively obtained." To do so required "a much freer use, a much fuller use, of the historical method...and it is in his sparing use of history that Mr. Bryce seems to me principally at fault." Whereas Bryce saw a need to avoid "straying off into history," Wilson held that "history belongs to the very essence" of the method Bryce used since "facts in comparative politics possess little value in the absence of clues to their development." As Wilson saw it, Bryce's minimizing of history resulted in "a partial failure to meet the demands of his own method."[38]

This disagreement expressed a new divide within, and over the future of, empirically and practically oriented political science. Bryce would personally thank Wilson for the "exercise of thought" and grasp of his aim that he found in Wilson's review of *The American Commonwealth*. But amity did not make disagreement less real, and Bryce also reaffirmed to Wilson his belief: "To treat either the institutions or national character of your country historically... might distract the average reader from the actualities of the State and people as they now stand."[39]

The divide between Bryce and Wilson marks a turning point in the evolution of political science. As a celebrated institutional historian who, when taking up America's political system, consciously chose to limit attention to the past in order to more fully portray the present, Bryce identified, legitimated, and modeled a

---

[35] Bryce, *American Commonwealth*, 1: 6.

[36] James Bryce, *The Holy Roman Empire* (Oxford: Shrimpton, 1864).

[37] Bryce, *American Commonwealth*, 1: 6. Restating this point again a little later in his text, Bryce explained that he was "anxious to avoid this danger [of straying into history], because the task of describing American institutions as they now exist is more than sufficiently heavy for one writer and one book." *American Commonwealth*, 1: 20.

[38] Wilson, "Bryce's *American Commonwealth*," 162–63.

[39] Bryce to Wilson, December 2, 1891, in *Papers of Woodrow Wilson*, 7: 343–44. Wilson's own reciprocation of Bryce's friendliness is evident in his response, which he closed by declaring "I wish I might some day have the pleasure of *talking* these points over with you!" Wilson to Bryce, December 18, 1891, in *Papers of Woodrow Wilson*, 7: 371.

way to pursue empirical political science that was distinct from institutional history. Bryce's pioneering of a posthistorical political science spurred Wilson to reaffirm the midcentury wide political science belief that history was integral, and hence "historical method" a banner under which scholars of politics could and should march together. This view would long retain a constituency among American political scientists. But the broader trend, from the appearance of *The American Commonwealth* onward, would be a steady rise of present-focused work in the vein of the new political science that Bryce pioneered.

The Study of Parties and Classical Liberalism: From Bryce's to Lowell's Political Science

The extended treatment of America's party system in Bryce's *American Commonwealth* is pivotal for locating the book within liberal debates about democracy. As Bryce was writing his book, Sir Henry Maine's 1885 *Popular Government* was already stressing to British liberals the inescapable but understudied role of parties in democracy:

> The truth is, that the inherent difficulties of democratic government are so manifold and enormous that, in large and complex modern societies, it could neither last nor work if it were not aided by certain forces which are not exclusively associated with it, but of which it greatly stimulates the energy. Of these forces, the one to which it owes most is unquestionably Party.
>
> No force acting on mankind has been less carefully examined than Party, and yet none better deserves examination.... Party disputes were originally the occupation of aristocracies, which joined in them because they loved the sport for its own sake; and the rest of the community followed one side or the other as its clients. Now-a-days, Party has become a force acting with vast energy on multitudinous democracies, and a number of artificial contrivances have been invented for facilitating and stimulating its action.[40]

Recognition that parties are inescapable combined with the belief that they operate differently in mass than in limited suffrage political systems to give studies of mass-based parties great import for British liberal debates over the promise or peril of their nation's growing suffrage. As Bryce well knew, a British audience awaited his portrait of America's parties.

---

[40] Henry Sumner Maine, *Popular Government* (Indianapolis, IN: Liberty Fund, 1976), 112–13, 115.

The portrait Bryce painted had a discernibly democratized classical liberal temper, with the two-sidedness characteristic of this midcentury liberalism's analyses of
democracy. On the one hand, Bryce gave a stark depiction of spoils-centered party
machines that would disturb any classical liberal. But, on the other hand, while showing this dark side of America's democracy, he argued that this was not its only side. He
also recounted reform efforts by educated mugwump elites who, if the spoils and corruption produced by parties got too extreme, would enter politics for a limited time
and have some success in shaping public opinion and electoral results.[41] In Bryce's
portrait of America, despite the dark arts of professional politicians, democracy was
far from irremediable. In *The American Commonwealth*'s introduction, he carefully
rang a note of democratic hope as he announced "the existence in the American people of a reserve of force and patriotism more than sufficient to sweep away all the evils
which are now tolerated." Aware of both sides of the portrait that he painted, Bryce
explained: "A hundred times in writing this book have I been disheartened by the
facts I was stating: a hundred times has the recollection of the abounding strength
and vitality of the nation chased away these tremors."[42]

Bryce's 1888 classic offered multiple lessons to multiple audiences. For British
liberals he provided a rejoinder to the disenchantment with democracy prominent in the mid-1880s work of Spencer and Maine. *The American Commonwealth*
called into the question the lament that mass suffrage politics inevitably puts all
power in the hands of professional politicians who use corruption and excessive
public spending to win and retain their party's hold upon power. Bryce did not
deny the existence of such tendencies, but suggested a different response to them.
Rather than bemoan mass suffrage, liberals should respond by nurturing, among
public opinion-shaping educated elites, enough criticism and independence of
professionalized parties to temper these tendencies.[43]

---

[41] For an extended study of Bryce's treatment of American political parties and their relation to public opinion, see Hugh Tullock, *James Bryce's American Commonwealth: The Anglo-American Background*
(Bury St. Edmunds, UK: Royal Historical Society, 1988), chap. 5. In identifying Bryce's book as the
work of a democratized *classical* liberal I rely on his continuing commitment to laissez-faire as construed in the moderate midcentury sense of John Stuart Mill discussed in earlier chapters. On Bryce's
persistence in laissez-faire views, even as other British liberals increasingly departed from them in the
late nineteenth and early twentieth centuries, see Tullock, *James Bryce's American Commonwealth*,
211–17.

[42] Bryce, *American Commonwealth*, 1: 14.

[43] Bryce's lessons for those debating democracy in the British context would later be explicitly
stated in James Bryce, "Preface," in *Democracy and the Organization of Political Parties*, by Moisei
Ostrogorski (London: Macmillan, 1902). Ostrogorksi had taken up the topic of democracy and its
influence on parties in the late 1880s when pursuing graduate work at Sciences Po. Through the 1890s
Ostrogorski expanded his research, at Bryce's encouragement, with detailed inquiry into political parties in England. Disappointed that Ostrogorski's work ended up infused with classical liberal disillusionment, Bryce had used his preface to try to counterbalance the body of the work with his own
views. On the tense relation between Bryce and Ostrogorski, and a contextualizing in light of it, of

For America's political scientists what Bryce's book offered was less a substantive lesson about democracy—a lesson they already knew since Bryce drew so much of it from discussions with them and their writings—than a new method. By limiting his focus to the present Bryce was able to broaden the range of contemporary phenomena he addressed and to pioneer a shift from historical toward systems-centered explanatory strategies. Whereas institutional history located present political institutions within lines of descent running back to an often-distant past, Bryce covered a wider set of present-day phenomena conceived as interacting parts of a complex whole: the "political system." After first discussing "The National Government," Bryce took up "The State Governments" (and local government), and then "The Party System," which he saw as essential to grasping how the formal institutions of government worked in actual practice. Yet, for Bryce, the parties were "not the ultimate force in the conduct of affairs," because "[b]ehind and above them stands the people." He thus continued on from "The Party System" to "Public Opinion" as the final part, and indeed the centerpiece, of America's political system.[44]

The American Commonwealth did not create the concept of the "political system." But it modeled a way to analyze political phenomena that developed the concept's potential. In doing so, Bryce inaugurated a new agenda for American political scientists. The following of Bryce's lead by Americans was quickly evident in A. L. Lowell's work. Lowell had already invoked the "political system" in criticizing Wilson's *Congressional Government* in 1886, but his approach shifted notably in the early 1890s in the wake of Bryce's book. He was, moreover, personally primed to engage Bryce by the friendship of his father, Augustus, with Bryce, which dated from Augustus Lowell's inviting the British scholar to give Lowell Institute lectures in 1881.[45] In the early 1890s, in Lowell Institute lectures of his own, A. L. Lowell followed Bryce's example of integrating studies of government institutions with examinations of political parties and public opinion. After further research, the lectures became Lowell's 1896 *Governments and Parties in Continental Europe.* This study of France, Italy, Germany, Austria-Hungary, and Switzerland focused on "the relation between the development of parties and the mechanism of modern government." The "systematic order of arrangement" it

Bryce's more rewarding relationship with A. Lawrence Lowell, see Paolo Pombeni, "Starting in Reason, Ending in Passion: Bryce, Lowell, Ostrogorski and the Problem of Democracy," *Historical Journal* 37, no. 2 (1994), 319–41.

[44] Bryce lays out this synchronic explanatory movement in his introduction. See *American Commonwealth,* 1: 6–8.

[45] Bryce and the younger Lowell later became frequent correspondents and friends in the years after Augustus Lowell died in 1900, when A. Lawrence Lowell was working, with Bryce's encouragement and feedback, on his magnum opus, his 1908 *Government of England,* which sought to do for England what Bryce had done for America.

followed largely paralleled the order in which Bryce's *American Commonwealth* proceeded: "The treatment of each country begins with a description of its chief institutions, or political organization; this is followed by a sketch of its recent history, in order to show how the parties actually work; and, finally, an attempt is made to find the causes of the condition of party life."[46]

Lowell's study was framed by the absence in continental countries of the "division into two great parties" found in most "Anglo-Saxon countries."[47] By viewing continental Europe in contrast to Britain and its colonial offspring, Lowell trod a well-worn path. But in revisiting this old line of contrast Lowell refashioned its content to engage a transformed political world. Most European countries now had representative assemblies elected by wide suffrage. By attending to party system differences, Lowell remade a contrast that had previously been centered on formal institutions. In an era in which elected parliaments had become the norm, "[a] study of the nature and development of parties" had become, Lowell pronounced, "the most important one [study] that can occupy the student of political philosophy today."[48] Whereas in the previous chapter we saw Wilson's focus on administration combine with the cross-national spread of mass suffrage to inform a progressive liberal convergence narrative, Lowell's focus on party systems helped him, by contrast, to formulate updated comparisons that offered more disenchanted perspectives on the present and future.

Lowell's focus led him to a series of claims about how party systems affect the working of political systems. His lead example was France. Under the Third Republic, France now had parliamentary institutions similar in general form, if not all details, to those of England.[49] But the actual working and outcomes of its political system differed greatly, and much of this difference was, for Lowell, due to the multiplicity and unstable contours of French parties. In recentering the contrast between England and France on party systems, he carried forward the evaluative weight this contrast had traditionally held. England served Lowell, as it had served earlier classical liberals like Lieber, as a standard against which France fell short. Lowell saw his comparison as teaching a more general lesson: "The normal condition of the parliamentary system... is a division into two parties," such a division is "necessary in order that the parliamentary form of government should permanently produce good results," and the system had therefore, in France, "not worked well, because this condition has not been fulfilled."[50]

---

[46] A. Lawrence Lowell, *Governments and Parties in Continental Europe*, 2 vols. (Boston: Houghton, Mifflin, 1896), 1: vii.

[47] Lowell, *Governments and Parties*, 1: vii.

[48] Lowell, *Governments and Parties*, 1: 69.

[49] Lowell, *Governments and Parties*, 1: 2–7.

[50] Lowell, *Governments and Parties*, 1: 69–74.

Lowell did, however, cautiously suggest that France could be moving toward the "normal condition" found in England. He noted an incipient consensus in support of the existing form of government—a consensus the lack of which had helped make France an exemplar of instability and revolution for a century. More specifically, lack of consensus about the rules of the game (to use a key phrase of twentieth-century political scientists) had historically, Lowell held, been a major cause of the multiplicity of parties in France. The growth of consensus might hence open the way to two-party politics as found in the Anglo-Saxon world.[51] Lowell here, as Bryce did in dealing with America, studied the party system alongside phenomena of public opinion, seen as a more basic force shaping the character of parties in a mass suffrage political system.

In moving beyond France to examine other nations of continental Europe, Lowell also identified an additional line of contrast that cut across the traditional Anglo-Saxon versus continental contrast. Although he portrayed France and Italy as having political systems that did not function as well as England's, Lowell did categorize them, along with England and the United States, as examples of "popular government." But he pointedly excluded Germany and Austria from this category. Lowell did so on the grounds that monarchs in Germany and Austria retained, and were if anything increasing, their control over governments that were not actually responsible to elected parliaments, or via them, to public opinion.[52]

This novel contrast was interwoven with differences in Lowell's judgments of the future political prospects of continental European nations. On one side, he cautiously saw prospects in the long term for stable and functioning popular government in France and Italy.[53] On the other side, by contrast, he looked with foreboding on the future of Germany and Austria.[54] Prospects for popular government in Germany were, he argued, vitiated by a party system that cut along, rather than across, class lines. The situation was, moreover, tending to get worse over time due to the growing divide between supporters of the growing socialist party and supporters of the "new monarchical theory...that decries universal suffrage and proclaims the military monarchy the best possible form of government."[55] In Austria, division of political parties along ethnic lines ruled out

[51] Lowell, *Governments and Parties*, 1: 101–5, 137–42.

[52] Lowell, *Governments and Parties*, 2: 67–77. Lowell's mid-1890s argument that imperial Germany did not have popular government because its parliament had no real power anticipates a point Max Weber later made. Max Weber, "Parliament and Government in Germany under a New Political Order," in *Political Writings*, ed. Peter Lassman and Ronald Speirs (Cambridge: Cambridge University Press, 1994), 130–271.

[53] Lowell, *Governments and Parties*, 1: 137–45, 229–31.

[54] Lowell, *Governments and Parties*, 2: 52–69, 119–23.

[55] Lowell, *Governments and Parties*, 2: 54; see also 1: 376–77 on the "vitality of the monarchical principle" in Germany.

popular government as a viable option. In Lowell's anxious judgment, division on these lines marked out the kingdom as the place where tides of "race feeling" on the rise across Europe cast their darkest "shadows."[56] With benefit of hindsight, it is all too easy to see in Lowell's mid-1890s reflections about Germany and Austria prescient insight into political tensions that fueled the descent, less than two decades later, into the shattering calamity of World War I.

Lowell's comments on Germany and Austria embody a hard-edged realism that pervades his disenchanted classical liberal political science. Even when offering reasons to view favorably the prospects of France's Third Republic, Lowell cautiously made these prospects contingent on French politicians leaving behind their historically passionate commitments to competing social and political ideals in favor of a willingness to work with an existing system that was far from realizing any high hopes.[57] In the hands of Lowell, a political science of the actual working of "political systems" was developing, more specifically, into a disenchanted liberal science that offered cold doses of the facts to temper enthusiasm for potentially disruptive political agendas.

The Progressive Liberal Political Science of Frank Goodnow

Although Lowell shows how Bryce's methodological approach could be put in the service of disenchanted classical liberalism, there was no one-to-one mapping between any single liberal political vision and the new political science that Bryce pioneered. To suggest how Bryceian analysis of political systems could be used in articulating a progressive liberal political science, I now take up the late-century scholarship of Frank J. Goodnow, a core faculty member of Columbia's School of Political Science and the future first president of the APSA.

While earning a law degree at Columbia in the early 1880s, Goodnow took courses in the recently founded School of Political Science and was offered a faculty post there conditional on his first undertaking further study in Europe. After spending time both at Sciences Po in Paris and the University of Berlin, he returned to start teaching in fall 1884. Goodnow's primary responsibility was teaching administration, and along with Woodrow Wilson, he helped to shape this as a new, growing, and quickly prominent area of specialization among political scientists. Like Wilson, Goodnow approached administration in a transatlantic fashion that took German and French scholarship and practices as

---

[56] Lowell, *Governments and Parties*, 2: 122–23. For Lowell, as for many other thinkers of his time, talk of "race" and "race feeling" played roles that have since been largely subsumed by talk of "nations" and "nationalism."

[57] Lowell, *Governments and Parties*, 1: 137–41.

a starting point and drew on these to forge an American scholarly agenda that placed American administrative practices in transatlantic perspective and used comparison to inform and encourage reforms in those practices.[58] If in Wilson's hands this agenda came with a qualifying emphasis that European influences must be adapted to America's democratic commitments, Goodnow at times stated his admiration for Europe so forcefully that Lowell in 1896 would caustically pronounce him "completely imbued with continental ideas."[59]

Goodnow's scholarship was, again like Wilson's, infused with a progressive liberal view of "modern" society and its imperatives. In the preface to his 1893 *Comparative Administrative Law*, which continued the series began by Burgess's 1891 *Political Science and Comparative Constitutional Law*, Goodnow made clear that his transatlantic comparisons were pursued with concerns different from the venerating American exceptionalism of Burgess:

> While the age that has passed was one of constitutional, the present age is one of administrative reform. Our modern complex social conditions are making enormous demands of the administrative side of the government, demands which will not be satisfied at all or which will be inadequately met, unless a greater knowledge of administrative law and science is possessed by our legislators and moulders of opinion. This knowledge can be obtained only by study, and by comparison of our own with foreign administrative methods.[60]

As we will see, Goodnow conceived "modern complex social conditions" more specifically in terms of industrialization and its impacts. In doing so he illustrates further the progressive liberal belief that industrialization was so transformative as to necessitate major changes in government.

---

[58] While Wilson's 1887 "Study of Administration" is the most celebrated published example of the inauguration of this area of specialization, Goodnow actually slightly beat him into print, publishing a more technical article that preceded Wilson's in *Political Science Quarterly* by two issues. Frank J. Goodnow, "The Executive and the Courts: Judicial Remedies against Administrative Action," *Political Science Quarterly* 1, no. 4 (1886), 533–59.

[59] Lowell, *Governments and Parties*, 60n.

[60] Frank J. Goodnow, *Comparative Administrative Law: An Analysis of the Administrative Systems, National and Local, of the United States, England, France and Germany*, 2 vols. (New York: Putnam's, 1893), 1: iv. Compare Burgess's American exceptionalism: "[W]hile we feel the pressure upon all sides to expand the powers of government in accordance with European practice, let us never forget that constitutional civil liberty is the peculiar product of our own political genius; and let us sacrifice no part of it, until the evidence becomes indisputable that, as to that part, individual autonomy has become either dangerous to the public security or detrimental to the general welfare." Burgess, *Political Science*, 1: 264.

What we can chart in Goodnow is the way in which the progressive liberalism forged during the 1880s subsequently came to be expressed in the idiom of the new political science pioneered by Bryce. During the 1890s Goodnow's works moved toward systems-centered analysis in a way that paralleled, and was partly indebted to, Lowell's Bryce-inspired study of parties. By the time he published his 1900 *Politics and Administration*, Goodnow's persistent progressive liberalism had fully cross-fertilized with the newer analytical orientation. The result was a book that exemplifies how the progressive liberal political vision, earlier stated in terms of the wide political science of the 1880s, became a leading, arguably the primary, political vision articulated in the new political science that would, in 1903, be given a national-level institutional home with the founding, under Goodnow's leadership, of the APSA.

LOCAL GOVERNMENT AND MUNICIPAL REFORM: FROM TRANSFORMATIVE HISTORICISM TO SYSTEMS ANALYSIS

The shift in Goodnow's scholarship is well displayed in his works on local government, the most frequent substantive topic of his late-century writing. Of ten articles Goodnow authored for *Political Science Quarterly* during the first decade after its 1886 founding, half were on local government. His 1893 *Comparative Administrative Law* was tellingly subtitled *An Analysis of the Administrative Systems, National and Local, of the United States, England, France and Germany*, with the part devoted to local administration over half again as long as that devoted to national administration. In treating local government as central to the study of administration, Goodnow paralleled a key trait of Wilson's lectures on administration at Hopkins in 1888–1896.

Goodnow's works on local government were, from the start, informed by the progressive liberal interpretation of industrialization as a transformative process. Writing in 1887, Goodnow declared that English local government was "wholly revolutionized" soon after the 1832 Reform Bill as part of a larger "movement... in great part due to social changes":

> The application of steam-power to manufactures and the very general introduction of machinery revolutionized industrial methods, massed large populations in the cities, and gave to the possessors of personal property—that is, the commercial and industrial classes—an importance they never had before. This change in the relative importance and power of property-owning classes led first to change in the method of representation in Parliament... it was only natural that the new political masters sought to discover some plan of local government by which their local influence might be increased.[61]

[61] Frank J. Goodnow, "Local Government in England," *Political Science Quarterly* 2, no. 4 (1887), 648–49.

Turning to Prussian local government in subsequent articles, Goodnow again situated the topic within a socioeconomically based grand narrative of nineteenth-century political development:

> In Prussia as in England the nineteenth century ushered in great social changes. The industrial development that began in this century and the long peace that followed the revolutionary and Napoleonic wars had favored the accumulation of a vast amount of personal property. The industrial and commercial classes thought that the power which they possessed in the affairs of every-day life was not sufficiently recognized in the government system; and the refusal by the nobility of their just demands for recognition led to the revolutionary events of the year 1848. The revolution of that year was really little more than a protest on the part of the possessors of personal property, i.e. the mercantile and manufacturing classes, against the monopoly of governing enjoyed by the possessors of large estates in land, i.e. the nobility.[62]

Goodnow's local government articles of 1887–1890 also singled out the later developing Prussia as achieving better results. In England earlier and more incremental changes created a convoluted "machinery of local government" that Goodnow suggested needed a "reorganization" in which "the new system adopted by Prussia might well serve as a model." He went on in a pair of articles to historicize, summarize, and trumpet Prussia's reform of local government between 1872 and 1883 as "one of the most notable administrative reforms that the world has ever been called upon to witness." Declaring it "the duty of the administrative system" to minimize "conflict between social classes," Goodnow judged that "no other reform shows as well how to reconcile apparently irreconcilable social interests." In closing his Prussia articles, Goodnow finally drew America explicitly into his discussion. He suggested that the "excellence in results of Prussian city organization" as compared to that of America should be credited less to Prussia's unequal suffrage system than to "the care that has been taken by the municipal law to force the well-to-do classes into the service of the city," and the fact "that the interference of the central legislature of the state in local affairs is infinitesimal if it exists at all."[63]

Goodnow here staked out a position in a burgeoning political science conversation about the governance and reform of America's cities. While it began with

---

[62] Frank J. Goodnow, "Local Government in Prussia I," *Political Science Quarterly* 4, no. 4 (1889), 657.

[63] Goodnow, "Local Government in England," 664–65; Goodnow, "Local Government in Prussia I," 648; Frank J. Goodnow, "Local Government in Prussia II," *Political Science Quarterly* 5, no. 1 (1890), 155–56.

a more historical approach, this conversation was, by 1890, increasingly focusing on the present, its problems, and reforms. Municipal government had been an organizing theme for the *Johns Hopkins University Studies in Historical and Political Science* in both 1886 and 1887, with articles appearing on the past development and contemporary character of local government in Washington, New Haven, Philadelphia, Boston, and St. Louis. In 1888, Wilson stressed the importance "in this age of cities... of municipal organization," and noted: "It almost seems as if city government, instead of national government, were to be the field of experiment and revolution for the future." He then devoted about half his twenty-five lectures in 1890 to examining the "modern industrial city" and proposed that the city be reconceived as "*a humane economic society*" and reformed in light of this.[64] As Wilson made municipal government a centerpiece of his administration lectures, his fellow Hopkins PhD Albert Shaw was, in 1888–1889, traveling in Britain and continental Europe investigating city governance.[65] Returning to America, Shaw published an article that presented Britain's large industrial cities (e.g., Glasgow, Manchester, and Birmingham) as offering "valuable lessons" for American cities "becoming too large and too densely populated to be indifferent any longer to the problems that all cities sooner or later must face and solve."[66]

Shaw's 1889 article appeared, as did Goodnow's 1887–1890 articles, in the increasingly prominent *Political Science Quarterly* published by Columbia's School of Political Science. At the same time that the focus of political science's conversation about cities shifted to the present and reforms, Columbia was supplanting Hopkins as the lead academic base of this conversation. Both shifts received a boost from Bryce's *American Commonwealth*. In a series of chapters on local government, Bryce summarized years of articles in the *Johns Hopkins University Studies*—from H. B. Adams's developmental historicist studies of rural towns to recent articles on cities—into a general assertion that, in America, "rural government" stood out "for its merits" and "city government for its faults."[67] After judging that "the government of cities is the one conspicuous failure of the United States,"[68] Bryce made this failure a recurring theme in later chapters. These

[64] Woodrow Wilson, "Lecture I: Systems of Municipal Organization," in *Papers of Woodrow Wilson*, 5: 697; Woodrow Wilson, "Notes for Lectures on Administration," in *Papers of Woodrow Wilson*, 6: 488–505, quote from 490.

[65] On Shaw's transatlantic travel, see Lloyd J. Graybar, *Albert Shaw of the "Review of Reviews": An Intellectual Biography* (Lexington: University Press of Kentucky, 1974), 39–42. Graybar also notes that, while in England in 1888, Shaw commented on the manuscript of Bryce's *American Commonwealth* and met leading British liberals such as Gladstone and Lord Action during dinners at Bryce's home.

[66] Albert Shaw, "Municipal Government in Great Britain," *Political Science Quarterly* 4, no. 2 (1889), 229.

[67] Bryce, *American Commonwealth*, 1: 7. This introductory statement sums up chapters 48–51 in 2: 220–95.

[68] Bryce, *American Commonwealth*, 2: 281.

included two chapters authored by Americans, who both were, or soon would be, at Columbia. Seth Low—a recent proreform mayor of Brooklyn, who would serve as Columbia's president from 1890 until he became mayor of the recently consolidated City of New York in 1901—provided "An American View of Municipal Government in the United States."[69] And Goodnow wrote a chapter titled "The Tweed Ring in New York City." His chapter's account "of a band of 'statesmen' of more than average ability and of quite phenomenal dishonesty, whose career constitutes the greatest reproach that has ever been cast upon popular government," was damning enough to spur libel litigation that kept it out of later editions of *The American Commonwealth*.[70]

Bryce in his book also advanced his own notably analytical explanation of the varying quality of American local government. Abstracting from the history and institutions of any single local government, he sought out "general and widespread causes" conceived as properties of the structure and practical working of America's political system as a whole. These causes included the "spoils system" and the character it gave the "party system," variation in how nominations and elections actually worked in practice in local electorates of differing sizes and education, and variation in the level of participation in local politics by more educated and wealthy elites. Taken together these factors made up Bryce's explanation: in America, "a particular form of democratic government acting under certain peculiar conditions" put governmental power, in large cities characterized by these conditions (which included "a mass of ignorant and pliable voters," and "insufficient participation in politics of the 'good citizens'") into the hands of "rings and bosses," who maintained and profited from power by behaving in ways that led to "the extravagance, corruption, and mismanagement which mark the administration of most of the great cities."[71]

While post-1888 editions of *The American Commonwealth* lacked the vivid chapter on New York's Tweed Ring Goodnow had authored, Goodnow's own writings in the course of the 1890s showcased his adoption of Bryce's moves. In surveying local administration in his 1893 *Comparative Administrative Law*, Goodnow structured his American chapters (but not those on England, France, or Prussia) using a rural/municipal distinction.[72] After dutifully finishing his

---

[69] Seth Low, "An American View of Municipal Government in the United States," in *The American Commonwealth*, by James Bryce, vol. 2 (London: Macmillan, 1888), 296–317.

[70] Frank J. Goodnow, "The Tweed Ring in New York City," in *The American Commonwealth*, by James Bryce, vol. 3 (London: Macmillan, 1888), 176.

[71] Bryce, *American Commonwealth*, 2: 281–88, 3: 467–68. In supporting his explanation Bryce provided evidence from multiple localities in a qualitative application of what he himself (using language J. S. Mill had coined) called "the method of concomitant variations." *American Commonwealth*, 3: 468. Goodnow's chapter on New York might be treated alongside Bryce's subsequent chapter on Philadelphia as a paired comparison providing evidence that variation in whether the Democratic or Republican Party was dominant was not a significant factor affecting the quality of urban governance.

[72] Goodnow, *Comparative Administrative Law*, book 3.

contribution to the series begun by Burgess, Goodnow fully devoted his next two books—his 1895 *Municipal Home Rule* and 1897 *Municipal Problems*—to municipal government and its reform. Each cause identified in Bryce's explanation of failure in city governance was elaborated upon in these books. Goodnow identified the spoils system as a "fault in municipal organization…to which until of recent years little attention has been directed," hailed reforms to limit it in the federal government, called for it to "be corrected as well in our municipal organization," and warned that "until that is accomplished little hope of improvement can be entertained."[73] Turning to elections, he used the rural/municipal contrast to argue that the "success of universal suffrage and majority rule in the rural towns…show[s] that neither system is inherently bad," and hence he promoted reform of election details (e.g., number of posts elected, election timing, if ballots were secret) rather than suffrage. In a further Bryceian move, Goodnow declared the nominating primary "an apparently democratic institution, but in reality the tool of the party machine," and proposed reforms to make it easier to get onto the ballot without party support.[74] However, he also doubted that anything could alter the American "social conditions," most fully evident in cities, that drew elites into a "race for wealth" that "caused the more intelligent, if not the better classes of the communities, to look down upon, or at least to look with indifference upon, civic honours," thus often leaving city offices to be "monopolized by persons of inferior intelligence and character."[75]

Goodnow also followed Bryce's methodological lead when he propounded a redirection of the municipal reform conversation toward system-centered analysis. This push to redirect the conversation grew out of his critical reaction to new books by Albert Shaw. Between 1889 and 1892 Shaw had published a series of articles based on his observations of British and European cities, and then, following another transatlantic trip in 1893, brought all his findings together in a pair of 1895 books surveying multiple British and continental European cities.

---

[73] Frank J. Goodnow, *Municipal Home Rule: A Study in Administration* (New York: Macmillan, 1895), 5.

[74] Frank J. Goodnow, *Municipal Problems* (New York: Macmillan, 1897), chap. 8. Goodnow's views on parties, elections, nominating process, and reforms to all these were further elaborated in a chapter contributed to the report accompanying the program formally adopted in late 1899 by the National Municipal League. Frank J. Goodnow, "Political Parties and City Government under the Proposed Municipal Program," in *A Municipal Program*, adopted by the National Municipal League (New York: Macmillan, 1900), 129–45. For more on the extensive role of political scientists in the National Municipal League and municipal reform more generally, and how these efforts created network connections that aided the formation soon thereafter of the APSA, see Frisch, "Urban Theorists"; Helene Silverberg, "A Government of Men: Gender, the City, and the New Science of Politics," in *Gender and American Social Science: The Formative Years*, ed. Helene Silverberg (Princeton, NJ: Princeton University Press, 1998), 156–84.

[75] Goodnow, *Municipal Home Rule*, 7–8.

When reviewing the books in *Political Science Quarterly*, Goodnow praised the quality of their description of the organization and working of particular cities, but complained that Shaw failed to sufficiently attend to the national-level conditions influencing municipal government, how these differed cross-nationally, and how such differences affected any transatlantic lessons that might be drawn.[76]

Goodnow then set out in his 1897 *Municipal Problems* to elaborate an analytical system-centered approach and its payoff for reform. Announcing in his preface his endeavor "to treat the city rather as a part of the governmental system than as an isolated phenomenon," Goodnow stressed his "hope" that doing so would "throw light on most of the important municipal problems of the present day."[77] The "light" that might be shed by attending to the interplay among levels of government was displayed in Goodnow's nuanced argument that, as national and state-level posts were being removed from the "spoils system," the "spoils of municipal office" was presently acquiring even "greater importance" as the remaining domain in which parties could strengthen themselves by directly rewarding their supporters.[78]

Goodnow's goal in pursuing his "new line of investigation" in the study of cities involved more than attaining novel empirical insights. By examining "the position which the city occupies in our system of government" and comparing this to the position "it occupies in those countries in which municipal government has been successful," Goodnow aspired "to ascertain what is the correct position which the city should occupy."[79] When he embraced system-centered analysis as pioneered by Bryce, Goodnow did so, not as an end in itself, but as a tool that could help identify "the ideal form of organization of municipal government for this country."[80] Rather than reject, he was renewing, the grand mission—assigned to political science by Burgess—to identify and disseminate ideals that could elucidate, elevate, and rationalize the path of liberal progress.

GOODNOW'S CLASSIC: *POLITICS AND ADMINISTRATION*

As the 1890s drew to a close Goodnow further extended his developing system-centered approach when he wrote his 1900 classic *Politics and*

---

[76] Albert Shaw, *Municipal Government in Great Britain* (New York: Century, 1895); Albert Shaw, *Municipal Government in Continental Europe* (New York: Century, 1895). Goodnow's reviews appeared in *Political Science Quarterly* 10, no. 1 (1895), 171–75 and *Political Science Quarterly* 11, no. 1 (1896), 158–63. Shaw and Goodnow are treated as "two poles" of the 1890s political science conversation on municipal reform in Frisch, "Urban Theorists," 304–8.

[77] Goodnow, *Municipal Problems*, v.

[78] Goodnow, *Municipal Problems*, 202.

[79] Goodnow, *Municipal Problems*, 19–20.

[80] Goodnow, *Municipal Problems*, 280–81.

Administration. Goodnow here built on his prior treatment of local and central government as interrelated parts of a "governmental system." By now relating the "governmental system" more fully to the "party system," he sought, in turn, to study them together as interacting parts of the "political system" as a whole. In his first pages Goodnow paid homage to Bryce's pioneering use of this approach to give "the best description of the actual political system obtaining in the United States." But he also turned, in addition, to his fellow American Lowell's "recent and most excellent work on *Government and Parties in Continental Europe*" as "a shining example of the value of the study of parties to the student of government."[81] Goodnow wielded transatlantic comparisons throughout *Politics and Administration,* and in doing so he repeatedly drew on Lowell's 1896 work for substantive claims about the relations between party systems and governments in Europe.

Even as Goodnow engaged specific claims of Lowell's, major differences between these two American scholars exemplified the varied purposes that a Bryce-informed systems-centered approach could serve. There was contained, but nonetheless real, room for variety—political and methodological—in the conversation of the new posthistorical political science on the rise in the turn-of-the-century American academy. Goodnow, in contrast to Lowell, wielded transatlantic comparisons with a progressive liberal reformer's goal of elucidating criticisms of America's political system and offering "concrete remedies." His comparisons, as a result, focused on suggestive examples of selected features of European political systems: both positive features that progressive reform might move America toward, and negative features to be avoided. There remained in Goodnow's classic, moreover, a lingering legacy of the philosophical idealism favored by Burgess. *Politics and Administration* unapologetically advanced claims about "the political ideas" on which the American political system "was based," and presented its "concrete remedies" as "changes in the formal system of the United States that must be made, in order to make the actual system conform, more closely than it does at present" to these political ideas.[82]

Probably the most famous feature of Goodnow's classic is the duality of "politics" and "administration" in its very title. Goodnow unpacked this duality in terms of a contrast between the "expression" and the "execution" of the "will" of "the state," embedded in a sociological framing that held that, as societies became more "complex," these "political functions" were or should be handled by more differentiated "organs."[83] The duality was used by Goodnow to structure both

---

[81] Frank J. Goodnow, *Politics and Administration: A Study in Government* (New York: Macmillan, 1900), 4–5, 28.

[82] Goodnow, *Politics and Administration,* preface.

[83] Goodnow, *Politics and Administration,* chap. 1. Goodnow had earlier propounded the expression/execution contrast within the theory of the state in terms more tied to those of Burgess, but by the

his descriptions and his reform proposals. If certain methodological elements of Goodnow's approach show lingering legacies of Burgess's political science, in its substance his central duality was infused by a progressive liberalism familiar to us from Wilson. Goodnow viewed progress in the institutions and actions of governments during recent centuries as having developed along two historical trajectories: one in England and its American offspring, the other in continental Europe. Thus, he had held in 1897,

> While the Anglo-American race has taught the world a valuable lesson in showing them how government should be organized in order to secure civil liberty and provide for the expression of the will of the people, it is certainly true that continental Europe, with its Roman legal traditions, has done much towards the solution of purely administrative problems.[84]

Against this backdrop, the task of the present appeared, for Goodnow like Wilson, to be wedding "popular government," as developed in Anglo-American history, with "efficient administration," as developed in continental Europe. Grasping the distinction between politics and administration, and making reforms to better realize it in practice, was the key, for Goodnow, to reconciling the potential tensions between these ends, and thus achieving them both in a given political system.[85]

Goodnow's conception of "popular government" (which he thought "unquestionably the political ideal of the nineteenth century") exemplified again the progressive liberal intertwining of liberalism with democracy we saw earlier in Wilson's works. This is evident in the prior quote when Goodnow, in summing up the achievements of the "Anglo-American race," stressed both "civil liberty" *and* providing for the "expression of the will of the people." He left little, if any, theoretical space here in which to acknowledge possible trade-offs between these achievements. It is thus unclear what to make of the shift between his 1897 language and his 1900 *Politics and Administration*, where the democratic commitment to "expression of the will of the people" carried forward into his talk of "popular government," but "civil liberty" (which classical liberals like Lieber, and more recently, Burgess made much of) was no longer invoked. Did Goodnow's concept of "popular government" in *Politics and Administration* assume that such government is coexistent with civil liberty, or did it allow conflict between them and

---

late 1890s the influence of another Columbia colleague, sociologist Franklin Giddings, had reshaped Goodnow's framing. Cf. Goodnow, *Comparative Administrative Law*, 2: book 5.

[84] Goodnow, *Municipal Problems*, 86.

[85] *Politics and Administration* is pervaded by discussion of "popular government," "efficient administration," and what it takes to realize each of them, and both of them together. For specific examples, see Goodnow, *Politics and Administration*, 24, 36–38, 43–44, 72, 77, 82–93, 131, 136–37, 148–52, and 255–63.

democratically prioritize popular government?[86] It is, however, perhaps in just such ambiguity that Goodnow most fully embodied, and most effectively promoted, the political vision of progressive liberalism.

The progressive liberalism distinguishing Goodnow's *Politics and Administration* from Lowell's work is further evident in the way each used the "actual" versus "formal" contrast central to the rising political science conversation. Goodnow endorsed Lowell's view that, despite the universal manhood suffrage formal basis of the Reichstag, the strength of Germany's monarch and weakness of its parties, and resulting subordinate position of the legislature in the actual working of German government, meant that Germany did not have "popular government." But at the same time, in a move Lowell would quickly contest, Goodnow extended this style of analysis to also argue, twenty pages or so later, that America's own political system did not currently "satisfy the demands of popular government." For the progressive liberal Goodnow, America's "formal governmental systems" were based on an "ideal of democracy" that, he critically held, "was not realized in actual political practice."[87]

Goodnow charged that popular government was undermined in America by the character of its political parties. The parties were, indeed, such a hindrance that, he argued, popular government was better realized in practice in England than America, even though the House of Commons was based on a less extensive suffrage. England's system provided for an "immediate responsiveness to the public will" lacking in America.[88] In conceiving such "responsiveness" as a necessary feature of "popular government," and England's political system as paradigmatic of it, Goodnow echoed Wilson's *Congressional Government*. But details of Goodnow's argument moved away from Wilson's criticism of the separation of legislature and executive powers in America. Drawing instead on claims about how separation of powers related to the organization and operation of political parties,[89] *Politics and Administration* advocated promoting responsiveness by reforming the party system, rather than the separation of legislative and executive powers, with the goal of making American parties "responsible" to public opinion, such as parties in England were assumed to be.[90]

---

[86] Goodnow, *Politics and Administration*, chap. 7.

[87] Goodnow, *Politics and Administration*, 137–38, 158–67.

[88] Goodnow, *Politics and Administration*, 163.

[89] Goodnow, *Politics and Administration*, chaps. 2, 5–6. Goodnow here drew on an 1898 book by journalist Henry Jones Ford. Henry Jones Ford, *The Rise and Growth of American Politics: A Sketch of Constitutional Development* (New York: Macmillan, 1898). The book impressed Wilson also, who subsequently brought Ford into the academy to teach politics at Princeton.

[90] Goodnow devotes the last four chapters of *Politics and Administration* to his critical comparison of America with England as regards popular government and parties, to articulating proposed reforms to the party system in America that grow out of this comparison, and then, finally, to arguing that these proposed reforms in the political sphere will only be a success if pursued alongside reforms he also proposed for the administrative sphere. Goodnow, *Politics and Administration*, chaps. 7–10.

The Contained Contention of the New Political Science

We have seen in his chapter how the posthistorical analytical study of "modern political systems" pioneered by Bryce's 1888 *American Commonwealth* was taken up and extended in the 1890s by American political scientists. Two traits of their conversation should be at the fore of our attention when we take up, in this book's conclusion, the 1903 founding of the APSA. First, it accommodated, indeed it to a large degree was constituted by, debate among alternative liberal political visions over topics closely related to the proposed local-, state-, and national-level reforms of American democracy whose late-century upswing opened what is often called the Progressive Era. Second, if contention was substantively lively and practically relevant, it was, at the same time, conducted in a contained manner that participants understood to be distinctively scientific. Discussion centered on advancing empirical claims about, and usually comparisons between, Western nations with mass suffrage politics and then drawing out implications for American reform agendas.

The contained contention characteristic of the conversation of the new political science can be illustrated by contrasting Goodnow's claim that popular government was better realized in England than America with the views of Bryce and Lowell. When Goodnow argued in *Politics and Administration* that party "machines" and "bosses" were so powerful as to forestall popular government in America, he broke with Bryce. Even while particular chapters of *The American Commonwealth* helped to spread such claims about American parties, the overarching portrait Bryce offered was of a political system in which public opinion was "the great source of power, the master of servants who tremble before it." When stepping back from specific details to make transatlantic comparisons, Bryce held that the "will of the people" acted "directly and constantly upon its executive and legislative agents" to a far greater extent in America. This made America "materially" more democratic in the actual working of its political system than were other "free countries"—such as France and England—in which elected office holders were more able to act independently of public opinion.[91] Bryce stated his own view of the relation of parties to public opinion in America eloquently during his book's introduction:

> Public opinion, that is the mind and conscience of the whole nation, is the opinion of persons who are included in the parties, for the parties taken together are the nation; and the parties, each claiming to be its true exponent, seek to use it for their purposes. Yet it stands above the parties, being cooler and larger minded than they are; it awes party leaders

---

[91] Bryce, *American Commonwealth*, 3: 14–33.

and holds in check party organizations. No one openly ventures to resist it. It determines the direction and the character of national policy. It is the product of a greater number of minds than in any other country, and it is more indisputably sovereign. It is the central point of the whole American polity.[92]

The progressive liberal Goodnow and democratized classical liberal Bryce thus disagreed over whether America or England better realized a democratic ideal of government responsive to the public will. Goodnow's reversal of Bryce's position called forth, in turn, a vigorous criticism from Lowell. In responding Lowell reframed the terms of discussion. His disenchanted classical liberalism made him more skeptical than Bryce or Goodnow about the extent to which there is a "public will," and in the limited situations when talk of such a will is viable, about the extent to which government should be directly responsive to it. Setting aside the overarching question of whether America or England more fully realized popular government, Lowell devoted his 1902 "The Influence of Party upon Legislation in England and America" to critically assessing more specific empirical premises that Goodnow's recent argument assumed as given.[93]

Lowell here redeployed an intellectual tactic he had earlier used in criticizing the England versus America comparison of Wilson's *Congressional Government*. Just as he had when criticizing Wilson, Lowell challenged the accuracy of empirical claims about America that were essential for Goodnow's transatlantic comparison, and thereby indirectly promoted skepticism about the reform proposals informed by that comparison. Lowell opened his study by juxtaposing "the growing sense of the importance of party in public life" in "the discussion of observers and reformers" and the accompanying rising tide of legislation regulating parties, against the scarcity of empirical knowledge about parties, their influence, or lack thereof. He then set out "to show that the vehemence in the outcry against party and in complaint of its despotism by no means always corresponds with the actual extent of its power." Analyzing the level of party cohesion found in recorded votes in the House of Commons, Congress, and five American state legislatures, Lowell argued that, "it is manifest that the influence of party over legislation in public matters is less by far in America than in England." On this basis he rejected "the prevalent impression that party is more powerful and despotic in America than

[92] Bryce, *American Commonwealth*, 1: 7–8.

[93] A. Lawrence Lowell, "The Influence of Party upon Legislation in England and America," in *Annual Report of the American Historical Association for the Year 1901*, vol. 1 (Washington DC: Government Printing Office, 1902), 319–541. The footnotes on 348–49 spell out that the argument about parties the article calls into question is specifically that forged by Henry Jones Ford and then extended by Goodnow.

in England" as based on a failure to differentiate party control over patronage (greater in America) from party control over legislation (greater in England).[94]

If Lowell is remembered among American political scientists today, it is perhaps most for the way he used statistics to support his claim about the influence of parties over legislation. Holding that this influence could not be assessed "without thorough statistics,"[95] Lowell himself compiled over two hundred pages of data tables and charts that he published along with the thirty pages of his actual article. Yet, if he deserves recognition for an exacting (for its time) empirical analysis, we should not allow this recognition to overshadow the practical purpose that motivated Lowell's labors. As Bernard Crick perceptively observed, Lowell pursued statistics, "not for the advancement of a possible social science, but to provide some evidence, amongst other evidence, for practical judgments."[96] What spurred his study was observing a belief that had growing practical import, and wanting to question if that belief was plausible. As Lowell explained in a 1901 letter:

> You know it is the habit to speak of parties in this country as if they had a peculiar monopoly on legislation, as compared, for example, with England. People talk as if everything was done by party here. A good many political theories are founded upon the idea, and a good deal of the political action of the reformers is based on it. It seemed, therefore, worth while to investigate the matter thoroughly.[97]

Even as Lowell deftly wielded empirical work to undermine a key premise of Goodnow's reform-promoting England versus America comparison, he contained his contentiousness. There was no trace here of the caustic edge of Lowell's aside, in the 1896 first edition of *Governments and Parties*, characterizing

---

[94] Lowell, "Influence of Party," 321, 342, 348–50.

[95] Lowell, "Influence of Party," 321. Lowell was, it bears noting, far from seeing statistics as always essential or superior to other research tools. The primary approach of his magnum opus, *The Government of England*, was that of a field research scholar: drawing together wide reading, much travel in the country under study, and conversations and letter exchanges with scholars and politicians there. In the book's preface, Lowell explained: "The forces to be studied do not lie upon the surface, and some of them are not described in any document or found in any treatise. They can be learned only from men connected with the machinery of public life. A student must, therefore, rely largely upon conversations which he can use but cannot cite as authorities, and the soundness of his conclusions must be measured less by his references in footnotes than by the judgment of the small portion of the public that knows at first-hand the things whereof he speaks." Lowell, *Government of England*, 1: vi.

[96] Crick, *American Science of Politics*, 105.

[97] Lowell to Haskins, April 15, 1901, in letterpress book (March 19, 1901–Jan. 25, 1905), box 21, Abbott Lawrence Lowell Papers, Harvard University Archives. Quoted courtesy of the Harvard University Archives.

Goodnow as "completely imbued with continental ideas."[98] Despite that aside, Goodnow had used, and even generously praised, Lowell's book in his own *Politics and Administration*. Goodnow had, in effect, treated Lowell as a fellow participant in a conversation with a code of conduct that allowed contention, but contained its form. Lowell's own recognition of that code of conduct is suggested by the fact that, while his 1902 study criticized Goodnow on a substantive point, newer editions of *Government and Parties* expunged the caustic aside of its first edition. Indeed, by 1903, Lowell had enough respect for Goodnow as a political scientist to invite him (albeit unsuccessfully) to leave Columbia to join Harvard's Department of Government.[99]

In sum, as we note the contention between alternate liberal visions in turn-of-the-century exchanges between Goodnow and Lowell, we should, at the same time, note how the character of this contention came to be contained. Lowell and Goodnow had become, by the first years of the twentieth century, participants in a common conversation who recognized one another as major contributors to that conversation. There was much overlap in the works they cited and concepts they used, in the types of institutions and other political phenomena they analyzed, and in the nations and time periods they found relevant for students of "modern political systems." Each exemplified, and added momentum to, the new political science agenda of relating a broad array of contemporary institutions and phenomena as interacting parts of a system, which was starting to supplant the earlier historicist agenda of relating institutions to developmental antecedents in a grand narrative reaching through centuries or even millennia. In sum, Goodnow and Lowell had started to do political science in its twentieth-century sense, and both, in doing so, followed the transatlantic lead of Bryce, "the master and guide of all students of modern political systems."[100]

[98] Lowell, *Governments and Parties*, 60n.

[99] Lowell to Goodnow, May 23, 1903, in letterpress book (March 19, 1901–Jan. 25, 1905), box 21, Abbott Lawrence Lowell Papers, Harvard University Archives. Referenced courtesy of the Harvard University Archives.

[100] Lowell, *Government of England*, 1: vii.

Conclusion

THE AMERICANIZATION OF POLITICAL SCIENCE
AND THE AMERICANIZATION OF "LIBERALISM"

This book has followed two narrative and thematic trajectories. First, we have followed the emergence of a self-conscious "political science" in America's academy from the antebellum era to the opening of the twentieth century. This trajectory reaches a narrative closing point in the first part of this conclusion, where I selectively sketch some key traits of the American Political Science Association (APSA) and the process that led to its 1903 founding. Considered against the earlier history of political science in America as presented in this book, the new association embodied both innovation and inheritances. By institutionalizing political science as a specialized field, the APSA constituted a critical turning point in the Americanizing shift from the older wide sense of political science inaugurated in Europe, to a newer, narrower America-led conception of what political science is. But this reframing was accompanied by simultaneous vigorous reaffirmation of the long-standing aspiration that political science could and should play a broad public role in addressing pressing questions of the day.

Our second trajectory has presented the pioneers of political science in America as active participants in a transatlantic liberal tradition, who adapted beliefs, hopes, and fears of European liberals in order to address American political and economic realities. In following this trajectory we have advanced from the 1830s crystallization of democratized classical liberalism through the late-nineteenth-century development of the alternative political visions of progressive liberalism and disenchanted classical liberalism. In the second part of this conclusion, I showcase how this divergence in liberal thought, already articulated among American political scientists in the late nineteenth century, illuminates particular meanings given to "liberal" and "liberalism" as these words acquired American political use between the 1910s and 1930s. Americanization of the language of "liberalism" unfolded upon terrain already structured by the Americanization of liberalism as a transatlantic tradition of political thought.

Americanizing Political Science: Innovation and Inheritances in the APSA

As we have seen in this book, political science in America precedes the founding of the APSA. But the APSA's founding was a—arguably *the*—pivotal event in the *Americanization* of political science in America. Formal establishment of the APSA on December 30, 1903 was the culmination of a yearlong initiative. A year earlier a conference had been held in Washington, DC, to consider the desirability of founding an American Society of Comparative Legislation. At the conference attendees had decided instead that "a National Association should, if possible, be created, whose province should embrace the whole field of Political Science, and thus include Comparative Legislation as one of its special topics." This project was entrusted to a committee of fifteen, which conducted a letter campaign in 1903 to announce the initiative, assess support for it, and then promote participation in the meeting that officially established the APSA during the American Historical Association and American Economics Association conferences, held together in New Orleans that December.[1]

Viewed in transatlantic perspective, the shift from the initial plan to create an American Society of Comparative Legislation to the more expansive initiative that produced the APSA was an American innovation. The initial plan followed European precedents. A Société de Législation Comparée had been created in Paris in 1867; its first president was the French liberal Edouard Laboulaye, whom we met briefly at the end of chapter 3 as a correspondent of Lieber. The older French society had more recently served as a model for the mid-1890s founding in London of a Society of Comparative Legislation.[2] Establishment of an American Society of Comparative Legislation would hence have been another instance of the transatlantic modeling we have seen often during the emergence of American political science.

The situation was very different with regard to the APSA. There was no European model for such an association. When the Washington conference attendees in December 1902 directed their organizing effort toward a national political science association, they envisioned something that would be created, for the first time ever, in America. This was a watershed in the history of political science seen in transatlantic perspective. If we were to carry that history up through the twentieth century we would tell a narrative of how political science,

---

[1] "The Organization of the American Political Science Association," *Proceedings of the American Political Science Association* 1 (1904), 5–14.

[2] On the English society and its activities, see Munroe Smith, "Review of Journal of the Society of Comparative Legislation," *Political Science Quarterly* 12, no. 3 (1897), 537–43.

in the sense institutionalized in the APSA, later came to be exported to Europe. The American Century in political science had begun.

What then was new, and what not new, about political science as institutionalized in the APSA? One principal novelty was the belief, trumpeted in the October 1903 letter encouraging attendance at APSA's upcoming founding, that "Political Science, as distinguished from History and Economics," had its own "special interests" that would be best "represented and advanced" by its own national association.[3] This belief stands out in contrast to earlier views that had held that the interests of political science were served by the American Historical Association (AHA) and American Economics Association (AEA). In chapter 5 we saw such a view expressed in Albert Shaw's 1888 hailing of the founding of the AHA and the AEA as developments that, in coordination with the programs in wide political science at Hopkins and Columbia, were helping to give "the study of political science so remarkable an impetus in this country."[4]

An explanation of why Americans who associated themselves with political science came to see their interests as distinguishable from and unmet by the AHA and the AEA would have to address multiple factors. But one such factor that we have seen develop in the closing chapters of this book is the rise of specialized agendas that were neither historical nor economic in character. A first example of such an agenda we have noted is the development of administration as a focus of substantive specialization within the remit of political science in the years following Wilson's pioneering 1887 "The Study of Administration." A second example is the innovative approach to studying parties that we charted, in chapter 8, taking shape between the late 1880s and the start of the twentieth century. The methodological orientation of Bryce, Lowell, and Goodnow highlighted there—notably concentration upon the present, and analysis in terms of the political system—produced specialized works that were not reliant on the established methods of history or economics. It is thus especially telling that Goodnow, whose 1900 *Politics and Administration* interwove these two rising agendas, became the first president of the APSA.[5] In the association's inaugural presidential address he would disavow attempting to "define political science" and instead characterize "the field of the American Political Science Association" by surveying the specialized

[3] "Organization of the APSA," 9. This phrasing appeared in the circular letter sent to several hundred individuals in October 1903 inviting them to attend the meeting that formally founded APSA that December.

[4] Albert Shaw, "Introductory," in *The National Revenues*, ed. Albert Shaw (Chicago: McClurg, 1888), 28–30.

[5] As second president of the APSA, Albert Shaw explicitly held up Goodnow as representing the emergence "of a body of trained and competent men… who are primarily political scientists rather than historians or economists." He presented the emergence of such men as "a comparatively recent fact" and one reason for the formation of the APSA. Albert Shaw, "Presidential Address," *American Political Science Review* 1, no. 2 (1907), 177–78.

agendas—including, among others, the two I have just noted—that "have not yₑₜ been systematically treated by the other societies already in existence."[6]

The APSA's founding as an autonomous association assumed and accelerated departure from the older wide sense of political science that Lieber and others had imported from Europe. Wide political science had encompassed political economy and allied itself with history, as areas of specialized knowledge and methods to be drawn upon in order to inform practical judgments about what was possible and preferable in present-day politics and policy. A conceptual shift had to be made to structure the narrower sense of "political science" that located it *alongside* history and economics as another area of specialization. In chapter 4 we saw that William Graham Sumner and Munroe Smith had each articulated a narrowed sense of political science already in the 1880s. But it was only during the decades *after* the APSA gave a national-level institutional embodiment to this conceptual reframing that the narrower sense became decidedly dominant in America. The now long-familiar view of political science as one specialized field set alongside an array of others that together make up the "social sciences" is not what "political science" has always meant in America and its academy. It is what the APSA helped to make it.

At the same time that we recognize the founding of the APSA as a watershed moment in articulating and advancing a narrowed sense of political science's remit, we must also pay heed to the association's inheritances from the wide political science of earlier decades. In the October 1903 letter circulated to promote attendance at the APSA's founding, the announcements of its founding, and the speeches of its early presidents at the annual meetings that began in December 1904, we find an aspiration to serve a broader public purpose that we have seen throughout this book. In chapter 4, when considering Andrew D. White's mid-1860s arguments for including education in political science at the soon to open Cornell University, we flagged his contention that political science promotes better decision-making about "great public questions." We find a parallel argument in the published announcement of the new APSA by the University of Wisconsin's Paul Reinsch, who had served on the committee that led the new association's founding. Reinsch ended the announcement by declaring: "In short, problems in every branch of governmental activity are pressing for solution. In the study and discussion which are so essential to a right understanding of these difficult questions, an important part will be borne by the American Political Science Association."[7]

---

[6] Frank J. Goodnow, "The Work of the American Political Science Association," *Proceedings of the American Political Science Association* 1 (1905), 35.

[7] Paul S. Reinsch, "The American Political Science Association," *Iowa Journal of History and Politics* 2, no. 2 (1904), 161.

Throughout my account of nineteenth-century wide political science we have, moreover, persistently found this aspiration to improve decision-making about public questions interwoven with a commitment to nonpartisanship. That commitment was reiterated, even as it varied in its details, as we moved from Andrew D. White appealing to nonpartisanship to the 1860s, to William Graham Sumner doing so in the 1870s, and Richard T. Ely in the 1880s. In dealing with the early years of the AEA, we recounted the controversy that followed Ely's attempt to commit that association to disavow any "partisan attitude" on charged economic policy questions while also simultaneously endorsing the state as an agent of progress. The compromise that ended this controversy eliminated from the AEA's constitution its initial positive statement about the state, but retained in isolation a formal disavowal of partisanship. When the APSA was established a generation later, it built directly on this precedent. Looking explicitly to the AEA as an example, drafters of the APSA's constitution produced language closely following the postcompromise AEA constitution.[8] The "Statement of Objects" in Article II of the AEA constitution included the following:

> The encouragement of perfect freedom of economic discussion. The Association, as such, will take no partisan attitude, nor will it commit its members to any position on practical economic questions.[9]

Article II of the new APSA constitution read, in turn:

> ARTICLE II. OBJECT.
> The encouragement of the scientific study of Politics, Public Law, Administration, and Diplomacy.
> The Association as such will not assume a partisan position upon any question of practical politics, nor commit its members to any position thereupon.[10]

There are two take-away points especially worth noting with regard to the APSA's stance on partisanship.[11] First, in approaching the APSA in light of the

---

[8] Reinsch, "American Political Science Association," 157.

[9] "Constitution, By-Laws, and Resolutions of the American Economic Association with List of Officers and Members," *Publications of the American Economic Association* 4, Supplement (July, 1889), 3.

[10] "Constitution of the American Political Science Association," *Proceedings of the American Political Science Association* 1 (1904), 16.

[11] For another interpretation, see John G. Gunnell, "The Founding of the American Political Science Association: Discipline, Profession, Political Theory, and Politics," *American Political Science Review* 100, no. 4 (2006), 479–86. I diverge from Gunnell in seeing little novelty in the association's stance on partisanship, but follow him closely in interpreting the stance as one that political scientists themselves

wide political science preceding it, we should see the new association's disavowal of partisanship as extending an attitude integral to political science in America for many decades. Second, we should recognize that disavowal of "a partisan position" on questions of "practical politics" was no disavowal of engagement with pressing public questions. On the contrary, the disavowal expressed political scientists' belief that they had a distinctive contribution to make to decision-making about such questions. This belief was vigorously affirmed by Albert Shaw in his December 1906 address as APSA's second president. Turning for examples to questions about how "governmental policy" hinders or aids "industrial prosperity," Shaw held that, precisely because "[t]his Association is not partisan, is not a body of reformers, is concerned with no propaganda; it could therefore study with absolute calmness and impartiality" particular policy choices in this charged domain. More generally, he extolled the promise of political science to "bring to a hundred questions now under discussion in the affairs of the nation, of the States, or of the municipalities, the spirit of calmness, of inquiry, of reasonable discussion—in short, the scientific spirit."[12]

Viewed against the longer-term history of political science in America, what stands out about the aspiration to public influence at the time of the APSA's founding is less the aspiration than the accompanying confidence in its ability to be realized. One basis for this confidence was a belief that there was a public audience for political science. The October 1903 letter promoting APSA's establishment identified reaching a broader audience as a primary reason favoring a new association over establishing a political science section in one of the older national associations. A section would give "an opportunity to read papers and have them published in the reports of the annual proceedings." But this would "not satisfy the needs of the political scientists," which called ambitiously for "the establishment of some representative body that can take the scientific lead in all matters of a political interest." Such a body would, the letter proposed, "attract the support not only of those engaged in academic instruction, but of public administrators, lawyers of broader culture, and in general, all those interested in the scientific study of the great and increasingly important questions of practical and theoretical politics."[13]

The APSA was founded to be this "representative body," and its annual conferences were meant to provide a venue for interaction with a broader public. Addressing the inaugural APSA conference in 1904 as its first president, Goodnow presented the association's conferences as a "common meeting ground" offering "an opportunity for those whose work savors somewhat of the closet, to meet

understood as buttressing their claim to speak with authority on pressing public questions, rather than as a reason to avoid such questions.

[12] Shaw, "Presidential Address," 183–84.
[13] "Organization of the American Political Science Association," 11.

those engaged in the active walks of political life." The APSA was, in sum, created with confidence that it would promote interaction between "those engaged in the work of instruction in political science" and "those who are immediately responsible for the solution of the many pressing political problems of our day."[14]

The process by which the APSA had been founded provided support for confidence in the association's extra-academic appeal. The series of events that culminated in the APSA's creation had been initiated at the nexus between the federal government and the academy. The call for the 1902 Washington conference about comparative legislation had been issued by three prominent Washingtonians—Carroll Wright (commissioner of labor), Martin Knapp (chairman of the Interstate Commerce Committee), and Charles Needham (president of Columbian University, soon to be renamed George Washington University)— as well as professors at major East Coast schools—including Cornell, Princeton, and Columbia's School of Political Science. As attention turned toward establishing a national political science association, nonacademics remained prominent. They made up almost half the fifteen-person committee charged with the project: in addition to the aforementioned chairman of the Interstate Commerce Commission, the committee included two judges, a census official, a legislative librarian, and a minister nationally prominent in social service.[15] The APSA today is an association of professors for professors. But it was first founded as an association of professors with other professionals who were similarly attracted to the belief that pressing public problems could and should be influentially addressed by a nonpartisan science.

The confidence of the early APSA in its ability to provide a nexus between the academy and government service should, finally, also be situated in light of the extent of career moves between these activities at the time. In Part II of this book we saw Andrew Dickson White exemplify such movement during the mid- to late-nineteenth century heyday of wide political science. The later shift toward a narrower sense of political science was initially accompanied, if anything, by greater interconnectedness. Just as White's career had earlier led from Cornell to his diplomatic service as America's minister to Germany at a critical stage in that nation's history, so the University of Wisconsin political scientist Paul Reinsch would spend most of the 1910s as America's minister to the new Republic of China. More generally, if we look into the details of the careers of academics prominently involved in the early APSA, we repeatedly find that they also engaged in significant extra-academic activities. Woodrow Wilson's famous service as the nation's president is only the most remembered example of the sweeping array of engagements that political scientists had across multiple levels of government in an era

---

[14] Goodnow, "Work of the American Political Science Association," 45–46.
[15] "Organization of the American Political Science Association," 7.

in which interaction and movement between the academy and public service was more the norm than the exception in American political science.

The Americanization of "Liberalism": Connecting Political Visions to Political Language

We turn, finally, to the issue—both historical and methodological—with which this book began: what is involved in interpreting nineteenth-century American political scientists as agents of the Americanization of liberalism. Over many chapters now I have analyzed political visions articulated during the emergence of political science in America as *liberal* visions. This entails, as I stressed in my introduction, projecting the words "liberalism" and "liberal" onto Americans who did not themselves talk about American thought and politics in these terms. I first justified that projection, in Part I, based upon how "liberalism" and "liberal" were used as they entered European political discourse in the early and middle nineteenth century. Specifically, I argued that, as political science first secured a niche in America's antebellum academy in the hands of the émigré Francis Lieber, it presented a political vision also characteristic of a distinct strand of contemporaneous European "liberalism": the democratized classical liberalism of Tocqueville and J. S. Mill. In Parts II and III, as I followed political science's expansion and evolution from the Civil War up through the dawn of the twentieth century, I supported my continuing analysis of liberal political visions among American political scientists by documenting the transatlantic intellectual influences tying these Americans to Europeans who were explicitly "liberals" in the political terms of their own countries.

I now offer a final justification for analyzing American political scientists as participants in the development of liberal thought, by briefly suggesting how that analysis prefigures ways in which Americans came to apply the words "liberalism" and "liberal" to their own politics between the 1910s and 1930s. Scholars of political language in America have agreed that these words acquired mass political resonance in the 1930s when Franklin D. Roosevelt successfully framed himself and his policies as the embodiment of "liberalism."[16] But FDR selectively extended and shaped the long-term outcome of a preceding *Americanization of "liberalism"*—a process of some two decades during which "liberalism" and "liberal" had already been given a succession of American uses in more limited intellectual and political circles. Scholars diverge over some minor details of this

---

[16] Ronald Rotunda, *The Politics of Language: Liberalism as Word and Symbol* (Iowa City: University of Iowa Press, 1986), chap. 4; David Green, *Shaping Political Consciousness: The Language of Politics in America from McKinley to Reagan* (Ithaca, NY: Cornell University Press, 1987), chap. 5.

process. But they agree that it started in the mid-1910s, during the presidency of Woodrow Wilson, and involved claims upon the language of "liberal" and "liberalism" being made from varied political positions, with all sides positively valuing the words they competed over.[17]

I will briefly note certain episodes from this period of linguistic ferment to show how the late-nineteenth-century divergence between liberal visions recounted in this book can be mapped onto competing moments in the early-twentieth-century Americanization of "liberalism." First, in the 1910s, we find "liberalism" applied to American politics in relation to the vision that I called progressive liberalism. Second, from the 1920s into the 1930s, we see the alternative vision that I called disenchanted classical liberalism articulated in later uses of "liberalism" that opposed the meaning advanced in the 1910s. The novelty of Americans applying the words "liberalism" and "liberal" to their own politics was not, in either moment, accompanied by any major innovation in the contours of political thought. Rather, their uses extended themes explored in Part III of this book. Much of the linguistic battle during the Americanization of "liberalism" was thus fought on terrain already structured by a prior cleavage within the longer-term process of the Americanization of liberalism as a tradition of political thought—a process I have examined in this book through the lens of American political science.

One of the earliest examples of an American application of "liberalism" occurred at the nexus between the academy, government, and progressive reform so central to the early APSA. In Washington, DC, in late December 1913, political scientist William F. Willoughby gave the presidential address of the proreform American Association for Labor Legislation at its annual meeting. The meeting overlapped—as it had several times before—with the APSA's own annual conference, and the address, "The Philosophy of Labor Legislation," was shortly thereafter published in the February 1914 *American Political Science Review*.[18] It is thus in the pages of the APSA's official journal that we find Willoughby claiming "liberalism" for American purposes when he forthrightly declares: "Modern liberalism, in the United States as well as in England, looks to state action as the means, and

---

[17] Rotunda, *Politics of Language*, 41–51; Green, *Shaping Political Consciousness*, 76–109.

[18] When he gave the address, William F. Willoughby was faculty in Princeton's Department of Politics during a short academic respite after having spent almost a quarter-century in federal government posts, and before his return to Washington, DC, to become first director of the Institute for Government Research (forerunner of the Brookings Institution). William had been a member of APSA since it was founded, and later served as association president. His twin brother, Westel W. Willoughby, was APSA president at the same time that William was president of the AALL, and their presidential addresses were published alongside one another in the February 1914 *APSR*.

the only practical means, now in sight, of giving to the individual, all individuals, not merely a small economically strong class, real freedom."[19]

Willoughby's application of the term "liberalism" to the United States was novel. But the political vision he advanced in connection with it displayed features familiar to us from chapter 7's analysis of Woodrow Wilson as an exemplar of progressive liberalism: rejection of laissez-faire, locating of America as a transatlantic laggard, and a distinctive conception of the "modern state." Willoughby argued that the "great problem" confronting the "modern social reformer" in America was that "the American people" were "still dominated by the dogmas of laissez-faire and individualism as preached by the Manchesterian and utilitarian school of the middle nineteenth century." Looking across the Atlantic, he noted admiringly that "scarcely a vestige of this old philosophy" remained in Europe, and hailed the "transformation" in recent decades of "the political principles of the Liberal party" in Britain as a model for the change he hoped to see in America.[20] In connection with this desired transformation, and in terms akin to those we saw in Wilson's 1889 *The State*, Willoughby advocated conceiving the "function of the state," and its relation to the individual, in such a manner as to promote "a fuller recognition of the province of the modern state."[21]

Willoughby's view of "the province of the modern state" differed from Wilson's *The State*, however, in that it advanced a *more* demandingly progressive standpoint. Going beyond Wilson's support of state action to prevent "unfair competition" and equalize "the conditions of endeavor,"[22] Willoughby also declared that "there is a minimum of economic independence and comfort that must obtain if an individual is to be measurably free," and held that "this minimum can only be secured by the State."[23] He went on to spell out policy implications of this principle. For example, speaking against the backdrop of the British Liberal Party's recent enactment of the 1908 Old Age Pensions Act and 1911 National Insurance Act, Willoughby argued that a modern state should provide security against "accident, sickness, old age, and inability to find work." He then justified this policy

---

[19] William F. Willoughby, "The Philosophy of Labor Legislation," *American Political Science Review* 8, no. 1 (1914), 17.

[20] Willoughby, "Philosophy of Labor Legislation," 16–17.

[21] Willoughby, "Philosophy of Labor Legislation," 16, 20.

[22] Woodrow Wilson, *The State: Elements of Historical and Practical Politics, a Sketch of Institutional History and Administration* (Boston: Heath, 1889), 653–54, 664–65.

[23] Willoughby, "Philosophy of Labor Legislation," 19. William F. Willoughby's treatment of this theme pairs well with the more philosophical treatment of his brother Westel's APSA presidential address, "The Individual and the State." Westel put the point as follows: "[I]t is a proper province of the state not only to raise the level of competition and thus permit individuals to contest with one another upon fair and open terms, and under conditions of life that are morally and physically satisfactory, but to secure the realization of a general scheme of distributive justice." Westel Woodbury Willoughby, "The Individual and the State," *American Political Science Review* 8, no. 1 (1914), 10.

prescription as demanded by traditional liberal ideals by asserting that it was needed to fulfill "the prime function of a constitutional government... the protection of the individual against oppression and the guaranteeing to him of the fullest possible enjoyment of life, liberty and the pursuit of happiness."[24]

The difference between Wilson's *The State* and William F. Willoughby's *APSR* piece is more than a nuance in the development of progressive liberal political science between the 1880s and the 1910s. It directly evokes the political dynamic that would accompany broader diffusion of "liberal" and "liberalism" among American intellectuals—a diffusion that occurred via the influential *New Republic* (NR), founded in 1914.[25] As plans for the NR came together, its lead editor, Herbert Croly, wrote to fellow editor Walter Lippmann: "The fundamental object of this paper would be to give a more vigorous, consistent, comprehensive and enlightened expression to the progressive principle... it would try itself to embody a single-minded, whole-hearted and well-balanced liberalism." The transition from "progressive" to "liberalism" already on display in Croly's letter was made in the pages of the NR itself during mid-1916, from which point on the paper commonly presented its editorial stances as the views of "liberals" and "liberalism."[26]

This shift occurred during the 1916 presidential election as the NR pondered if "liberals" should support Woodrow Wilson's bid for re-election. The editors took as given that, as the NR had just declared, "American liberalism is seeking a radical transformation of the political and economic structure of this country."[27] The starting point for the NR's evaluation was criticism of Wilson for expressing, in his 1912 campaign, "confidence in free competition among individuals as the most effective means of securing the public welfare—provided only the competition was automatically regulated in the interest of fair play." This criticism was tempered, however, by an editorial claim that, in actual office, as Wilson created the Federal Reserve and the Federal Trade Commission, he had "yielded to a more active and positive attitude." He was hence now "a wiser and safer political leader today than he was four years ago—one who has a better claim on the support of intelligent liberals."[28]

---

[24] William F. Willoughby, "Philosophy of Labor Legislation," 20.

[25] Rotunda, *Politics of Language*, 38–41.

[26] Edward A. Stettner, *Shaping Modern Liberalism: Herbert Croly and Progressive Thought* (Lawrence: University Press of Kansas, 1993), 108–9, 113. While I highlight its domestic policy concern, the *New Republic* also gave liberalism content in relation to foreign policy, and in this domain its usage appears to have influenced Woodrow Wilson's beginning to apply the term "liberal" in early 1917. Stettner, *Shaping Modern Liberalism*, chap. 7.

[27] Stettner, *Shaping Modern Liberalism*, 113. Quoting *New Republic*, June 24 (1916), 181.

[28] *New Republic*, June 24 (1916), 185–87. Full text of original editorial appears in John B. Judis, "'Liberal' Enters the American Political Lexicon," http://www.newrepublic.com/article/liberal-enters-the-american-political-lexicon (accessed March 12, 2013).

Both in William F. Willoughby's late 1913 address, and thereafter in the more influential setting of the *New Republic*, we find "liberalism" given American application at the intersection of intellectual and political discourse. Use of the word was inaugurated within the framework of the political vision that I have labeled progressive liberalism, and it specifically favored further reforms to give government a greater economic role. To be "liberal" meant, as such, to view the progressive reforms already made in the earlier presidency of Theodore Roosevelt, and the first term of Wilson, as simply first steps toward yet more far reaching reforms to come.

The 1920s saw, however, a classical liberal counterclaim on the language of liberalism. Again innovative usage appeared at the intersection between intellectual and political discourse. Especially noteworthy were two figures who had unsuccessfully sought the Republican Party's presidential nomination in 1920: Nicholas Murray Butler, president of Columbia University and, after 1925, also of the Carnegie Endowment for International Peace; and Herbert Hoover, who in 1928 would win the Republican Party's nomination and in turn the presidency. Each attacked the equation of "liberalism" with a "radicalism" that held, as Hoover critically put it in 1922, "that all reform and human advancement must come through government."[29] Each sought to supplant any such equation by positively expounding a classical liberal vision as the "true liberalism."[30]

The "true liberalism" of Butler and Hoover extended a political vision whose substantive contours we earlier sketched in chapter 6's analysis of disenchanted classical liberalism. What made this vision disenchanted was a shared decline narrative about the, as A. L. Lowell had put it, "drift towards paternal government" evident in a "great increase in the functions of the state" and the "widespread faith in the possibility of regenerating the world by legislation."[31] In 1880s Britain, Herbert Spencer and Sir Henry Maine had denounced trends in this direction as a betrayal of "liberalism." After "liberalism" had entered into American political language in the 1910s, so in its wake followed this specific disenchanted refrain. We find it as Butler declares in the 1920s, "at the moment liberalism is in eclipse which is visible, either as partial or total, over pretty much the whole surface of

---

[29] Herbert Hoover, *American Individualism* (Garden City, NY: Doubleday, Page, 1922), 67. Butler claimed forthrightly soon thereafter: "Radicalism is not a form of Liberalism." Nicholas Murray Butler, *The Faith of a Liberal: Essays and Addresses on Political Principles and Public Policies* (New York: Scribner's, 1924), xi.

[30] For their explicit invocations of "true liberalism" see, for example, Butler, *Faith of a Liberal*, xii, and Herbert Hoover, quoted from *Two Faces of Liberalism: How the Hoover-Roosevelt Debate Shapes the 21st Century*, ed. Gordon Lloyd (Salem, MA: Scrivener Press, 2006), 37.

[31] A. Lawrence Lowell, "Oscillations in Politics," *Annals of the American Academy of Political and Social Science* 12 (July 1898), 95.

the earth."[32] We find it yet again as Hoover holds forth in the 1930s, "Liberalism is now under beleaguered attack even in the great countries of its origins."[33]

Though Butler and Hoover wielded the word "liberalism" in a way novel for Americans, in doing so they expressed particular anxieties continuous with those we saw earlier in Lowell's political science. When presenting Lowell I stressed the practical concern that informed much of his innovative empirical work: he sought, with cold statements of fact, to temper the confidence that progressive legislation could remake the world. Butler thus translated an older anxiety into fresh terminology when he targeted the "passion for law-making, which has for some time past prevailed in the United States" as "a flat denial of Liberalism," and judged there to be "little hope for true Liberalism in the United States" until that passion "subsides or is cured."[34] An additional classical liberal anxiety of Lowell's took as its focus a "bureaucratic system where everything is regulated by the state."[35] We also find this older anxiety translated into explicit language about liberalism as Butler declares, "The liberal resists the building up of a still more huge bureaucracy at Washington," and as Hoover contends that "liberalism should be found not striving to spread bureaucracy but striving to set bounds to it."[36]

Such specific classical liberal anxieties, and the grand cross-national decline narrative they inform, constitute shared contours of disenchanted classical liberalism. But the placement of America relative to that narrative marks, I have argued, a key point of differentiation *within* this political vision. In concluding chapter 6 I grouped the British Maine and American Lowell in a distinct subgenre of disenchanted classical liberalism because they tempered disenchantment with an exceptionalist belief that America was less susceptible than European nations to the drift toward "paternalism." This had led Lowell to present America in 1889 as facing an open choice "between individualism and paternal government."[37] Some four decades later, we find Hoover, on the 1928 presidential campaign trail, speaking similarly of a "choice between the American system of rugged individualism and a European philosophy of diametrically opposed doctrines—doctrines of paternalism and state socialism." In 1920 America had, he contended, by electing a Republican president returned to "individualism" after being "regimented...temporarily into a socialistic state" during participation in the world war under Woodrow Wilson. The election of 1928 now again offered, Hoover held, a choice between the Democratic Party's "state socialism" and his own commitment, as the Republican Party's nominee, to "the principles of our American

---

[32] Butler, *Faith of a Liberal*, 6.

[33] Herbert Hoover, *The Challenge to Liberty* (Scribner's: New York, 1935), 14.

[34] Butler, *Faith of a Liberal*, xii.

[35] A. Lawrence Lowell, *Essays on Government* (Boston: Houghton, Mifflin, 1889), 10.

[36] Butler, *Faith of a Liberal*, 12; Hoover, quoted from Lloyd, *Two Faces of Liberalism*, 37.

[37] Lowell, *Essays on Government*, 19.

political economic system, upon which we have advanced beyond all the rest of the world."[38]

What was especially novel about Hoover's 1928 campaign language was his parsing of American exceptionalism explicitly in terms of "liberalism," as he proclaimed: "For a hundred and fifty years liberalism has found its true spirit in the American system, not in European systems."[39] We are far here from the transatlantic frame of W. F. Willoughby, who had claimed "liberalism" for contemporary American purposes by hailing what the British Liberal Party had become in recent decades as an ideal for aspiring reformers of a laggard America. It is a dramatic reorientation to find Hoover, by contrast, wielding transatlantic comparison to venerate America as the truly liberal side of the Atlantic. It is, in addition, perhaps even more dramatic to find him grandly projecting that comparison back through time as having been true ever since America's revolutionary era. Yet the scale of Hoover's projection into the past pales in comparison to that already favored by Butler, who had pronounced in 1924: "The American spirit has been liberal from the outset. It was not tories but liberals who crowded the decks of the *Mayflower*."[40]

The *Mayflower* had crossed the Atlantic almost three centuries before the onset of the process I have called in this conclusion the Americanization of "liberalism." Yet within a decade of that process starting, some Americans were already projecting liberal language back across all three centuries to find "liberals" among their earliest forefathers. The impulse expressed in this projection—to restate American exceptionalism in terms of America being the fullest exemplar of a "liberal" society, with "liberalism" something most fully embodied in American ideals and institutions—was to become, in the decades ahead, a common trope among academics. Political scientists would be especially prominent in its mid-twentieth-century propagation.[41] My book has told the story of how, long before American political scientists started to explicitly characterize America as "liberal," they had interpreted America in light of identifiably liberal beliefs, hopes, and fears, and in doing so, acted as lead agents in the Americanization of liberalism.

---

[38] Hoover, quoted from Lloyd, *Two Faces of Liberalism*, 36.

[39] Hoover, quoted from Lloyd, *Two Faces of Liberalism*, 37.

[40] Butler, *Faith of a Liberal*, 6. Hoover would later extend his own projection into the American past of the "great philosophy of society—Liberalism" all the way back to "Plymouth Rock." Hoover, *Challenge to Liberty*, 3.

[41] On the midcentury rise of the "liberal" society interpretation of America and political science's relationship to this interpretation, see John G. Gunnell, "The Archaeology of American Liberalism," *Journal of Political Ideologies* 6, no. 2 (2001), 125–45; John G. Gunnell, *Imagining the American Polity: Political Science and the Discourse of Democracy* (University Park: Pennsylvania State University Press, 2004).

BIBLIOGRAPHY

Abbott, Philip. "Still Louis Hartz after All These Years: A Defense of the Liberal Society Thesis." *Perspectives on Politics* 3, no. 1 (2005), 93–109.

Adams, Charles Kendall. *Democracy and Monarchy in France: From the Inception of the Great Revolution to the Overthrow of the Second Empire.* New York: Holt, 1874.

Adams, Henry. "Civil-Service Reform." *North American Review* 109, no. 225 (1869), 443–75.

———. *The Education of Henry Adams.* New York: Oxford University Press, 1999.

Adams, Henry, Henry Cabot Lodge, Ernest Young, and J. Laurence Laughlin. *Essays in Anglo-Saxon Law.* Boston: Little, Brown, 1876.

Adams, Henry C. "Relation of the State to Industrial Action." *Publications of the American Economic Association* 1, no. 6 (1887), 7–85.

Adams, Herbert Baxter. *The College of William and Mary: A Contribution to the History of Higher Education, with Suggestions for Its National Promotion.* Circulars of Information of the Bureau of Education no. 1. Washington, DC: Government Printing Office, 1887.

———. "Cooperation in University Work." *Johns Hopkins University Studies in Historical and Political Science* 1, no. 2 (1882), 39–57

———. "The Germanic Origin of New England Towns." *Johns Hopkins University Studies in Historical and Political Science* 1, no. 2 (1882), 5–38.

———. "Jared Sparks and Alexis de Tocqueville." *Johns Hopkins University Studies in Historical and Political Science* 16, no. 2 (1898), 1–49.

———. "Maryland's Influence upon Land Cessions to the United States." *Johns Hopkins University Studies in Historical and Political Science* 3, no. 1 (1885), 1–54.

———. "New Methods of Study in History." *Johns Hopkins University Studies in Historical and Political Science* 2, nos. 1–2 (1884), 25–137.

———. "Norman Constables in America." *Johns Hopkins University Studies in Historical and Political Science* 1, no. 8 (1883), 1–38.

———. "Origin of the Baltimore and Ohio Railroad." *Johns Hopkins University Studies in Historical and Political Science* 3, no. 1 (1885), 97–102.

———. "Saxon Tithingmen in America." *Johns Hopkins University Studies in Historical and Political Science* 1, no. 4 (1883), 1–23.

———. "Secretary's Report of the Organization and Proceedings." *Papers of the American Historical Association* 1, no. 1 (1885), 5–44.

———. "Special Methods of Historical Study." *Johns Hopkins University Studies in Historical and Political Science* 2, nos. 1–2 (1884), 5–23.

———. *The Study of History in American Colleges and Universities.* Bureau of Education Circular of Information no. 2. Washington, DC: Government Printing Office, 1887.

———. "Village Communities of Cape Anne and Salem." *Johns Hopkins University Studies in Historical and Political Science* 1, no. 9–10 (1883), 1–81.

————. "Washington's Interest in the Potomac Company." *Johns Hopkins University Studies in Historical and Political Science* 3, no. 1 (1885), 79–91.

————. "Washington's Interest in Western Lands." *Johns Hopkins University Studies in Historical and Political Science* 3, no. 1 (1885), 55–77.

Adcock, Robert. "A Disciplinary History of Disciplinary Histories." Paper presented at the annual meeting of the Midwest Political Science Association, Chicago, April 11, 2013.

————. "The Emergence of Political Science as a Discipline: History and the Study of Politics in America, 1875–1910." *History of Political Thought* 24, no. 3 (2003), 459–86.

Adcock, Robert, Mark Bevir, and Shannon C. Stimson, eds. *Modern Political Science: Anglo-American Exchanges since 1880*. Princeton, NJ: Princeton University Press, 2007.

Appleby, Joyce. "America as a Model for the Radical French Reformers of 1789." *William and Mary Quarterly* 3rd Series, 28, no. 2 (1971), 267–86.

Appleton, Nathan. *The Introduction of the Power Loom and the Origin of Lowell*. Lowell, MA: Penhallow, 1858.

————. "Labor, Its Relations, in Europe and the United States, Compared." *Merchants' Magazine* 11, no. 3 (1844), 217–23.

Aristotle. *The Politics, and the Constitution of Athens*. Edited by Stephen Everson. Cambridge: Cambridge University Press, 1996.

Artz, Frederick B. "The Electoral System in France during the Bourbon Restoration, 1815–30." *Journal of Modern History* 1, no. 2 (1929), 205–18.

Ball, Terence. "An Ambivalent Alliance: Political Science and American Democracy." In *Political Science in History: Research Programs and Political Traditions*, edited by James Farr, John S. Dryzek, and Stephen T. Leonard, 41–65. Cambridge: Cambridge University Press, 1995.

Beaumont, Gustave de, and Alexis de Tocqueville. *On the Penitentiary System in the United States, and Its Application in France*. Translated by Francis Lieber. Philadelphia: Carey, Lea & Blanchard, 1833.

Bellamy, Richard. *Liberalism and Modern Society: A Historical Argument*. University Park: Pennsylvania State University Press, 1992.

Bernal, Martin. *Black Athena: The Afroasiatic Roots of Classical Civilization*. Vol. 1, *The Fabrication of Ancient Greece, 1785–1985*. New Brunswick, NJ: Rutgers University Press, 1987.

Bevir, Mark. *The Logic of the History of Ideas*. Cambridge: Cambridge University Press, 1999.

Biography of an Ideal: A History of the Federal Civil Service. Washington, DC: Government Printing Office, 2003. http://www.opm.gov/biographyofanideal/ (accessed June 24, 2011).

Bledstein, Burton J. "Noah Porter versus William Graham Sumner." *Church History* 43, no. 3 (1974), 340–49.

Bluntschli, Johann Caspar. *Allgemeines Statsrecht Geschichtlich Begründet*. Munich: J. G. Cotta, 1852.

————. *Lehre vom Modernen Stat*. 3 vols. Stuttgart: J. G. Cotta, 1875.

————. "Lieber's Service to Political Science and International Law." In *Miscellaneous Writings of Francis Lieber* 2: 7–14.

————. *The Theory of the State*. Kitchner, ON: Batoche Books, 2000.

Blyth, Mark. *Great Transformations: Economic Ideas and Institutional Change in the Twentieth Century*. New York: Cambridge University Press, 2002.

Bock, Kenneth E. "Comparison of Histories: The Contribution of Henry Maine." *Comparative Studies in Society and History* 16, no. 2 (1974), 232–62.

Brown, Bernard Edward. *American Conservatives: The Political Thought of Francis Lieber and John W. Burgess*. New York: Columbia University Press, 1951.

Bryce, James. *The American Commonwealth*. 3 vols. London: Macmillan, 1888.

————. *The Holy Roman Empire*. Oxford: Shrimpton, 1864.

————. "The Predictions of Hamilton and de Tocqueville." *Johns Hopkins University Studies in Historical and Political Science* 5, no. 9 (1887), 5–57.

————. "Preface." In *Democracy and the Organisation of Political Parties*, by Moisei Ostrogorski. London: Macmillan, 1902.

Burgess, John W. "The American Commonwealth: Changes in Its Relation to the Nation." *Political Science Quarterly* 1, no. 1 (1886), 9–35.

———. "The Ideal of the American Commonwealth." *Political Science Quarterly* 10, no. 3 (1895), 404–25.

———. *Political Science and Comparative Constitutional Law*. Boston: Ginn, 1890.

———. "Political Science and History." In *Annual Report of the American Historical Association for the Year 1896*, vol. 1: 203–19. Washington, DC: Government Printing Office, 1897.

———. *The Reconciliation of Government with Liberty*. New York: Scribner's, 1915.

———. *Reminiscences of an American Scholar: The Beginnings of Columbia University*. New York: Columbia University Press, 1934.

———. "Review of *Government and Parties in Continental Europe* by A. Lawrence Lowell." *Political Science Quarterly* 12, no. 1 (1897), 161–63.

Burke, Edmund. *The Portable Edmund Burke*. Edited by Isaac Kramnick. New York: Penguin, 1999.

Burrow, John. *Evolution and Society: A Study in Victorian Social Theory*. Cambridge: Cambridge University Press, 1966.

Butler, Leslie. *Critical Americans: Victorian Intellectuals and Transatlantic Liberal Reform*. Chapel Hill: University of North Carolina Press, 2007.

Butler, Nicholas Murray. *The Faith of a Liberal: Essays and Addresses on Political Principles and Public Policies*. New York: Scribner's, 1924.

Chiu, Yvonne, and Robert Taylor. "The Self-Extinguishing Despot: Millian Democratization." *Journal of Politics* 73, no. 4 (2011), 1239–50.

Clinton, David. *Tocqueville, Lieber, and Bagehot: Liberalism Confronts the World*. New York: Palgrave Macmillan, 2003.

Coats, A. W. "Henry Carter Adams: A Case Study in the Emergence of the Social Sciences in the United States, 1850–1900." *Journal of American Studies* 2, no. 2 (1968), 177–97.

Collini, Stefan, Donald Winch, and John Burrow. *That Noble Science of Politics: A Study in Nineteenth Century Intellectual History*. Cambridge: Cambridge University Press, 1983.

Constant, Benjamin. *Political Writings*. Edited by Biancamaria Fontana. Cambridge: Cambridge University Press, 1988.

———. *Principles of Politics Applicable to All Governments*. Edited by Etienne Hofmann. Translated by Dennis O'Keeffe. Indianapolis, IN: Liberty Fund, 2003.

"Constitution, By-Laws and Resolutions of the American Economic Association." *Publications of the American Economic Association* 1, no. 1 (1886), 33–46.

"Constitution, By-Laws and Resolutions of the American Economic Association with List of Officers and Members." *Publications of the American Economic Association* 4, Supplement (July 1889).

"Constitution of the American Political Science Association." *Proceedings of the American Political Science Association* 1 (1904), 16–17.

Coulanges, Fustel de. *The Ancient City: A Study of the Religion, Laws, and Institutions of Greece and Rome*. Translated by Willard Small. Garden City, NY: Doubleday, 1956.

Craiutu, Aurelian. *Liberalism under Siege: The Political Thought of the French Doctrinaires*. Lanham, MD: Lexington Books, 2003.

Craiutu, Aurelian, and Jeremy Jennings, eds. *Tocqueville on America after 1840: Letters and Other Writings*. New York: Cambridge University Press, 2009.

Crick, Bernard. *The American Science of Politics: Its Origins and Conditions*. Berkeley: University of California Press, 1959.

Croce, Benedetto. *History as the Story of Liberty*. New York: Meridian Books, 1955.

Crook, David Paul. *American Democracy in English Politics, 1815–1850*. Oxford: Clarendon Press, 1965.

Crook, Malcolm. *Elections in the French Revolution: An Apprenticeship in Democracy, 1789–1799*. Cambridge: Cambridge University Press, 1996.

Cunningham, Raymond J. "The German Historical World of Herbert Baxter Adams: 1874–1876." *Journal of American History* 68, no. 2 (1981), 261–75.

Dorfman, Joseph. *The Economic Mind in American Civilization, 1606–1865*. 2 vols. New York: Viking, 1946.

———. *The Economic Mind in American Civilization*. Vol. 3, *1865–1918*. New York: Viking Press, 1949.

Dryzek, John S., and Stephen T. Leonard. "History and Discipline in Political Science." *American Political Science Review* 82, no. 4 (1988), 1245–60.

Ellis, Richard E. *The Jeffersonian Crisis: Courts and Politics in the Young Republic*. New York: Oxford University Press, 1971.

Ely, Richard T. *French and German Socialism in Modern Times*. New York: Harper, 1883.

———. *Ground under Our Feet: An Autobiography*. New York: Macmillan, 1938.

———. *An Introduction to Political Economy*. New York: Chautauqua Press, 1889.

———. *The Labor Movement in America*. New York: Crowell, 1886.

———. "The Past and the Present of Political Economy." *Johns Hopkins University Studies in Historical and Political Science* 2, no. 3 (1884), 5–64.

———. "Political Economy in America." *North American Review* 144, no. 363 (1887), 113–19.

———. "Recent American Socialism." *Johns Hopkins University Studies in Historical and Political Science* 3, no. 4 (1885), 5–74.

———. "Report of the Organization of the American Economic Association." *Publications of the American Economic Association* 1, no. 1 (1886), 5–32.

———. *Socialism: An Examination of Its Nature, Its Strength and Its Weakness, with Suggestions for Social Reform*. New York: Crowell, 1894.

Emerton, Ephraim. "History." In *Development of Harvard University since the Inauguration of President Eliot, 1869–1929*, edited by Samuel Eliot Morison, 150–77. Cambridge, MA: Harvard University Press, 1930.

Everett, Edward. *Orations and Speeches on Various Occasions*, vol. 2. Boston: Little, Brown, 1850.

Farnam, Henry W. "Review of *The Labor Movement in America*." *Political Science Quarterly* 1, no. 4 (1886), 683–87.

Farr, James. "The Estate of Political Knowledge: Political Science and the State." In *The Estate of Social Knowledge*, edited by JoAnne Brown and David K. van Keuren, 1–21. Baltimore: Johns Hopkins University Press, 1991.

———. "Francis Lieber and the Interpretation of American Political Science." *Journal of Politics* 52, no. 4 (1990), 1027–49.

———. "From Modern Republic to Administrative State." In *Regime and Discipline: Democracy and the Development of Political Science*, edited by David Easton, John G. Gunnell, and Michael B. Stein, 131–67. Ann Arbor: University of Michigan Press, 1995.

———. "From Moral Philosophy to Political Science: Lieber and the Innovations of Antebellum Political Thought." In Mack and Lesesne, *Francis Lieber*, 113–26.

———. "The Historical Sciences of Politics." In Adcock, Bevir, and Stimson, *Modern Political Science*, 66–96.

———. "The History of Political Science." *American Journal of Political Science* 32, no. 4 (1988), 1175–95.

———. "Political Science and the Enlightenment of Enthusiasm." *American Political Science Review* 82, no. 1 (1988), 51–69.

Farr, James, John G. Gunnell, Raymond Seidelman, John S. Dryzek, and Stephen T. Leonard. "Can Political Science History Be Neutral?" *American Political Science Review* 84, no. 2 (1990), 587–607.

Fiske, John. *American Political Ideas: Viewed from the Standpoint of Universal History*. New York: Harper & Brothers, 1885.

———. *The Beginnings of New England, or the Puritan Theocracy in Its Relation to Civil and Religious Liberty*. Boston: Houghton, Mifflin, 1889.

Ford, Henry Jones. *The Rise and Growth of American Politics: A Sketch of Constitutional Development*. New York: Macmillan, 1898.

Francis, Mark. *Herbert Spencer and the Invention of Modern Life*. Stocksfield, UK: Acumen, 2007.

Freeman, Edward. *Comparative Politics.* London: Macmillan, 1873.

———. "An Introduction to American Institutional History." *Johns Hopkins University Studies in Historical and Political Science* 1, no. 1 (1882), 13–39.

Freidel, Frank. *Francis Lieber: Nineteenth-Century Liberal.* Baton Rouge: Louisiana State University Press, 1947.

French, John C. *A History of the University Founded by Johns Hopkins.* Baltimore, MD: Johns Hopkins Press, 1946.

Frisch, Michael H. "Urban Theorists, Urban Reform, and American Political Culture in the Progressive Period." *Political Science Quarterly* 97, no. 2 (1982), 295–315.

Furet, François. *The French Revolution, 1770–1814.* Oxford: Blackwell, 1996.

Furner, Mary O. *Advocacy & Objectivity: A Crisis in the Professionalization of American Social Science, 1865–1905.* Lexington: University Press of Kentucky, 1975.

Gentz, Friedrich von. *The Origin and Principles of the American Revolution, Compared with the Origin and Principles of the French Revolution.* Translated by John Quincy Adams. Indianapolis, IN: Liberty Fund, 2009.

Goodnow, Frank J. *Comparative Administrative Law: An Analysis of the Administrative Systems, National and Local, of the United States, England, France and Germany.* 2 vols. New York: Putnam's, 1903.

———. "The Executive and the Courts." *Political Science Quarterly* 1, no. 4 (1886), 533–59.

———. "Local Government in England." *Political Science Quarterly* 2, no. 4 (1887), 638–65.

———. "Local Government in Prussia. I." *Political Science Quarterly* 4, no. 4 (1889), 648–66.

———. "Local Government in Prussia. II." *Political Science Quarterly* 5, no. 1 (1890), 124–58.

———. *Municipal Home Rule: A Study in Administration.* New York: Macmillan, 1895.

———. *Municipal Problems.* New York: Macmillan, 1907.

———. "Political Parties and City Government under the Proposed Municipal Program." In *A Municipal Program*, adopted by the National Municipal League, 129–45. New York: Macmillan, 1900.

———. *Politics and Administration: A Study in Government.* New York: Macmillan, 1900.

———. "Review of *Municipal Government in Continental Europe*, by Albert Shaw...." *Political Science Quarterly* 11, no. 1 (1896), 158–63.

———. "Review of *Municipal Government in Great Britain*, by Albert Shaw...." *Political Science Quarterly* 10, no. 1 (1895), 171–75.

———. "The Tweed Ring in New York City." In *The American Commonwealth*, by James Bryce, vol. 3: 173–98. London: Macmillan, 1888.

———. "The Work of the American Political Science Association." *Proceedings of the American Political Science Association* 1 (1904), 35–46.

Gray, Walter D. *Interpreting American Democracy in France: The Career of Edouard Laboulaye, 1811–1883.* Newark: University of Delaware Press, 1994.

Graybar, Lloyd J. *Albert Shaw of the Review of Reviews: An Intellectual Biography.* Lexington: University Press of Kentucky, 1974.

Green, David. *Shaping Political Consciousness: The Language of Politics in America from McKinley to Reagan.* Ithaca, NY: Cornell University Press, 1987.

Green, Thomas Hill. "Lecture on Liberal Legislation and Freedom of Contract." In *The Works of Thomas Hill Green*, vol. 3, *Miscellanies and Memoir*, edited by Richard Lewis Nettleship, 365–86. London: Longmans, Green, 1888.

Gregory, Frances W. *Nathan Appleton: Merchant and Entrepreneur, 1779–1861.* Charlottesville: University Press of Virginia, 1975.

Grimmer-Solem, Erik. *The Rise of Historical Economics and Social Reform in Germany, 1864–1894.* Oxford: Clarendon Press, 2003.

Guizot, François. *History of Civilization in Europe.* Edited by George Wells Knight. New York: Appleton, 1896.

———. *The History of the Origins of Representative Government in Europe.* Translated by Andrew R. Scoble. Indianapolis, IN: Liberty Fund, 2002.

Gunnell, John G. "American Political Science, Liberalism, and the Invention of Political Theory." *American Political Science Review* 82, no. 1 (1988), 71–87.

———. "The Archaeology of American Liberalism." *Journal of Political Ideologies* 6, no. 2 (2001), 125–45.

———. *The Descent of Political Theory: The Genealogy of an American Vocation*. Chicago: University of Chicago Press, 1993.

———. "The Founding of the American Political Science Association: Discipline, Profession, Political Theory, and Politics." *American Political Science Review* 100, no. 4 (2006), 479–86.

———. "The Historiography of Political Science." In *The Development of Political Science: A Comparative Survey*, edited by David Easton, John G. Gunnell, and Luigi Graziano, 13–33. London: Routledge, 1991.

———. *Imagining the American Polity: Political Science and the Discourse of Democracy*. University Park: Pennsylvania State University Press, 2004.

———. "Louis Hartz and the Liberal Metaphor: A Half-Century Later." *Studies in American Political Development* 19 (Fall 2005), 196–205

Haddow, Anna. *Political Science in American Colleges and Universities, 1636–1900*. New York: Appleton Century, 1939.

Hanson, Russell L. *The Democratic Imagination in America: Conversations with Our Past*. Princeton, NJ: Princeton University Press, 1985.

Hart, Albert Bushnell. "Government." In *The Development of Harvard University since the Inauguration of President Eliot, 1869–1929*, edited by Samuel Eliot Morison, 178–86. Cambridge, MA: Harvard University Press, 1930.

Hartford, William F. *Money, Morals, and Politics: Massachusetts in the Age of the Boston Associates*. Boston: Northeastern University Press, 2001.

Hartz, Louis. *The Liberal Tradition in America: An Interpretation of American Political Thought since the Revolution*. New York: Harcourt, Brace, and World, 1955.

Haskell, Thomas L. *The Emergence of Professional Social Science: The American Social Science Association and the Nineteenth-century Crisis of Authority*. Baltimore, MD: Johns Hopkins University Press, 2000.

Hawkins, Hugh. *Pioneer: A History of the Johns Hopkins University, 1874–1889*. Ithaca, NY: Cornell University Press, 1960.

Hayek, Friedrich A. *Law, Legislation and Liberty*. Vol. 3, *A New Statement of the Liberal Principles of Justice and Political Economy*. Chicago: University of Chicago Press, 1973.

Hegel, G. W. F. *Elements of the Philosophy of Right*. Translated by H. B. Nisbet. Cambridge: Cambridge University Press, 1991.

———. *Political Writings*. Edited by Laurence Dickey and H. B. Nisbet. Translated by H. B. Nisbet. Cambridge: Cambridge University Press, 1999.

———. *The Philosophy of History*. Translated by J. Sibree. New York: Dover, 1956.

Heilbron, Johan, Nicolas Guilhot, and Laurent Jeanpierre. "Toward a Transnational History of the Social Sciences." *Journal of the History of the Behavioral Sciences* 44, no. 2 (2008), 146–60.

Hennis, Wilhelm. "Tocqueville's 'New Political Science'" In *Politics as a Practical Science*, translated by Keith Tribe. New York: Palgrave Macmillan, 2009.

Herbert B. Adams Tributes of Friends, with a Bibliography of the Department of History, Politics and Economics, 1876–1901. Baltimore: Johns Hopkins Press, 1902.

Holland, Catherine A. "Hartz and Minds: The *Liberal Tradition* after the Cold War." *Studies in American Political Development* 19 (Fall 2005), 227–33.

Holmes, Oliver Wendell. *The Common Law*. Boston: Little, Brown, 1881.

Hoover, Herbert. *American Individualism*. Garden City, NY: Doubleday, Page, 1922.

———. *The Challenge to Liberty*. New York: Scribner's, 1935.

Horsman, Reginald. *Race and Manifest Destiny: The Origins of American Racial Anglo-Saxonism*. Cambridge, MA: Harvard University Press, 1981.

Howe, Daniel Walker. *The Political Culture of the American Whigs*. Chicago: University of Chicago Press, 1979.

Howe, Mark DeWolfe. "Introduction." In *The Common Law*, by Oliver Wendell Holmes, xi–xxvii. Boston: Little, Brown, 1881.

Hoxie, R. Gordon. *A History of the Faculty of Political Science*. New York: Columbia University Press, 1955.

Hulliung, Mark, ed. *The American Liberal Tradition Reconsidered: The Contested Legacy of Louis Hartz*. Lawrence: University Press of Kansas, 2010.

Huntington, Samuel P. *The Third Wave: Democratization in the Late Twentieth Century*. Norman: University of Oklahoma Press, 1991.

Iggers, Georg G. *The German Conception of History: The National Tradition of Historical Thought from Herder to the Present*. Middletown, CT: Wesleyan University Press, 1968.

Ions, Edmund S. *James Bryce and American Democracy, 1870–1922*. London: Macmillan, 1968.

Jewett, Andrew. *Science, Democracy, and the American University: From the Civil War to the Cold War*. Cambridge: Cambridge University Press, 2012.

Johns Hopkins University Official Circular no. 3 (June 1876).

Johnson, John W. *Historic US Court Cases: An Encyclopedia*. 2nd ed. New York: Routledge, 2001.

Judis, John B. " 'Liberal' Enters the American Political Lexicon." http://www.newrepublic.com/article/liberal-enters-the-american-political-lexicon (accessed March 12, 2013).

Kalyvas, Andreas, and Ira Katznelson. *Liberal Beginnings: Making a Republic for the Moderns*. Cambridge: Cambridge University Press, 2008.

Kant, Immanuel. *Political Writings*. 2nd ed. Edited by Hans Reiss. Cambridge: Cambridge University Press, 1991.

Kenny, Michael. "History and Dissent: Bernard Crick's *The American Science of Politics*." *American Political Science Review* 100, no. 4 (2006), 547–53.

King, Ronald F. "A Most Corrupt Election: Louisiana in 1876." *Studies in American Political Development* 15 (Fall 2001), 123–37.

Kloppenberg, James T. *Uncertain Victory: Social Democracy and Progressivism in European and American Thought, 1870–1920*. Oxford: Oxford University Press, 1986.

Knight, George W. "The Political Science Association of the Central States." *Annals of the American Academy of Political and Social Science* 5 (March 1985), 144–45.

Lieber, Francis, ed. *Encyclopedia Americana*. 13 vols. Philadelphia: Carey, Lea & Carey, 1829–33.

Lieber, Francis. *On Civil Liberty and Self-Government*. Philadelphia: Lippincott, 1853.

———. *On Civil Liberty and Self-Government*. 3rd ed. Edited by Theodore D. Woolsey. Philadelphia: Lippincott, 1874.

———. *Essays on Property and Labour as Connected with Natural Law and the Constitution of Society*. New York: Harper & Brothers, 1841.

———. "History and Political Science Necessary Studies in Free Countries." In *Miscellaneous Writings of Francis Lieber* 1: 329–68.

———. "On History and Political Economy, as Necessary Branches of Superior Education in Free States." In *Miscellaneous Writings of Francis Lieber* 1: 179–203.

———. *On International Copyright: In a Letter to the Hon. William C. Preston, Senator of the United States*. New York: Wiley and Putnam, 1840.

———. "Introductory Letter." In Frédéric Bastiat, *Sophisms of the Protective Policy*, translated by D. J. McCord. New York: Putnam, 1848.

———. *Letters to a Gentleman in Germany, Written after a Trip from Philadelphia to Niagara*. Philadelphia: Carey, Lea & Blanchard, 1834.

———. *Manual of Political Ethics: Designed Chiefly for the Use of Colleges and Students at Law*. 2 vols. Boston: Little, Brown, 1838–39.

———. *The Miscellaneous Writings of Francis Lieber*. 2 vols. Edited by Daniel C. Gilman. Philadelphia: Lippincott, 1881

———. *Notes on Fallacies Peculiar to American Protectionists, or Chiefly Resorted to in America*. New York: American Free Trade League, 1869.

———. *Reminiscences of an Intercourse with Mr. Niebuhr the Historian, During a Residence with Him in Rome, in the Years 1822 and 1823*. Philadelphia: Carey, Lea & Blanchard, 1835.

————."Some Truths Worth Remembering, Given, as a Recapitulation, in a Farewell Lecture to the Class of Political Economy of 1849." Published by the class, 1849.

————. *The Stranger in America, Comprising Sketches of the Manners, Society, and National Peculiarities of the United States, in a Series of Letters to a Friend in Europe*. London: Bentley, 1835.

Lindenfeld, David F. *The Practical Imagination: The German Sciences of State in the Nineteenth Century*. Chicago: University of Chicago Press, 1997.

Lloyd, Gordon, ed. *The Two Faces of Liberalism: How the Hoover-Roosevelt Debate Shapes the 21st Century*. Salem, MA: Scrivener Press, 2006.

Low, Seth. "An American View of Municipal Government in the United States." In *The American Commonwealth*, by James Bryce, vol. 2: 296–317. London: Macmillan, 1888.

Lowell, A. Lawrence. *Colonial Civil Service: The Selection and Training of Colonial Officials in England, Holland, and France*. New York: Macmillan, 1900.

————. "The Colonial Expansion of the United States." *Atlantic Monthly* 83 (February 1899), 145–54.

————. *Essays on Government*. Boston: Houghton, Mifflin, 1889.

————. *The Government of England*. 2 vols. New York: Macmillan, 1908.

————. *Governments and Parties in Continental Europe*. 2 vols. Boston: Houghton, Mifflin, 1896.

————. "The Influence of Party upon Legislation in England and America." In *Annual Report of the American Historical Association for the Year 1901*, vol. 1: 319–541. Washington, DC: Government Printing Office, 1902.

————. "The Limits of Sovereignty." *Harvard Law Review* 2, no. 2 (1888), 70–87.

————. "Ministerial Responsibility and the Constitution." *Atlantic Monthly* 57 (February 1886), 180–93.

————. "Oscillations in Politics." *Annals of the American Academy of Political and Social Science* 12 (July 1898), 69–97.

————. *Public Opinion and Popular Government*. New York: Longmans, 1913.

————. "The Responsibilities of American Lawyers." *Harvard Law Review* 1, no. 5 (1887), 232–40.

————. "Review of James K. Hosmer, *A Short History of Anglo-Saxon Freedom. The Polity of the English-Speaking Race: Outlined in Its Inception, Development, Diffusion, and Present Condition*." *Annals of the American Academy* 1 (January 1891), 492–95.

Lowell, Francis Cabot, and A. Lawrence Lowell. *The Transfer of Stock in Private Corporations*. Boston: Little, Brown, 1884.

Macaulay, Thomas Babington. "Lord Macaulay on American Institutions." In *The Life and Letters of Lord Macaulay*, by George Otto Trevelyan, vol. 2: 407–12. New York: Harper & Brothers, 1875.

————. "Mill on Government." In *Macaulay: Prose and Poetry*, edited by G. M. Young. Cambridge, MA: Harvard University Press, 1952.

Mack, Charles R., and Henry H. Lesesne, eds. *Francis Lieber and the Culture of the Mind*. Columbia: University of South Carolina Press, 2005.

Mahoney, Dennis J. *Politics and Progress: The Emergence of American Political Science*. Lanham, MD: Lexington Books, 2004.

Maine, Henry Sumner. *Ancient Law: Its Connection with the Early History of Society, and Its Relation to Modern Ideas*. New York: Scribner, 1864.

————. *Popular Government*. Indianapolis, IN: Liberty Fund, 1976.

————. *Village-Communities in the East and West*. 3rd ed. New York: Holt, 1876.

Mantena, Karuna. *Alibis of Empire: Henry Maine and the Ends of Liberal Imperialism*. Princeton, NJ: Princeton University Press, 2010.

Mehta, Uday Singh. *Liberalism and Empire: A Study in Nineteenth-Century British Liberal Thought*. Chicago: University of Chicago Press, 1999.

Meinecke, Friedrich. *Historism: The Rise of a New Historical Outlook*. Translated by J. E. Anderson. London: Routledge and Kegan Paul, 1972.

Menger, Carl. *Investigations into the Method of the Social Sciences, with Special Reference to Economics*. Translated by Francis J. Nock. New York: New York University Press, 1985.

Merriam, Charles Edward. *American Political Ideas: Studies in the Development of American Political Thought 1865–1917*. New York: Macmillan, 1920.

Mill, John Stuart. *Autobiography*. New York: Liberal Arts Press, 1957.

———. *Collected Works of John Stuart Mill*. 33 vols. Edited by John M. Robson. Toronto: University of Toronto Press, 1963–91.

———. *Considerations on Representative Government*. In *Essays on Politics and Society, Collected Works of John Stuart Mill* 19: 371–577.

———. "De Tocqueville on Democracy in America [II]." In *Essays on Politics and Society, Collected Works of John Stuart Mill* 18: 153–204.

———. "Grote's History of Greece [2]." In *Essays on Philosophy and the Classics, Collected Works of John Stuart Mill* 11: 307–38.

———. "Guizot's Essays and Lectures on History." In *Essays on French History and Historians, Collected Works of John Stuart Mill* 20: 257–94.

———. "Inaugural Address Delivered to the University of St. Andrews." In *Essays on Equality, Law, and Education, Collected Works of John Stuart Mill* 21: 215–57.

———. *The Principles of Political Economy with Some of Their Applications to Social Philosophy, Collected Works of John Stuart Mill* 2–3.

———. "Reorganization of the Reform Party." In *Essays on England, Ireland, and the Empire, Collected Works of John Stuart Mill* 6: 465–96.

———. "State of Society in America." In *Essays on Politics and Society, Collected Works of John Stuart Mill* 18: 91–115.

Montesquieu. *The Spirit of the Laws*. Translated by Anne M. Cohler, Basia C. Miller, and Harold Stone. Cambridge: Cambridge University Press, 1989.

Müller, Max. "Aryan, as a Technical Term." In *Selected Essays on Language Mythology and Religion*. London: Longmans, Green, 1881.

Niebuhr, G. B. *The History of Rome*. Vol. 1. Translated by Julius Charles Hare and Connop Thirlwall. Philadelphia: Thomas Wardle, 1835.

"The Organization of the American Political Science Association." *Proceedings of the American Political Science Association* 1 (1904), 5–15.

Perry, Thomas Sergeant, ed. *The Life and Letters of Francis Lieber*. Boston: Osgood, 1882.

Peterson, Merrill D., ed. *Democracy, Liberty, and Property: The State Constitutional Conventions of the 1820s*. Indianapolis, IN: Liberty Fund, 2010.

Philipp, Michael. "The 'Politica' of 17th Century Germany, as Reflected in the 'dissertationes politicae': Some Aspects of the Older Tradition in Academic Political Science." Paper presented at the "Sciences of Politics" International Conference, Tulane University, New Orleans, January 9, 2004.

Pitts, Jennifer. *A Turn to Empire: The Rise of Imperial Liberalism in Britain and France*. Princeton, NJ: Princeton University Press, 2005.

Pölitz, Karl Heinrich Ludwig. *Die Staatswissenschaften im Lichte unsrer Zeit*. 5 vols. Leipzig: J. C. Hinrichs, 1827–28.

Pombeni, Paolo. "Starting in Reason, Ending in Passion: Bryce, Lowell, Ostrogorski and the Problem of Democracy." *Historical Journal* 37, no. 2 (1994), 319–41.

Priddat, Birger P. "Intention and Failure of W. Roscher's Historical Method of National Economics." In *The Theory of Ethical Economy in the Historical School*, edited by Peter Koslowski, 15–34. Berlin: Springer-Verlag, 1995.

Reinsch, Paul S. "The American Political Science Association." *Iowa Journal of History and Politics* 2, no. 2 (1904), 157–61.

Robson, Charles B. "Papers of Francis Lieber." *Huntington Library Bulletin* 3 (February 1933), 135–55.

Rodgers, Daniel T. *Atlantic Crossings: Social Politics in a Progressive Age*. Cambridge, MA: Harvard University Press, 1998.

Ross, Dorothy. "On the Misunderstanding of Ranke and the Origins of the Historical Profession in America." In *Leopold Von Ranke and the Shaping of the Historical Discipline*, edited by Georg G. Iggers and James M. Powell, 154–213. Syracuse, NY: Syracuse University Press, 1990.

———. *The Origins of American Social Science.* Cambridge: Cambridge University Press, 1991.

———. "Socialism and American Liberalism: Academic Social Thought in the 1880s." *Perspectives in American History* 11 (1977–78), 5–80.

Rotunda, Ronald. *The Politics of Language: Liberalism as Word and Symbol.* Iowa City: University of Iowa Press, 1986.

Ruggiero, Guido de. *The History of European Liberalism.* Translated by R. G. Collingwood. London: Oxford University Press, 1927.

Sauvigny, G. de Bertier de. "Liberalism, Nationalism and Socialism: The Birth of Three Words." *Review of Politics* 32, no. 2 (1970), 147–66.

Say, Jean Baptiste. *A Treatise on Political Economy; or the Production, Distribution, and Consumption of Wealth.* 6th ed. Translated by C. R. Prinsep and Clement C. Biddle. Philadelphia: Grigg, Elliot, 1834.

Schleifer, James T. *The Making of Tocqueville's Democracy in America.* 2nd ed. Indianapolis, IN: Liberty Fund, 2000.

Schmidt, Brian C. *The Political Discourse of Anarchy: A Disciplinary History of International Relations.* Albany: State University of New York Press, 1998.

Seidelman, Raymond, and Edward J. Harpham. *Disenchanted Realists: Political Science and the American Crisis, 1884–1984.* Albany: State University of New York Press, 1985.

Shaw, Albert. "The American State and the American Man." *Contemporary Review* 51 (May 1887), 695–711.

———. "Coöperation in a Western City." *Publications of the American Economic Association* 1, no. 4 (1886), 7–106.

———. "Coöperation in the Northwest." *Johns Hopkins University Studies in Historical and Political Science* 6, no. 4–6 (1888), 195–359.

———. "The Growth of Internationalism." *International Review* 14 (April 1883), 267–83.

———. *Icaria: A Chapter in the History of Communism.* New York: Putnam's, 1884.

———. "Introduction." In *President Wilson's State Papers and Addresses.* Edited by Albert Shaw. New York: Doran, 1918.

———. "Introductory." In *The National Revenues: A Collection of Papers by American Economists.* Edited by Albert Shaw. Chicago: McClurg, 1888.

———. "Local Government in Illinois." *Johns Hopkins University Studies in Historical and Political Science* 1, no. 3 (1883), 5–19.

———. *Municipal Government in Continental Europe.* New York: Century, 1895.

———. *Municipal Government in Great Britain.* New York: Century, 1895.

———. "Municipal Government in Great Britain." *Political Science Quarterly* 4, no. 2 (1889), 197–229.

———. "New Studies in Political and Social Science." *The Dial* 6 (July 1885), 72–74.

———. "Presidential Address." *American Political Science Review* 1, no. 2 (1907), 177–86.

———. "Recent Economic Works." *The Dial* 6 (December 1885), 210–13.

———. "Review of *Congressional Government.*" In *Papers of Woodrow Wilson* 4: 309–15.

Silverberg, Helene. "A Government of Men: Gender, the City, and the New Science of Politics." In *Gender and American Social Science: The Formative Years,* edited by Helene Silverberg, 156–84. Princeton, NJ: Princeton University Press, 1998.

"Sketch of William Graham Sumner." *Popular Science Monthly* 35 (June 1889), 261–68.

Smith, Goldwin. "The Experience of the American Commonwealth." In *Essays on Reform,* 217–37. London: Macmillan, 1867.

Smith, Harriette Knight. *The History of the Lowell Institute.* Boston: Lamson, Wolffe, 1898.

Smith, Munroe. "Introduction: The Domain of Political Science." *Political Science Quarterly* 1, no. 1 (1886), 1–5.

———. "Review of *Journal of the Society of Comparative Legislation.*" *Political Science Quarterly* 12, no. 3 (1897), 537–43.

Somit, Albert, and Joseph Tanenhaus. *The Development of American Political Science: From Burgess to Behavioralism.* Boston: Allyn and Bacon, 1967.

Spencer, Herbert. *Descriptive Sociology; or, Groups of Sociological Facts, Classified and Arranged by Herbert Spencer.* 8 vols. London: Williams and Norgate, 1873–81.

——. *The Man versus the State, with Six Essays on Government, Society, and Freedom.* Indianapolis, IN: Liberty Fund, 1982.

——. *The Principles of Sociology.* Vol. 1. London: Williams and Norgate, 1876.

——. *The Principles of Sociology.* 3 vols. New York: Appleton, 1898.

——. "Specialized Administration." In *The Man versus the State,* 435–86.

——. *The Study of Sociology.* New York: Appleton, 1874.

Staël, Germaine de. *Considerations on the Principal Events of the French Revolution.* Edited by Aurelian Craiutu. Indianapolis, IN: Liberty Fund, 2008.

Starr, Harris E. *William Graham Sumner.* New York: Holt, 1925.

Stears, Marc. *Progressives, Pluralists, and the Problems of the State: Ideologies of Reform in the United States and Britain, 1909–1926.* Oxford: Oxford University Press, 2002.

Stern, Fritz, ed. *The Varieties of History: From Voltaire to the Present.* New York: Meridian Books, 1956.

Stettner, Edward A. *Shaping Modern Liberalism: Herbert Croly and Progressive Thought.* Lawrence: University Press of Kansas, 1993.

Story, Joseph. *Joseph Story and the Encyclopedia Americana.* Clark, NJ: Lawbook Exchange, 2006.

——. "The Science of Government." In *The Miscellaneous Writings of Joseph Story,* edited by William W. Story. Boston: Little, Brown, 1852.

Story, William W., ed. *Life and Letters of Joseph Story.* 2 vols. Boston: Little, Brown, 1851.

Sumner, William Graham. "The Absurd Effort to Make the World Over." In *Liberty, Society, and Politics,* 251–61.

——. "Advancing Social and Political Organization in American History." In *Challenge of Facts,* 287–344.

——. *Alexander Hamilton.* New York: Dodd, Mead, 1890.

——. *Andrew Jackson as a Public Man.* Boston: Houghton Mifflin, 1882.

——. "The Argument against Protective Taxes." In *Collected Essays,* 58–76.

——. *The Challenge of Facts and Other Essays.* Edited by Albert Galloway Keller. New Haven, CT: Yale University Press, 1914.

——. *Collected Essays in Political and Social Science.* New York: Holt, 1885.

——. "Democracy and Plutocracy." In *Liberty, Society, and Politics,* 137–48.

——. *Earth-Hunger and Other Essays.* Edited by Albert Galloway Keller. New Haven, CT: Yale University Press, 1913.

——. "Federal Legislation on Railroads." In *Challenge of the Facts,* 175–82.

——. *The Financier and the Finances of the American Revolution.* New York: Dodd, Mead, 1891.

——. *Folkways: A Study of the Sociological Importance of Usages, Manners, Customs, Mores, and Morals.* New York: Mentor Book, 1960.

——. "For President?" In *Challenge of Facts,* 363–80.

——. "The Forgotten Man." In *Liberty, Society and Politics,* 201–22.

——. *A History of American Currency.* New York: Holt, 1874.

——. *History of Banking in the United States.* New York: Journal of Commerce and Commonwealth Bulletin, 1896.

——. "Introductory Lecture to Courses in Political and Social Science." In *Challenge of Facts,* 389–404.

——. "Laissez-Faire." In *Liberty, Society, and Politics,* 227–33.

——. *Lectures on the History of Protection in the United States.* New York: Putnam's, 1877.

——. "Legislation by Clamor." In *Challenge of Facts,* 183–90.

——. "Memorial Day Address." In *Challenge of Facts,* 345–62.

——. *On Liberty, Society and Politics: The Essential Essays of William Graham Sumner.* Edited by Robert C. Bannister. Indianapolis, IN: Liberty Fund, 1992.

——. "Politics in America, 1776–1876." *North American Review* 122, no. 250 (1876), 47–87.

——. "Presidential Elections and Civil-Service Reform." In *Collected Essays,* 140–59.

————. "Professor Sumner's Speech." In *Herbert Spencer on the Americans and the Americans on Herbert Spencer*, edited by E. L. Youmans, 35–40. New York: Appleton, 1883.

————. "Republican Government." In *Liberty, Society, and Politics*, 81–92.

————. *Robert Morris*. New York: Dodd, Mead, 1892.

————. "Socialism." In *Liberty, Society, and Politics*, 159–82.

————. "Sociology." In *Collected Essays*, 77–97.

————. "Solidarity of the Human Race." In *Liberty, Society, and Politics*, 26–36.

————. "Speculative Legislation." In *Challenge of Facts*, 213–20.

————. "State Interference." *North American Review* 145, no. 369 (1887), 109–19.

————. "The Survival of the Fittest." In *Liberty, Society, and Politics*, 223–26.

————. "The Theory and Practice of Elections." In *Collected Essays*, 98–139.

————. "Wages." In *Collected Essays*, 36–57.

————. *What Social Classes Owe to Each Other*. Caldwell, ID: Caxton Printers, 1989.

Sumner, William Graham, David A. Wells, W. E. Foster, R. L. Dugdale, and G. H. Putnam, comps. *Political Economy and Political Science*. New York: Society for Political Education, 1881.

Swedberg, Richard. *Tocqueville's Political Economy*. Princeton, NJ: Princeton University Press, 2009.

Taussig, F. W. *The Tariff History of the United States*. New York: Putnam's, 1888.

Thayer, M. Russell. "The Life, Character, and Writings of Francis Lieber." In *Miscellaneous Writings of Francis Lieber* 1: 14–44.

Theriault, Sean M. "Patronage, the Pendleton Act, and the Power of the People." *Journal of Politics* 65, no. 1 (2003), 50–68.

Thorsen, Niels. "The Origins of Woodrow Wilson's 'The Study of Administration.'" *American Studies in Scandinavia* 21 (1989), 16–29.

Throntveit, Trygve. "The Higher Education of Woodrow Wilson." In *The Educational Legacy of Woodrow Wilson: From College to Nation*, edited by James Axtell, 407–43. Charlottesville: University of Virginia Press, 2012.

Tocqueville, Alexis de. *Democracy in America*. Translated by Harvey C. Mansfield and Delba Winthrop. Chicago: University of Chicago Press, 2000.

————. *Memoir, Letters, and Remains of Alexis de Tocqueville*. 2 vols. London: Macmillan, 1861.

————. *The Old Regime and the French Revolution*. Translated by Stuart Gilbert. New York: Anchor Books, 1983.

————. "Speech Given to the Annual Public Meeting of the Academy of Moral and Political Sciences on April 3, 1852." In *Alexis de Tocqueville and the Art of Democratic Statesmanship*, edited by Brian Danoff and L. Joseph Hebert Jr., 17–30. Lanham, MD: Lexington Books, 2011.

Tomasi, John. *Free Market Fairness*. Princeton, NJ: Princeton University Press, 2012.

Tribe, Keith. "Continental Political Economy from the Physiocrats to the Marginal Revolution." In *Cambridge History of Science*, vol. 7, *The Modern Social Sciences*, edited by Theodore M. Porter and Dorothy Ross, 154–70. Cambridge: Cambridge University Press, 2003.

Tullock, Hugh. *James Bryce's American Commonwealth: The Anglo-American Background*. Bury St. Edmunds, UK: Royal Historical Society, 1988.

Turner, Brandon P. "John Stuart Mill and the Antagonistic Foundation of Liberal Politics." *Review of Politics* 72, no. 1 (2010), 25–53.

Veysey, Laurence R. *The Emergence of the American University*. Chicago: University of Chicago Press, 1965.

Vitalis, Robert. "The Noble American Science of Imperial Relations and Its Laws of Race Development." *Comparative Studies in Society and History* 52, no. 4 (2010), 909–38.

Weber, Max. "Parliament and Government in Germany under a New Political Order." In *Political Writings*, edited by Peter Lassman and Ronald Speirs, 130–271. Cambridge: Cambridge University Press, 1994.

White, Andrew D. *Autobiography of Andrew Dickson White*. 2 vols. New York: Century, 1905.

———. "Do the Spoils Belong to the Victor?" *North American Review* 134, no. 303 (1882), 111–33.

———. *Education in Political Science: An Address.* Baltimore, MD: John Murphy, 1879.

———. "Inaugural Address." In *Builders of American Universities: Inaugural Addresses,* edited by David Andrew Weaver. Vol. 1. Alton, IL: Shurtleff College Press, 1950.

———. *Paper-Money Inflation in France.* New York: Appleton, 1876.

———. "The Provision for Higher Instruction in Subjects Bearing Directly on Public Affairs." In *Reports of the United States Commissioners to the Paris Universal Exposition 1878,* vol. 2. Washington, DC: Government Printing Office, 1880.

———. "The Relation of National and State Governments to Advanced Education." *Journal of Social Science* 7 (September 1874), 299–322.

———. *Report of the Committee on Organization, Presented to the Trustees of the Cornell University, October 21st 1866.* Albany, NY: C. Van Benthuysen and Sons, 1867.

———. "Studies in General History and the History of Civilization." *Papers of the American Historical Association* 1, no. 2 (1885), 5–28.

Willoughby, Westel Woodbury. "The Individual and the State." *American Political Science Review* 8, no. 1 (1914), 1–13.

Willoughby, William F. "The Philosophy of Labor Legislation." *American Political Science Review* 8, no. 1 (1914), 14–24.

Wilson, Woodrow. "An Address to the Princeton Alumni of New York." In *Papers of Woodrow Wilson* 5: 137–41.

———. "Bryce's American Commonwealth." *Political Science Quarterly* 4, no. 1 (1889), 153–69.

———. "Cabinet Government in the United States." In *Papers of Woodrow Wilson* 1: 493–510.

———. "Character of Democracy in the United States." *Atlantic Monthly* 64 (November 1889), 577–88.

———. "Committee or Cabinet Government?" In *Papers of Woodrow Wilson* 2: 614–40.

———. "Congressional Government." In *Papers of Woodrow Wilson* 1: 548–74.

———. *Congressional Government: A Study in American Politics.* Boston: Houghton, Mifflin, 1885.

———. "Draft of a Report to the Historical Seminary." *Papers of Woodrow Wilson* 4: 422–24.

———. "John Bright." In *Papers of Woodrow Wilson* 1: 608–21.

———. "Leaders of Men." In *Papers of Woodrow Wilson* 6: 644–71.

———. "A Lecture on Democracy." In *Papers of Woodrow Wilson* 7: 344–69.

———. "Lecture I. Systems of Municipal Organization." In *Papers of Woodrow Wilson* 5: 697–705.

———. "Lecture II. The Functions of Government." In *Papers of Woodrow Wilson* 5: 677–90.

———. "The Modern Democratic State." In *Papers of Woodrow Wilson* 5: 58–92.

———. "Mr Gladstone, A Character Sketch." In *Papers of Woodrow Wilson* 1: 624–42.

———. "Nature of Democracy in the United States." In *Papers of Woodrow Wilson* 6: 221–39.

———. "New Southern Industries." In *Papers of Woodrow Wilson* 2: 119–25.

———. "Notes for a Course in Public Law: Introductory." In *Papers of Woodrow Wilson* 7: 7–9.

———. "Notes for Lectures on Administration." In *Papers of Woodrow Wilson* 6: 484–521.

———. "Notes Taken in Dr. Ely's Minor Course in Political Economy." In *Papers of Woodrow Wilson* 2: 506–08.

———. "Of the Study of Politics." *New Princeton Review* 3, no. 2 (1887), 188–99.

———. *An Old Master and Other Political Essays.* New York: Scribner's, 1893.

———. *The Papers of Woodrow Wilson.* 69 vols. Edited by Arthur S. Link. Princeton, NJ: Princeton University Press, 1966–94.

———. "Responsible Government under the Constitution." In *Papers of Woodrow Wilson* 5: 107–24.

———. "Review of John W. Burgess, *Political Science and Comparative Constitutional Law.*" In *Papers of Woodrow Wilson* 7: 195–203.

———. "Self-Government in France." In *Papers of Woodrow Wilson* 1: 515–39.

———. "Socialism and Democracy." In *Papers of Woodrow Wilson* 5: 559–63.

———. "Some Thoughts on the Current State of Public Affairs." In *Papers of Woodrow Wilson* 1: 347–54.

———. *The State: Elements of Historical and Practical Politics, a Sketch of Institutional History and Administration.* Boston: Heath, 1889.

———. "Stray Thoughts from the South." In *Papers of Woodrow Wilson* 2: 19–25

———. "The Study of Administration." *Political Science Quarterly* 2, no. 2 (1887), 197–222.

———. "Testimony before the Tariff Commission." In *Papers of Woodrow Wilson* 2: 140–43.

———. "Three Essays on Administration." In *Papers of Woodrow Wilson* 5: 44–54.

———. "What Can Be Done for Constitutional Liberty." In *Papers of Woodrow Wilson* 2: 33–40.

———. "Wilson's Section for a *History of Political Economy in the United States.*" In *Papers of Woodrow Wilson* 4: 631–63.

Winegarten, Renee. *Germaine De Staël & Benjamin Constant: A Dual Biography.* New Haven, CT: Yale University Press, 2008.

Wolin, Sheldon S. *Politics and Vision: Continuity and Innovation in Western Political Thought.* Boston: Little, Brown, 1960.

Wood, Dennis. *Benjamin Constant: A Biography.* London: Routledge, 1993.

Woolsey, Theodore Dwight. *Introduction to the Study of International Law.* Boston: Munroe, 1860.

———. *Political Science: Or the State Theoretically and Practically Considered.* 2 vols. New York: Scribner Armstrong, 1877.

Yeomans, Henry Aaron. *Abbott Lawrence Lowell, 1856–1943.* Cambridge, MA: Harvard University Press, 1948.

Ziblatt, Daniel. "How Did Europe Democratize?" *World Politics* 58, no. 2 (2006), 311–38.

INDEX